UNDERSTANDING HUMAN RIGHTS VIOLATIONS

Ethics and Global Politics

Series Editors: Tom Lansford and Patrick Hayden

Since the end of the Cold War, explorations of ethical considerations within global politics and on the development of foreign policy have assumed a growing importance in the fields of politics and international studies. New theories, policies, institutions, and actors are called for to address difficult normative questions arising from the conduct of international affairs in a rapidly changing world. This series provides an exciting new forum for creative research that engages both the theory and practice of contemporary world politics, in light of the challenges and dilemmas of the evolving international order.

Also in the series

International Environmental Justice
A North-South Dimension
Ruchi Anand
ISBN 0 7546 3824 3

Understanding Human Rights Violations

New Systematic Studies

Edited by

SABINE C. CAREY
and
STEVEN C. POE

ASHGATE

Published by
Ashgate Publishing Limited
Gower House
Croft Road
Aldershot
Hants GU11 3HR
England

Ashgate Publishing Company
Suite 420
101 Cherry Street
Burlington, VT 05401-4405
USA

Ashgate website: http://www.ashgate.com

British Library Cataloguing in Publication Data
Understanding human rights violations : new systematic
studies. - (Ethics and global politics)
1.Human rights 2.Human rights - Government policy 3.Human
rights - Economic aspects
I.Carey, Sabine C. II.Poe, Steven C.
323

Library of Congress Cataloging-in-Publication Data
Understanding human rights violations : new systematic studies / edited by Sabine C. Carey and Steven C. Poe.
p. cm. -- (Ethics and global politics)
Includes bibliographical references and index.
ISBN 0-7546-4026-4
1. Human rights. 2. International relations--Decision making. I. Carey, Sabine C., 1974- II. Poe, Steven C. III. Series.

J571.U53 2004
323'.044--dc22

2003024698

ISBN 0 7546 4026 4

Printed and bound in Great Britain by MPG Books Ltd, Bodmin, Cornwall

Contents

PART IV: LEGAL AND INSTITUTIONAL DETERMINANTS OF HUMAN RIGHTS

PART V: NEW DIRECTIONS IN THE RESEARCH ON HUMAN RIGHTS VIOLATIONS

PART VI: CONCLUSION

List of Figures

List of Tables

List of Contributors

M. Rodwan Abouharb is a Ph.D. student at Binghamton University, New York. His research is principally interested in the determinants and consequences of structural adjustment policies on political, socio-economic development and human rights. His other interests include the relationship between culture and intrastate violence.

Bethany Barratt is an Assistant Professor at Roosevelt University. Her primary research interests are human rights and foreign policy, as well as the role of media and public opinion in foreign policy, gender and international politics and the correlates of societal intolerance toward minority groups.

Rhonda L. Callaway is an Assistant Professor at Rochester Institute of Technology, Rochester, NY, who completed this research while she was Tower Fellow at Southern Methodist University in Dallas, Texas. Her main research interests include the relationship between globalization and human rights, democratization, international organizations and American foreign policy. Some of her research with Julie Harrelson-Stephens was recently published in *International Interactions*.

Sabine C. Carey is lecturer at the School of Politics, University of Nottingham. Her research concentrates on life integrity violations, dissent, intrastate conflict and the role of political institutions in conflict situations. Previous work include studies evaluating European foreign aid and the impact of regime transition on human rights violations and has appeared in *Journal of Peace Research*, *European Union Politics, Democratization* and *Human Rights Quarterly*.

David L. Cingranelli is Professor of Political Science at Binghamton University, New York. He has published numerous influential books and articles on the human rights practices of governments from a cross-national comparative perspective and American foreign policy.

Julie Harrelson-Stephens is a Senior Lecturer at the University of Texas at Dallas, specializing in International Relations. She recently finished her dissertation on globalization and human rights, at the University of North Texas. Her previous research on human rights (with Rhonda Callaway) has been published in *International Interactions*.

Linda Camp Keith is Professor of Political Science at Collin County Community College in Plano, Texas. Her current research interests are human rights and the rule of law. She has published articles on this topic in *Political Research Quarterly, Journal of Peace Research* and *Judicature*. She has also co-authored human rights articles in *International Studies Quarterly* and two edited volumes. She has co-authored articles on the U.S. Supreme Court in *American Journal of Political Science, Political Research Quarterly, Social Science Quarterly* and *Social Science History.*

Kimi L. King is Associate Professor of Political Science at the University of North Texas. Her current research interests include international law and human rights, gender issues in international law and judicial decision making in the area of fair housing. Her works have been published in *Social Science Research*, *Political Research Quarterly*, *American Politics Research*, *Presidential Studies Quarterly* and the *International Criminal Law Review.*

David Leblang is an Associate Professor at the University of Colorado, Boulder, focusing on International Political Economy. His current research examines the relationship between political information and volatility in international financial markets. He recently received a grant from the National Science Foundation to study the causes and consequences of speculative attacks against fixed exchange rate regimes in emerging economies. Some of his work has been published in the *American Journal of Political Science*, the *British Journal of Political Science*, *International Organization*, and *International Studies Quarterly.*

Chris Lee is an Assistant Professor of Comparative Politics at the University of Minnesota Morris. Research interests include dissent, repression, political conflict and violence and terrorism.

Ronny Lindström has previously published in *International Interactions* and *Journal of Political and Military Sociology*. Since 1998 Dr. Lindström has worked for the United Nations Population Fund, first in the organization's Tashkent, Uzbekistan, office as a Programme Officer and currently at the New York Headquarters where his work focuses on U.N. reform issues. This article is not related to his work for the U.N.

James D. Meernik is Associate Professor of Political Science at the University of North Texas. He has specialized in research on United States foreign policy, judicial politics and international law. His research has been published in *International Studies Quarterly*, the *Journal of Politics*, *Political Research Quarterly, Journal of Peace Research*, *Conflict Management and Peace Science*, *International Criminal Law Review* and the *American Journal of Political Science.*

Dawn Miller is a Ph.D. student at Penn State University, who was formerly a student at the University of North Texas. She is the assistant to the Director of the Peace Science Society. Her research interests include human rights, civil war, conflict resolution, and third party intervention.

Wesley T. Milner is Director of International Studies and Austin S. Igleheart Professor of Political Science at the University of Evansville. His research integrates international political economy and broadly defined aspects of human rights. His work has appeared in *Human Rights Quarterly*, *Journal of Private Enterprise* and edited books.

Will H. Moore is an Associate Professor in the Department of Political Science at the Florida State University. His research and teaching interests include violent political conflict, human rights and refugee movements. Recent examples of his work can be found in *American Journal of Political Science*, *International Interactions*, *Journal of Conflict Resolution* and *Journal of Politics*.

Steven C. Poe is Professor of Political Science and Director of the Undergraduate Peace Studies Program at the University of North Texas, in Denton, Texas. He formerly taught at William Penn College in Oskaloosa, Iowa. His research on human rights related issues has been published in numerous scholarly anthologies and journals. He is on the Editorial Review Board of *Human Rights Quarterly*, and he recently began a five-year term as Chief Editor of *International Studies Quarterly*.

Pablo Policzer is a Research Fellow at the University of British Columbia's Institute of International Relations. He studies human rights violations by non-state armed groups and civilian control over military forces in Latin America. He has published in *Canadian Foreign Policy,* the *Journal of Interamerican Studies and World Affairs*, the *Canadian Journal of Political Science*, *Estudos Históricos* (Rio de Janeiro) and the *Revista Jurídica de la Universidad de Palermo* (Buenos Aires).

Alette Smeulers is a Lecturer in International Criminal Law at the Department of Criminal Law and Criminology at Maastricht University. She has worked with PIOOM (Leiden University, the Netherlands) on a research project on the Gross Human Rights Violator. Her main research areas are international criminal law and causes of gross human rights violations. She has published various Dutch and English articles on torture, extradition and human rights.

Kara Smith was a participant in the McNair Program at the University of North Texas, which has assisted numerous first generation college students in their efforts to prepare for graduate school. After receiving her undergraduate degree at North Texas, she taught government and economics in the Czech Republic. She currently is applying for admittance into graduate schools.

Kürşad Turan is a Ph.D. candidate in the Department of Political Science at the Florida State University. His research and teaching interests are conflict, ethnicity and political development. His dissertation addresses the impact of democratization on ethnic violence levels in multinational countries.

Acknowledgements

The idea for this edited book was born during our preparation for a workshop that we organized at the ECPR Joint Sessions in Turin, Italy, in March 2002. Several chapters of this volume were presented at this workshop. We would like to thank Cynthia Colley and Mehmet Gurses for their fine editorial support and Nicolas Rost for his invaluable proof-reading and professional assistance in preparing the index. Cynthia's work was supported by the McNair Program, and Mehmet's contribution was made possible by the Christian Family Peace Endowment, both at the University of North Texas. We are very grateful to Patrick Hayden and Tom Lansford, the editors of this book series, for their valuable input and their timely responses to our queries. We would like to thank Kirstin Howgate, Irene Poulton and Rosalind Ebdon at Ashgate Publishing for working with us as we prepared the manuscript for publication. Last but not least, we are especially grateful to our spouses, Sean Carey and SunJu Poe, for endless proof-reading, patience and support throughout the whole publication process.

To our parents,
Werner and Waltraud Zanger
and
Jack, Liz and Mickey Poe

PART I
HUMAN RIGHTS RESEARCH AND THE QUEST FOR DIGNITY

Chapter 1

Human Rights Research and the Quest for Human Dignity

Sabine C. Carey and Steven C. Poe

There can be no doubt that systematic, social scientific scholarly research on human rights has proliferated in the last two decades. Research on human rights related topics has been published in the major journals of the political science discipline. The scholarly movement to study and promote human rights has grown and is quickly being institutionalized.[1]

In fact, scholars have been interested in human rights for quite some time, but until relatively recently most have adopted political theory, philosophical or legalistic perspectives (e.g., Van Dyke, 1973; Dworkin, 1978, and sources cited therein).[2] Today, there are two complementary and interrelated veins of social science research adopting different approaches to studying human rights. The first stems from a movement by social science scholars who began to use systematic, qualitative methods to study human rights behaviours (e.g., Claude, 1976, Forsythe, 1983; Donnelly, 1989). A second vein of research has developed from early works that sought to overcome data availability problems in order to empirically test theories relating human rights to other phenomena (e.g., Strouse and Claude, 1976; Schoultz, 1981; Stohl, Carleton and Johnson, 1984).

It is undeniable that violations of human rights are causing pain, anguish and oftentimes death to citizens of most countries in the world most of the time. Yet even today human rights are given far less attention by empirical social science researchers than international wars and numerous other issues that seem much less important when one considers their relative human costs. Indeed, in terms of killing, human rights violations outside of a state of war are arguably more destructive of life than those that occur when wars are ongoing. Rummel once estimated that in the twentieth century far more people have been killed by democide, which includes acts of genocide, politicide and mass murder and other public killing by governments' actions (which are the most serious abuses of the human right to personal integrity), than were killed in combat by governments in a state of war.[3] The quickly developing human rights literature, of which each of the pieces in this volume is an example, is an illustration of recent scholarly work that attempts to remedy this historical imbalance.[4]

The reasons why human rights have been afforded much less attention by empirical social scientists than is warranted are not firmly established. However, several factors may be considered as likely suspects. It seems undeniable that much social scientific academic inquiry is a reaction to real-world political events and discourse. According to this line of thinking, systematic studies of human rights may be late to develop relative to the study of war because until very recently it was thought that, consistent with the dictates of national sovereignty, what governments did within their own borders was their own business. Indeed, it was not until the Universal Declaration of Human Rights, passed in 1948, that a meaningful challenge was made to this line of thought. And though the Declaration increasingly took on law-like status, the two U.N. Covenants that established many of the rights declared in the Universal Declaration as law did not enter into force until 1976.

So, while the likes of Louis Fry Richardson, Quincy Wright and later Kenneth Boulding, J. David Singer and others were looking systematically at the causes of wars, gathering data and institutionalizing a field of study around that issue, the concept of human rights had not yet appeared on most social scientists' maps.

Perhaps another part of the story is the belief held by many in the social sciences that normative judgments should be avoided, since they are apt to introduce a systematic bias into research that is supposed to be scientific and therefore objective.[5] To be fair, many students of international war and others in the international relations field are open about their own normative biases, but those biases frequently go unmentioned in their writings. In contrast, studies of human rights are normative from the outset, as is made clear even in the titles of publications on this topic. They are open about their assumption that there is something called human rights and that people are entitled to be treated with dignity, simply as a result of them being human (i.e., Donnelly, 1989). Proceeding from this value judgment, they set out to produce replicable, valid research that would be accepted by knowledgeable social scientists.

While we cannot speak for other human rights researchers, the editors of this collection are quite comfortable doing research of this kind in part because we believe that some normative judgments are made by social scientists at the beginning of any research programme, unless the choice of topics is either random or made by one's instructor. Almost everyone who studies human behaviour chooses a topic based partly on what they consider to be important and/or interesting, and such judgments are naturally based partly on what that researcher values. This is no less the case for someone doing a game theoretic study of countries' bargaining behaviour on trade issues, than it is for someone studying human rights or international war. What is different about human rights scholars is that they are open about their own normative assumptions, usually making them clear in the titles and abstracts of their research, where they choose to use the 'human rights' terminology. Should someone not accept these assumptions, they might still find value in the work, by substituting 'repression' or 'starvation' or other more value neutral terms for the term violation of human rights where appropriate.

A third explanation why empirical research on human rights has been relatively late to develop has to do with the predominant theoretical orientation of the field. A quarter of a century ago, Roy Preiswerk (1981) charged that at that time international relations scholars were ignoring human suffering and failing to do research 'as if people really matter.' Preiswerk's criticism had some merit then, and perhaps even today, since most international relations scholars have approached their subject from realist and neo-realist theories, which primarily focus on the nation-state, or on the relations between nation-states in the international system. Even the liberal movement in international relations seems to stay mostly at that nation-state level of analysis. As such, most international relations scholars and their theories address the effects on actual peoples' lives only rather indirectly. This is not to say that international relations research does not relate to issues that are of importance. Research on wars and the use of force, trade and a variety of international economic phenomena clearly addresses important issues that affect peoples' lives, but frequently the linkages are indirect and not explicitly tackled.

On this score, research on human rights provides a much needed contrast to the thrust of mainstream international relations research. Like the human rights movement more generally, the scholarly movement that examines human rights asserts that *people and their suffering* are important and worthy of the attention of international relations scholars and those in other disciplines, and that governments and other entities should be held responsible for living up to certain standards in their treatment of people. Human rights researchers tie their intellectual and theory-building efforts to individuals' suffering and to international efforts to ensure that people are treated with dignity.

The systematic human rights research conducted to date, including each of the following twelve chapters, may be seen as researchers' efforts to respond *systematically* to Preiswerk's challenge. The studies in this volume seek to apply the analytical tools of social science research, both qualitative and quantitative, to answer questions of why human dignity is so frequently being violated. They combine scholarly rigour with the desire to further our understanding of human rights violations in the hope that we will be better equipped in the future to prevent such suffering.

What do we mean by human rights? Human rights are those rights that people have just as a result because of being human and that are necessary to live a life of dignity (Donnelly, 1989). This volume concentrates on human rights that are internationally recognized in the Universal Declaration of Human Rights and in the International Human Right Covenants.[6] More specifically, it focuses on personal (or physical) integrity rights and subsistence rights. Personal integrity rights, or security rights (Shue, 1980), are those rights that protect the integrity of a person's life. They include the right to be free from torture, arbitrary imprisonment and murder. Subsistence rights, or basic human needs, refer to the right to an adequate standard of living, such as access to housing, food, clothing and medical care. Concentrating on these universally accepted rights allows us to generalize our arguments and findings across different regions and cultures of the world. By focusing on security and subsistence rights, we do not mean to suggest that these are the only rights necessary for a life in dignity. But without the respect of these rights, the enjoyment of other rights, such as social and cultural rights, is impossible (see also Shue, 1980).

In the remainder of this chapter, we briefly summarize the research that has been conducted on these issues to date, what has been learned and the goals that remain to be achieved. Then we briefly discuss how each chapter in this volume contributes to these goals. The volume is organized into five parts, including the present one. We provide more in-depth discussions in the beginning of each part, discussing the contributions of each chapter and putting them into context.

Empirical Human Rights Research

Early Studies of Foreign Aid Allocation

The first efforts to use quantitative methods to investigate human rights issues dealt with the allocation of U.S. foreign aid. In the 1970s, the Harkin Amendment to the U.S. foreign assistance act mandated that U.S. aid be tied to human rights issues, but observers of U.S. foreign policy questioned whether the purpose of this law was actually reflected in foreign policy outputs. The pioneer of empirical and quantitative human rights research was Lars Schoultz (1981). In his early studies, Schoultz asked whether the United States paid attention to human rights issues when allocating its foreign aid. Investigating U.S. aid allocation and the human rights performance of Latin American countries during the mid-1970s, he was led to conclude that during this time period, 'United States aid was clearly distributed disproportionately to countries with repressive governments' (Schoultz, 1981, p.167). This research was fraught with difficulties, but it did provide a starting point for later work. Soon, research looking at other periods and other parts of the world began to appear, and incremental improvements in the research approach and methods were achieved. Others were led by their analyses to conclude that human rights were ignored or overlooked by U.S. foreign policymakers (Stohl, Carleton, and Johnson, 1984; Stohl and Carleton, 1985).

However, in 1985 an important study by Cingranelli and Pasquarello appeared in the *American Journal of Political Science*. This article was an improvement over previous research in that it used multivariate methods to investigate the effects of human rights practices on U.S. aid allocation to a number of Western Hemispheric countries. After excluding El Salvador, an outlier, as a 'nonroutine' case, and accounting for a number of control variables, they found that human rights did appear to affect the allocation of U.S. foreign aid. Their findings were called into question by subsequent studies (Carleton and Stohl, 1987; McCormick and Mitchell, 1988) and demonstrated to result mainly from the exclusion of El Salvador. Some subsequent studies suggest that human rights do affect aid allocation by the U.S. government, but that they are weighed against strategic and economic concerns (e.g., Poe, 1992; Poe and Sirirangsi, 1994; Apodaca and Stohl, 1999). More recent research has sought to extend this research by focusing on and comparing other governments (Zanger, 2000; Neumayer, 2003). For example, the chapter by Bethany Barratt in this volume analyzes how human rights considerations influence aid allocation by Great Britain. Thus far the findings, as indicated by the more sophisticated recent research employing multivariate models, are that human rights appear to be considered. But what is most clear is that even if human rights are taken into consideration, they are frequently 'trumped' by strategic or political concerns, and thus human rights policies, for example of the U.S., are applied inconsistently at best. The idea that human rights are 'trumped,' some would persuasively argue, is antithetical to the idea of what a 'right' is (see Dworkin, 1978).

Looking back at the literature on this issue that has been conducted to date, we would say that thus far its contributions have not yet led to a substantial refinement in international relations or foreign policy theory, but its findings are important nevertheless. This literature rehearses theories and tests hypotheses, but its greatest contribution is more descriptive. Governments, especially that of the United States, have frequently called other governments to task for not living up to international human rights standards. In demonstrating empirically that the U.S. frequently aids human rights abusers, it is shown that this country fails to live up to its own standards, failing to act in accordance with its own laws. Demonstrating this incongruity is an important contribution in and of itself, which is relevant to real-world political debates. The charge of hypocrisy is one that carries heavy weight in political debates, and arguably much of the success made by minorities and women in realizing their rights stems from the persuasiveness of such arguments. For example, the message of Martin Luther King, in his famous 'I Have a Dream' speech, was that the Declaration of Independence stated that all men were created equal, but that African-Americans were still not accorded these rights. This speech was the continuation of a long American tradition. Indeed, more than a century earlier, prior to the Emancipation Proclamation, a similar charge of hypocrisy was made by Frederick Douglass, regarding the American celebration of 'independence' on 4 July when most Black Americans were still owned as slaves (Douglass, 1852). Charges of hypocrisy may be less effective in the realm of international politics, where claims related to national sovereignty and military and economic considerations tend to reside, but they certainly are made frequently and are persuasive to many. International and domestic criticism of U.S. and British actions in Iraq shows us this, though it evidently has not succeeded in changing the policies of those countries, at least at the time of our writing this chapter.

Research on other U.S. policies, such as the granting of asylum by the U.S. (e.g., Gibney and Stohl, 1988), has been given much less attention in empirical human rights research. Arms transfers are another example that has received little attention by academics, despite its obvious importance for the well-being of people. The chapter by Dawn Miller builds upon the important studies by Blanton (1999a, 1999b; 2000) on U.S. arms transfers and investigates their impact on different types of human rights.

Research Explaining Why Human Rights Abuses Happen

A few years after the first scholarly exchanges on human rights and foreign aid, more researchers began to turn their attention to the issue of why human rights are abused in the first place (e.g., Park, 1987; Henderson, 1991). Most of the literature explaining human rights abuses has focused on the rights to personal (or physical) integrity, including the right not to be imprisoned, tortured, murdered or disappeared, either arbitrarily or for political purposes. Since the following chapter by Steven Poe addresses this literature in some depth, we will not go into its findings here. Suffice it to say that the goals of this burgeoning literature are three-fold: 1) to lead to a better understanding of why human rights abuses occur; 2) to make useful prescriptions to decisionmakers based on the findings at hand and 3) to allow us to forecast or assess the risk of human rights abuses in particular locales in the future.

Does the research conducted to date meet the challenge of Preiswerk? Does it study their subject as if people really matter? Though research on these issues is still rather infrequent, it is headed in the right direction. Regarding the first goal, a theoretical understanding of human rights abuse would seem to be a vital step toward addressing Preiswerk's challenge. Such an understanding is crucial for our efforts to stop or avoid human rights abuses, in much the same way that understanding the genetic structure of man is vital to our efforts to cure various diseases.

Making prescriptions to policymakers by suggesting ways to decrease human rights abuses might increase respect for human dignity, if they were to be heeded. Clearly, a number of prescriptions can already be made based on existing research. Do you want greater respect of personal integrity rights? Existing literature (e.g., Henderson, 1993; Poe and Tate, 1994) says that governments should be assisted in their efforts to democratize, to develop economically and to manage domestic and international conflicts short of war. Unfortunately, finding ways to fulfil these prescriptions is an extremely tall order. So far, not much of the advice offered by social science scholars involves variables that can easily be manipulated by government policymakers or human rights activists. Some headway has been made, however, as researchers have begun to investigate the effects of manipulable foreign policy outputs such as foreign aid (e.g., Regan, 1995). Some chapters in this volume also investigate the impact of factors that can be manipulated by various actors. As mentioned above, Dawn Miller researches the impact of arms transfers on the respect for human rights in the developing world. The chapter by Rhonda Callaway and Julie Harrelson-Stephens analyzes how trade affects human rights by changing the political and economic development of countries. Rodwan Abouhard and David Cingranelli investigate the determinants of IMF and World Bank Loans, and the chapter by Linda Keith addresses the role of constitutional provisions in protecting human rights.

Unfortunately, little headway has been made toward forecasting and assessing the risk of human rights abuse. There can be little doubt that successfully constructing a system that would allow us to predict or assess such risk is studying international relations as if people matter. Like many human rights activists, as scholars we hope that someday human institutions will provide the means to address potential humanitarian emergencies before they even begin. At present, such assessment would at least allow IGOs, NGOs and interested governments to allocate resources more efficiently and to better prepare themselves for relief efforts prior to humanitarian emergencies.

It would appear that researchers already have at their disposal many of the tools needed to achieve these aims, but they have been addressed only sparingly in print.[7] Models of repression and human rights abuses have explained up to 80 per cent of the variance in those variables and regularly explain over 50 per cent of the variance. While it is questionable whether researchers will ever be able to 'predict' repression with anything near certainty, such models would appear to provide a foothold to researchers who would wish to identify countries at risk, relative to others. Like medical researchers investigating cancer, heart and many other ailments, we know many of the more important risk factors and are still identifying others.[8]

Each chapter of this book is an example of systematic, social science research that addresses one or more of these aims. Below we further discuss the original contributions in this volume.

New Avenues in Human Rights Research

As the overview of empirical social scientific research on human rights shows, the systematic analyses into why human rights violations occur and how they affect foreign policies have made substantial progress over the last two decades. What is needed now is to pull the gained knowledge together in an overarching theoretical framework and address newly raised questions in a way that employs the latest research techniques and makes the findings accessible to both the academic community and a general audience. The collected works of this volume advance the systematic study of human rights violations around the world, addressing those human rights issues that have received little attention in previous work. The collection applies the tools of social scientific research to the study of human rights violations, while presenting it in a way that is both accessible to a general audience and of interest to the more advanced research community.

The following chapters address what are perhaps the most important and frequently asked questions in the political science research on human rights. How can we explain the occurrence of human rights violations in an encompassing theoretical framework? How do certain foreign policy decisions affect, and are affected by, the respect for human rights in developing countries? What general constitutional characteristics, and those of democracies in particular, are conducive for good human rights records? And how are basic subsistence rights influenced by international actors and their economic policies? All contributions share a concern for first and second generation human rights, examining political institutions and the impact of national and international policy making in an effort to learn more about the violation, and ultimately the protection, of such human rights.

The chapter by Steven Poe sets the stage by building a theoretical framework for the following contributions. He develops a process-oriented decisionmaking model that integrates previous human rights research. The model, which builds upon work by Most and Starr (e.g., Starr, 1978; Most and Starr, 1989), consists of four main elements: perceived levels of strength of the regime, perceived levels of threat to the domestic regime, perceived opportunities to act and the willingness to choose repression as one option of response to times of alarm, i.e. times in which the Strength/Threat ratio changes for the disadvantage for the government. Steven Poe shows how this unified and parsimonious model can integrate previously developed hypotheses about the violation of life integrity rights and how divergent and unexpected findings might be explained by concentrating on the decisionmaking process of the political regime.

The chapters by Bethany Barratt and Dawn Miller build upon the second strand of human rights research, which attempts to ascertain whether, and under what conditions, human rights influence foreign policy decisions. Both studies seek to understand how and why human rights influence decisionmakers' deliberations. The aim is to examine claims made by government decisionmakers that human rights issues are important and to expose inconsistencies between their rhetoric and reality, should incongruities be found.

After the introductory part and the section on foreign policy analysis, the third part addresses a related aspect, investigating how economic development and trade influence the respect for human rights. The three chapters in this part extend the concept of human rights from a more narrow definition of life integrity and security rights, which make up the first generation of human rights, to subsistence rights, the second generation of human rights. They question how their respect can be improved, or harmed, by economic development and international trade and, as such, provide some insight into how certain actors would be able to influence the protection of human rights. The first contribution by Rhonda Callaway and Julie Harrelson-Stephens analyzes the relationship between trade, economic development, democracy and human rights. It compares and empirically investigates the two main contradicting theories, liberal and radical theory, in the field of international political economy. The second chapter in the section on development and trade focuses on the provision of subsistence rights. Wesley Milner et al. investigate whether personal integrity rights, political liberties and subsistence rights are mutually reinforcing, as suggested by previous research, or whether there are trade-offs between different categories of rights. Rodwan Abouharb and David Cingranelli tackle the issue of development and trade from a different angle. Complementing Barratt's analysis of how human rights influence British foreign aid allocation, they investigate how World Bank and IMF decide which countries receive their financial assistance and whether they favour dictatorships over democracies, making an important contribution to policy evaluations performed by academic researchers.

The fourth section of the volume addresses an increasingly important issue, which has received little attention from the academic community. The two chapters in this section investigate legal and institutional aspects of human rights. The call for institutionalizing both the provision of human rights and the punishment of their violations has constantly grown over the past few years. For example, part of the motivation of the coalition forces for the recent war in Iraq was to bring democracy to the country in order to improve the life of the Iraqis. The question is what constitutional elements are most conducive to the respect of human rights and what aspects of democracy account for the generally better respect of the integrity of the life of its citizens in such regimes.

Apart from institutionalizing the respect of human rights, the legal prosecution of perpetrators has also been further implemented over recent years. In 1995 the International Criminal Tribunal for Rwanda has been set up by the U.N. Security Council to prosecute serious violations of international humanitarian law during the genocide in 1994, and in 2002 the United Nations and Sierra Leone set up a special court for war crimes committed during the 10 year civil war. The chapters in the fourth section of this collection address these issues of legal and institutional determinants of human rights. The contribution by Jim Meernik and Kimi King is one of the very first empirical studies to examine sentencing by International Criminal Tribunals. It represents an important innovation in the study of the punishment of human rights abuses by investigating sentencing by the International Criminal Tribunals for Former Yugoslavia. Linda Camp Keith analyzes the linkage between constitutional provisions and the violation of human rights between 1973 and 1996. She investigates the effect of constitutional provisions, such as the provision for fair trial and formal judicial independence, in various regions of the world, resulting in the most comprehensive examination of the effect of constitutions to date.

The final section asks where we go from here and what new avenues need to be explored to alleviate human suffering at the hands of their governments. It introduces new approaches and new areas to the research on human rights. It contains analyses of conditions that facilitate human rights violations, as well as inquiries into how human rights violations by the state influence the behaviour of domestic opposition in the form of protest and dissent. The last section also addresses a new issue on how human rights are violated and what the structural and individual mechanisms behind such violations are.

Chris Lee et al. explore the impact of the ethnic composition of a country on the extent to which the government violates human rights. They analyze the impact of the ethnic composition of a country on state violations of human rights using a global database ranging from 1976 to 1993, presenting the most comprehensive examination of the effects of ethnic composition on human rights to date.

Research on the conditions of human rights violations has largely concentrated on structural factors, such as economic development and regime type. However, it is not merely the structure of political regimes and the environment that influence governments' decision to repress, but also the behaviour of the population, such as the display of dissent and protest against the rulers. Sabine Carey analyzes how different types of domestic protest influences state repression, using data from Latin America and sub-Saharan Africa between 1977 and 1994. It offers a new approach to the study of domestic dissent and state repression by differentiating between five types of dissent and employing a statistical tool that allows for non-linear relationships between the different forms of dissent and repression.

The last two chapters address two unique questions about the dynamics behind coercion. They ask, firstly, what the characteristics of organizations are that are behind the human rights violations and how different organizational structures influence the nature of human rights violations, and secondly, what transforms ordinary people into gross human rights violators and what characterizes this process.

Pablo Policzer focuses on the characteristics of organizations and Alette Smeulers on the individuals that carry out human rights violations. Policzer's study is based on the argument that state-sponsored coercion does not appear in a vacuum but has to be organized. It concentrates on the question of how different types of organizations affect the intensity and types of human rights violations perpetrated by them. His chapter presents a new framework to describe the various ways states can organize coercion. Similarly, Smeulers also addresses the road to repression from a new perspective. It turns the focus of the previous chapter from the organization to the individual and the group. This qualitative study analyzes how ordinary people are transformed into human rights violators. Smeulers distinguishes a specific set of phases of the transformation process that turns ordinary people into gross human rights violators. This especially provocative study puts the perpetrators of gross human rights violations in the centre of the analysis and develops theories, mechanisms and processes to outline and explain this transformation.

Continuing the Quest for Human Dignity

The present volume brings together studies that apply the tools of social scientific inquiry to the quest for human dignity. Starting from the assumption that people matter and that they have human rights simply because of their being human, these studies set out to investigate how the protection of human rights has influenced policy decisions and what factors are likely to threaten the respect of such rights. At the heart of this venture lies the desire to contribute to our understanding of human rights violations, and ultimately to assist in improving the prospects for people around the world to live their lives with dignity. Over the past two decades human rights and their violations have attracted increasing attention from the social science community. The studies in this volume build on this effort and highlight new directions in this line of research. Hopefully their publication will increase further the movement's momentum, adding to our knowledge and, at the same time, stimulating future scholarly inquiry on these important issues.

Notes

1 Recently a Human Rights section was added to the American Political Science Association and an increasing number of human rights undergraduate and graduate programmes are being created at Western universities.

2 See Donnelly (1989) for a discussion of various philosophical traditions on human rights. Donnelly's work, of which this book is cited as an example, is difficult to classify as it has elements of the philosophical and qualitative, as well as some simple quantitative analysis.

3 See Table 4, 'Genocide and Power,' htttp://www.hawaii.edu/powerkills/power.tab4.gif accessed 28 June 2003. This comes from a 1986 pilot study, in which Rummel compared numbers who died from international and domestic wars to those killed by democide, attempting to separate those who died in combat from those who were intentionally killed by governments outside of combat (democide). Rummel includes the intentional bombing of civilian areas in interstate wars to kill people in the category of international democides (i.e, the fire-bombing of Dresden). Since such bombings arguably are against international laws, one could easily formulate an argument that they are violations of human rights. But even if these events are excluded, those killed in domestic democides (estimated at over 129 million) far outweigh those killed in all wars and international democides conducted in connection with those wars (just under 74 million). Rummel later warned that the statistics from the pilot study were badly underestimated, but he gives us no reason to believe that the basic finding regarding the overall importance of domestic democide would change with more accurate data.

4 The recent increase in research on civil war is another example of scholars addressing human suffering that occurs as a result of conflicts within countries' borders (e.g., Elbadawi and Sambanis, 2000; Collier and Hoeffler, 2002; Fearon and Laitin, 2003).

5 Some would substitute the term 'intersubjective' for objective, arguing that objectivity is hard if not impossible to establish. Intersubjectivity, however, is possible to establish. This would represent agreement by numerous persons holding a variety of viewpoints that a study appears to be valid.

6 The Universal Declaration of Human Rights is available online in numerous languages at http://www.unhchr.ch/udhr/ (last accessed: 24 October 2003). The International Covenants and numerous other existing human rights instruments are available at http://www.unhchr.ch/html/intlinst.htm (last accessed: 24 October 2003) as well as some which are currently in development.

7 Notable exceptions are the work of the State Failure Task Force (1999) and the replication by King and Zeng (2001) by forecasting state failure, where genocides are a part of the definition of state failure.

8 Our focus here on physical integrity rights is not meant to imply that other human rights are unimportant. There is a tradition of research on basic human needs and the chapter by Wesley Milner et al. in this volume contributes to this line of inquiry. Social science research on women's rights has begun (see Apodaca, 1998), and is an important frontier to which more scholarly attention should be given.

References

Apodaca, C. (1998), 'Measuring Women's Economic and Social Rights Achievements', *Human Rights Quarterly*, Vol. 20(1), pp. 139-72.

Apodaca, C. and Stohl, M. (1999), 'United States Human Rights Policy and Foreign Assistance', *International Studies Quarterly*, Vol. 43(1), pp. 185-98

Blanton, S.L. (1999a), 'Instruments of Security or Tools of Repression? Arms Imports and Human Rights Conditions in Developing Countries', *Journal of Peace Research*, Vol. 36(2), pp. 233-44.

Blanton, S.L. (1999b), 'The Transfer of Arms and the Diffusion of Democracy: Do Arms Promote or Undermine the "Third Wave"?' *The Social Science Journal*, Vol. 36(3), pp. 413-29.

Blanton, S.L. (2000), 'Promoting Human Rights and Democracy in the Developing World: U.S. Rhetoric versus U.S. Arms Exports', *American Journal of Political Science*, Vol. 44(1), pp. 123-31.

Carleton, D. and Stohl, M. (1987), 'The Role of Human Rights in U.S. Foreign Assistance Policy', *American Journal of Political Science*, Vol. 31(4), pp. 1002-18.

Cingranelli, D.L. and Pasquarello, T. (1985), 'Human Rights Practices and the U.S. Distribution of Foreign Aid to Latin American Countries', *American Journal of Political Science*, Vol. 29(3), pp. 539-63.

Claude, R.P. (ed.) (1976), *Comparative Human Rights,* Baltimore, Johns Hopkins University Press.

Collier, P. and Hoeffler, A. (2002), 'On the Incidence of Civil War in Africa', *Journal of Conflict Resolution*, Vol. 46(1), pp. 13-28.

Donnelly, J. (1989), *Universal Human Rights in Theory and Practice,* Ithaca, Cornell University Press.

Douglass F. (1852), 'The Hypocrisy of American Slavery', 4 July 1852, *Modern History Sourcebook* http://washington.uwc.edu/faculty/dhuehner/his101/douglass.htm, accessed 30 June 2003.

Dworkin, R. (1978), *Taking Rights Seriously*, Cambridge, MA, Harvard University Press.

Elbadawi, I. and Sambanis, N. (2000), 'Why are there so many Civil Wars in Africa? Understanding and Preventing Violent Conflict', *Journal of African Economies*, Vol. 9(3), pp. 244-69.

Fearon, J.D and Laitin, D.D. (2003), 'Ethnicity, Insurgency, and Civil War', *American Political Science Review*, Vol. 97(1), pp. 75-90.

Forsythe, D. (1983), *Human Rights and World Politics*, Lincoln, University of Nebraska Press.

Gibney, M. and Stohl, M. (1988), 'Human Rights and U.S. Refugee Policy', in M. Gibney (ed.) *Open Borders? Closed Societies? The Ethical and Political Issues*, Westport, Greenwood Press.

Henderson, C.W. (1991), 'Conditions Affecting the Use of Political Repression', *Journal of Conflict Resolution*, Vol. 35(1), pp. 120-42.

Henderson, C.W. (1993), 'Population Pressures and Political Repression', *Social Science Quarterly*, Vol. 74(2), pp. 322-33.

King, G. and Zeng, L. (2001), 'Improving Forecasts of State Failure', *World Politics*, Vol. 53(4), pp. 623-58.

McCormick, J.M and Mitchell, N. (1988), 'Is U.S. Aid Really Linked to Human Rights in Latin America?' *American Journal of Political Science*, Vol. 32(1), pp. 231-9.

Most, B.A. and Starr, H. (1989), *Inquiry, Logic and International Politics*, Columbia, SC, University of South Carolina Press.

Neumayer, E. (2003), 'Do Human Rights Matter in Bilateral Aid Allocation? A Quantitative Analysis of 21 Donor Countries', *Social Science Quarterly*, Vol. 84(1), pp. 650-66.

Park, H.S. (1987), 'Correlates of Human Rights: Global Tendencies', *Human Rights Quarterly*, Vol. 9(3), pp. 405-13.

Poe, S.C. (1992), 'Human Rights and Economic Assistance under Ronald Reagan and Jimmy Carter', *American Journal of Political Science*, Vol. 36(1), pp. 147-67.

Poe, S.C. and Tate, C.N. (1994), 'Human Rights and Repression in the 1980s: A Global Analysis', *American Political Science Review*, Vol. 88(4), pp. 853-72.

Poe, S.C. and Sirirangsi, R. (1994), 'Human Rights and U.S. Economic Aid During the Reagan Years', *Social Science Quarterly*, Vol. 75(3), pp. 494-509.

Preiswerk, R. (1981), 'Could We Study International Relations as if People Mattered', in *Peace and World Order Studies: A Curriculum Guide,* New York: Transnational Academic Program, Institute for World Order, New York City, 1981.

Regan, P.M. (1995), 'United States Economic Aid and Political Repression: An Empirical Evaluation of United States Foreign Policy', *Political Research Quarterly*, Vol. 48(3), pp. 613-28.

Schoultz, L. (1981), 'US Foreign Policy and Human Rights', *Comparative Politics*, Vol. 13(2), 149-170.

Shue, H. (1980), *Basic Rights: Subsistence, Affluence, and U.S. Foreign Policy*, Princeton, NJ, Princeton University Press.

Starr, H. (1978), '"Opportunity" and "Willingness" as Ordering Concepts in the Study of War', *International Interactions*, Vol. 4, pp. 363-87.

State Failure Task Force (1999), 'State Failure Task Force Report: Phase II Findings', in *Environmental Change and Security Project Report*, Washington, D.C., The Woodrow Wilson Centre.

Stohl, M. and Carleton, D. (1985), 'The Foreign Policy of Human Rights: Rhetoric and Reality from Jimmy Carter to Ronald Reagan', *Human Rights Quarterly*, Vol. 7(2), pp. 205-29.

Stohl, M., Carleton, D. and Johnson, S. (1984), 'Human Rights and U.S. Foreign Assistance from Nixon to Carter', *Journal of Peace Research*, Vol. 21(3), pp. 215-26.

Strouse, J. C. and Claude, R.P. (1976), 'Empirical Comparative Rights Research: Some Preliminary Tests of Development Hypotheses', in R. P. Claude (ed.) *Comparative Human Rights*, Baltimore, Johns Hopkins University Press.

Van Dyke, V. (1973), 'Human Rights Without Discrimination', *The American Political Science Review*, Vol. 67(4), pp. 1267-74.

Zanger, S.C. (2000), 'Good Governance and European Aid: The Impact of Political Conditionality', *European Union Politics*, Vol. 1(3), pp. 293-317.

Chapter 2

The Decision to Repress: An Integrative Theoretical Approach to the Research on Human Rights and Repression

Steven C. Poe

Introduction

Beginning in the mid-1970s, international relations, comparative politics, and public policy scholars began to build statistical models in order to answer the question of why countries abuse human rights and repress their citizens. This movement, spurred by the development and proliferation of international human rights law and reporting, and a growing popular interest and concern for human rights, has recently gained considerable momentum. Empirical studies and their findings have quickly accumulated.[1]

Still, as is almost always the case in any area of inquiry, much hard work remains to be done. The vast majority of studies conducted to date have adopted an approach consistent with that recommended by Blalock's *Theory Construction* (1969), whereby an inventory of hypotheses is compiled from a variety of theories that are then tested in a single multivariate model. This 'scavenger hunt' approach has provided a very good base from which to work, as researchers have compiled empirical findings on the effects of many variables, thus achieving an additive cumulation of findings (Zinnes, 1976) on why repression occurs. Unfortunately, a by-product of the nearly exclusive adoption of this approach is that the theoretical linkages between the many hypotheses, drawn from diverse and seemingly unrelated theoretical perspectives, are as yet quite unclear. Though we can identify several of the variables that influence levels of repression, no model has been put forward to tie them together. Therefore, here I shall concern myself with the task of integrating the hypotheses and findings extant in the empirical literature on human rights and repression into a single, process-oriented decisionmaking model, in order to achieve what Zinnes (1976) called 'integrative cumulation'.

In integrating these findings, this study will move forward our understanding of states' use of human rights abuses and repression in at least three ways. First, this unified model will be much less complex than the many diverse and seemingly unrelated theories that have been tested using the additive approach, and thus, much more parsimonious and easier to comprehend. Second, I will demonstrate that the model can provide analysts with theoretical insights as to why divergent and unexpected findings have arisen, thus indicating directions for their future queries. And third, as a result of the particular model I adopt, from Most and Starr (1989), I will improve over previous research by moving toward a more process-oriented understanding of the dynamics underlying regimes' decision to repress, taking into account the logical difficulties posed by substitutability (Most and Starr, 1984, 1989). Development of this approach could take researchers toward a more sophisticated, process-oriented understanding of why repression occurs.[2]

The Most-Starr Decisionmaking Model

My theoretical point of departure is a variant of the rational actor decisionmaking approach already adopted by others to approach the study of repression and dissent (e.g., DeNardo, 1985; Lichbach, 1987; Simon, 1994).[3] I will employ a conceptual model first presented by Most and Starr (1989), and expanded upon by Starr and his colleagues (e.g., Starr, 1994; Simon, Starr and McGinnis, 1994; Simon and Starr, 1996). The model assumes that decisionmakers can be represented as 'unified and value-maximizing actors who possess perfect information regarding all options and their consequences' (Most and Starr, 1989, p.126). According to the domestic governmental model that relates most closely to my topic (presented in Table 2.1) the main foci of decisionmakers who make domestic policy decisions are their perceptions of their regimes' political *Strength* in the domestic domain (S), and their perception of the probability that a domestic *Threat* (T) will topple their regime. Regime leaders are motivated (or willing) to take an action to increase their Strength, or decrease the Threat to their regime, posed by their political opponents in times of *alarm*, when they perceive the regime's Strength is less than the Threat '($S_{nt1}<T_{nt1}$)', or if they perceive Threat is increasing relative to Strength, that is, '[S_{nt1}/T_{nt1}] < [S_{nt0}/T_{nt0}]' (Most and Starr, 1989, pp.126-8).[4] The regime will be moved to take an action to the end of increasing the Strength/Threat ratio, if such willingness is present *and* if it is presented with the opportunity to do so. The axioms and postulates of the model that are most relevant to our undertaking are presented in Table 2.1. Seen in light of this model, repression and human rights abuse are tools that can be used by leaders to respond when they are alarmed by the S/T ratio.

One should be careful not to take as truth the rhetoric of government leaders and politicians. That being said, their public statements can sometimes provide a window to their perceptions or rationalizations. The rare statements made by officials in repressive regimes appear to indicate that such decisions may focus on the strength of the regime *vis-à-vis* the perceived seriousness of the threat, just as the Most and Starr model suggests. For example, a former Minister of Justice of South Africa, quoted in the work of the Rabie Commission constituted after the death of Steve Biko, was very forthcoming in his statement that 'Over the past almost thirty years, it was necessary, from time to time, to place statutory measures

Table 2.1 A Most-Starr unified actor/governmental stability model

Axiom 1 The decisionmakers of an nth state are - or can be treated as - unified and value-maximizing actors...*

Axiom 2 At any given point in time, the decisionmakers in an nth state perceive that their government has a certain degree of political Strength (S_{nt}) and is confronted by some degree of Threat that it will be toppled by domestic forces (T_{nt}).

Axiom 3a The decisionmakers of an nth state are motivated or willing to establish the following inequality:

$$[S_{nt} > T_{nt}]$$

Axiom 3b The decisionmakers of an nth state are motivated or willing to establish the following inequality:

$$[S_{nt}/T_{nt}] \geq [S_{nt-1}/T_{nt-1}]$$

The postulates of the model most relevant to our undertaking are the following:

Postulate 1 Only if the decisionmakers of an nth state command the necessary objective capability or opportunity (O) to adopt some unilateral policy initiative, then the adoption of that initiative.

Postulate 2 If the decisionmakers of an nth state perceive that their government's Strength has been neglected or allowed to deteriorate between t_0 and t_1 they will perceive that $S_{nt_0} > S_{nt_1}$

Postulate 3 If a given domestic opponent of the government increases its capacity between t_0 and t_1 and the decisionmakers in an nth state perceive that action as a Threat to their government, they will perceive that $T_{nt0} < T_{nt1}$.

Postulate 4a If $[S_{nt_1} < T_{nt_1}]$ then the decisionmakers of the nth state will be motivated to adopt some policy initiative which is designed to increase S_n and/or decrease T_n at t_2.

Postulate 4b If $[S_{nt_1}/T_{nt_1}] < [S_{nt_0}/T_{nt_0}]$ then the decisionmakers of the nth state will be motivated to adopt some policy initiative which is designed to increase S_n and/or decrease T_n at t_2

Postulate 5 If and only if the decision makers of an nth state command the necessary capacity (or opportunity) to adopt some unilateral policy alternative and they are motivated (or willing) to do so, then the adoption of that initiative.

* This is an amalgamation of Models 3 and 4, presented in Most and Starr (1989, pp. 126-8). Some of the notation has been changed, but the postulates and axioms are essentially identical to those presented in that source, with one exception. Part of Axiom 1, which assumes perfect information, has been left out because that is an assumption I do not wish to make here.

on the lawbook to counteract the constantly changing threats to the internal security of the republic' (quoted in Foster and Davis, 1987, p.31).

According to that official, the statutes (which did result in many of the human rights abuses borne by the black majority in South Africa) were put in place in reaction to threats *perceived* by the white minority in power. Or, put in terms of the model, a decrease in the S/T ratio was perceived as a result of the perception of an increase in Threat. Then repressive measures were enacted with an eye toward decreasing T, thus tending to increase the S/T ratio to what, from the regime's standpoint, would be a more favourable value.

For further evidence taken from the context of a totalitarian government, consider this quote from probably the worst violator of human rights in modern times, Adolf Hitler:

> I shall spread terror through the surprising application of all means. The sudden shock of a terrible fear of death is what matters. Why should I deal otherwise with all my political opponents? These so-called atrocities save me hundreds of thousands of individual actions against the protesters and discontents. Each one of them will think twice to oppose us when he learns what is [awaiting] him in the [concentration] camp (Hitler, quoted in Gurr, 1986, pp.46-7).

In Hitler's eyes then, it seems that some of his murder was but an expedient way of decreasing the threats that he perceived (whether they be real or imagined) increasing the S/T ratio by decreasing T. Finally, for an example from yet another region, statements by former Philippine President Ferdinand Marcos cited by Ruiz (1989) also imply that his attention was on the S/T ratio, when he determined to enact repressive national security laws.

The model outlined in the table and discussed in the text is an amalgamation of two of the four models presented in the Most and Starr book dealing with regimes' decisionmaking processes in domestic and international level games (e.g., Putnam, 1988). Underlying these models is the assumption that variables may exercise effects on repression and other policy outputs either because they constrain leaders' choices, i.e., environmental possibilism in the Sprout's terms, and/or because they are perceived by decisionmakers and are therefore transformed into ideas or information that are considered and brought to bear in some way on decisions, as with environmental probabalism (Sprout and Sprout, 1969). For example, in the model dealing with the international level game, which is the major focus of the majority of Most and Starr's research, the use of force is conceived of as being but one option, or opportunity among many possibilities, or substitutable items on the menu (e.g., Russett and Starr, 1992) of *some* decisionmakers to deal with their international security dilemma. In a similar way, repression is but one option of several courses of action that *can be chosen* by leaders to deal with their domestic dilemma: how to keep control when there are those who would threaten to topple the regime.

Though decisionmakers usually have the capability to repress and often believe repression to be a viable tool to use in dealing with this dilemma, there are almost certainly other tools at their disposal that could be used to accomplish that same purpose. To rehearse some examples, governments may make concessions in reaction to the opposition in the hope of diffusing the threat. In some cases decisionmakers may, by taking particular actions on a critical issue, be able to shift some portion of public support from the opposition to the government, thereby increasing Strength while decreasing Threat. For example, scapegoating a minority political opponent, as Hitler did to Jews as he rose to power, may have been part of his way of consolidating Strength, by appealing to anti-semitic sentiments in pre-war Germany, drawing support to his regime. Also, since they are involved in a two-level game, regime leaders may seek foreign aid from abroad with the idea of increasing their Strength in the domestic sphere.

Because such options are substitutable, Most and Starr point out, the results stemming from analyses using one item of the menu alone as the dependent variable (e.g., use of force, or repression) may prove misleading (1989). This is particularly true if we are looking for a generally applicable linear relationship between an independent variable and one policy output, as is typically done, since leaders may choose different options at different times and conditions in response to the same stimulus. According to this line of reasoning, we should conceive of the problem more broadly, as is done in this model.

In the remainder of this chapter I will briefly review the empirical literature on human rights and repression. Then I will use the model to bring some order to the many propositions and findings arising from this literature.

Previous Literature on Human Rights, Repression and State Terror

It would be impossible to offer an in-depth and complete coverage and critique of the methodologies, operationalizations, designs and findings of each empirical study of repression in the available space, and therefore such a review must be beyond the scope of this paper. That being said, though, an overview and characterization of the major attributes of these studies is in order.

In his recent review of the repression literature Davenport (1997) argues that empirical and theoretical research on repression tends to come from one of three separate traditions: human rights (e.g., Mitchell and McCormick, 1988; Henderson, 1991, 1993; Poe and Tate, 1994; McNitt, 1995), state terror (e.g., Stohl, Carleton and Johnson, 1984; Lopez, 1984, 1986; Gurr, 1986) and negative sanctions (e.g., Rasler, 1986; Ziegenhagen, 1986; Davenport, 1995a, 1995b, 1996a, 1996b, 1997). A reading of these studies leads inexorably to the conclusion that the three veins of research do, in fact, have much in common, and that many of the differences are in terminology only. This becomes especially evident when one or more of the labels are used interchangeably (e.g., Gurr, 1986; Poe and Tate, 1994). Indeed, in spite of their rhetorical differences, most of the studies cited above refer to the dependent phenomenon at some point as 'repression' (e.g., Pion-Berlin, 1984; Davis and Ward, 1990). I will therefore use that term to describe literature in each of these three veins throughout the remainder of the paper.

Though each research tradition deals with some aspect of repression, there are certainly non-trivial differences in the studies' operationalizations of that phenomenon. The negative sanctions literature has adopted what Lopez and Stohl (1992) have called an events-based approach to measurement. These studies use a simple count of the number of repressive events, or negative sanctions, occurring in a particular country during a chosen time frame to represent repression. Most often used are measurements that tap the number of instances of censorship and political restrictions, including restrictions on the media and instances of limitation and/or restrictions of political parties or individuals (e.g., Davenport, 1995b). Thus this approach is primarily concerned with government actions that take away civil and political liberties, and it assumes that the number of events during a chosen time frame is a theoretically interesting indicator of repression.

Statistical studies from the human rights literature, by contrast, have tended to use standards-based measures. These measures are generated by trained coders who read human rights organizations' and governmental agencies' reports on human rights conditions in the world's countries. Those readers then categorize countries based on a predetermined set of criteria. The bulk of human rights studies have focused primarily on violations of personal (or physical) integrity, where persons are imprisoned, tortured, executed or disappeared either arbitrarily or due to their political views (e.g., Cingranelli and Pasquarello, 1985; Mitchell and McCormick, 1988; Poe, Tate and Keith, 1997; Zanger, 2000, Carey 2004, Keith 2004). Somewhat different coding criteria have been employed by the various researchers, but they have commonly used one of two sources of information; the annual Reports of Amnesty International (e.g., 1996) and of the U.S. State Department (e.g., 1997). Though there are few statistical studies which explicitly choose the state terror terminology the most commonly used measure in the human rights literature is the Political Terror Scale (Gibney and Dalton, 1996) which was originally gathered by Michael Stohl, a scholar who has written articles using both the human rights and state terror terminologies (e.g., Stohl, Carleton and Johnson, 1984; Mitchell, Stohl, Carleton and Lopez, 1986; Lopez and Stohl, 1992). This makes sense, since one could argue, as Poe and Tate (1994) did, that state terror and serious abuses of the human right to physical integrity are but two sides of the same coin, since human rights violations are the result of regimes' terrorists acts. More closely related to the negative sanctions literature are empirical human rights studies using the Freedom House scales (e.g., Gastil, 1989), standards-based measures which capture the degree to which a broad range of political rights and civil liberties are realized around the world (e.g., Strouse and Claude, 1976; Park, 1987; Boswell and Dixon, 1990; Meyer, 1996).

Clearly the measures used by the negative sanctions and the human rights/state terror approaches differ, but put in terms of the domestic model there is an underlying similarity; each taps decisionmakers' choice of repressive actions from the menu of behaviours, both repressive and nonrepressive, that can often be employed by regimes with an eye toward dealing with perceived threats. Therefore, the commonality in hypotheses and findings that appears in these literatures (to be discussed in greater depth later) is to be expected.

Another similarity is that the vast majority of these studies employ similar methodologies. With but a few exceptions they use ordinary leasr squares (O.L.S.) multiple regression, which allows the researcher to isolate the effects of one variable on repression, while holding the effects of other factors constant and assuming linear relationships.[5] The vast majority of research designs have a cross-national component (meaning they are either cross-national or pooled cross-sectional time series studies), though there are some exceptions that analyse exclusively time series data (e.g., Pion-Berlin, 1984; Rasler, 1986; Davis and Ward, 1990).

Toward an Integrative Cumulation of Findings on Repression

A necessary first step toward integration is to take inventory of the hypotheses that have been tested and the findings which have accumulated. When one examines these studies, one is struck by the variety of hypotheses that have been tested. Though findings are mixed on a number of hypotheses, research seems to have reached a consensus on the effects of several variables. Multivariate research conducted with both events and standards-based approaches strongly supports the conclusion that past repression influences current levels of repression (Poe and Tate, 1994; Davenport, 1995, 1996a, 1995a; Poe, Tate and Keith, 1997; Richards, Gelleny and Sacko, 2001). The clear majority of findings from each of these approaches indicate that democratic political institutions are associated with less political repression (Henderson, 1991, 1993; Davenport, 1995b, 1996a, 1996b; Poe and Tate, 1994; Poe, Tate and Keith, 1997; Richards, 1997; Zanger 2000; Callaway, 2001; Sherborne, 2003; Harrelson-Stephens, 2003; Keith, 2004; Carey, 2004).[6] Economic development has generally been found to be associated with somewhat fewer negative sanctions and less human rights abuse (e.g., Strouse and Claude, 1976; Mitchell and McCormick, 1988; Boswell and Dixon, 1990; Poe and Tate, 1994; Davenport, 1995b; McNitt, 1995; Meyer, 1996; Poe, Tate and Keith, 1997; Carey 2004) once other relevant factors have been controlled (but see Davenport, 1996a and Henderson, 1993). Research with standards-based human rights measures strongly support the conclusion that countries' involvement in international war is associated with greater repression of human rights (Poe and Tate, 1994; Poe, Tate and Keith, 1997) as does a study using a negative sanctions approach, focusing on the twentieth century United States (Rasler, 1986), and a recent multivariate cross-national study (Sherborne, 2003). Finally, quite consistent with the axioms and postulates of the Most and Starr (1989) model, hypotheses linking the presence of various forms of threats and dissent with increased repression have received quite strong support in quantitative analyses using both events and standards-based repression variables (e.g., Ziegenhagen, 1986; Boswell and Dixon, 1990; Davis and Ward, 1990; Alfatooni and Allen, 1991; Davenport, 1995, 1996a, 1996b, 1997; Poe and Tate, 1994; Poe, Tate, Keith and Lanier, 1997; Poe, Tate and Keith, 1999; Zanger, 2000; Sherborne, 2003; Carey 2004) and the existence of an important linkage is widely accepted (Davenport, 1995b). Some analyses with standards-based measures indicate that population size is an important determinant of repression (Poe and Tate, 1994; Poe, Tate and Keith, 1997; Carey 2004). Finally, the results provide some support for the hypothesis that military presence in government is associated with repression (McKinlay and

Cohan, 1975, 1976; Ziegenhagen, 1986; Poe and Tate, 1994; Davenport, 1995b; McNitt, 1995; Poe, Tate and Keith, 1999).

More mixed findings have been yielded with regard to the effects of numerous other variables, including population growth (e.g., Henderson, 1993, Poe and Tate, 1994; Poe, Tate and Keith, 1997), economic growth (Strouse and Claude, 1976; Poe and Tate, 1994; McNitt, 1995; Poe, Tate and Keith, 1999), British cultural influence (e.g., McCormick and Mitchell, 1988; Boswell and Dixon, 1990; Poe and Tate, 1994; Poe, Tate and Keith, 1997), leftist government (McCormick and Mitchell, 1988; Boswell and Dixon, 1990; Davenport, 1995b; Poe and Tate, 1994; McNitt, 1995; Poe, Tate and Keith, 1997), international trade and investment variables (Meyer, 1996; Smith, Bolyard and Ippolito, 1999; Richards et al., 2001; Harrelson-Stephens 2003; Harrelson-Stephens and Callaway, 2003), cultural diversity (Walker and Poe, 2002; Lee, Lindstrom, Moore and Turan, 2004) and a variety of external, international environmental variables (e.g., Pion-Berlin, 1984; Ziegenhagen, 1986; Boswell and Dixon, 1990; Davis and Ward, 1990; Henderson, 1995; Meyer, 1996; Davenport, 1995b; Keith and Poe, 1996; Blanton, 1999; Sherborne, 2003; Miller 2004).

An additive cumulation of findings is clearly present, but what is lacking is a theory to integrate them, thus making them easier to comprehend. The Most and Starr domestic decisionmaking model provides us with just such a theoretical tool, as each of the many hypotheses outlined above can be integrated into it in at least one of four possible ways. First, variables may affect repression because they increase or decrease the levels of Threat perceived by decisionmakers. Second, variables may affect repression because they increase or decrease leaders' perceptions of Strength. Third, they may affect the kinds of opportunities that are available to decisionmakers who are acting in response to their perceptions of the Strength/Threat ratio. Fourth and finally, variables may affect regime leaders' willingness to adopt the option of repression as opposed to other available options on the menu, once those leaders are alarmed. To illustrate the utility of this model as an integrative device I will focus mainly on the variables that have received support as determinants of repression.

Entry Point One: Variables that Influence Perceptions of Threat

One of the most frequently examined and strongly supported linkages in the literature is the connection between democracy and repression. Though it is not reflected in the statistical models tested thus far, descriptions of the theoretical underpinnings of the democracy hypothesis often appear to posit the effect for that variable to travel through the intervening variable of Threat. Consider, for example, the following quote from Henderson (1991):

> Democracy 'offers a meaningful alternative for handling conflict if leaders choose to use it. Democracy should not be viewed as an idealistic process, but as a realistic way to accommodate demands with a minimum of conflict [citations omitted]. With a large measure of democracy, conflict should not grow so sharp as to invite repression' (Henderson, 1991, pp.123-4).

Other variables found to be important by past studies seem likely to influence repression levels through their impact on perceived Threat. These are contextual factors such as economic development, population size and population growth. With regard to the effect of population growth, Henderson argues that countries burdened with large population growth rates are apt to be confronted with 'burgeoning demands' (1993, p.4), which would lead to a greater probability of threats occurring, other factors being equal. With regard to population size, it has been argued that large numbers of people tend to place a stress on resources and, as a matter of probability, that a larger number of citizens increases the probability that entrepreneurs will be present to successfully form dissident movements (Poe and Tate, 1994). So while democracy would tend to decrease threat, by making alternative (and peaceful) pathways to power available to the opposition, large populations might tend to increase the level of Threat. Each would exercise an indirect effect on the probability of increased repression, through their effect on Threat.

Economic development has been one of the variables most commonly linked to repression by previous empirical works.[7] In presenting their theoretical reasons for posing this hypothesis, Mitchell and McCormick suggest the importance of Threat as an intervening factor, arguing that 'The poorest countries, with substantial social and political tensions created by economic scarcity, would be most unstable and thus most apt to use repression in order to maintain control' (1988, p.478). Along the same lines, Henderson argues that 'It is only logical to think that, with a higher level of development, people will be more satisfied' (1991, p.126). This, of course, would tend to decrease levels of Threat, as it is unlikely that those who are satisfied will mobilize against the regime.

External threats, in the form of participation in international wars, may affect internal dissent and therefore levels of domestic threat perceived by regime leaders, consistent with the logic of Putnam's (1988) two-level game. Though an initial rally-around-the-flag effect may occur in some instances, it is likely that as losses mount the populace will tend to tire of war efforts (e.g., Mueller, 1973), as was apparently the case in the U.S. during the War in Vietnam. This would increase the probability that movements against the regime will arise, increasing T, decreasing S/T, and therefore increasing the probability that the regime will choose to enact repressive responses.

Finally, decisionmakers' belief systems enter the model through their effect on leaders' perceptions of reality. The model leaves open the possibility (or, perhaps more accurately, the strong likelihood) that decisionmakers' perception of an increased Threat are in part the result of their viewing events through the filter of ideology. Hitler's Nazism identified Jews as a serious threat, both internally and internationally. This accepted state ideology played a part in the horrific human rights violations in part because it led Hitler and his followers to *perceive* Jews to be a serious threat to his regime, whether they were one or not (see Arendt, 1951). Similarly, military regimes in Latin America may have been moved to undertake coups in part by ideologies that emphasize their positions as defenders of national security against threats, both at home and abroad.[8] In the case of Argentina, this sort of worldview, which Pion-Berlin and Lopez (1991) call the 'National Security

Doctrine' was combined with a free market ideology. Perhaps as a result the Dirty War was undertaken to eviscerate the alleged threat – members of particular unions that were 'perceived by the government to have obstructed its achievement of economic and security goals' (Pion-Berlin and Lopez, 1991, p.63).

Entry Point Two: Variables that Influence Perceived Levels of Strength

The second path by which variables may affect levels of repression is by decreasing the strength of the regime in decisionmakers' minds, thereby decreasing the Strength/Threat ratio. It is more difficult to find implicit evidence of this path being important in existing theoretical discussions. Still, several of the variables found to be important in explanations of repression (as well as some variables whose effects have not been supported so well by the literature, to be discussed later) may affect Strength and/or regimes' perceptions of Strength. For example, economic development is one variable that would tend to affect both Threat and Strength. Its impact on Strength is apt to be positive because a strong economy allows the demands made by the populace to be better accommodated. Also, leaders' perception of their own strength would tend to be greater in economically developed countries in part because their countries are typically perceived to be better risks by investors and financial institutions at home and abroad. This means that the regime of a developed country is apt to be able to obtain more capital from other sources than it would if it were a less developed country.

The fact that a particular country is ruled by a military regime that took power through a coup probably also decreases Strength in that country for a couple of reasons. In some cases, their taking power through the use of force or the threat to use force has led parties in the international environment to question the legitimacy of the regime, and in some cases even to enact sanctions that would tend to decrease Strength. Further, the fact that the regime gained power through extra-constitutional means would not be completely lost on members of the regime either, for they would often realize that they would enjoy greater legitimacy, and therefore strength, if they had been put in power by the will of the people. Perhaps this is one reason why military coups are often followed by increases in repression, as was the case in Argentina and Chile in the mid-1970s.

Finally, it would seem that involvement in an international war is another factor that would tend to decrease Strength, either because limited resources are spent on the war effort or because of losses in manpower and capital in connection with that war effort.

Entry Point Three: Variables that Affect the Alternatives on Decisionmakers' Menu

One of the contributions of the Most and Starr model to our understanding of repression is that it reminds us that a consideration of opportunities is a necessary step in the decisionmaking process. Surely all countries have the capability to undertake some repressive measures such as stabbing opponents with a pointed stick, or imprisoning them for political purposes, but some countries may not have the security forces necessary to undertake large-scale human rights violations against the entire citizenry. A bureaucracy with individuals willing to commit human rights violations is important in this context, a necessary condition for higher levels of repression to occur. (See both Smeulers in this volume on how individuals are convinced to commit human rights violations and Policzer in this volume on the bureaucracies of which many of those individuals are a part.)

The statistical analyses that have been conducted in the literature thus far, however, are not very well suited to finding necessary conditions, because they assume a general linear relationship, inconsistent with the logic of the likely effects of a necessary condition (Davenport, 1995a, 1996a).[9] Perhaps methods better suited to isolating necessary conditions (Braumoeller and Goertz, 1997) would yield more supportive statistical results.

Structural dependence may be another factor entering the decisionmaking process at this point. As Mason and Krane (1989) point out, dependent development may leave countries without the institutions or the political machinery to address demands from opposition elements through accommodation. Thus the accommodating options on their decisionmaking menus are constrained and, perhaps, repressive measures made more likely. They find support for this proposition in a case study of El Salvador. Similarly, the lack of sufficient economic development (perhaps as a result of dependence) may decrease decisionmakers' ability to choose accommodation over repression.

Entry Point Four: Variables that Affect the Choice among the Alternatives on the Menu

Fourth and finally, the factors hypothesized to impact levels of repression may affect the likelihood that the regime will adopt particular options as opposed to others once it is in a state of alarm, and thus has the willingness to take an action. Consider again that repression may be but one of several tools available to decisionmakers to increase the Strength/Threat ratio in a particular country at a given moment in time. Being in a state of alarm, a regime is willing to take an action but may have several alternatives on its menu from which to choose. Here the decisionmakers' perception of the consequence of repression as compared to the perceived results of other available options is highly relevant. The type of political system, and the attributes of political culture, have an effect in the definition of the pay-off structure that decisionmakers face, and therefore on the option(s) that will be apt to lead to an increase of the S/T ratio. So, too, the campaigns by international non-governmental organizations such as Amnesty International, and coordinated efforts between groups and foreign governments in the form of Transnational Advocacy Networks (Keck and Sikkink, 1998), may lead a regime to perceive an increase in the costs associated with repression, thus leading them to be more moderate in their actions than they would otherwise be. Later case studies seem to support this claim (e.g., Keck and Sikkink, 1998; Risse, Ropp and Sikkink, 1999), but thus far no statistical analyses have been conducted on this issue.

Variables that would seem to enter the decisionmaking process here, as well as other entry points, include previous levels of repression, democracy and military control, and economic development. Previous levels of repression have been shown to be an extremely important determinant of present personal integrity abuse. That bureaucracies tend to make decisions incrementally, using past decisions as a baseline for the present, is well known and widely held. Further, organizations are held to have an inertia because they tend to resist change (e.g., Allison, 1971; Bendor and Hammond, 1992). For both of these reasons there is apt to be less cost associated with repression when it is already being used as a tool in the prior period, other things being equal. Further, if repression has not been used in the previous period the choice of this option is apt to be more costly than it would otherwise be, other factors being equal.

Apart from its effects that enter at points one and two, democracy also puts in place an incentive structure that is apt to discourage the choice of repression by government officials. As William Dixon (1994) maintains, both the citizenry and the leaders of a democracy are socialized into democratic norms that conflicts should be resolved peacefully, through bargaining and negotiation instead of violence, in a system that adheres to the rules of 'bounded competition'. The presence of these norms, coupled with the use of elections to choose key decisionmakers, means that leaders are apt to forego repression as a tool. If they do not, they are apt to be punished for the excessive use of repression when people go to the polls. Elections thus give citizens of democratic governments a check on leaders that is not present when a non-democratic government is in place, a key difference in the incentive structures of democratic and nondemocratic leaders.

Whether the decisionmakers are a part of a military regime might also enter the decisionmaking process at this point. Recent findings indicate that military government may have some effect on states' propensities to repress basic human rights even after controlling for levels of democracy (Poe and Tate, 1994; Davenport, 1995a; Poe Tate, and Keith, 1997). Military governments are, of course, nondemocratic governments, so we would expect that military governments would be more repressive than others for this reason. If that were the only reason to pose the military government–human rights hypothesis, we should not expect military government to exercise an impact on repression independent from that of democracy. However, the existence of militarily controlled government might also serve to remove obstructions to the use of force that would be present in civilian governments, thus decreasing the cost of repression relative to other available options.

Another variable that may enter the picture at this point is economic development. Consistent with the argument of John Mueller (1990), one might argue that developed nations have evolved to the point where certain behaviours are proscribed as being inhumane. If, as Mueller argued, major war has become unsavoury to decisionmakers in those countries, and thus is unlikely in the future, then we would surely expect that major human rights abuses would be viewed with similar disdain by those at the helm of the same regimes. Though repression may be on the menu of the decisionmakers of those countries, leaders may be less willing to undertake it than in countries where no such norms are in place, other factors being equal.[10]

Resolving Existing Puzzles

Though still other linkages of the model to other hypotheses might be made, I have illustrated how the Most and Starr model provides us with a means to integrate the empirical findings in the repression literature into a single theoretical structure. What remains to be seen, however, is whether this model will be a useful tool in helping to resolve empirical contradictions and puzzling findings existing in this field of study. A complete explanation of all negative and ambiguous findings in the repression subfield is well beyond the scope of this chapter. However, in the section that follows, I will further demonstrate the utility of the Most-Starr model by addressing two of the problems in the field, pertaining to the effects of economic growth and foreign aid allocations on repression.

The Effect of Economic Growth

One of the variables on which mixed and puzzling findings have been found is economic growth. Previous studies have yielded contradictory findings, including coefficients that are statistically insignificant in both unexpected and expected directions (Poe and Tate, 1994; McNitt, 1995).

Some of the variables discussed in the sections above (e.g., democracy, economic development) may reasonably be expected to affect Strength and Threat in opposite directions, leading one to the expectation (consistent with empirical findings) that the Strength/Threat ratio will either increase or decrease in response to changes in those variables. However, a complication may arise in the case of economic growth because an increase in that variable could reasonably be expected to simultaneously increase both Strength and Threat. Mancur Olson's theoretical work would lead us to expect that economic growth will tend to increase the probability of dissent, and therefore threats, both because it rarely is rapid enough to outstrip the growth of expectations that is also occurring, and because it increases the number of *déclassé* individuals and groups that are most prone to promote instability (Olson, 1963; Gurr, 1970; Poe and Tate, 1994). According to these lines of reasoning we would expect that economic growth would increase dissatisfaction with government and, therefore, Threat to the government and the probability of greater repression. Alternatively, though, we might expect that economic growth would serve to strengthen the regime in the eyes of the economic and military elites and others not dislocated by the growth at home and in the view of foreign governments, corporations and financial institutions abroad. If this is indeed the case, then economic growth would lead to a regime's perceiving increased Strength, which might well make up for the increases in perceived levels of Threats, such that $[S_{nt_1}/T_{nt_1}] \geq [S_{nt_0}/T_{nt_0}]$. Thus, we should not necessarily expect that leaders will be alarmed by economic growth and therefore be willing to enact measures such as repression with an eye toward decreasing Threat. Considered in this light, it is not too surprising that repression studies have found mixed evidence on this variable's effect. An important linkage of repression to economic growth could be missed if both of these effects are present in a sample, weighing differently depending on the country and their different circumstances.

The Impact of Foreign Aid on Repression

Much research has been done on the linkage between human rights and foreign aid, asking the question whether donor nations take into account human rights when allocating their aid moneys (e.g., Cingranelli and Pasquarello, 1985; Stohl and Carleton, 1987; McCormick and Mitchell, 1988; Poe, 1991, 1992; Poe and Sirirangsi, 1993, 1994; Blanton, 1994; Poe, Pilatovsky, Miller and Ogundele, 1994; Poe and Meernik, 1995; Sterken, 1996; Apodaca and Stohl, 1997; Barratt, 2004). Given the amount of research on the effect of human rights considerations on foreign aid, it is somewhat surprising that little research has been conducted on the policy relevant question of whether the donation or revocation of aid influences human rights in recipient countries. In the first published multivariate quantitative study on this question of which I am aware, Regan (1995) examined a cross-national data set including 32 less developed countries, using multiple regression, to ascertain whether changes in U.S. foreign aid allocation result in changes in their respect for human rights. From the results of these analyses he concludes that the lagged effect of aid on human rights conditions, though statistically significant in the context of a multivariate model, is rather small and unimportant. In a second study, William Meyer (1996) investigates the effects of U.S. aid allocated in 1983 and 1987, as one of a variety of economic variables explaining variations in the Freedom House Civil Liberties and Political Rights scores, for the years of 1985 and 1990, and samples of 52 and 39 developing countries, respectively. His findings show positive relationships between aid and levels of respect for human rights, statistically insignificant for the 1985 analyses, but statistically significant or bordering on statistical significance for the year of 1990. Taken together, these studies appear to show that U.S. aid might have a small effect on human rights practices, or on changes in repression levels, though those effects are at best only minuscule. I will argue, however, that though these analyses are useful first explorations of the issue, because they tend to show that aid does not have a large effect on repression generally, they fail to provide us with evidence sufficient to confidently conclude that foreign aid is 'not an effective mechanism for altering the human rights records in recipient countries' (Regan, 1995, p.625).

To illustrate, let us first assume that the U.S. decreases a country's aid package by 20 million dollars. What effect would this likely have on the S/T ratio, and therefore the likelihood of increases or decreases in repression, in a particular recipient country? The most reasonable answer to this question, with the information given, is 'It depends'. That is, the effect of such a decrease on the S/T ratio might be either great or negligible, depending on a set of factors not yet considered in the analyses conducted to date. One such factor is the degree to which a country is dependent on the foreign aid being cut. We might expect that a decrease of this magnitude would have a greater effect on the S/T ratio of a regime that is highly dependent on that aid, as compared to one where the aid is not that important to the regime. In the more dependent of the two countries the likely immediate result of the decrease in aid would be a corresponding decrease in the strength of the regime. If other factors are held constant, this would have the effect of alarming the regime, $[S_{nt_1}/T_{nt_1}] < [S_{nt_0}/T_{nt_0}]$, giving leaders the willingness to take action to increase the S/T ratio. Thus, ironically, the model suggests that the cut-off of aid sometimes undertaken due to human rights concerns could result in a condition of alarm in the targeted nation, which would in some cases lead to greater repression.[11]

When might foreign aid be used as a tool to improve human rights? A credible threat by the donor nation to take away the 20 million dollars might affect the decisionmaking calculus of an aid-dependent offending regime, making the costs of repression greater than the costs of other instruments to deal with alarming situations (entry point four). Or if the donor offers aid under the condition that repression levels are decreased, the recipient regime might be led to decrease its abuses in the expectation that the increase in Strength associated with aid will compensate for any increase in Threat due to its decreased use of repression. Another factor not considered by the analyses conducted to date, then, is that the donor must communicate to the recipient that it has expectations regarding the recipients' human rights practices for the revocation to have any effect. If not, then there is no reason to expect that the aid will affect levels of repression in the recipient country. For a concrete example, consider the serious human rights violations undertaken by the Salvadoran regime and their surrogates when U.S. aid was at very high levels to that country in the early 1980s. The Reagan administration framed El Salvador as a Cold War battlefield, of vital importance to U.S. security interests in the Western hemisphere. Perceiving this, the Salvadoran regime was not apt to take very seriously either the complaints regarding their crimes heard in the halls of Congress, or the statutes that body had passed years before, tying U.S. aid to human rights concerns. Had the issue been framed differently by the administration, and if there had been a believable threat that aid would have been cut-off, then perhaps the expectations of that regime would have been different, and its repressive policies moderated more quickly.

What becomes clear from the above discussion is that the communication process between the donor and recipient, the messages sent, and their strategic interactions are apt to be important to our understanding of the linkage between aid and repression overlooked by the analyses conducted to date. A better understanding of the effect of foreign aid on human rights would be gained if we were to use models that would allow us to better grasp the strategic interaction between donor and the recipient regimes across time.

Another insight we have gained from our application of the Most and Starr model to this problem is that conditional relationships may exist, where the effect of foreign aid on human rights conditions is contingent on other factors that, as yet, may have been unspecified in statistical analyses testing for the presence of general laws. Empirical searches for domain-specific 'Nice Laws' (Most and Starr, 1989), whereby it is hypothesized that the effect of aid on repression is dependent on the degree of dependence of countries on U.S. foreign aid, might well bear fruit.

Summary and Conclusions

Numerous studies of the determinants of repression have been conducted, a variety of hypotheses have been tested and a plethora of empirical findings have accumulated. As a result of these studies we can confidently identify several variables that are apt to affect the likelihood that regimes will choose repression. What has thus far been lacking, though, is a theoretical tool that allows researchers to tie together the various, seemingly unconnected hypotheses. What Zinnes called 'integrative cumulation' (1976) has been missing.

In this chapter my goal was to achieve integrative cumulation by using a decisionmaking model developed by Most and Starr (1989). This model did in fact show us that each of the hypotheses and findings present in the field can be integrated into a single, parsimonious decisionmaking model, in which the regime's perception of its strength and the threats to its rule are key foci. Secondly, the model helps us to draw theoretical insights regarding the processes behind some of the mixed and negative findings that have arisen to date. Drawing on these insights it should be possible to conduct new empirical analyses that will better explicate the nature of the effects of factors such as economic growth and foreign aid.

This exercise also showed that there is good reason to believe that important relationships are being hidden because most analysts search exclusively for general laws, holding across all cases. Our understanding of repression might be moved forward if we were to look for laws that hold in particular domains, defined by factors that as yet are unspecified in statistical models.

Finally, the examples illustrated that a better understanding of the effect of foreign aid on human rights (and perhaps other international factors such as economic sanctions or efforts of Transnational Advocacy Networks) rests on our adoption of models that allow researchers to move beyond simply identifying factors that have linear effects on repression, to models that can capture the dynamic effects of these variables on regimes' decisionmaking processes as they unravel across time. The model we adopted has certain advantages in this regard, because in it is imbedded the element of time. [12] Maybe in future work it can be adapted further, to help us to grasp the interactions between two or more international actors.

Notes

1 E.g., McKinlay and Cohan, 1975, 1976; Strouse and Claude, 1976; Park, 1987; Ziegenhagen, 1986; Mitchell and McCormick, 1988; Boswell and Dixon, 1990; Davis and Ward, 1990; Alfatooni and Allen, 1991; Cingranelli, 1992; Henderson, 1991, 1993; Poe and Tate, 1994; Davenport, 1995a, 1995b, 1996a, 1996b; Fein, 1995; McNitt, 1995; Regan, 1995; Meyer, 1996; Richards, 1996; Poe, Tate and Keith, 1999; Poe, Tate, Keith and Lanier, 1997; Gartner and Regan, 1996; King, 1997; Richards, 1999; Cingranelli and Richards, 1997, 1999; Keith, 1999; Blanton, 1999; Smith,

Bolyard, and Ippolito, 1999; Zanger, 2000; Richards, Gelleny and Sacko, 2001; Walker and Poe, 2002.

2 See Panning (1983, pp.484-90) for a cogent argument that our understanding of political phenomena could be improved if we were to aim toward building process-oriented models, as opposed to merely collecting generalizations.

3 The use of Threat as a central concept is a similarity between my model and that of Gartner and Regan (1996). It should be noted, though, that in focusing only on the seriousness of demands placed by opposition groups, those researchers adopt a very narrow, and I think, incorrect operationalizational definition of threat which overlooks important factors that are apt to color perceptions of the regime, such as the size and strength of the group, and the methods they choose to use.

4 The term 'alarm' is mine.

5 But see Gartner and Regan (1996) and Fein (1995) for exceptions. Also, see Richards (1999) and Richards et al. (2001), Sherborne (2003) and Harrelson-Stephens (2003) for examples of studies using alternative methodologies.

6 Fein (1995) presents bivariate statistical results which indicate that there may be 'more murder in the middle', that the transition of non-democracies to democratic states may be paved with greater human rights abuse. Though this topic cannot be dealt with in much depth here, I believe that insight into these findings can be gained with the Most and Starr model. Countries in transition periods might be apt to have more threats occurring, and new leaders may be apt to perceive greater threats until their rule is consolidated (and the S/T ratio increased to remove the state of alarm). If this is the case, the curvilinear, bivariate relationship uncovered by Fein may be the result of the alteration of the governing arrangements as opposed to the move toward democracy in particular.

7 A dissenting voice is the Richards et al. (2001) study. However, this study included only less developed countries, thus constraining the variance on the independent variable. This would seem to be the likely reason behind the difference in results.

8 Of course such ideologies are preceded by sets of interests, and they may be developed as a rationalization for giving the armed forces more power and to take control. Even if this were the case, though, the diffusion of such destructive ideologies to rank and file members of the police and military forces and to the public would still make repression more likely by affecting the decisionmaking calculus in other ways. Ideologies would enter the decisionmaking process at entry points three and four, at entry point three by constraining security forces' willingness to question the regimes' repressive actions, thus, perhaps increasing the menu of feasible repressive options available to the regime. If such ideologies were adopted by members of the public at large, this would be apt to decrease the cost of repression relative to other choices on the menu, since persons subscribing to such ideologies would not be apt to question the government's repressive actions.

9 Davenport tested models in which a variable tapping coercive capacity (Defense expenditures/Total government expenditures) was employed, and statistically insignificant results were yielded. Still that variable is certainly an important part of the story of why repression occurs and should be considered in our future efforts to build process-oriented models of decisionmaking processes.

10 Here I should note that the republican governmental systems of most developed countries may be an important reason why such norms are developed, and thus there may be some difficulty in disentangling, empirically, the effects of democracy and development.

11 Alternatively, though, the withheld aid could decrease Strength to the extent that the old regime falls (i.e., Schoultz, 1981; Regan, 1995) ushering in either a more repressive or a less repressive revolutionary regime.

12 Clearly the variables in this literature could have been integrated to other sorts of frameworks. For example, we might have adopted a 'levels of analysis' approach similar to that of Waltz (1954) or Levy (1996). However useful such categorizations are as heuristic devices, they do not have this advantage.

References

Alfatooni, A. and Allen, M. (1991), 'Government Sanctions and Collective Protest in Periphery and Semiperiphery States', *Journal of Political and Military Sociology,* Vol. 19(1), pp. 29-45.

Allison, G. (1971), *Essence of Decision*, Boston, Little, Brown and Company.

Amnesty International (1996), *Amnesty International Report*, London, Amnesty International Publications.

Apodaca, C. and Stohl, M. (1997), 'United States Human Rights Policy and Foreign Assistance Allocations from Carter to Clinton: Plus ça change, plus c'est la meme chose?', unpublished manuscript.

Arendt, H. (1951), *The Origins of Totalitarianism*, New York, Harcourt Brace.

Barratt, B. (2004), 'Aiding or Abetting: British Foreign Aid Decisions and Recipient Country Human Rights', in S.C. Carey and S.C. Poe (eds), *Understanding Human Rights Violations: New Systematic Studies*, Aldershot, Ashgate, pp. 43-62.

Bendor, J. and Hammond, T.H. (1992), 'Rethinking Allison's Models', *American Political Science Review*, Vol. 86(2), pp. 301-22.

Blalock, H.M., Jr. (1969), *Theory Construction: From Verbal to Mathematical Formulation*, Englewood Cliffs, NJ, Prentice-Hall, Inc.

Blanton, S.L. (1994), 'Impact of Human Rights on U.S. Foreign Assistance to Latin America', *International Interactions*, Vol. 19(4), pp. 339-58.

Blanton, S.L. (1999), 'Instruments of Security or Tools of Repression? Arms Imports and Human Rights Conditions in Developing Countries', *Journal of Peace Research*, Vol. 36(2), pp. 233-244.

Boswell, T. and Dixon, W.J. (1990), 'Dependency and Rebellion: A Cross-National Analysis', *American Sociological Review*, Vol. 55(4), pp. 540-59.

Braumoeller, B F. and Goertz, G. (1997), 'The Methodology of Initial Conditions', Paper presented at the meeting of the International Studies Association, Toronto, Canada, 18-22 March 1997.

Callaway, R.L. (2001), 'Is the Road to Hell paved with Good Intentions?: The Effect of U.S. Foreign Assistance and Economic Policy on Human Rights', Unpublished Ph.D. dissertation, University of North Texas, Denton, Texas.

Carey, S. (2004), 'Domestic Threat and Repression: An Analysis of State Responses to Different Forms of Dissent', in S.C. Carey and S.C. Poe (eds), *Understanding Human Rights Violations: New Systematic Studies*, Aldershot, Ashgate, pp. 201-19.

Cingranelli, D.L. (1992), 'Democracy and Human Rights in Less Developed Countries', Presented at the annual meeting of the American Political Science Association, Chicago.

Cingranelli, D.L. and Pasquarello, T. (1985), 'Human Rights Practices and the U.S. Distribution of Foreign Aid to Latin American Countries', *American Journal of Political Science*, Vol. 29(3), pp. 539-63.

Cingranelli, D.L. and Richards, D.L, Jr. (1997), 'Which Personal Integrity Rights Does a State Choose to Violate and Why?', Paper presented at the Comparative Human Rights and Repression Conference, Boulder CO, 10-11 June 1997.

Cingranelli D.L. and Richards, D.L. (1999), 'Measuring the Level, Pattern and Sequence of Government Respect for Physical Integrity Rights', *International Studies Quarterly*, Vol. 43(2), pp. 407-17.

Davenport, C. (1995a), 'Assessing the Military's Influence on Political Repression: An Examination of Different Hypotheses', *Journal of Political and Military Sociology*, Vol. 23, pp. 119-144.

Davenport, C. (1995b), 'Multidimensional Threat Perception and State Repression: An Inquiry into Why States Apply Negative Sanctions', *American Journal of Political Science*, Vol. 39(3), pp. 683-713.

Davenport, C. (1996a), 'The Weight of the Past: Exploring the Lagged Determinants of Political Repression', *Political Research Quarterly*, Vol. 49(2), pp. 377-405.

Davenport, C. (1996b), 'Constitutional Promises and Repressive Reality: A Cross-National Time Series Investigation of Why Political and Civil Liberties are Suppressed', *Journal of Politics*, Vol. 58(3), pp. 627-54.

Davenport, C. (1997), 'Regime Change and Political Repression: Direction, Coherence and Persistence', unpublished manuscript.

Davis, D.R. and Ward, M.D. (1990), 'They Dance Alone: Deaths and Disappeared in Contemporary Chile', *Journal of Conflict Resolution*, Vol. 34(3), pp. 449-75.

DeNardo, J. (1985), *Power in Numbers*, Princeton, NJ, Princeton University Press.

Dixon, W. (1994), 'Democracy and the Peaceful Settlement of International Conflict', *American Political Science Review,* Vol. 88(1), pp. 14-32.

Fein, H. (1995), 'More Murder in the Middle: Life Integrity Violations and Democracy in the World, 1987', *Human Rights Quarterly*, Vol. 17(1), pp. 170-91.

Foster, D. and Davis, D. (1987), *Detention & Torture in South Africa: Psychological, Legal & Historical Studies*, New York, St. Martin's Press.

Gartner, S.S. and Regan, P.M. (1996), 'Threat and Repression: The Non-Linear Relationship between Government and Opposition Violence', *Journal of Peace Research*, Vol. 33(3), pp. 273-87.

Gurr, T.R. (1970), *Why Men Rebel*, Princeton, NJ, Princeton University Press.

Gurr, T.R. (1986), 'The Political Origins of State Violence and Terror: A Theoretical Analysis', in M. Stohl and G. A. Lopez (eds.), *Government Violence and Repression: An Agenda for Research*, Westport, CT, Greenwood Press, pp. 45-71.

Gibney, M. and Dalton, M. (1996), 'The Political Terror Scale,' In David Louis Cingranelli (Ed.) *Human Rights and Developing Countries*. Greenwich/London, JAI Press, pp. 73-84.

Harrelson-Stephens, J. (2003) 'The Value of Human Rights on the Open Market: Liberal Economic Policies and the Achievement of Personal Integrity Rights', Unpublished Ph.D. Dissertation, University of North Texas, Denton, Texas.

Harrelson-Stephens, J. and Callaway, R.L. (2003), 'Does Trade Openness Promote Security Rights in Developing Countries? Examining the Liberal Perspective', *International Interactions,* Vol. 29(2), pp. 143-58.

Henderson, C. (1991), 'Conditions Affecting the Use of Political Repression', *Journal of Conflict Resolution*, Vol. 35(1), pp. 120-42.

Henderson, C. (1993), 'Population Pressures and Political Repression', *Social Science Quarterly*, Vol. 74(2), pp. 322-33.

Keck, M. and Sikkink, K.A. (1998), *Activists Beyond Borders: Advocacy Networks in International Politics*, Ithaca, NY, Cornell University Press.

Keith, L.C. (1999), 'The United Nations International Covenant on Civil and Political Rights: Does It Make a Difference in Human Rights Behavior?' *Journal of Peace Research*, Vol. 36(1), pp. 95-118.

Keith, L.C. (2004), 'National Constitutions and Human Rights Protection: Regional Differences and Colonial Influences', in S.C. Carey and S.C. Poe (eds), *Understanding Human Rights Violations: New Systematic Studies*, Aldershot, Ashgate, pp. 162-80.

Keith, L.C. and Poe, S.C. (2000), 'The U.S., the IMF, and Human Rights: A Policy Relevant Approach', in D. P. Forsythe (ed.) *The U.S. and Human Rights: Looking Inward and Outward*, Lincoln, NB, University of Nebraska Press.

King, J. (1997), 'Ameliorating Effects of Democracy on Political Repression as Seen in 51 Countries Across 35 Years', presented at the Comparative Human Rights and Repression Conference, at the University of Colorado, Boulder, 20-21 June 1997.

Lee, R., Lindstrom R., Moore, W. and Turan, K. (2004), 'Ethnicity and Repression: The Ethnic Composition of Countries and Human Rights Violations,' in S.C. Carey and S.C. Poe (eds), *Understanding Human Rights Violations: New Systematic Studies*, Aldershot, Ashgate, pp. 186-200.

Levy, J.S. (1996), 'Contending Theories of International Conflict', in C.A. Crocker, F. O. Hamson and P. Aall (eds.) *Managing Global Chaos: Sources of and Responses to International Conflict*, Washington DC, U.S. Institute of Peace.

Lichbach, M.I. (1987), 'Deterrence or Escalation? The Puzzle of Aggregate Studies of Repression and Dissent', *Journal of Conflict Resolution*, Vol. 31(2), pp. 266-97.

Lopez, G. and Stohl, M. (1992), 'Problems of Concept and Measurement in the Study of Human Rights', in T.B. Jabine and R.P. Claude (eds.), *Human Rights and Statistics: Getting the Record Straight*, Philadelphia, University of Pennsylvania Press.

Mason, T.D. and Krane, D.A. (1989), 'The Political Economy of Death Squads: Toward a Theory of the Impact of State-Sanctioned Terror', *International Studies Quarterly*, Vol. 33(2), pp. 175-98.

McCormick, J.M., and Mitchell, N. (1988), 'Is U.S. Aid Really Linked to Human Rights in Latin America?' *American Journal of Political Science*, Vol. 32(1), pp. 231-9.

McKinlay, R.D. and Cohan, A.S. (1975), 'A Comparative Analysis of the Political and Economic Performance of Military and Civilian Regimes', *Comparative Politics*, Vol. 7(1), pp. 1-30.

McKinlay, R.D. and Cohan, A.S. (1976), 'Performance and Instability in Military and Nonmilitary Regimes', *American Political Science Review*, Vol. 70(3), pp. 850-64.

McNitt, A.D. (1995), 'Government Coercion: An Exploratory Analysis', *The Social Science Journal*, Vol. 3(2), pp. 195-205.

Meyer, W. (1996), 'Human Rights and MNCs; Theory versus Quantitative Analysis', *Human Rights Quarterly*, Vol. 18(2), pp. 368-97.

Miller, D. (2004), 'Security and What Cost? Arms Tranfers to the Developing World and Human Rights', in S.C. Carey and S.C. Poe (eds), *Understanding Human Rights Violations: New Systematic Studies*, Aldershot, Ashgate, pp. 63-81.

Mitchell, C., Stohl, M., Carleton, D. and Lopez, G.A. (1986), 'State Terrorism: Issues of Concept and Measurement', in M. Stohl and G. A. Lopez (eds.), *Government Violence and Repression: An Agenda for Research*, New York, Greenwood Press.

Mitchell, N.J. and McCormick, J.M. (1988), 'Economic and Political Explanations of Human Rights Violations', *World Politics*, Vol. 40(4), pp. 476-98.

Most, B.A. and Starr, H. (1984), 'International Relations Theory, Foreign Policy Substitutability and "Nice" Laws', *World Politics*, Vol. 36(3), pp. 383-406.

Most, B.A. and Starr, H. (1989), *Inquiry, Logic and International Politics*, Columbia, SC, University of South Carolina Press.

Mueller, J. (1973), *War, Presidents and Public Opinion,* New York, Wiley.

Olson, M. (1963), 'Rapid Growth as a Destabilizing Force', *Journal of Economic History*, Vol. 23(4), pp. 529-52.

Panning, W. (1983), 'What Does it Take to Have a Theory? Principles of Political Science', in J.S. Nelson (ed.), *What Should Political Theory Be Now?* Albany, NY, State University of New York.

Park, H.S. (1987), 'Correlates of Human Rights: Global Tendencies', *Human Rights Quarterly*, Vol. 9, pp. 405-13.

Pion-Berlin, D. (1984), 'The Political Economy of State Repression in Argentina' in M. Stohl and G.A. Lopez, (eds.), *The State as Terrorist: The Dynamics of Governmental Violence and Repression*, Westport, CT, Greenwood Press.

Pion-Berlin, D. and Lopez, G. (1991), 'Of Victims and Executioners: Argentine State Terror, 1975-1979', *International Studies Quarterly*, Vol. 35(1), pp. 63-86.

Poe, S.C. (1992), 'Human Rights and Economic Assistance under Ronald Reagan and Jimmy Carter', *American Journal of Political Science*, Vol. 36(1), pp. 147-67.

Poe, S.C. and Meernik, J. (1995), 'U.S. Military Aid During the Eighties: A Two-Stage Model', *Journal of Peace Research*, Vol. 32(4), pp. 399-412.

Poe, S.C, Pilatovsky, S, Miller, B. and Ogundele, A. (1994), 'Human Rights and U.S. Foreign Aid Revisited: The Latin American Region', *Human Rights Quarterly*, Vol. 16(4), pp. 539-58.

Poe, S.C. and Sirirangsi, R. (1993), 'Human Rights and U.S. Economic Aid to Africa', *International Interactions*, Vol. 18, pp. 309-22.

Poe, S.C. and Sirirangsi, R. (1994), 'Human Rights and U.S. Economic Aid During the Reagan Years', *Social Science Quarterly*, Vol. 75(4), pp. 494-509.

Poe, S.C. and Tate, C.N. (1994), 'Repression of Human Rights to Personal Integrity in the 1980s: A Global Analysis', *American Political Science Review*, Vol. 88(4), pp. 853-72.

Poe, S.C, Tate, C.N. and Keith, L.C. (1999), 'Repression of the Human Right to Personal Integrity Revisited: A Global Crossnational Study Covering the Years 1976-1993', *International Studies Quarterly*, Vol. 43(2), pp. 291-315.

Poe, S.C, Tate, C.N, Keith, L.C. and Lanier, D. (1997), 'The Continuity of Suffering: Domestic Threat and Human Rights Abuse Across Time', presented at the Comparative Human Rights and Repression Conference, at the University of Colorado, Boulder, 20-21 June 1997.

Policzer, P. (2004), 'Organization Effects on Patterns of Human Rights Violations', in S.C. Carey and S.C. Poe (eds), *Understanding Human Rights Violations: New Systematic Studies*, Aldershot, Ashgate, pp. 220-37.

Putnam, R.D. (1988), 'Diplomacy and Domestic Politics: The Logic of Two-Level Games', *International Organization*, Vol. 42(3), pp. 427-60.

Rasler, K. (1986), 'War, Accommodation, and Violence in the United States, 1890-1970', *American Political Science Review*, Vol. 80(4), pp. 921-45.

Regan, P.M. (1995), 'U.S. Economic Aid and Political Repression: An Empirical Evaluation of US Foreign Policy', *Political Research Quarterly*, Vol. 48(4), pp. 613-28.

Richards, D.L. (1999), 'Perilous Proxy: Human Rights and the Presence of National Elections', *Social Science Quarterly*, Vol. 80(4), pp. 648-665.

Richards, D.L, Gelleny, R.D. and Sacko, D.H. (2001), 'Money with a Mean Streak? Foreign Economic Penetraton and Government Respect for Human Rights in Developing Countries', *International Studies Quarterly*, Vol. 45(2), pp. 219-39.

Risse, T., Ropp, S.C. and Sikkink, K. (1998), *The Power of Human Rights: International Norms and Domestic Change*, Cambridge, Cambridge University Press.

Ruiz, L.E.J. (1989), 'An Archaeology of State Terrorism: The Philippines under Marcos', in G.A. Lopez and M. Stohl (eds.), *Dependence, Development, and State Repression*, New York, Greenwood Press.

Russett, B, and Starr, H. (1992), *World Politics: The Menu for Choice*. New York, W.H. Freeman and Company.

Schoultz, L. (1981), *Human Rights and U.S. Policy toward Latin America*, Princeton, NJ, Princeton University Press.

Sherborne, L. (2003), 'An Integrated Model of Political Repression: Theory and Model Development', Unpublished Ph.D. Dissertation, University of Houston, Houston, Texas.

Simon, M.V. (1994), 'Hawks, Doves, and Civil Conflict Dynamics: A "Strategic" Action-Reaction Model', *International Interactions*, Vol. 19(3), pp. 213-39.

Simon, M.V., Starr, H. and McGinnis, M.D. (1994), 'A Two-Level Analysis of War and Revolution: A Dynamic Simulation of Response to Threat', Paper presented at a conference held at Texas A.M. University, College Station TX, March 1994.

Simon, M.V. and Starr, H. (1996), 'Extraction, Allocation and the Rise and Decline of States: A Simulation Analysis of Two-Level Security Management', *Journal of Conflict Resolution*, Vol. 40(2), pp. 272-97.

Smeulers, A. (2004), 'What Transforms Ordinary People into Gross Human Rights Violators?', in S.C. Carey and S.C. Poe (eds), *Understanding Human Rights Violations: New Systematic Studies*, Aldershot, Ashgate, pp. 238-52.

Smith, J., Bolyard, M. and Ippolito, A. (1999), 'Human Rights and the Global Economy: A Response to Meyer', *Human Rights Quarterly*, Vol. 21(1), pp. 207-19.

Sprout, H. and Sprout, M. (1969), 'Environmental Factors in the Study of Politics', in J. N. Rosenau (ed.) *International Politics and Foreign Policy: A Reader in Research and Theory*, New York, The Free Press.

Starr, H. (1994), 'Revolution and War: Rethinking the Linkage between Internal and External Conflict', *Political Research Quarterly*, Vol. 47(3), pp. 481-507.

Sterken, R.E. (1996), *An Empirical Analysis of the Impact of Economic Interests on Overseas Development Assistance in Latin America, 1972-1993,* Ph.D. Dissertation, Texas Tech University.

Stohl, M. and Carleton, D. (1985), 'The Foreign Policy of Human Rights: Rhetoric and Reality from Jimmy Carter to Ronald Reagan' *Human Rights Quarterly*, Vol. 7, pp. 205-29.

Stohl, M., Carleton, D. and Johnson, S. (1984), 'Human Rights and U.S. Foreign Assistance from Nixon to Carter', *Journal of Peace Research*, Vol. 21(3), pp. 215-26.

Strouse, J. C. and Claude, R.P. (1976), 'Empirical Comparative Rights Research: Some Preliminary Tests of Development Hypotheses', in R. P. Claude (ed.) *Comparative Human Rights*, Baltimore, Johns Hopkins University Press.

U.S. State Department, (1977-1984), *Country Reports on Human Rights Practices*, Washington DC, U.S. Government Printing Office.

Walker, S. and Poe, S.C. (2002), 'Does Cultural Diversity Affect Countries' Respect for Human Rights?' *Human Rights Quarterly*, Vol. 24(1), pp. 237-63.

Waltz, K.N. (1954), *Man, the State and War*, New York, Columbia University Press.

Ziegenhagen, E.A. (1986), *The Regulation of Political Conflict*, New York, Praeger.

Zanger, S. (2000), 'A Global Analysis of the Effect of Political Regime Changes on Life Integrity Violations, 1977-1993', *Journal of Peace Research*, Vol. 37(2), pp. 213-33.

Zinnes, D.A. (1976), 'The Problem of Cumulation', in J.N. Rosenau (ed.) *In Search of Global Patterns,* New York, Free Press.

PART II
FOREIGN POLICY ANALYSIS

Introduction to Part II

The second part of this volume builds upon human rights research that attempts to ascertain whether, and under what conditions, human rights influence foreign policy decisions. Both studies in this part seek to understand how and why human rights influence decision-makers' deliberations. The aim is to examine claims made by government decision-makers that human rights issues are important and to expose inconsistencies between their rhetoric and reality, should incongruities be found.

The chapter by Bethany Barratt analyzes British foreign aid decisions between 1980 and 1996, testing the impact of the human rights conditions in the recipient country on British aid allocation. This study fills an important gap in the literature on European foreign aid allocation and human rights, which is mainly dominated by descriptive studies with only few exceptions (e.g., Zanger, 2000; Neumayer, 2003). Barratt analyzes whether human rights considerations influence British aid allocation, but also under what conditions repressive regimes are most likely to be punished with decreasing aid. She addresses two questions. Firstly, what distinguishes countries that receive aid from the UK from those countries that do not receive aid from Great Britain? And secondly, what factors influence the amount of aid a country receives from the UK? The study investigates the realist argument that strategic concerns are the main factors behind states' behaviours, as well as the impact of trade and democracy, based on neoliberal and globalization perspectives. One of the main contributions of this chapter is that it takes into account that heavily publicized humanitarian crises might influence foreign aid decisions due to an increased public awareness created by special attention of the media. Barratt finds that perceived recipient needs and domestic political considerations are most important in deciding whether a country is included as an aid recipient of the UK. Human rights do not appear to have an impact on the levels of foreign aid, but trade interests clearly play a role in aid allocation. The study also highlights that the UK is more likely to punish repressive regimes with a decrease in aid if the country is not important to its economic interests.

The second chapter in this part focuses on a different aspect of foreign policy by analyzing arms transfers from the largest manufacturer of arms in the world, the United States, to developing countries. This chapter by Dawn Miller is an extension of previous research on this issue (Blanton, 1999a, 1999b). It investigates how three different sets of human rights are affected by arms transfers from the United States. She analyzes the impact on those human rights, which pertain to personal integrity, democratic and civil rights, economic and social rights, over a dataset that covers a more recent time period than previous research on this issue. The findings indicate that arms transfers do generally influence the realization of human rights negatively, although findings regarding personal integrity rights are somewhat more mixed than in previous studies. Miller's contribution is an example of research on a neglected topic, which yields results that should be of interest to many. At the same time it shows how current social scientific research is building on previous studies, and as such it is evidence that the much-desired 'cumulation' of research, which is the aim of social science studies, is actually occurring. Such cumulation is a clear signal of the maturation of the field.

References

Blanton, S.L. (1999a), 'Instruments of Security or Tools of Repression? Arms Imports and Human Rights Conditions in Developing Countries', *Journal of Peace Research*, Vol. 36, pp. 233-44.

Blanton, S.L. (1999b), 'The Transfer of Arms and the Diffusion of Democracy: Do Arms Promote or Undermine the "Third Wave"?' *The Social Science Journal*, Vol. 36, pp. 413-29.

Neumayer, E. (2003), 'Do Human Rights Matter in Bilateral Aid Allocation? A Quantitative Analysis of 21 Donor Countries', *Social Science Quarterly*, Vol. 84(1), pp. 650-66.

Zanger, S.C. (2000), 'Good Governance and European Aid: The Impact of Political Conditionality', *European Union Politics*, Vol. 1(3), pp. 293-317.

Chapter 3

Aiding or Abetting: British Foreign Aid Decisions and Recipient Country Human Rights

Bethany Barratt

Introduction

When do policy makers take human rights into account in foreign policy formation? This chapter examines the relative role of human rights and economic self-interest in shaping aid policy in an era of globalization. I develop an argument that human rights abuses in the recipient state will prompt aid reduction or cessation by donors only when the recipient is of little economic value to the donor, and when the government of the donor state is politically weak. I then assess the hypotheses I have derived through quantitative and qualitative analyses of British foreign aid policy during the 1980s and 1990s. In doing so, I move beyond extant analyses of US foreign aid policy and expand the purview of my own past research into these trade-offs. I trace overall patterns in the relationships between aid, trade and domestic politics, as well as changes occurring as the state-centered, strategically defined world of the Cold War era dissolved into the interconnected politico-economic world of the mid- to late-1990s.

This research is designed to shed light on a question often raised in debate about the role of human rights in the foreign policies of democracies. Are these rights, ostensibly at the heart of the democratic form of governance, something for which states are willing to sacrifice gains in other arenas – or are they only pursued when it is not costly to do so? This research is motivated by the often-observed inconsistencies in the foreign policies of aid-giving states towards countries that have dubious human rights records (for instance, the stark contrast between the U.S.'s engagement with China and ostracism of Cuba). I attempt to account for inconsistencies both in the treatment of different states with similar problems, as well as between official rhetoric and action.

Determining under what conditions human rights actually have an effect *vis à vis* other potential explanations of foreign policy decisions is important for at least two reasons. First, if states with the ability to send the international agenda fail to do so, a clear signal will be sent to leaders of other states that human rights can be costlessly sacrificed. Second, in countries where respect for democratic values is supposed to be the basis of governmental legitimacy, a failure to respect and protect these rights internationally (let alone at home) represents an apparent contradiction of core principles.

Are human rights, ostensibly at the heart of the democratic form of government, something for which states are willing to sacrifice gains in other arenas, or are they only pursued when it is not costly to do so? This question is often posed about the role of human rights in foreign policy but rarely addressed systematically. It is an especially critical question in a post-Cold War world, where policy makers and academics alike celebrate the spread of democracy – because when terms like 'human rights' become hollow, so does one of the organizing principles that defines democracy. More importantly, aid generally serves to prop up whatever regime is in power in recipient states. It tends not to go to the poorest members of society, and therefore ultimately exacerbates societal inequalities.

This work fills a lacuna in the human rights literature by looking beyond the United States and in a comparative perspective at the bilateral aid decisions in another major donor state, the UK.[1]

The Question and Some Extant Answers

Democracies have a long record of committing blood and treasure to the cause of political and civil rights. While realists argue that ethical concerns never matter in foreign policy, still democratic states and multilateral organizations provide billions of dollars in aid to non-strategic countries.

Britain is a particularly interesting case in that it provides a unique test of many of the key factors often argued to be driving foreign aid policy. First, British policy makers are often accused of solely following the US in terms of putting strategic interests at the top of its policy agenda (perhaps never so much as during the lead-up to Gulf War II). Second, Britain's history as a colonial power may make former ties more important than some current economic concerns. Third, it has been among the first signatories to a number of international human rights instruments and has instituted more explicit and far-reaching human rights instruments than is the case for many other Western democracies. On the other hand, it is a capitalist nation that in a globalized world might be expected to put its economic interests before ethical concerns.

There are several bodies of international relations literature that can help explain these inconsistencies.

Realism

Seldom, from a realist perspective, is the status of individual rights in another country important unless it affects state power. And realism has often given short shrift to the importance of domestic considerations to foreign policy makers.

The results of this research, therefore, have interesting implications for testing the realist assumption that the imperative to survive in an anarchic international arena subsumes all other concerns. If realist assumptions are valid, internal characteristics of states can only have the most minor impact. The British case may prove an especially interesting test, as political discourse in Britain in the 1980s took a distinct realist turn. Says Larsen: 'Power politics was seen as the true nature of international relations' (1997, pp.93-4). In fact, the realist view would still be confirmed if rhetoric acknowledges human rights but is not backed up by policy commitments.

Idealism and Legal Protections of Human Rights

Respect for civil and political human rights is at the heart of democratic governance. International legal incentives to take human rights into account are supplemented in Britain by official Government rhetoric entailing a commitment to using human rights as criteria for aid disbursement. For example, in 1990, John Major, then Chancellor of the Exchequer, advocated making aid conditional on democratic reforms in recipient countries (Burnell, 1991). That same year, Foreign Secretary Douglas Hurd claimed that promotion of good government and political pluralism was Britain's official development assistance goal (Stokke, 1995b, p.22). And the Foreign and Commonwealth Office (FCO) has declared that foreign aid should be used to foster the 'observance of human rights' as well as democratic government (Burnell, 1997, p.156).

Neoliberalism/Globalization Perspectives

If trade and economic cooperation for mutual benefit between nations is a paramount concern of policy makers (Keohane, 1993; Lipson, 1993; Axelrod and Keohane; 1993), some relations may be so valuable that the donor would rather continue to generate good will through aid than jeopardize access to the recipient by cutting it off. These are countries that offer significant trade potential to the donor, provide fertile export markets, and have large or expanding economies. These countries are less likely to be punished and, if they are, punished less severely than are other states for commensurate human rights abuses (Gillies, 1989; Scharfe, 1996).

The General Context of British Foreign Policy Making

Formal Policy-Making Institutions and Structure

Several characteristics of British foreign policy have particular relevance for the aid allocation process. Institutional inertia exists in every decision-making apparatus, but may exert a particularly strong effect in the British civil service. According to Wallace (1975, p.8), 'the high morale and prestige of the British civil service, and its successful resistance of the bypassing of its regular procedures by political channels, make the problem of organizational inertia particularly acute for policy makers in Britain'. Additionally, the decision-making process about aid is one of the most difficult to trace in terms of its official institutional channels;

looking at long-term overall factors in the aid decision can help one induce what one could not derive from official institutional arrangements.

History of Human Rights in British Foreign Policy

Scholars of the role of human rights in British foreign policy often trace the roots of an explicit role for human rights in British foreign policy to the mid-1970s (Vincent, 1986). But the late 1970s and 1980s saw little evidence that such rhetoric was incorporated into policy practice. In 1989, Cunliffe (1989, p.115) could conclude that 'analysis of the flow of economic aid from London to the less developed world over the past fifteen years does not reveal any enduring, concerted effects by successive British Governments to utilize the flow of concessional finance for the promotion of international human rights.' In fact, as of the late 1970s, the UK had only cut off aid completely to two countries in response to human rights abuses. Moreover, when human rights had any effect at all, it was highly conditional:

> London's relations with the Third World ...have been dominated by ...political, historical, and economic constraints which have drastically limited the extent to which ...concern for...human rights has led to changes in...aid relations...[human rights] concerns are subservient to other political and economic ambitions in determining the quantity and direction of the aid programme (Cunliffe, 1985, pp.112, 116).

There is evidence of some improvement over the past decade, at least rhetorically. The Blair government has argued that human rights should have a more significant role in British foreign policy. Many of Blair's initiatives reflect programmes begun under the preceding Conservative government, suggesting some linkage between aid policy and rights performance during the years of this study.

Public Opinion/Interest Groups.

Three categories of interest groups have been particularly well organized around aid issues.

Human rights NGOs Policy results often turn on how the national interest is defined in a given situation. Therefore, one of the primary goals of human rights interest groups is to make human rights aspects of a particular aid decision appear to be of higher salience than other kinds of considerations. Issue definition also establishes which components of the British policy-making machinery will assume responsibility for an issue.

Business interests Wallace claims that 'promotional groups and economic interests are as active in foreign policy issues as they are [in] questions of transport or educational policy' (Wallace, 1975, p.3). Some trace the influence of business interests in foreign policy to Britain's status as a middle-power state.

> By 1970... British policy makers and observers had alike accepted that Britain could no longer aspire to world status, but was rather a 'major power of the second order.' Their perception of the national interest which foreign policy should pursue reflected the more commercial orientation appropriate to a middle power (Wallace, 1975, p.4).

Immigrant populations Immigrant populations, while generally comprising a very small percentage of total population, can make a real impact if they are well organized and concentrated, as in the UK around the urban centers of, most notably, London and Birmingham, the largest current countries of origin being Pakistan, India, and Nigeria, in descending order.

Characteristics of the Aid Decision and Considerations Therein

The decision-making process consists of two stages: will the UK give the recipient aid, and how much will it give?

Theoretically, the two decisions need to be modelled separately because in most donors, a different set of actors interacts – in a different process – for each decision. Most studies of the aid-human rights relationship have been based on the US, where the decision-making process is described in two stages by the members of the policy community (Cingranelli and Pasquarello, 1985).[2]

Although the UK's government does not entail the same separation of powers that underpins the differences between the two decisions in the US, it still seems that different processes drive the two decisions. It appears that the FCO (and particularly the Department for International Development) has greater potential leverage in making recommendations on whether a state receives aid, while Parliament has more say in the amount to be allocated (*Human Rights in United States and United Kingdom Foreign Policy: A Colloquium*, 1979).[3]

Since the end of World War II, the major donors' *aims* for aid have been contested. Generally, however, there have been four major goals: 1) Assisting strategic allies (this often includes former colonies or members of the Commonwealth, whose 'strategic' value might be debatable, but who are allies due to historical cultural, political and economic ties, and whom the U.K wants to maintain as allies); 2) securing trade benefits for domestic businesses (this is pursued largely as a result of the efforts of large, well-organized, and well-funded business lobbies in the UK. Such trade advantages are usually pursued through strategies like 'tied aid' and special aid-for-trade deals or legislation such as the Aid and Trade Provision in Britain)[4]; 3) pursuing general global stability through development and economic growth, though there is often a failure to distinguish between the two in practice; 4) achieving democratization and increased respect for human rights (development goals which do not have concurrent benefits to some sector of the UK's economy are generally given far less attention than are strategic and economic goals. Where they are taken into account, they are largely justified with reference to their utility as a means, rather than as an end.).

Most authors argue that the first two of these are much higher on donors' agendas than is the last.

Hypotheses

From the foregoing considerations, I derive the following hypotheses:

Gatekeeping

1) States that are more economically valuable are more likely to receive aid.
2) States that are more economically valuable are less likely to have human rights taken into account in decisions about their aid status.

Allocation

3) States that are more economically valuable will receive higher levels of aid.
4) States that are more economically valuable are less likely to have human rights taken into account in decisions about their aid amounts.

Methods

Assessing the goodness of fit of these hypotheses necessitates three different sets of analyses. The first assesses the determinants of whether in any given year the recipient state received aid (1 if yes, 0 otherwise) from the UK I also analyze the determinants of amount of aid allocated to each recipient in a given year. Finally, I divide recipient states into groups based on their economic importance to the UK, and analyze whether human rights matter more for some kinds of states than others.

Time Period to Be Covered

The unit of analysis is the recipient-year. My analyses include the years 1980-1996, the years for which quantitative data on human rights is available. This is a particularly useful time period to examine for a number of reasons. It gives us over 1000 cases in the decade before the Cold War ended and over 700 in the six years after the breakup of the Soviet Union. Finally, this time period includes aid responses of the West to genocide in both Africa and in the backyard of Europe.

Equations to Be Estimated

The quantitative component of this research design has two parts. For the gatekeeping decision, a model of the determinants of overall OECD aid is estimated using pooled cross-sectional time series logit analysis, appropriate to dichotomous dependent variables for which the distribution of the error-terms is roughly log-linear, where one is interested in a large number of cases at several temporal points. A variable is included for aid at year t-1 to control for past aid and serial autocorrelation. For the allocation decision, pooled cross-sectional time-series regression analysis is conducted of the factors influencing amount of aid given is conducted.

Dependent Variable

The operational forms of the dependent variable for the gatekeeping decision are discussed above. For the allocation decision, aid is operationalized as total aid from Britain to that state in the given year. Annual aid data was obtained from the OECD (various years).

If a state was a non-creditor country in a given year, it was included as a potential aid recipient. It is more unusual to *not* to be granted aid than to be granted it. In a sample year, 1996, 119 of the 180 potential recipients received aid. Therefore, a consideration of the 69 states that did *not* receive aid is in some ways more revealing. Eight of these were oil exporters and relatively wealthy; it is not surprising that they would not be aid priorities. Many others were island nations who receive large amounts of aid from geographically proximate states. There are also few clear patterns evident in terms of the human rights records of the states that are left off the list. Only five, or less than ten per cent have relatively poor human rights scores of 4 or 5 (categories discussed below). Clearly human rights do not matter for every aid decision. The question is: *when does it?*

Independent Variables

Human rights abuses in recipient country Human rights abuses, which I expect to matter only when a recipient is of little economic value to the UK, are measured using the Purdue Political Terror Index, originally compiled by Michael Stohl and including two ratings derived, respectively, from the US State Department's annual country reports and those of Amnesty International. This is a 5-point scale ranging from 1 ('Countries... under a secure rule of law, people are not imprisoned for their views, and torture is rare or exceptional... Political murders are extraordinarily rare') to 5 ('The violence of Level 4 has been extended to the whole population...The leaders of these societies place no limits on the means or thoroughness with which they pursue personal or ideological goals') (Stohl, 1983). The State Department measure was chosen, though not without trepidation. Key differences between the two scales are discussed in Barratt (2002).

To provide an idea of what the State scales look like in real-world terms, Table 3.1 provides examples of the countries who received the best (1) and worst (5) human rights scores for the last year in the study (of all potential OECD aid recipients). This variable is lagged one year to allow for collection of data in the UK, as well as for the budgeting process to take place.[5]

Table 3.1 US State Department's best and worst human rights performers, 1996

Level 5 (worst) records, 1996, n=12	Level 1 (best) records, 1996, n=21
Afghanistan	Benin
Algeria	Comoros
Angola	Costa Rica
Burundi	Cyprus
Colombia	Czech Republic
Iraq	Eritrea
Liberia	Hungary
Rwanda	Jordan
Sierra Leone	Kyrgyzstan
Somalia	Laos
Venezuela	Latvia
Zaire	Lesotho
	Macedonia
	Mali
	Poland
	Seychelles
	Singapore
	Slovakia
	Taiwan
	United Arab Emirates
	Uruguay

Many studies of human rights treat 'democracy' and 'respect for human rights' as nearly synonymous (Beitz, 1979, p.179; Franck, 1992, pp.46-7; Ray, 1998, pp.442-3). However, one might also expect that democratic recipients might be less able to reciprocate aid with preferential trade agreements than are autocratic ones. This variable is included to test whether democracy is indeed a proxy for respect for human rights and is measured as the recipient's polity score on Jaggers and Gurr's (1996) Polity III index. However, I expect democracy to be of lesser significance in predicting aid amounts than are economic and strategic measures. Additionally, many donors are reluctant to sink aid funds into unstable regions, which are often either undemocratic or transitional.

Potential and actual economic value of the recipient state Potential economic value of the recipient to the UK, which I expect to be positively associated with recipient aid, is measured in two ways: size of the economy of the recipient (GDP) and annual growth rate of GDP. Together, these two figures should give us some idea of how promising a trade partner the recipient looks to be. The recipient state's population is also taken into account (CIA, various years).

In addition, measurements of economic value are constructed that more specifically measure the recipient country's *trade* potential. Volume and percentage of imports and exports between Britain and each recipient are drawn from the International Monetary Fund's Direction of Trade Statistics (various years) data. Since not all trades are created equal, I also take into account whether a recipient is an oil-exporting state.

Strategic value of the recipient state Realists would predict that strategic interests trump human rights concerns. A recipient with whom the UK has had recent conflict or sees possibility of future conflict should be less likely to receive aid because that conflict would disrupt any benefit the UK would derive from its investment. However, such conflicts, at least militarized ones, are relatively rare.

The strategic value of the recipient is measured in several other ways. These measures include the geographic location of the recipient, proximity to trade intersections, location in areas of instability (CIA, various years) and whether the recipient possesses nuclear capabilities (*Historical Statistics of the United States*, 1997). If a state is listed as a participant in an interstate dispute, as a site of substantial civil unrest, or if it borders on such a state, it is coded as a site of instability. A state is coded as located at a key trade intersection if it contains major pipelines, key ports, or is on a major shipping route.

I also take into account military commitments, measured as shared alliance membership taken from the alliance subset of the Correlates of War data set. In addition, donors that are geographically proximate to a recipient have a greater stake in that recipient's fate. Geographical proximity is measured as distance in kilometers between London and the capital of each recipient.

I expect strategic value of the recipient to be taken into account to a greater extent than human rights records, but to a lesser extent than trade value.

Additional Control Variables: Both Gatekeeping and Allocation Decisions

Five other categories of variables are included as controls:

Mass mediated humanitarian crises Determining whether a recipient suffered a humanitarian crisis (that was widely publicized in the mass media) allows one to measure economically-based altruism[6] as well as public awareness. This variable is a count of headlines in print news as compiled under the coding scheme used for the Kansas Events Data Set (KEDS) and its Protocol for the Assessment of Nonviolent Direct Action (PANDA) subset.[7] If states are taking into account the needs of recipients, the presence of a humanitarian crisis should be positively associated with a recipient's aid status.

Domestic politics Convincing policy makers that human rights is the most important lens through which to examine a particular decision is often the goal of human rights NGOs, and I therefore include a count of all reported demonstrations in Britain in a given year regarding the human rights record of the recipient.[8] In addition, the presence of a large immigrant diaspora in the UK may be successful in lobbying for aid for its country of origin; therefore, I also include the number of immigrants in the past 10 years to the UK from the recipient country.

Former colonial status of recipient I control for whether a recipient is a former British colony (*Flags of the World*, 2003); colonial ties promote a tradition of financial support and account for a good deal of variation in aid amounts between recipients (Maizels and Nissanke, 1984; Lumsdaine, 1993).

End of the Cold War British policymakers might see themselves as less constrained by strategic concerns and freer to allocate aid according to either economic or human rights criteria. In addition, with the end of the Cold War, British policymakers have aspired to restore its role as a major player in world politics, using aid as one instrument. Finally, with shrinking security budgets, aid becomes a more versatile (and available) policy tool than was heretofore the case. Whether the aid year occurs during the Cold War is measured as a dummy variable - 1 before and including 1991 (when the Soviet Union finally broke apart), 0 after. I expect more states to get aid, but less of it, after the Cold War ends.

Because it is probable that in the less rigid strategic atmosphere of the post-cold war world, human rights would have a better chance of being a criterion in aid decisions, I include an interaction term to determine whether the effect of human rights considerations is greater after the Cold War.

Past aid Past aid is a key determinant of present aid because appropriations are often left unchanged as a result of institutional inertia. In the gatekeeping model, whether a state received aid in the previous year is measured as a 0,1 dummy. In the allocation model, past aid is measured as the overall aid amount to that state in the previous year.

Despite the fact that I use several measures of economic importance of the recipient and strategic importance of the recipient, and two measures of some other characteristics of recipient or of the donor-recipient relationship, there is little collinearity between the independent variables. In fact, out of 220 pairs, there are only 7 sets of variables that correlate at over 0.4,[9] and none that correlate at under -0.4.

Results

The Gatekeeping Decision

Scholars have expressed much of the same skepticism about humanitarian rhetoric in the UK (and elsewhere in Europe) as they have in the case of the US, arguing that 'calls for the protection of others' rights have not led to serious commitments' (Brewin, 1986, p.189). In addition, scholars of British foreign policy have clearly perceived that allocation of foreign policy resources almost always necessitates tradeoffs (Vincent, p.1986).

Table 3.2 Pooled cross-sectional logit analysis of whether a state received aid

Variable	Coefficient	(Robust Std. Error)
Human Rights Measures		
Human rights	-0.932**	(0.318)
Recipient polity score	0.023	(0.013)
Economic Value Measures		
Trade intersection	-0.176	(1.095)
UK exports to recipient	-0.000	(0.001)
UK imports from recipient	-0.000	(0.001)
Recipient is oil exporter	-0.018	(0.009)
Recipient GDP	-0.000	(0.001)
Recipient GDP growth	-0.083*	(0.034)
Recipient population	-0.000	(0.000)
Strategic Value Measures		
Recipient nuclear capabilities	-35.588	(1.09E+09)
Recipient instability	0.179	(0.592)
Distance from UK	-0.001***	(0.000)
Dispute with UK	-38.896	(none reported)
Alliance with UK	0.269	(1.684)
Cold War	-1.566	(0.844)
Humanitarian Need Measure		
Humanitarian crisis	-0.030	(0.027)
Domestic Politics Measures		
Human rights activism	-42.914	(none reported)
Immigrants from this recipient	0.000	(0.000)
Colonial History Measure		
Former colony	0.968	(0.741)
Interaction Terms		
Cold War* human rights	-0.849*	(0.335)
Policy History		
Aid previous year?	2.136***	(0.329)
Significance of Model	0.000	
N	1468 (#groups=103)	
% Predicted Correctly	46.71	
Proportional Reduction in Error (Lambda)	0.00	

***=significant at p<0.001; **=p<0.01; *=p<0.05 (one-tailed).

Table 3.3 Pooled cross-sectional regression analyses of determinants of raw aid amounts

Variable	Coefficient	(Robust Std. Error)
Human Rights Measures		
Human rights	3351.976	(3017.031)
Recipient polity score	-45.086	(125.186)
Economic Value Measures		
Trade intersection	13164.320	(10344.240)
UK exports to recipient	-15.588	(8.202)
UK imports from recipient	19.909*	(10.026)
Recipient is oil exporter	-68.821	(77.558)
Recipient GDP	-6.215	(13.624)
Recipient GDP growth	394.401	(260.202)
Recipient population	0.102	(0.103)
Strategic Value Measures		
Recipient nuclear capabilities	Dropped	
Recipient instability	-3680.894	(3789.185)
Distance from UK	2.704*	(1.114)
Dispute with UK	Dropped	
Alliance with UK	-16786.450	(15534.060)
Cold War	-3449.831	(8498.734)
Humanitarian Need Measure		
Humanitarian crisis	603.392	(241.538)
Domestic Politics Measures		
Human rights activism	Dropped	
Immigrants from this recipient	4.272	(2.603)
Colonial History Measure		
Former colony	1053.222	(5482.960)
Interaction Terms		
Cold War* human rights	-189.926	(3326.189)
Policy History		
Aid amount previous year	0.320	(0.115)
Significance of Model	0.000	
N	120 (# states: 24)	
R^2 overall	0.43	
R^2 within groups	0.15	
R^2 between groups	0.83	

***=significant at p<0.001; **=p<0.01; *=p<0.05 (one-tailed).

For the first analysis of the gatekeeping decision, the dependent variable took the value of 0 if no aid was given, and 1 if aid was given. Hypothesis 1 stated that: *States that are more economically valuable are more likely to receive aid.*

The results of a logit analysis designed to test the relative relationships to aid of human rights versus economic concerns are presented in Table 3.2. Human rights have a strong effect on likelihood that a state receives aid; in fact, its effect is more significant than are any of the measures of recipient economic importance. Interestingly, states with worse human rights records are *more* likely to receive aid than are ones with better human rights records, perhaps because UK policy makers perceive that they will have greater potential to influence these states if they maintain relationships with them (Matthews and Pratt, 1988). The characteristics of a recipient's economy that have the most significant impact are whether or not it is an oil exporter (marginally significant, in a negative direction) and the growth rate of the economy (which also has a negative effect on its likelihood of receiving aid).

Most measures of strategic relations with the recipient make little difference, except that closer states are more likely to receive aid. Additionally, fewer states received aid during the Cold War, perhaps reflecting a more focussed targeting of aid resources.

Whether the state received aid in the previous year was the single most important predictor of current aid status.

The Allocation Decision

Hypothesis 2 states: *Recipient states that are more economically valuable will receive higher levels of aid.* Table 3.3 presents regression results for aid levels. While recipients with poor human rights records were more likely to receive aid, human rights do *not* appear to be related to aid levels. This suggests that though policy makers realize they have greater potential to influencing states with whom they maintain relations, those aid amounts are largely symbolic. At this stage, the status of the UK's trade relations with the recipient does appear to impact aid amounts, as a trade-driven explanation predicts. Strategic considerations take a back seat to economic ones in explaining aid amounts – except that geographically proximate recipients receive more aid.

Overall measures of explanatory power (especially PPC/PRE (percent predicted correctly/proportional reduction in error) at the gatekeeping stage) are low for this model at both stages. Much of this is driven by the underlying skew in the variables – most states receive aid, and most states tend to get relatively small aid amounts.

Are Calculations Really Different For Different Categories of States?

I predicted that states that are more potentially economically valuable would be less likely to be 'punished' for human rights violations by having aid terminated or decreased. In order to test this, one would need to choose a measure of economic importance, disaggregate the pool of recipients based on these measures, and examine whether human rights was more strongly associated with the aid fortunes of 'unimportant' states than of 'important' ones.

What is the best measure of economic importance of a state? Measures based on trade are in some ways the most natural choice since they clearly capture the issue of interest for this argument and empirically speaking seem to be more influential than any other measure of 'economic value' in the analyses above. Since export initiatives are most frequently mentioned in British FCO policy statements, volume of total exports from the UK to the recipient is used (these analyses have also been run for categories of states divided by GDP and GDP growth, with similar results).

Gatekeeping decision The results presented in the following two tables offer some support for the above predictions. Table 3.4 presents results for the gatekeeping decision. For recipients with below-average trade with the UK, human rights have an impact in the expected direction on the likelihood that a state receives aid. Few economic factors have an effect. States with more stagnant economies are more likely to receive aid, as was the case in the pooled sample. This seems to indicate that states that are more likely to need aid are more likely to receive it.

States in areas of instability may be seen as risky bets and are less likely to receive aid. States that are closer to the UK and former colonies are more likely to receive aid, as was the case for the pooled sample. Past aid status is the most significant predictor of current status. So past relationships are good predictors of the strength of current ones.

As would be predicted, the effect of recipient human rights disappears in aid decisions regarding states with higher trade volumes with the UK. This is one of the major differences between the two categories of potential recipients. In addition, recipient economic growth continues to be negatively associated with likelihood of receiving aid (and continues to be the only economic consideration that is). States close to the UK continue to be more likely to receive aid. A third difference between these two categories of recipients is the greater focusing of aid as a tool during the Cold War is more evident in these important trade partners. This presents a puzzle, in that we would expect aid to trading partners to be *less* sensitive to the changing status of East-West tensions. Finally, trade relations mitigate the importance of past colonial history.

So far, these results are consistent with a trade-driven model of aid disbursement.

Allocation decision Table 3.5 presents determinants of aid amounts for the two categories of recipients according to their status as export markets for the UK. At this stage, far fewer factors appear to be taken into account in the decision process. For states which provide a lower than average share of the UK's export volume, decisions do not appear to be based on human rights records or on additional measures of the recipient's economic importance, but rather on domestic politics factors such as whether that recipient has a large immigrant diaspora in the UK. In addition, recipients which have been the site of humanitarian catastrophes get more aid overall, evidence that the altruistic considerations that were historically the

Table 3.4 Recipients with strong versus weak trade relations with UK pooled cross-sectional logit analyses of whether a state received aid

Variable	Potential Recipients with Below-Average Imports from UK		Potential Recipients with Above-Average Imports from UK	
Human Rights Measures				
Human rights	0.822	(0.442)	0.774	(0.531)
Recipient polity score	0.015	(0.020)	0.017	(0.015)
Economic Value Measures				
Trade intersection	4.213	(2.512)	-38.086	(3.72E+07)
UK imports from recip.	-0.000	(0.001)	-0.003	(0.003)
Recipient is oil exporter	-0.021	(0.016)	0.007	(0.013)
Recipient GDP	-0.010	(0.006)	-0.000	(0.001)
Recipient GDP growth	-0.117*	(0.053)	-0.078	(0.041)
Recipient population	0.000	(0.000)	0.000	(0.000)
Strategic Value Measures				
Recipient nuclear cap.	-62.704	(19.10E+07)	1.436	(2.66E+07)
Recipient instability	-2.884	(1.589)	0.384	(0.556)
Distance from UK	-0.001**	(0.000)	-0.001***	(0.000)
Dispute with UK	-29.998	(25.30E+07)	-31.394	(4.70E+07)
Alliance with UK	1.881	(1.956)	-28.393	(3.03E+07)
Cold War	-0.018	(1.165)	-3.110*	(1.377)
Humanitarian Need Measure				
Humanitarian crisis	-0.009	(0.033)	-0.085	(0.053)
Domestic Politics Measures				
Human rights activism	-37.222	(28.90E+07)	-31.687	(4.24E+07)
Immigrants from recipient	-0.000	(0.000)	0.000	(0.000)
Colonial History Measure				
Former colony	3.009*	(1.455)	-0.216	(0.875)
Interaction Terms				
Cold War* human rights	-0.031	(0.483)	-1.555**	(0.577)
Policy History				
Aid previous year?	2.931***	(0.483)	2.107***	(0.423)
Significance of Model	0.0000		0.0000	
N	848 (#groups=80)		620 (#groups=63)	
% Predicted Correctly	64.57		35.30	
Proportional Reduction in Error (Lambda)	0.00		0.00	

***=significant at p<0.001; **=p<0.01; *=p<0.05 (one-tailed).

Table 3.5 Recipients with strong versus weak trade relations with UK pooled cross-sectional regression analyses of raw levels of aid

Variable	Recipients with Below-Average Exports from UK		Recipients with Above-Average Exports from UK	
Human Rights Measures				
Human rights	1947.318	(4345.855)	-196.234	(6172.266)
Recipient polity score	71.183	(202.797)	-11.578	(148.285)
Economic Value Measures				
Trade intersection	15659.090	(15333.240)	Dropped	
UK imports from recip.	7.284	(5.717)	10.836	(34.704)
Recipient is oil exporter	45.054	(122.996)	92.570	(103.627)
Recipient GDP	-119.929	(82.312)	-2.608	(10.772)
Recipient GDP growth	780.097	(475.892)	199.151	(299.584)
Recipient population	0.129	(0.220)	0.073	(0.119)
Strategic Value Measures				
Recipient nuclear cap.	Dropped		Dropped	
Recipient instability	-12290.640	(9307.580)	-1254.602	(5203.269)
Distance from UK	1.755	(2.226)	1.845	(1.546)
Dispute with UK	Dropped		Dropped	
Alliance with UK	-25060.940	(23852.670)	Dropped	
Cold War	-10526.980	(12756.090)	5850.708	(14235.080)
Humanitarian Need Measure				
Humanitarian crisis	725.605*	(344.021)	683.394	(402.337)
Domestic Politics Measures				
Human rights activism	Dropped		Dropped	
Immigrants from recipient	9.072*	(3.821)	1.804	(4.695)
Colonial History Measure				
Former colony	4494.396	(9859.380)	-9116.358	(11840.900)
Interaction Terms				
Cold War * human rights	584.347	(5814.503)	3583.601	(6276.194)
Policy History				
Aid amount previous year	0.233	(0.146)	0.313	(0.325)
Significance of Model	0.0000		0.8365	
N	76 (#groups=15)		44 (#groups=15)	
R^2 overall	0.47		0.28	
R^2 between groups	0.95		0.54	
R^2 within groups	0.17		0.06	

***=significant at p<0.001; **=p<0.01; *=p<0.05 (one-tailed).

original reason for aid are still in play. A more complex process appears to be in effect for states with lower than average trade volumes with the UK; it may be that for states that are more important trade partners, that relationship is the overwhelming reason they receive the aid they do.[10]

It appears that at the gatekeeping stage, in fact UK policy makers only *do* take human rights into account in the case of potential recipients with which they will not be endangering and important export market. But this effect disappears at the allocation stage, perhaps because all states that have made it to this stage tend to be of high economic value to the UK (export volumes are almost twice as high on average for states that do get aid than for those that do not).

Conclusion and Implications

Examination of British aid decisions yields mixed support for predictions that human rights will only be taken into account in aid decisions when donors can 'afford' to. When all potential aid recipients were examined together, states with worse human rights records were actually *more* likely to receive aid than the ones with better human rights records, perhaps because UK policy makers perceive that they will have greater potential to influence these states if they maintain relationships with them. Several characteristics of a recipient's economy also appear to be significant to whether it will receive aid. Most measures of strategic relations do not make much difference at the gatekeeping phase.

At the allocation stage for the pooled sample, recipient human rights record does not appear to be related to aid levels. Status of the UK's trade relations with the recipient does appear to be a factor, as a trade-driven explanation of aid decisions predicts. Strategic considerations also appear to take a back seat to economic ones in explaining aid amounts.

When I turned to the question of whether different calculi appeared to be at work for different categories of recipients, the analyses offered some support for the predictions made above. For recipients with below-average trade with the UK, human rights records have an impact in the expected direction on whether a state receives aid. For this category, few economic factors have an effect, except that states whose economies are less robust (and who are more likely to need aid) are more likely to receive aid. In addition, past relationships appear good predictors of the strength of current ones.

As would be predicted, the effect of human rights conditions in the recipient country disappears in aid decisions regarding states with more significant trade relations with the UK. So far, the results of these analyses are consistent with a trade-driven model of aid disbursement. At the allocation stage, far fewer factors appear to be taken into account in the decision process.

At the gatekeeping stage, UK policy makers only take human rights into account in the case of potential recipients with which they will not be endangering and important export market. But this effect disappears at the allocation stage.

Realists predict that human rights should never matter to foreign policy makers in other states, while neoliberal scholars and legal constraints would lead one to believe that they are of the highest priority. A survey of the general context of British foreign policy making would lead one to believe that human rights should be taken into account – at least in some aid decisions. The answer is, human rights *do* matter – but only when it is not too expensive.

Human rights abuses continue apace despite the fact that policy makers and activists in democratic states profess a firm commitment to civil and political rights. Determining when and why states take action in defense of those goals helps us understand why so many continue to be denied basic political and civil liberties, and what can be done about it by states that possess the resources to encourage change.

Notes

1 Similar questions have been ably addressed in the US context by a number of scholars (Lumsdaine, 1993; Milner, Poe, and Leblang, 1999; Poe, 1992; Poe. Tate, and Keith, 1999).

2 Policy makers describe the first decision as a 'gatekeeping' one in which certain countries were systematically excluded and others systematically included. The second decision is described as being more complex, with a higher level of give-and-take amongst actors.

3 In addition, such an approach provides maximum comparability with previous studies (Poe, 1990, 1992; Poe, Tate and Keith, 1999).

4 An important side effect of this characteristic is that it is biased towards helping richer developing countries, something found in several of my analyses.

5 In addition, these analyses were run substituting other proxies for the status of rights in the recipient states, such as levels of democracy and counts of internal disorder incidents (riots, demonstrations, etc.). Similar results were observed.

6 This control is also included in the interest of replicability (it is included in many studies of US aid, such as Cingranelli and Pasquarello (1985) and Poe (1990, 1991)).

7 See http://www.wcfia.harvard.edu/ponsacs/panda.htm.

8 See http://www.wcfia.harvard.edu/ponsacs/panda.htm. Ideally, I would have obtained measures of the amount and intensity of campaigning done on behalf of particular human rights crises from the major human rights interest groups themselves. However, both Amnesty and Human Rights Watch claim not to keep records of this kind or any other that would lend itself to systematic analysis – not even a financial audit that would contain country-specific line items.

9 Recipient's nuclear capabilities and location at a trade intersection, recipient's location in an area of instability and at a trade intersection, size of immigrant population in the UK and the recipient's location at a trade intersection, UK exports to the recipient and imports from it, UK exports to the recipient and whether the recipient was a location of humanitarian crisis, UK imports to the recipient and whether the recipient was a location of humanitarian crisis, the recipient's population and whether it possesses nuclear capabilities, the recipient's population and its immigrant presence in the UK and the interaction variable with one of its components (the Cold War period).

10 However, we do run into some statistical problems in estimating the sources of aid allocation amounts for this latter group of recipients; because so few states actually

receive aid from the UK in this group, the estimations are not as robust (see the high p>Chi^2 figure) as for the other analyses presented.

References

Axelrod, R. and Keohane, R.O. (1993), 'Achieving Cooperation Under Anarchy: Strategies and Institutions', in D.A. Baldwin (ed.), *Neorealism and Neoliberalism: The Contemporary Debate*, New York, Columbia University Press.

Barratt, B.A. (2002), *Aiding or Abetting: The Comparative Role of Human Rights in Foreign Aid Decisions*, Ph.D. dissertation, University of California, Davis.

Beitz, C.R. (1979), *Political Theory and International Relations*, Princeton, NJ, Princeton University Press.

Brewin, C. (1986), 'Europe', in R.J.Vincent (ed.), *Foreign Policy and Human Rights: Issues and Responses,* Cambridge, Cambridge University Press.

Burnell, P. (1991), 'Introduction', in A.Bose and P.Burnell (eds), *Britain's Overseas Aid since 1979: Between Idealism and Self-Interest*, Manchester, Manchester University Press.

Burnell, P. (1997), *Foreign Aid in A Changing World,* Buckingham, Open University Press.

Central Intelligence Agency (Various Years), *CIA World Factbook*, Washington, DC, US Government Printing Office.

Cingranelli, D.L. and Pasquarello, T.E. (1985), 'Human Rights Practices and the Distribution of US Foreign Aid to Latin American Countries', *American Journal of Political Science*, Vol. 29(3), pp. 539-63.

Cunliffe, S.A. (1989), 'Economic Aid as and Instrument for the Promotion of International Human Rights', in D.M.Hill (ed.), *Human Rights and Foreign Policy: Principles and Practice,* London, The Macmillan Press.

Flags of the World Project. (2002), http://www.crwflags.com/fotw/flags/gb-colon.html#list, accessed 9 February 2003.

Franck, T.M. (1992), 'The Emerging Right to Democratic Governance', *American Journal of International Law*, Vol. 86(1), pp. 46-91.

Friedman, T. (1999), *The Lexus and the Olive Tree: Understanding Globalization*, New York, Farrar, Strauss, and Giroux.

Gillies, D. (1989), 'Do Interest Groups Make a Difference? Domestic Influences on Canadian Development Aid Policies', in I. Brecher (ed.), *Human Rights, Development, and Foreign Policy: Canadian Perspectives*, Halifax, Nova Scotia, The Institute for Research on Public Policy.

Historical Statistics of the United States On CD-ROM : Colonial Times to 1970. [computer file] Bicentennial ed, (1997), New York, Cambridge University Press.

International Monetary Fund (Various Years), *Direction of Trade Statistics, 1948-1990*, Washington, DC, International Monetary Fund.

Jaggers, K. and Gurr, T.R. (1996), *Polity III: Regime Change and Political Authority, 1800-1994* [Computer file]. 2nd ICPSR version. Boulder, CO: Keith Jaggers/College Park, MD: Ted Robert Gurr [producers], Ann Arbor, MI: Inter-university Consortium for Political and Social Research [distributor].

Keohane, R.O. (1993), 'Institutional Theory and the Realist Challenge After the Cold War', in D.A. Baldwin (ed.), *Neorealism and Neoliberalism: The Contemporary Debate*, New York, Columbia University Press.

Larsen, H. (1997), *Foreign Policy and Discourse Analysis: France, Britain, and Europe*, London, Routledge.

Lipson, C. (1993), 'International Cooperation in Economic and Security Affairs', in D.A. Baldwin (ed.), *Neorealism and Neoliberalism: The Contemporary Debate*, New York, Columbia University Press.

Maizels, A. and Nissanke, M.K. (1984), 'Motivations for Aid to Developing Countries', *World Development,* Vol. 12(3), pp. 879-900.

Matthews, R.O., and Pratt, C. (1988), 'Introduction', in R.O. Matthews and C. Pratt (eds.), *Human Rights in Canadian Foreign Policy,* Kingston, McGill-Queen's University.

Poe, S.C. (1990), 'Human Rights and United States Foreign Aid - A Review of Quantitative Studies and Suggestions for Future Research', *Human Rights Quarterly*, Vol. 12(4), pp. 499-512.

Poe, S. C. (1991), 'Human Rights and the Allocation of US Military Assistance', *Journal of Peace Research*, Vol. 28(2), pp. 205-216.

Poe, S.C. (1992), 'Human Rights and Economic Aid Allocation Under Ronald Reagan and Jimmy Carter', *American Journal of Political Science*, Vol. 36(1), pp. 147-67.

Poe, S.C., Tate, C.N. and Keith, L.C. (1999), 'Repression Of The Human Right To Personal Integrity Revisited: A Global Cross-National Study Covering The Years 1976-1993', *International Studies Quarterly*, Vol. 43(2), pp. 291-313.

Purdue University Political Terror Scale. (1999), Purdue, IN, Purdue University Global Studies Program, Global Governance and Human Rights, Michael Stohl, Convenor. http://www.ippu/purdue.edu/info/gsp/govern.htm. Last accessed 28 March 2001.

Ray, J.L. (1998), *Global Politics*, Boston, Houghton Mifflin.

Scharfe, S. (1996), *Complicity-Human Rights and Canadian Foreign Policy: The Case of East Timor*, Montreal and New York, Black Rose Books.

Stokke, O. (1995), 'Introduction', in O. Stokke (ed.), *Aid and Political Conditionality,* London, Frank Cass.

Stohl, M. (1983), *The Purdue Political Terror Scale*, Codebook.

Vincent, R.J. (1986), 'Introduction', in R.J. Vincent (ed), *Foreign Policy and Human Rights: Issues and Responses*, Cambridge, Cambridge University Press.

Wallace, W. (1975), *The Foreign Policy Process in Britain,* London, The Royal Institute of International Affairs.

Wilson, Woodrow (2 April 1917), message to Congress asking for declaration of war.

Chapter 4

Security at What Cost? Arms Transfers to the Developing World and Human Rights

Dawn Miller

Introduction

Arms have often been seen as a way for a nation to preserve its security. Particularly, arms transfers to developing nations have been portrayed as a way to bolster defence. 'If you seek peace, prepare for war' (Bremer and Hughes, 1990, p. 33). Realists argue that the threat of force is fundamentally a stabilizing factor in international relations (Bremer, 1980; Bremer and Hughes, 1990; Pearson, 1994). 'Arms transfer have been one of the most critical aspects of international politics since the Second World War' (Maniruzzaman, 1992, p.733). Major arms suppliers such as the United States have historically shared the view of arms transfers as a tool of security (Betts, 1980). However, these arms transfers can have devastating impacts on the internal dynamics of the receiving country. They may provide the tools for political repression, lead to repeal of civil and political rights and may take away valuable revenues that could be spent on healthcare and education. Alarmingly, the acquisition of arms for security may lead to what Renner (1997) describes as a domestic arms race. If a country relies upon arms transfers to bolster its security, it may never reach a point where it perceives itself as completely secure. As a result, the country continues to import weapons to satisfy an ever-increasing need for arms. Such an arms race may send developing nations into an arms-seeking spiral and exacerbate the problems associated with the import of arms.

A large amount of the literature concerning the arms trade focuses on the world arms transfer system, however, much work must still be done on the impact the weapons have on the receiving states (Maniruzzaman, 1992). Developing countries have placed a strong emphasis on the import of arms to provide security at the expense of other governmental responsibilities. Deger and Smith (1983) discovered a negative relationship between military expenditure and economic growth. As a result of stunted economic development, export competitiveness is reduced and imports are increased, which in turn leads to unemployment (Wolpin, 1983). Brzoska (1982) found arms imports to be a large factor in the growth of the developing world's debt. Countries that devote a large part of their spending to arms are less likely to save which in turn stunts their economy (Sadowski, 1992). Developing nations are willing to sacrifice investments and market development to spend money on arms to improve their military forces (Kolodziej and Harkavy, 1982; Zonninsein, 1994). In addition to the negative impact on the economy and social spending, the spread of arms may also spark violence. 'Widespread unemployment, poverty, social inequity, and the pressures of environmental degradation and resource depletion in the presence of large quantities of small arms make a highly combustible combination' (Renner, 1997, p.8).

The acquisition of arms has not only affected developing nations' economies, but it has also affected the emphasis of the role of the military in the state. Stork and Paul investigated the link between arms transfers and increased militarization of the receiving country in the Middle East. 'Parallel to the growth of Middle East arms imports is a rapid increase in military expenditures' (Stork and Paul, 1983, p.5). Maniruzzaman (1992) identified similar links to increased militarization; he found that arms transfers encouraged *coups d'état* and may extend the length of military rule. Not only are arms transfers linked with militarization, they may also lead to actual conflict. Craft and Smaldone (2002) associated arms trade with the increased likelihood of conflict involvement in sub-Saharan Africa.

With the increased emphasis of the military and growing spending on weapons we may expect a decrease in democratic institutions and practices in developing nations. Blanton examined the link between level of democracy and arms transfers. Her findings tie arms with declining levels of democracy. Even low levels of arms imports may have a devastating impact on the provision of democratic rights (Blanton, 1999b). Interestingly, during the 1990s there has been a strong push for democratization in the developing world, yet developed nations continued to send arms transfers to the developing states (Blanton, 1999b).

Developing nations must make difficult choices in their budgeting decisions. In the past, developing states spent more of their economic resources than developed states on weapons (Kolodziej and Harkavy, 1982). Spending on arms transfers may divert funds from social programs. As large export markets for arms, these countries must make a difficult decision between spending limited revenues on arms or in other areas (Pearson, 1994). Although they are meant to provide security for the receiving state, arms transfers may have dire consequences for the internal stability of the country and well being of its citizens.

Arms Transfers and Human Rights

Little research has been done on the effect of arms transfers on human rights. One of the major researchers in this field is Shannon Lindsey Blanton. She found an association between arms transfers to the developing countries and the violation of personal integrity rights within those countries. Arms acquisitions appear to contribute to repression by making violent political acts more feasible. The import of these weapons provides the tools necessary for repression. To this end, arms may play a direct instrumental role in the infliction of human rights abuse, or they may represent the endpoint of a longer process of strengthening the military or fueling a national security mentality, which in turn leads to human rights repression (Blanton, 1999a).

In this chapter, I turn to Shannon Lindsey Blanton's model of arms transfers and human rights (1999a). I expand the model from 1992 to 1997 and introduce two more dimensions of human rights. For this chapter, I will employ Jack Donnelly's definition of human rights. Human rights are those rights people hold for simply being human (Donnelly, 1989). Although human rights have been described as interdependent and indivisible, human rights have been treated separately in the human rights literature and international organizations such as the United Nations. The bulk of research on human rights has focused on personal integrity rights. However, there is growing interest in other types of human rights. Also included in the literature on human rights are studies that investigate political and civil rights and social and economic rights. 'Since World War II, these rights and liberties have been incorporated in the core U.N. treaties and covenants' (Milner, Poe and Leblang, 1999, p.405), however, these rights have rarely been studied together. To truly gauge the effect of arms transfers on the provision of human rights, we must move beyond the investigation of rights against bodily harm to the impact weapons imports may have on civil and political rights and social and economic rights. In addition to looking at the effect of arms transfers on personal integrity rights, I will also look at its effect on two other types of human rights, civil and political rights and social and economic rights. Through expanding this conceptualization of human rights, I hope to increase our knowledge and provide a full understanding of the effect of arms transfers on the provision of human rights.

The rights discussed in this chapter range from the protection of the person to rights to education. All of these rights can be found within the Universal Declaration of Human Rights, which was adopted by the United Nations General Assembly on 10 December 1948. The Declaration was the first document to outline in detail the rights of all people. The right to personal integrity is the right of a person not to be 'subjected to murder, torture, mayhem, rape, or assault' (Shue, 1980, p.20). Political rights include the right to take part in government through free and fair election with universal and equal suffrage. Civil rights include 'freedom of thought, conscience, religion; opinion and expression; movement and residence; and peaceful assembly and association' (Donnelly, 1986, p.607). Due to unemployment and poverty sparking political upheavals, 'the United Nations Charter recognized the need to promote economic progress and social development' (Merali and Oosterveld, 2001, p.40). The International Covenant on Economic, Social and Cultural Rights was adopted in December 1966. Social and economic rights include the rights a citizen has to adequate food, education and healthcare (Donnelly, 1986).

The provisions of human rights in the developing world are threatened by arms imports. Arms transfers to developing countries provide the tools necessary for the government to exercise repression. The weapons developing countries receive provide the opportunity and capability for violent action (Blanton, 1999a). Since the end of the Cold War, the sale of heavy weapons has decreased while small arms have dominated the trade. 'As the number of internal wars has increased, the demand for small and light weapons has risen – to such proportions that some conclude the arms trade has been revolutionized' (Harkavy and Neuman, 2001, p.262). This increase in the importation of small arms makes repression even more likely, since such weapons are more easily used to repress citizens than tanks or jet fighters. Although people ultimately choose to engage in repression, the availability of weapons may make the choice of repression easier (Pearson 1994). The spread of arms 'has put guns in the hands of men willing to kill the innocent on their road to power' (Lewis, 2001, p.622).

Coupled with the transfer of arms are increased military personnel to wield those weapons (Maniruzzaman, 1992). The growth of the military may have dangerous consequences as the presence of a large military increases the probability that it may be used (Noel-Baker, 1958). In addition to providing the opportunity for action, arms transfers may transform the regime into a more militaristic government, which in turn leads to further repression, since military governments are more apt to engage in human rights abuse (McKinlay and Cohan, 1974; Brzoska and Ohlson, 1987). Therefore, I posit:

> H1: The more arms transfers a developing country receives, the greater the use of political repression by its government, *ceteris paribus*.

As a state becomes more militaristic, it may shift its emphasis from individual civil and political rights to greater centralization of the government and military control. Regardless of their size, arms transfers are associated with deteriorating levels of democracy (Blanton, 1999b). 'Any transfer of arms increases military firepower of military forces. More importantly, transfer of arms has multiplier effects; it initiates a chain of events that cumulate in strengthening the armed forces' (Maniruzzaman, 1992, p.738). The transfer of arms serves to strengthen the military through training and the building of the military's infrastructure. The specialized training of the soldiers increases their loyalty to the military. As the military's infrastructure is improved, existing bases are modernized while new ones are built. Maniruzzaman argues that these factors lead to an increased professionalism among the armed forces. This professionalism may lead to military coups and eventual military rule (Maniruzzaman, 1992). As military strength increases in the country, there is a greater likelihood that civil and political rights may be taken away. The import of arms has 'a pernicious effect on basic political rights,' (Kick, Davis, Kiefer and Burns, 1998, p.363) since revenues dedicated to arms in military regimes negatively affect political rights. Therefore, I posit:

> H2: The more arms transfers a developing country receives, the lower the level of civil and political rights provided to its citizens, *ceteris paribus*.

Not only do personal integrity and political rights suffer, nations tend to overemphasize the purchase of arms over important social programs and important human needs (Russett, 1969). Since civilian and military expenditures struggle for scant resources, developing nations seeking to bolster security may devote more of their budget to arms spending. Sadowski reports, (1992, p.6) 'By the late 1980s

Syria was spending 19 times as much on its military as it did on health and education. In Saudi Arabia this ratio was 38:1 and Iraq 56:1.' High arms burdens are associated with lowered health and educational expenditures (Wolpin, 1983). Developing nations have and continue to amass debt to import arms and reduce spending on social programs. Therefore, I posit:

> H3: The more arms a developing country imports, the lower the level of spending on social programs, such as education, healthcare and social programs, *ceteris paribus*.

To test these hypotheses, I constructed a model of human rights that will be explained in the next section.

A Model of Human Rights

Measuring Human Rights

Repression For the personal integrity rights portion of human rights, I turn to Stohl and Gibney's Political Terror Scale (PTS).[1] From Amnesty International and U.S. State Department reports countries' human rights practices are coded on a five-point scale, where one is the least repressive and five is the most repressive regime.[2] For 1997, I use the Political Terror Scale guidelines to code Amnesty International and State Department Reports. Like Blanton (1999a), I average the two scores. The scores are closely related to one another, as they are moderately correlated (0.736). However, the averaging of these two scores may be problematic for two reasons. First, the two scores may yield different results due to bias. Poe, Carey and Vazquez found the State Department and Amnesty International reports, 'have clearly converged in their assessments of human rights violations over time' (2001, p.677). However, researchers should be cautious; Poe et al., hypothesize that a new bias towards U.S. trading partners may have emerged in the State Department reports. Second, 'the scale requires ordinal judgments – distances between levels are not equal but a country at level 1 is doing better than a country judged to be at level 2' (Political Terror Scale website). Therefore, it may not be appropriate to average the two scores. To avoid these problems, I also analyze my hypothesis with the two measures of repression individually.

Political and civil rights To measure civil and political rights, I use Freedom House's *Freedom in the World Country Rankings*.[3] Freedom House ranks countries on their level of civil and political rights. Political rights and civil liberties are each measured on a one to seven scale; where one is the highest degree of freedom and seven the lowest. To create an increasing scale, I inverted the scores so that one is the lowest and seven is the highest degree of freedom.

Social and economic rights To operationalize my measure of social and economic rights I employ the Physical Quality of Life index gathered by Morris (1979, 1996) in conjunction with the Overseas Development Council. Three dimensions are captured in this index; countries' performances are evaluated on three dimensions: infant mortality, life expectancy at age one and literacy at age 15. These factors are placed on a scale from 0-100 and the mean of the three is calculated.[4] Milner et al. (2000), based on Morris's work (1979), argue that infant mortality and life expectancy at age one tap the effects of health, nutrition, family environment and social relations, while literacy rates capture the access to education, which enables people to share in economic development. The updated Physical Quality of Life data was generously furnished by Wesley Milner.

Operationalizing the Independent Variables

Arms transfers Many scholars have noted the problems of studying arms trade. Among the problems inherent to its subject of study are limited data, inaccurate reports and unverifiable figures, which lead to difficulties determining accuracy and validity (Kolodziej, 1979; Brzoska, 1982; Louscher and Salomone, 1987; Phillips and Racioppi, 1992). However, these problems should not keep us from engaging in research concerning arms trade. Many important questions call for the use of this imperfect data. Two of the major and often used sources of data for arms transfers are the Stockholm International Peace Research Institute (SIPRI) and the Arms Control and Disarmament Agency (ACDA), now the U.S. Bureau of Arms Control, a subsidiary of the State Department.

I obtained my arms transfer data from the ACDA and U.S. Bureau of Arms Control's *World Military Expenditures and Arms Transfers* (*WMEAT*). Arms transfers are defined as the import of military equipment by grant, credit or barter.[5] I use a measure of arms imports in constant 1997 dollars. Imports are defined as, 'the values for imports covers merchandise transactions and come mainly from International Financial Statistics published by the IMF' (*WMEAT*, 1998, p.207).

There are many aspects that may influence the provision and protection of human rights. In order to see if arms transfers truly have an impact on human rights, these factors must be held constant. Liberal democracies are less likely to abuse personal integrity rights (Poe and Tate, 1994). They are also more likely to provide a higher level of civil and political rights than other polities and less likely to violate these rights. Often in liberal democracies, constitutions serve as a protectors of their citizens' human rights. Countries that have constitutions outlining freedoms held by its citizens are less likely to violate human rights. 'Overall, constitutions do appear to offer a feasible path to pursue in regard to human right protection' (Keith, Tate and Poe, 2000, p.33). As for social and economic rights, democracies are more likely to provide social and economic programs. In democracies diverse groups are represented in the decision making process, they are more likely to have 'kinder and gentler qualities' (Lijphart, 1999). It can be expected that these qualities would lead to the provision of programs to provide for the social welfare and betterment of the country's citizens. To measure liberal democracy I use the Polity IV index and score all countries that receive a democracy score of eight or higher as one and all other as zero. This distinction captures the established, mature democracies in the international arena.

Conflict has been found to be a strong indicator of human rights abuse. During internal and external conflicts, governments may turn to repression to maintain control. Poe and Tate found 'international and domestic threats, in the form of international and civil wars, to an increased tendency to abuse personal integrity rights' (1994, p.866). During times of war, nations may also revoke civil and political rights in order to maintain order. In addition to scaling back rights, these governments may also decrease their spending on social programs, like education and healthcare, in order to channel more money to the war effort. To measure internal and external conflict I use the Militarized Interstate Disputes (MID) dataset version 3.0 to create two dichotomous variables.[6] For the internal conflict variable countries were coded one if they experienced a conflict that resulted in one thousand battle deaths and zero if they did not experience a war. For the external conflict variable, countries that were involved in an inter-state conflict were coded as one and zero if they had no involvement.

Perceived insecurity is another important factor that might affect governments' respect for human rights; not only may countries violate human rights during conflicts, but they may continue to violate human rights long after the conflict is over. 'The government is likely to remain concerned about being attacked or dominated by others and will retain its tight control over social order for some time' (Blanton, 1999a, p.238). To capture perceived insecurity, I created a dichotomous variable where countries were coded as one if they had been in an internal or external conflict any time in the previous five years and zero if they had not been involved a conflict during that period. For this variable I used the data I collected for internal and external variables from the MID dataset version 3.0.

Although developing nations depend on arms transfers for a bulk of their weapons, many have developed their own domestic source of arms (Looney and Frederiksen, 1986; Brzoska, 1989; Rosh, 1990). If a country wants to repress its citizens it does not need to rely on arms transfers from other countries. If it chooses, it may turn to domestic arms production to increase its ability to repress its citizens (Blanton, 1999a, p.238). Domestic arms production may also have a negative effect on civil and political rights and social and economic rights. The more militaristic a regime is, the less likely they are to support such rights. Domestic arms production is measured by a dichotomous variable where countries that had a history of arms production were coded as one and all other cases were coded as zero.[7] This variable was compiled from two studies (Looney and Frederiksen, 1986; Rosh, 1990) and the ACDA's *WMEAT*.

Economic development has been linked with lower levels of personal integrity abuses (Poe and Tate, 1994). Therefore, I expect the lower the level of economic development of a country, the lower its level of political and civil rights. 'A great many people in different countries of the world are systematically denied political liberty and basic civil rights. It is sometimes claimed that the denial of these rights help to stimulate economic growth and is 'good' for rapid economic development' (Sen, 2000, p.15). Additionally, I expect that economically developed nations are more likely to provide greater social and economic rights to their citizens. GNP per capita was used to capture a country's economic development. This variable was gathered from the World Bank's *World Development Indicators* (2001).

The greater a country's population, the more likely the government is to abuse personal integrity rights (Poe and Tate, 1994). I also expect the larger the nation, the lower its level of civil and political rights. In addition, I expect there to be a negative relationship between population and social and economic rights. The greater the population, the less able a country is to provide social programs. I gathered the population per capita for each country in the study using data from the *World Development Indicators* CD-ROM.

To test the multivariate models, I construct a data set spanning the period from 1982 to 1997 for 88 developing nations.[8] Developing nations are those defined as such in the 1994 UN Human Development Report (UNDP, 1994, pp. 102-3). Included in the dataset are countries with instances of arms transfers, as well as countries without any arms transfers.

Method of Analysis

To test the models, I employ Prais-Winsten regression[9] using panel corrected standard errors. I chose this method to control for correlation between the errors in different time periods and between countries. For my last model of social and economic rights, I also used a Generalized Estimating Equation(GEE) model since the previous year's physical quality of life level is the best predictor of the current level. This model accounts for correlation between time periods within country data. In addition to testing the contemporaneous effect of arms transfers on human rights, I also look at the lagged effect of the arms transfers. The effect of arms transfers may not be instantaneous, as the effects of the weapons imports may not be felt in the year they are received. To determine whether the previous year's arms transfers had an effect on the human rights practices of the current year, I test each of the hypotheses using data from the previous years' arms transfers with the current years' contributing factors.

Results

The contemporaneous effect of arms transfers on personal integrity rights are reported in Table 4.1. The results are consistent with Blanton's 1999a findings; arms transfers to developing countries are associated with increased levels of personal integrity violations. However, the impact is not very strong. Using the average of State Department and Amnesty International scores, the results indicate that a one per cent increase in arms transfers leads to a 0.00027 increase in repression. If arms transfers increase from 11 to 67 million dollars we would expect to see a 0.1664 increase in personal integrity violations. Using Amnesty International and State Department scores separately yields similar results. Amnesty International scores reveal that we may see a 0.0031 increase in repression for every one per cent increase in arms transfers. The State Department results produce a slightly higher impact; for every one per cent increase in arms, there is a 0.0043 increase in personal integrity violations. The control variables, liberal democracy, external conflict, internal conflict, perceived insecurity, domestic arms production and economic development, were all consistent with my expectations, except for population, which is not a statistically significant indicator of repression.

The results presented in Table 4.2 illustrate the effects of arms transfers on the next year's provision of personal integrity rights. Previous year's imports in arms leads to greater political repression in the next year. The effect of arms transfers on personal integrity rights is slightly larger than what we saw in the contemporaneous results. The average of Amnesty International and State Department scores indicate that a one per cent increase in arms will result in a 0.00046 increase in personal integrity violations the next year. Given an increase from 11 to 67 million dollars in arms transfers, we would expect to see a 0.28014 in the level of repression the country. Using the State Department and Amnesty International scores provides similar results. A 0.0006 increase in repression during the following year is associated with a one percent increase in arms transfers according to the Amnesty International model. The State Department model indicates a one per cent increase in arms transfers results in a 0.00045 increase in personal integrity violations in the following year.

In addition to harming personal integrity rights, arms transfers are also detrimental to civil and political rights. The contemporaneous results are reported in Table 4.3. For every one per cent increase in arms transfers there is a .0004 decrease in civil rights and a 0.00035 decrease in political rights. If a country increases its arms transfers from 11 to 52 million dollars, we would expect to see a 0.189 decrease in civil rights and a 0.166 decrease in political rights. Interestingly, domestic arms production has a positive impact on civil and political rights.

The effects of the prior year's arms transfers on the provision of civil and political rights are reported in Table 4.4. After lagging civil and political rights and the other independent variables one year, arms transfers continue to have a small, negative impact on both civil and political rights. If we saw an increase in arms transfers from 11 to 52 million dollars during this period, we would expect the countries level of civil rights to decrease by 0.265 and political rights by 0.095. As we saw in the contemporaneous effects, domestic arms production is linked with increased civil and political rights.

Table 4.1 The contemporaneous effect of arms transfers on personal integrity rights

	Political Terror Scale Average Coefficient		Political Terror Scale Amnesty International Coefficient		Political Terror Scale State Departmen Coefficient	
Arms Transfers[a]	0.027**	(0.016)	0.031**	(0.018)	0.043**	(0.018
Liberal Democracy	-0.126*	(0.089)	-0.087	(0.109)	-0.166**	(0.075
External Conflict	0.645***	(0.133)	0.726***	(0.156)	0.671***	(0.166
Internal Conflict	1.210***	(0.078)	1.190***	(0.097)	1.310***	(0.090
Perceived Insecurity	0.496***	(0.092)	0.410***	(0.103)	0.647***	(0.100
Domestic Arms	0.269***	(0.068)	0.293***	(0.065)	0.184**	(0.079
Economic Development	-0.072***	(0.001)	-0.065***	(0.010)	-0.081***	(0.008
Population	0.002	(0.002)	0.002	(0.002)	0.001	(0.002
Constant	2.625***	(0.078)	2.657***	(0.073)	2.567***	(0.085
N	1152		1152		1152	
Wald ch^2	367.61		348.97		386.08	
Prob > chi^2	0.000		0.000		0.000	

[a] The natural log was taken due to skewed distribution.

* indicates the level of statistical significance at $p < 0.1$, ** at $p < 0.05$ and *** at $p < 0.001$.

Table 4.2 The lagged effect of arms transfers on personal integrity rights

	Political Terror Scale Average Coefficient		Political Terror Scale Amnesty International Coefficient		Political Terror Scale State Department Coefficient	
Arms Transfers[a]	0.046**	(0.016)	0.060***	(0.018)	0.045**	(0.017)
Liberal Democracy	-0.177**	(0.088)	-0.158*	(0.109)	-0.159**	(0.073)
External Conflict	0.167	(0.146)	-0.022	(0.173)	0.519***	(0.162)
Internal Conflict	0.977***	(0.108)	0.970***	(0.114)	1.185***	(0.107)
Perceived Insecurity	0.591***	(0.107)	0.540***	(0.114)	0.665***	(0.111)
Domestic Arms	0.191**	(0.083)	0.195**	(0.078)	0.147**	(0.080)
Economic Development	-0.073***	(0.010)	-0.070***	(0.011)	-0.080***	(0.009)
Population	0.003	(0.002)	0.003	(0.002)	0.002	(0.003)
Constant	2.675***	(0.089)	2.676***	(0.086)	2.634***	(0.088)
N	1049		1049		1049	
Wald ch^2	244.22		267.07		316.09	
Prob > chi^2	0.000		0.000		0.000	

[a] The natural log was taken due to skewed distribution.

* indicates the level of statistical significance at $p < 0.1$, ** at $p < 0.05$ and *** at $p < 0.001$.

Table 4.3 The contemporaneous effect of arms transfers on civil and political rights

	Freedom House Civil Rights Coefficient		Freedom House Political Rights Coefficient	
Arms Transfers[a]	-0.040**	(0.017)	-0.035**	(0.19)
Liberal Democracy	1.333***	(0.165)	1.894***	(0.186)
External Conflict	-0.349**	(0.173)	-0.118	(0.157)
Internal Conflict	-0.447***	(0.106)	-0.268**	(0.138)
Perceived Insecurity	-0.170*	(0.113)	-0.350**	(0.140)
Domestic Arms	0.195**	(0.104)	0.303**	(0.144)
Economic Development	0.000***	(0.000)	0.000**	(0.000)
Population	-0.008***	(0.002)	-0.006*	(0.004)
Constant	3.196***	(0.141)	3.102***	(0.177)
N	1274		1274	
Wald ch^2	159.35		155.69	
Prob > chi^2	0.000		0.000	

[a] The natural log was taken due to skewed distribution.

* indicates the level of statistical significance at $p < 0.1$, ** at $p < 0.05$ and *** at $p < 0.001$.

Table 4.4 The lagged effect of arms transfers on civil and political rights

	Freedom House Civil Rights Coefficient		Freedom House Political Rights Coefficient	
Arms Transfers[a]	-0.056***	(0.018)	-0.020	(0.021)
Liberal Democracy	1.209***	(0.183)	1.555***	(0.222)
External Conflict	0.029	(0.184)	0.101	(0.189)
Internal Conflict	-0.126	(0.128)	-0.167	(0.156)
Perceived Insecurity	-0.319**	(0.133)	-0.145	(0.144)
Domestic Arms	0.280**	(0.125)	0.274**	(0.168)
Economic Development	0.000**	(0.000)	0.000***	(0.000)
Population	-0.009***	(0.002)	-0.007**	(0.003)
Constant	3.218***	(0.155)	3.119***	(0.171)
N	1194		1194	
Wald ch^2	125.03		75.48	
Prob > chi^2	0.000		0.000	

[a] The natural log was taken due to skewed distribution.

* indicates the level of statistical significance at $p < 0.1$, ** at $p < 0.05$ and *** at $p < 0.001$.

As shown in Table 4.5, my findings concerning the contemporary effect of arms transfers on social and economic rights are contrary to my expectations. My theory indicates that arms imports would have a damaging effect on social and economic rights, however, my results suggest otherwise. According to my models, arm transfers have a small, positive impact on social and economic rights. For every one percent increase in arms transfers, there is a 0.138 increase in social and economic rights. The results in the GEE model also indicate a small, positive relationship between arms transfers. There does not appear to be a budgetary tug-of-war contest between arms transfers and the provision of social and economic rights. It may be that those countries which import arms also have the resources to provide necessary social services such as healthcare and education. As with the civil and political rights model, domestic arms production has a strong impact on social and economic rights. This may be a reflection of jobs and income that such an industry would provide to citizens.

Table 4.5 The contemporaneous effect of arms transfers on social and economic rights

	Prais-Winsten Regression Model Coefficient		GEE Model Coefficient	
Arms Transfers[a]	0.138*	(0.104)	0.164*	(0.084)
Liberal Democracy	4.111***	(0.895)	0.875**	(0.457)
External Conflict	0.576	(1.218)	-0.095	(0.353)
Internal Conflict	-0.575	(0.746)	0.370	(0.665)
Perceived Insecurity	-0.254	(0.675)	0.508	(0.485)
Domestic Arms	8.621***	(1.286)	8.700**	(4.141)
Economic Development	0.001***	(0.000)	0.000*	(0.000)
Population	0.053***	(0.015)	0.100**	(0.056)
Constant	52.645***	(1.148)	55.263***	(3.111)
N	1167		107	
Wald ch^2	327.97		28.51	
Prob > chi^2	0.000		0.000	

a The natural log was taken due to skewed distribution.

* indicates the level of statistical significance at $p < 0.1$, ** at $p < 0.05$ and *** at $p < 0.001$.

The small impact arms transfers have on social and economic rights disappear when I test for the effect of arms transfers on the next year's social and economic rights. The results are shown in Table 4.6. Domestic arms production remains a strong indicator of social and economic rights. Although this variable is not highly associated with economic development the results may be an indirect indicator of the availability of jobs and economic opportunity within the country.

Table 4.6 The lagged effect of arms transfers on social and economic rights

	Prais-Winsten Regression Model Coefficient		GEE Model Coefficient	
Arms Transfers[a]	-0.026	(0.112)	-0.069	(0.067)
Liberal Democracy	4.242***	(0.934)	0.787**	(0.288)
External Conflict	0.815	(1.303)	0.596	(0.485)
Internal Conflict	-1.442**	(0.809)	0.282	(0.582)
Perceived Insecurity	-1.621**	(0.703)	-0.449*	(0.295)
Domestic Arms	9.174***	(1.149)	7.654**	(4.107)
Economic Development	0.001***	(0.000)	0.000**	(0.000)
Population	0.060***	(0.014)	0.113**	(0.058)
Constant	52.820***	(1.147)	56.535***	(3.196)
N	1087		950	
Wald ch^2	306.65		25.85	
Prob > chi^2	0.000		0.00	

a The natural log was taken due to skewed distribution.

* indicates the level of statistical significance at $p < 0.1$, ** at $p < 0.05$ and *** at $p < 0.001$.

Summary and Conclusions

In this chapter, I set out to answer the following question: do arms transfers to developing nations promote or enable the suppression of human rights? Adding two more types of human rights, I use Blanton's (1999a) model of human rights and arms transfers to examine the effects of arms transfers on 88 developing nations from 1982 to 1997. Arms transfers do not affect all three types of human rights equally. The results of my investigation illustrate that arms transfers have a small, damaging effect on personal integrity rights and civil and political rights. I did not find support for the proposition that transfers are detrimental to social and economic rights. The exact opposite was shown in my inspection of the contemporary relationship between social and economic rights and weapons imports. My analysis points to a small, positive interaction between social and economic rights and arms transfers. This puzzling result may be due to the economic health of the developing countries that are able to import weapons. This association warrants further exploration before more conclusive statements can be made about its cause.

Arms transfers contribute to increased repression and the decreased civil and political rights. Although arms transfers do not appear to carry a very large impact on either personal integrity rights or civil and political rights, this relationship should not be ignored. The effect of arms transfers on the human rights records of the country are dependent on the change in arms transfers the country receives. A large jump in weapons imports may spell trouble for the citizens of the receiving country. As a country increases its weapons imports, there is greater likelihood that the government will engage in repression and withdraw civil and political liberties. The imported arms provide the necessary tools for the government to engage in the suppression of human rights. As a result of these transfers we may also see greater militarization of the state, which in turn leads to an increased likelihood of repression and the possibility of the restriction of civil and political rights.

It is important to note that arms transfers are not the only factor affecting human rights practices of developing nations. Coupled with other factors damaging to the provision of human rights, such as external and internal threats, political instability, among others, arms transfers may exasperate the deterioration of personal integrity rights and civil and political rights. It is imperative for the countries that supply arms to the developing world to consider the potential hazard they introduce once delivered. The suppliers of these weapons should not only be concerned with the external stability of these states, but their internal health of developing states as well.

Notes

1 http://www.ippu.purdue.edu/global_studies/gghr/research_pts_terrorscale.cfm

2 (1) Countries...under a secure rule of law, people are not imprisoned for their views, and torture is rare or exceptional...Political murders are extraordinarily rare. (2) There is a limited amount of imprisonment for nonviolent political activity. However, few are affected, torture and beatings are exceptional ...Political murder is rare. (3) There is extensive political imprisonment, or a recent history of such imprisonment. Execution or other political murders and brutality may be common. Unlimited detention, with or without trial, for political views is accepted. (4) The practices of Level 3 are expanded to larger numbers. Murders, disappearances, and torture are a common part of life...In spite of its generality, on this level violence affects primarily those who interest themselves in politics or ideas. (5) The violence of Level 4 has been extended to the whole population...The leaders of these societies place no limits on the means or thoroughness with which they pursue personal or ideological goals (Gibney and Dalton, 1996).

3 http://www.freedomhouse.org/

4 Many scholars have criticized PQLI as a measure of human rights particularly because it weights all three components equally. However, other scholars defend its use as a human rights measure. Of the most convincing argument is Moon's 1991 defence of the measure. Moon found that different weighting schemes for PQLI did not result in significantly different test results.

5 Arms transfers 'represent the international transfer (under terms of grant, credit, barter, or cash) of military equipment, usually referred to as "conventional," including weapons of war, parts thereof, ammunition, support equipment, and other commodities designed for military use. Among the items included are tactical guided missiles and rockets, military aircraft, naval vessels, armored and nonarmored military vehicles, communications and electronic equipment, artillery, infantry weapons, small arms, ammunition, other ordnance, parachutes, and uniforms. Dual use equipment, which can have application in both military and civilian sectors, is included when its

primary mission is defined as military. The building of defence production facilities and licensing fees paid as royalties are included when they are contained in military transfer agreements. ... Military services such as training, supply operations, equipment repair, technical assistance, and construction are included when data are available. Excluded are foodstuffs, medical equipment, petroleum products and other supplies' (*WMEAT* 1998, p.205).

6 COW^2 Project Website: http://cow2.la.psu.edu/cow2dslist.htm

7 I employ a dichotomous variable because data on domestic arms production is very difficult to obtain. To err on the side of caution, I chose to consider a state to have domestic arms capability if they have ever produced arms.

8 The developing countries in the data set are: Algeria, Angola, Argentina, Bangladesh, Barbados, Benin, Bhutan, Bolivia, Botswana, Brazil, Burkina Faso, Burundi, Cambodia, Cameroon, Central African Republic, Chad, Chile, China, Colombia, Congo, Costa Rica, Cote d'Ivoire, Cyprus, Dominican Republic, Ecuador, Egypt, El Salvador, Ethiopia, Gabon, Ghana, Guatemala, Guinea, Guinea-Bissau, Haiti, Honduras, India, Indonesia, Iran, Jamaica, Jordan, Kenya, South Korea, Kuwait, Lao People Democratic Republic, Lebanon, Lesotho, Madagascar, Malawi, Malaysia, Mali, Mauritius, Mexico, Morocco, Mozambique, Nepal, Nicaragua, Niger, Nigeria, Oman, Pakistan, Panama, Papua New Guinea, Paraguay, Peru, Philippines, Rwanda, Saudi Arabia, Senegal, Sierra Leone, Singapore, Sri Lanka, Syrian Arab Republic, United Republic of Tanzania, Thailand, Togo, Trinidad & Tobago, Tunisia, Turkey, Uganda, United Arab Emirates, Uruguay, Venezuela, Viet Nam, Yemen, Zaire, Zambia, and Zimbabwe. The following countries were excluded from the personal integrity model due to missing values: Barbados, Botswana, Burkina Faso, Gabon and Mauritania. The following countries, although identified as developing countries in the UN Human Development Report (UNDP, 1994, pp.102-3) were excluded from all three models due to missing data: Afghanistan, Cuba, Iraq, Liberia, Libyan Arab Jamahiriya, Myanmar, Somalia and Sudan.

9 I chose to test my model with Prais-Winsten regression with panel corrected standard errors instead of using an ordered logit model. I chose this method to use panel corrected standard errors to control for correlation across my panels and serial correlation. To ensure that my results were accurate, I tested my model of personal integrity rights using ordered logit. The results from the ordered logit model were consistent with those generated with Prais-Winsten regression.

References

Betts, R.K. (1980), 'The Tragicomedy of Arms Trade Control', *International Security*, Vol. 5(Summer), pp. 80-110.

Blanton, S.L. (1999a), 'Instruments of Security or Tools of Repression? Arms Imports and Human Rights Conditions in Developing Countries', *Journal of Peace Research*, Vol. 36(2), pp. 233-44.

Blanton, S.L. (1999b), 'The Transfer of Arms and the Diffusion of Democracy: Do Arms Promote or Undermine the "Third Wave"?' *The Social Science Journal*, Vol. 36, pp. 413-29.

Bremer, S.A. (1980), 'National Capabilities and War Proneness' in J.D. Singer (ed.), *The Correlates of War II: Testing Some Realpolitik Models*, New York, Free Press.

Bremer, S.A. and Hughes, B.B. (1990), *Disarmament and Development: A Design for the Future?* Englewood Cliffs, N.J., Prentice Hall.

Brzoska, M. (1982), 'Arms Transfer Data Sources', *Journal of Conflict Resolution*, Vol. 26(1), pp. 77-88.

Brzoska, M. (1989), 'The Erosion of Restrain in West German Arms Transfer Policy', *Journal of Peace Research*, Vol. 26, pp. 165-77.

Brzoska, M. and Ohlson, T. (1987), *Arms Transfers to the Third World, 1971-1985*, Oxford, Stockholm International Peace Research Institute.

Bureau of Arms Control (2000), http://www.state.gov/www/global/arms/beaurac.html.

Craft, C. and Smaldone, J.P. (2002), 'The Arms Trade and the Incidence of Political Violence in Sub-Saharan Africa, 1967-97', *Journal of Peace Research*, Vol. 39(6), pp. 693-710.

Deger, S. and Smith, R. (1983), 'Military Expenditure and Growth in Less Developed Countries', *Journal of Conflict Resolution*, Vol. 27(2), pp. 335-53.

Donnelly, J. (1986), 'International Human Rights: A Regime Analysis', *International Organization*, Vol. 40(3), pp. 599-642.

Donnelly, J. (1989), *Universal Human Rights in Theory and Practice*, Ithaca, NY, Cornell University Press.

Freedom House (2001), *Freedom in the World Country Rankings*, http://www.freedomhouse.org.

Gibney, M. and Dalton, M. (1996), 'The Political Terror Scale', *Policy Studies and Developing Nations*, Vol. 4, pp. 73-84.

Harkavy, R.E. and Neuman, S.G. (2001), *Warfare and the Third World*, New York, Palgrave.

Keith, L.C., Tate, C.N. and Poe, S.C. (2000), 'Constitutional Protections, Judicial Independence and State Repression of Personal Integrity: Is the Law a Mere Parchment Barrier to Human Rights Abuse?', working paper.

Kick, E.L., Davis, B.L., Kiefer, D.M and Burns, T.J. (1998), 'A Cross-National Analysis of Militarization and Well-Being Relationships in Developing Countries', *Social Science Research*, Vol. 27(4), pp. 351-70.

Kolodziej, E.A. (1979), 'Measuring French Arms Transfers: A Problem of Sources and Some Sources of Problems with ACDA Data', *Journal of Conflict Resolution*, Vol. 23(2), pp. 195-227.

Kolodziej, E.A. and Harkavy, R. (1982), *Security Policies of Developing Countries*, Lexington, MA, Lexington Books.

Lewis, J.R. (2001), 'Arms Trade', *The Human Rights Encyclopedia,* in J.R. Lewis and C. Skutsch (eds.), Armonk, NY, Sharpe Reference.

Lijphart, A. (1999), *Patterns of Democracy: Government Forms and Performance in Thirty-Six Countries*, New Haven, CT, Yale University Press.

Looney, R.E. and Frederiksen, P.C. (1986), 'Profiles of Current Latin American Arms Producers', *International Organization*, Vol. 40(3), pp. 745-52.

Louscher, D.J. and Salomone, M.D. (1987), *Marketing Security Assistance: New Perspectives on Arms Sales*, Lexington, MA, Lexington Books.

Maniruzzaman, T. (1992), 'Arms Transfers, Military Coups, and Military Rule in Developing States', *Journal of Conflict Resolution*, Vol. 36(4), pp. 733-55.

McKinlay, R.D. and Cohan, A.S. (1975), 'A Comparative Analysis of the Political and Economic Performance of Military and Civil Regimes', *Comparative Politics*, Vol. 8, pp. 1-30.

Merali, I. and Oosterveld, V. (2001), *Giving Meaning to Economic, Social, and Cultural Rights*, Philadelphia, University of Pennsylvania Press.

Milner, W.T., Poe, S.C. and Leblang, D. (1999), 'Security Rights, Subsistence Rights, and Liberties: A Theoretical Survey of the Empirical Landscape', *Human Rights Quarterly*, Vol. 21(2), pp. 403-33.

Milner, W.T., Leblang, D., Poe, S.C. and Smith, K. (2000), 'Providing Subsistence Rights at the End of the Twentieth Century: Do States Make a Difference?' Paper presented at the Annual Meetings of the International Studies Association, Los Angeles, California, March 2000.

Morris, D.M. (1979), *Measuring the Condition of the World's Poor: The Physical Quality of Life Index*, New York, Pergamon.

Morris, D.M. (1996), *Measuring the Condition of the World's Poor: The Physical Quality of Life Index, 1960-1990*, Providence, RI, Thomas J. Watson, Jr. Institute for International Studies Working Paper (#23/24).

Noel-Baker, P. (1958), *The Arms Race: A Programme for World Disarmament*, London, John Calder.

Pearson, F.S. (1994), *The Global Spread of Arms: Political Economy of International Security,* Boulder, CO, Westview Press.

Phillips, W. and Racioppi, L. (1992), 'Soviet Arms Transfers with the Third World', *Seeking Security and Development: The Impact of Military Spending and Arms Transfers*, in N.A. Graham (ed.), Boulder, CO, Lynne Rienner Publishers.

Poe, S.C., Carey, S.C. and Vazquez, T. (2001), 'How are These Pictures Different? A Quantitative Comparison of the US Department and Amnesty International Human Rights Reports, 1976-1995', *Human Rights Quarterly*, Vol. 23(3), pp. 650-77.

Poe, S.C. and Tate, C.N. (1994), 'Repression of Human Rights to Personal Integrity in the 1980s: A Global Analysis', *American Political Science Review*, Vol. 88(4), pp. 853-72.

Purdue University Political Terror Scale. http://www.ippu.purdue.edu/global_studies/gghr/research_pts.cfm.

Renner, M. (1997), *Small Arms, Big Impact: The Next Challenge of Disarmament*, World Watch Paper.

Rosh, R.M. (1990), 'Third World Arms Production and the Evolving Interstate System', *Journal of Conflict Resolution*, Vol. 34, pp. 57–73.

Russett, B. (1969), 'Who Pays for Defense?' *American Political Science Review*, Vol. 63(2), pp. 412-26.

Sadowski, Y. (1992), 'Scuds versus Butter: The Political Economy of Arms Control in the Arab World', *Middle East Report*, Vol. 177(Jul-Aug), pp. 2-13.

Sen, A. (2000), *Development as Freedom*, New York, Anchor Books.

Shue, H. (1980), *Basic Rights: Subsistence, Affluence, and U.S. Foreign Policy*, Princeton, NJ, Princeton University Press.

Stork, J. and Paul, J. (1983), 'Arms Sales and the Militarization of the Middle East', *MERIP Reports*, Vol. 112, pp. 5-15.

United Nations Development Programme (UNDP) (1994), *Human Development Report 1994*, http://www.undp.org/hdro/hdrs/1994/english/94.htm.

United States Arms Control and Disarmament Agency (ACDA), (various issues), *World Military Expenditures and Arms Transfers*, Washington, D.C., ACDA.

Wolpin, M.D. (1983), 'Comparative Perspectives on Militarization, Repression, and Social Welfare', *Journal of Peace Research*, Vol. 20(2), pp. 129-55.

World Bank (2001), *World Development Indicators*, Washington, D.C., World Bank.

Zonninsein, J. (1994), 'Military Expenditures and Economic Growth', in *Seeking Security and Development: The Impact of Military Spending and Arms Transfers*, N.A. Graham, (ed.), Boulder, CO, Lynne Rienner Publishers.

PART III
DEVELOPMENT AND TRADE

Introduction to Part III

The third part of this volume addresses how economic development and trade influence the respect for human rights. The three chapters included here extend the concept of human rights from a more narrow definition of life integrity and security rights, which make up the first generation of human rights, to subsistence rights, the second generation of human rights. They ask how respect for these rights can be realized, or harmed, by economic development and international trade.

The first contribution by Rhonda Callaway and Julie Harrelson-Stephens analyzes the relationship between trade, economic development, democracy and human rights. Their chapter compares and empirically investigates the two main contradicting theories in the field of international political economy. It examines multiple channels through which trade influences both security rights and subsistence rights. In his study, they compare liberal and radical theory and develop two sets of arguments on how trade and development influence human rights. Motivated by the liberal perspective, the authors argue that international economic factors positively influence domestic conditions, including economic, social and political consequences. Critics of globalization, however, argue that international trade has negative effects, especially on the weak states in the system. They assume weak states are exploited by developed states and by the global capitalist structure. This chapter investigates those two opposing views by empirically analyzing 109 developing countries between 1976 and 1996. The findings support the liberal argument that trade, and exports in particular, leads to economic development, which leads to democracy and ultimately improves the realization of basic human needs.

The second chapter in the section on development and trade focuses on the provision of subsistence rights. Milner et al. investigate whether personal integrity rights, political liberties and subsistence rights are mutually reinforcing, as suggested by previous research, or whether there are trade-offs between different categories of rights. They analyze 114 non-OECD countries over the period from 1980 to 1993, which is the largest sample to date used to address this question. Milner et al. find no evidence of trade-offs between these categories of rights. Instead, their results suggest that democracy and the provision of political rights lead to better achievement in terms of subsistence rights. However, once democracy and other factors are accounted for, the existence of personal integrity rights does not appear to reinforce and encourage subsistence rights. The authors conclude that political liberties tend to reinforce subsistence rights, but no evidence is found that greater respect for physical integrity is associated with greater realization of subsistence rights. Numerous governments have argued that political rights or physical integrity rights must be limited in order to improve subsistence rights for the population at large, but there has been very little systematic research on the issue of trade-offs. The chapter by Milner et al. represents an important step towards systematically investigating the link between different categories of human rights and shedding light on this question.

Rodwan Abouharb and David Cingranelli tackle the issue of development and trade from a different angle. Complementing Barratt's analysis of how human rights influence British foreign aid allocation, they investigate how the World Bank and IMF decide which countries receive their financial assistance and whether they favour dictatorships over democracies. There is much speculation in the popular press and in the academic literature that the imposition of Structural Adjustment Loans induces recipient governments to reduce their level of respect for internationally recognized human rights. Abouharb and Cingranelli systematically address this question by empirically testing the arguments of classical economic theory, the theory of two-level games in international affairs and dependency theory to analyze the determinants of World Bank and IMF adjustment lending. Whereas previous large-N, cross-national studies have been conducted by scholars operating within the classical economics or critical economics schools, seeking to discover whether acceptance of IMF conditions leads to greater economic growth, the present study explicitly incorporates political considerations into the analysis. It is also the only study to date the addresses biases in the World Bank's selection of recipient countries. Their findings suggest that political factors played a major role in the negotiations for adjustment loans during 1981 and 1993.

Chapter 5

The Path from Trade to Human Rights: The Democracy and Development Detour

Rhonda L. Callaway and Julie Harrelson-Stephens

Introduction

The latter decades of the 20th century witnessed a merging of two distinct fields in international relations – human rights research and international political economy (IPE). In the IPE literature, the increasing forces of globalization that arose in the 1980s and continued in the post-Cold War era brought a concern about the consequences of the rapid movement of capital and goods on the human condition. The cry that we had reached the 'end of history' (Fukuyama, 1989) led many researchers and activists to become alarmed at the blurring of borders, boundaries and even identities. Researchers began to embark on inquiries related to the effects or consequences of globalization, particularly the impact on exchange rates, capital controls, political systems and social structures (Kentor, 2001; Richards et al., 2001; Leblang and Bernhard, 2002).

By the end of the century, a growing concern focused on the impact of globalization on the human condition. The many protests that accompany WTO and other international trade meetings, as well as growing discontent in Third World countries, call into question whether factors of globalization, especially trade, really provide any benefit to the average citizen, particularly those living in the global South. In this research, we examine both the direct and indirect effects of trade on two types of human rights, security and subsistence rights. The former refers to the personal integrity of the individual, while the latter considers those rights necessary for a minimal quality of life. Ultimately, we argue that there are multiple channels by which trade influences human rights.

This chapter contributes to the study and understanding of human rights and international political economy in several ways. First, we provide a more complete picture of the relationship between trade and human rights. Most of the previous research assumes and tests a direct relationship between external economic forces and human rights (Regan, 1995; Meyer, 1998; Richards et al., 2001). This specification results in researchers potentially ignoring indirect relationships. We address the empirical relationship between economic indicators and human rights conditions by utilizing path analyses models, whereby trade not only directly influences human rights, but also impacts human rights indirectly by influencing levels of economic development and democracy. Thus, we suggest that the impact of trade on human rights is augmented by its independent effects on both economic development and democracy.

Second, we address human rights from a more holistic approach, choosing to focus on both security rights and subsistence rights. Politicians, activists and social scientists alike have divided human rights into subsets of rights. It could be argued that one reason for the division of rights is for political expediency. The international community's response to incidence of torture and extra-judicial executions seem far more cut and dried than decisions regarding the plight of those wallowing in poverty, malnutrition and illiteracy. Political scientists find these divisions helpful as well. 'One way to avoid the problems caused by global measures of human rights is to concentrate on a small subset of core rights' (McNitt, 1986, p.73). Indeed, where developing states tend to concentrate on subsistence rights, developed states emphasize security rights. While no one measure can adequately capture the entire concept of human rights, the utilization of these two measures sheds light on human rights conditions in general.

We analyze security rights for several reasons. First, it is one of the prevalent conceptualizations used in empirical research on human rights (Cingranelli and Pasquarello, 1985; Poe and Tate, 1994; Gibney and Dalton, 1996). Security rights violations generally address the treatment of the political opposition within the state. This political opposition usually makes demands upon the state, of which the latter is unwilling to concede. Economic policy, concerns about economic development, democratization and human rights are undoubtedly included in many of the opposition's demands. Second, most states in the international system have made at least tacit agreements that these types of rights should be respected and thus are considered universal. Third, policymakers oftentimes attempt to link certain economic policies to human rights conditions, specifically to instances of torture and political imprisonment. This was seen, for example, in the annual debates in the U.S. Congress regarding China's trading status prior to their admission to the WTO.

Likewise, the focus on subsistence rights accomplishes several objectives. First, these types of rights are becoming more and more relevant in foreign policy as well as in missions undertaken by international organizations, as recent operations in Somalia and Afghanistan suggest. This is underscored by the increased emphasis on economic and development issues in the United Nations. Second, it is becoming more and more apparent that many of the political problems (e.g., genocide, conflict) are due to poverty, scarcity and other societal ills (Krain, 1997; Homer-Dixon, 1999). Human rights groups and intergovernmental organizations are also starting to shift their focus to these so-called second-generation rights.[1]

Finally, we contend that examining both security and subsistence rights provides an opportunity to explore tangible policy prescriptions. Specifically, this research allows us to explore the extent to which economic development and democratization influence the relationship between trade and human rights. Given a better identification of the exact nature of this relationship, policymakers can more accurately specify the effects of distinct trade policies.

In order to examine the relationship between trade and human rights, this chapter is organized in the following manner. The first section addresses the theoretical relationship between the variables of interest, specifically the causal path from trade to human rights. In the second section, we outline the data and measurements employed. The methodology and results are displayed and discussed in the third section. The last section is devoted to a discussion of the implications of the results for both future human rights research as well as future policy prescription.

Trade and Human Rights: The Theoretical Connection

Two broad literatures inform us on the theoretical connection between the international economy and human rights conditions within a state. The liberal perspective suggests that international economic factors positively influence domestic conditions, regardless of whether one is concerned about economic, social or political consequences. In essence, international forces such as trade serve as an engine of growth. On the other hand, critics contend that these same economic factors oftentimes lead to deleterious outcomes, particularly dependent trade relationships, stagnant economic growth, political disorder and poor human rights conditions. Thus, one can hypothesize from either a liberal or radical perspective that trade will influence human rights.

However, a more relevant question might be: how is it that trade might lead to either increases or decreases in the respect for human rights? One way is through economic development. We investigate this possibility along with the idea that trade influences democracy. In addition, economic development is oftentimes hypothesized to have an independent influence on democratization. This possibility is also included in our analysis. Lastly, we explore how all three of the factors (trade, economic development and democracy) might influence human rights. In the end, we believe that there are multiple channels by which trade influences human rights conditions.

The Liberal Ethos

The liberal ethos suggests that the presence of a free market system and the adoption of market-oriented domestic policies by Third World states is the best approach for economic development. Adoption of such policies will make up, in part, for inherent deficiencies in the host country, such as market imperfections and the unproductive use of the factors of production, improving both economic and social conditions. Classical economic thought suggests that open trade policies should increase wealth by forcing producers to concentrate on those items where they have a comparative advantage. Other scholars argue that the international 'market has caused the diffusion of wealth, technology, values, investment and capital' (Pease, 2000, p.233; see also Keohane and Nye, 1989, 2000).

Trade and economic development Liberals defend international trade as it relates to economic development on several points. International trade contributes to a state's transition from a traditional to a market economy by addressing certain deficiencies (the lack of an economic middle class, the presence of a predominantly agriculturally based economy and the inefficient use of natural resources) within the developing state. Specifically,

> export promotion has been considered an important instrument for growth. As the historical experience of East Asia shows, a developing country can specialize and export to promote its economic growth. Through an export-oriented development strategy, a country can raise factor productivity, can efficiently use its resources, and can increase its rate of technological innovation. Also, as the economy expands, the country tends to be integrated into international markets, which may increase capacity utilization and improve gains of scale effects (Feng, 1996, p.106).

Moreover, trade leads to efficiency in employment, which in turn leads to higher wages. These higher wages are reflected in the per capita GDP measures, a leading indicator of wealth. In addition, trade works to reduce inflation, thereby providing lower consumer prices. In sum, liberals point to international trade as a positive sum endeavour, whereby trading states shift resources away from low productivity industries resulting in households that enjoy more goods with less sacrifice. In fact, recent research finds that trade openness has long-term positive effects on economic development in less developed countries (Kentor, 2001).

Trade, economic development and democracy The liberal perspective suggests that trade might influence democracy directly. The interdependence that results from increases in trade levels facilitates both incentives to cooperate as well as a diffusion of norms and ideas (Keohane and Nye, 1989). While the incentives to cooperate refers to relations between states, the latter suggests that trade is a facilitator in the diffusion of democratic values within states. For example, the United States, as the current hegemon, argues that open markets are a path to democratic reforms.

In addition, the causal pattern suggests that wealth will have an independent effect on democracy. A well-known argument contends that wealth and economic development are requisites for democracy (Lipset, 1959). In fact, several theorists find economic development to be an important influence on democracy (Burkhart and Lewis-Beck, 1994; Helliwell, 1994; Londregan and Poole, 1996).[2] Specifically, Helliwell (1994, p.246) finds a positive relationship between per capita income and democracy, concluding that there is 'a strong tendency for democracy to become the choice and maintained form of government as countries get richer.' Furthermore, the increase in wealth among the citizenry leads to greater political participation. As citizens accumulate more wealth, there is growth in the middle class, as well as increased labour demands. This, in turn, leads citizens to call for greater respect of both political rights, as well as human rights (Richards et al., 2001).

Trade, economic development, democracy and human rights Thus far, we have explored how trade influences both economic development and democracy and subsequently, how economic development is related to democracy. Our next step is to address the influence of trade on subsistence and security rights. The liberal perspective suggests that trade is a significant component of a state's quest for national development. Trade represents an additional basket of goods available for consumption, separate from that provided by national production (Moon, 1991). In addition to the goods that result from trade, income generated from trade provides additional purchasing power for the goods necessary to improve quality of life. The result is an improvement in subsistence rights.

In terms of security rights, goods and income generated from increased levels of trade help to ease problems of scarcity in many Third World states. Oftentimes this economic scarcity brings about an increased level of social and political tension that leads regimes to implement repressive measures to maintain political control (Mitchell and McCormick, 1988). Furthermore, increases in trade relationships between states signify an inclusion in the international community, which may result in pressure for regimes to respect personal integrity rights. These factors point to improvements in both the basic welfare and physical quality of life of individuals.

In addition, liberals contend that both economic development and democracy are conducive to improvements in security and subsistence rights. In terms of security rights, a wealthier populace suggests a more satisfied constituency, resulting in less need for regime repression (Henderson, 1991). Likewise, democratic states seek non-violent means of conflict resolution rather than resort to abusive behaviour to silence political discontent. Wealthier and democratic states are also more likely to be able to provide the most basic human needs to the citizenry. In sum, the liberal perspective suggests a causal path where international trade contributes to economic development, democracy and human rights.

The Radical Counterpart

The radical perspective and the critics of globalization argue that there are several deleterious effects of foreign economic penetration on domestic conditions (Prebisch, 1950; Frank, 1966, 1979; Dos Santos, 1970). Integration into the global economy is viewed as a potential threat to the economic and social development of domestic industries, as less developed countries are systematically exploited by developed states.

Trade and economic development Critics argue that this exploitation leads to dependent trade relationships. Not only are Third World countries slow to develop, but also trade from the industrialized states blocks any development. The inability to develop domestic markets due to the influx of international commodities serves to restrict domestic economic growth and thus only perpetuates their economic stagnation. In turn, this stagnation suggests that dependent states have little additional income available for welfare programs aimed at alleviating poverty and malnutrition.

Trade, economic development and democracy This economic stagnation is further exacerbated by the relationship between trade and democracy. Critics suggest that domestic elites benefit from uneven trade relationships at the expense of the masses. 'Trade reliance is a rough indicator of the tendency of dominant classes to look outward for political resources, socio-economic orientation, and consumption goods, all to the detriment of the development of a political and social milieu likely to afford basic needs a high priority' (Moon, 1991, p.202). In addition, profits from trade add more power to the elite, creating a wider economic, political and social gulf between the rich and the poor. This schism in a developing society creates conditions that might lead to social unrest, domestic violence and ultimately poor human rights conditions.

Trade, economic development, democracy and human rights The competition between domestic and international products is believed to have negative consequences on vulnerable segments of the population, especially migrant and women workers, as well as indigenous populations. Specifically, globalization forces are said to impede both subsistence and security rights in a state. 'Globalization has been cited as a contributing factor in violations of the right to life, the right to protection of health, minority rights, freedom of association, the right to safe and healthy working conditions and the right to a standard of living adequate for health and well-being in many countries' (Leary, 1998, p.268). Moreover, radicals contend that the efforts of advanced countries to maintain favourable trade relationships with Third World countries hinder democratic reforms, such as the formation of trade unions. In essence, radicals characterize trade relationships between First and Third World as asymmetrical and neo-imperialistic. This exploitation pressures Third World governments to repress democratic reforms and movements aimed at improving living and working conditions. Oftentimes, this repression comes in the form of violent human rights abuses. Ultimately, radicals suggest that there is an increase in human rights violations by countries that are more involved with external capitalist interests (Chomsky and Herman, 1979; Mitchell and McCormick, 1988).

Thus, these critics suggest a causal model very different from that put forward by liberals. International trade does not lead to higher levels of economic development. In fact, critics argue reliance on external markets serves to disrupt or retard domestic economic development. Lower levels of economic development tend to be associated with lower levels of democracy and generally less respect for human rights.

We are left with competing hypotheses regarding the effect of trade on human rights. According to liberal theorists, trade has positive effects on recipient countries. Conversely, radical theorists point to the deleterious effects of trade. We examine the extent to which trade not only improves or hinders human rights directly, but also the extent to which trade improves or impedes human rights indirectly through economic development and democracy.

Data and Measurements

Human Rights Measures

One of the predominant measures for human rights in previous research has been personal integrity abuse or security rights violations utilizing the political terror scale based on the standards first established by Gastil 1980).[3] The Political Terror Scale (PTS) measures a country's proclivity to engage in the following types of repressive behaviour: politically motivated imprisonment, torture, political murder and politically motivated disappearances. Carleton and Stohl (1985) created an original dataset based upon Gastil's (1980) five level ranking criteria. Their effort yielded a dataset consisting of 59 countries for the years 1977-1983, which was updated through the year 1996.[4] In our data set, a one indicates countries that have the most abusive human rights records, while a five represents countries with the greatest respect for security rights. Developed countries tend to have much better security rights records. This is evidenced by an average human rights score of 4.76 in OECD countries, compared to 3.37 in non-OECD countries.

The physical quality of life index (Morris, 1979, 1996) is utilized to capture subsistence rights or basic human needs.[5] The variable is a weighted average of infant mortality, life expectancy at age one and basic literacy. These three individual measures address different aspects of basic human needs. Infant mortality reflects conditions of the home environment including water purity, maternal morbidity, basic well-being and cleanliness of the home. Life expectancy at age one, on the other hand, addresses the general health conditions outside the home, including nutrition and medical care. The literacy variable indicates the general level of development within a society. In particular, this measure reveals whether social benefits garnered from education actually extend to women and children (Morris, 1979; Dixon, 1984; Milner, 1998). This continuous variable potentially ranges from zero to 100, with low scores representing a low provision of subsistence rights and high scores representing a high provision of basic human needs. The physical quality of life index ranges from 7.3 to 92.5 in developing countries, with an average score of 65.01. In comparison in OECD countries, the index ranges from 87.4 to 95.3 with a mean of 91.6. Thus, the developing countries exhibit greatest variation as well as the greatest room for improvement of quality of life.

Trade Measures

Our variable of interest is the level of trade openness, which is calculated by the sum of imports and exports divided by the gross domestic product (GDP).[6] The purpose of this measure is to capture the extent to which a country's trade is liberalized or open to trade with other countries. This measure is used because it includes both exports and imports yielding an overall evaluation of a country's trade practices. Theoretically, a country with high imports and high exports will have a higher openness score, whereas a country with low imports and low exports will have a low openness score.

However, the use of trade openness, in some instances, presents a challenge to interpretation, as well as policy prescriptions. Countries with a disproportionate amount of exports may have the same level of trade openness to those countries with a disproportionate amount of imports assuming a comparable level of GDP. Should the relationship between trade and human rights be interpreted in the same fashion in this case? Consider the following scenario:

Table 5.1 The trade openness measure

	Country A	Country B
Exports	70 Billion	30 Billion
Imports	30 Billion	70 Billion
GDP	200 Billion	200 Billion
Openness Score	50	50

Country A and Country B have equivalent levels of GDP. They both have 100 billion in combined exports and imports, yielding an openness score of 50. The openness variable would lead us to conclude that Country A and Country B have equivalent levels of trade openness. However, as Table 5.1 illustrates, this conclusion is faulty. Country A has a much greater level of exports, whereas Country B is import dependent. As we can see, the level of trade openness can be misleading, as the openness score above would indicate identical trade practices, while in reality these two countries pursue drastically different trade strategies. This example illustrates the difficulty in capturing trade using any one measure. Thus, policy prescriptions advocating liberalized trade in general may yield an incomplete picture. As such, we include additional measures to capture the idea of the liberalization of trade. Two alternative measures for trade are the level of exports and the level of imports, relative to GDP. The average level of exports to GDP in developing countries is 31.21, whereas the average level of imports is 43.23. Separating the components of trade allow us to make more specific policy prescriptions.

Control Variables

A number of control variables prevalent in the literatures on economic development, democracy and human rights are included in the models. The control variables for the economic development model include education, urbanization and military expenditures. The democracy model control variables include British colonial influence, military spending, population growth, economic development, civil war and international war. The control variables for the security rights model include variables measuring the level of wealth, democracy, population and the presence of either a civil or international war. The subsistence rights model consists of all variables found in the security rights model plus dummy variables for the presence of a leftist regime, a military regime, the influence of British colonialism and the presence of a state religion. The variables, the source of the data and the expected direction of the coefficient are shown in the Appendix Table A.5.1.[7] The overall paths we are hypothesizing are shown in Figure 5.1 and Figure 5.2.

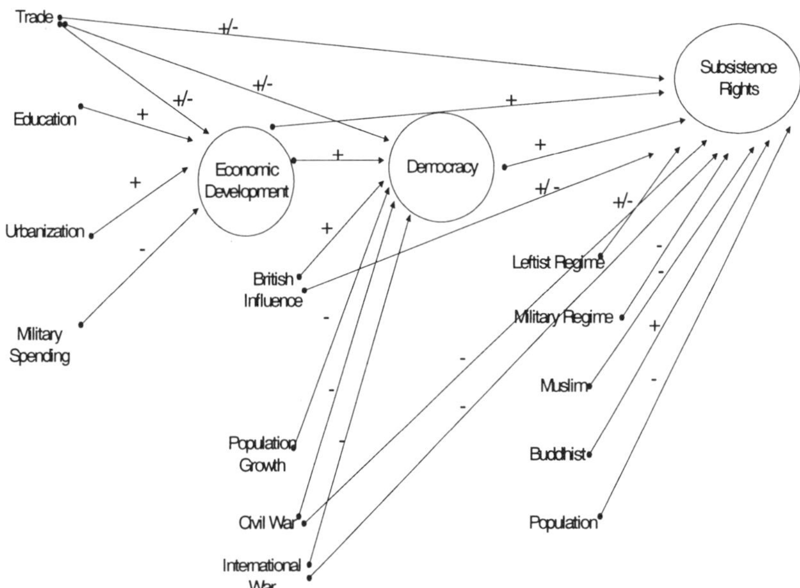

Figure 5.1 Hypothesized path analysis: Subsistence rights

Sample

We include all developing countries for which there are data. We focus on developing countries that exhibit lower levels of human rights and thus have the highest potential for improvement in human rights. Developing countries experience, on average, lower levels of personal integrity rights (PTS score 3.37) than developed countries (PTS score 4.76). This means that developing countries generally are more likely to experience extensive political imprisonment and political murders than developed countries. Governments of developing countries are also less likely to provide for their citizens' basic human needs. This is exemplified by the average subsistence rights score in developing countries of 65.01 compared to 91.6 in developed countries. Moreover, there is no expectation that developed countries will see significant improvements in human rights as these countries have already achieved a relatively high level of human rights. This is evidenced by the comparatively limited range in developed states for security rights (3 to 5) as well as subsistence rights (87.4 to 95.3). Developing countries have a much greater range in both security rights (1 to 5) and subsistence rights (7.3 to 92.5). Thus, it is in developing countries that we expect to see improvements in both types of human rights. The result is a sample of 109 developing countries, covering twenty years from 1976 to 1996.[8]

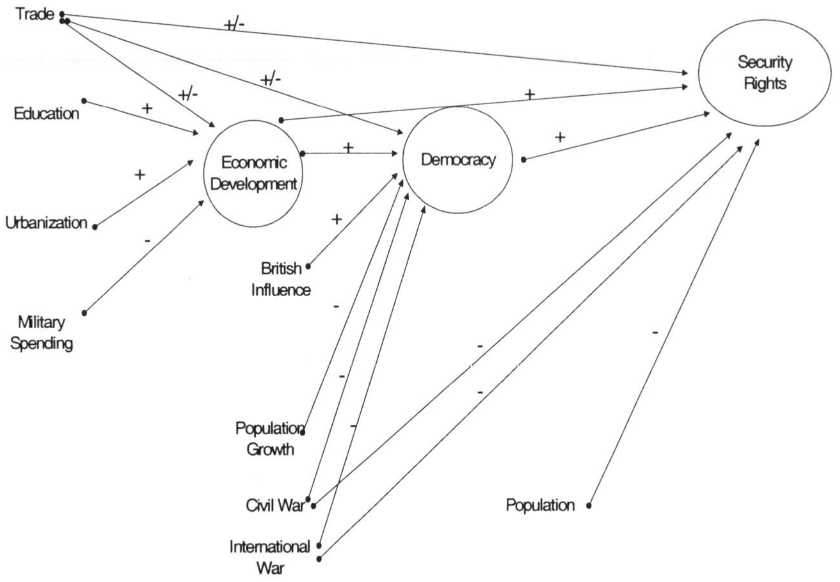

Figure 5.2 Hypothesized path analysis: Security rights

Results

In order to examine the hypothesized path between trade, economic development, democracy and human rights we utilize three models. These results are shown in Table 5.2.[9] The first model is designed to ascertain the extent to which trade is related to economic development. We find that even when education, urbanization and military spending are included in the analysis, countries with higher levels of trade openness are likely to be more economically developed. Moreover, the models that examine the level of imports and exports also have a positive effect on a country's level of economic development. Thus, we have consistent robust findings that indicate that trade is positively related to economic development.

Table 5.2 Summary of statistical results

	Economic Development	Democracy	Security Rights	Subsistence Rights
Trade Openness	Positive	Not Significant	Positive	Positive
Exports	Positive	Not Significant	Positive	Positive
Imports	Positive	Not Significant	Positive	Not Significant
Economic Development	N/A	Positive	Not Significant	Positive
Democracy	N/A	N/A	Positive	Positive

'Positive' and 'Negative' indicates that the variable was not statistically significant at the 0.05 level of significance. 'Not significant' indicates that the variable did not reach the 0.05 level of statistical significance.

The second model examines the impact of trade and economic development on democracy. As Table 5.2 indicates, higher levels of economic development are related to greater levels of democracy. The finding suggests support for the literature that argues that citizens in wealthier countries place greater demands upon their respective governments for civil and political liberties. Interestingly, each of our measures of trade does not appear to affect a country's level of democracy. This finding is counter-intuitive, as both the liberal and radical perspectives suggest a relationship between trade and a country's polity.[10]

Finally, we examine a model of subsistence rights and a model of security rights. The causal path suggests that democracy will have a direct impact on both types of human rights. The results displayed in Table 5.2 support the liberal contention that democratization is conducive to increases in the realization of human rights. In addition, economic development has a direct, positive influence on subsistence rights, but does not appear to be influential in improving security rights. As for the direct relationship between our trade variables and human rights, countries with a higher level of trade openness are significantly more likely to enjoy improved quality of life as well as more respect for security rights. Again, in order to ascertain the exact nature of the relationship between trade and human rights, trade is further broken down into imports and exports. Imports alone do not affect the level of basic human needs in a country; however, they do appear to positively influence security rights. By contrast, exports are positively related to the physical quality of life and security rights in a country. The models presented illustrate the intricate and complex nature of the relationship between trade and human rights. Path models are developed in the next section to better illustrate these multiple channels to human rights. In order to fully illustrate the impact of trade on human rights, we utilize causal models to examine economic development and democracy with each of the trade measures. The discussion of the various paths to human rights focuses on the economic variables.[11]

Path Analysis

The first model indicates that the effect of trade openness is intricate (Figure 5.3). As suggested by the liberal perspective, trade openness has a direct, positive impact on subsistence rights. Countries with liberalized trade strategies are more likely to provide for their citizens' basic human needs. We further examine the indirect effect of trade on human rights, through economic development as well as democracy. While we find no evidence for the hypothesized impact of trade on democracy, we do find trade openness impacts subsistence rights indirectly by increasing economic development. Examining the direct link alone is insufficient to explain the impact of trade on human rights (0.03). Increases in trade improve economic development (0.05), which in turn improves a state's provision of basic

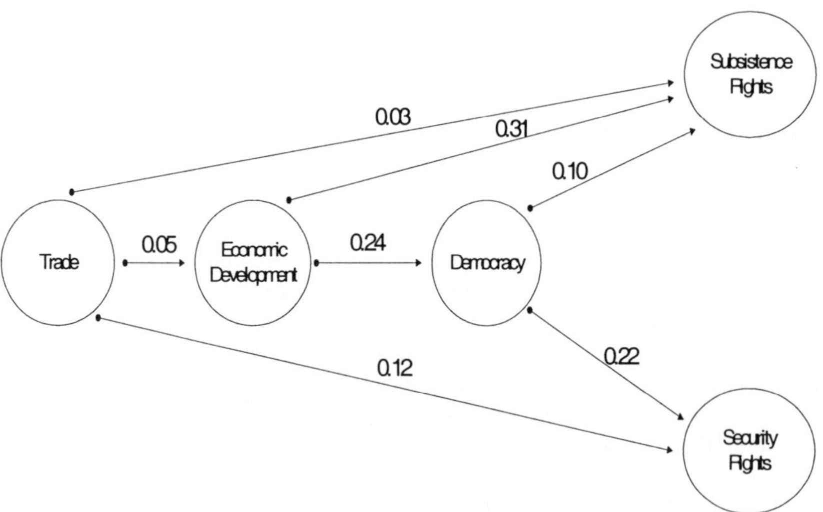

The coefficients used above are standardized by calculating the following: (sdx1/sdy) * b1. These coefficients allow us to compare their effects across models.

Figure 5.3 Trade openness

human needs (0.31). In addition, the consistent impact of trade on economic development is underscored by the positive influence of the latter on democracy (0.24), which, in turn, enhances subsistence rights (0.10). In sum, trade has an indirect impact on subsistence rights as well as an independent and direct impact on subsistence rights, even after we control for economic development.

There is also a direct and positive relationship between trade openness and security rights (0.12). As a country becomes more open to trade, its citizens realize improved personal integrity rights. We find no evidence for the hypothesized impact of trade on democracy, nor do we find support for the hypothesis that economic development directly affects security rights. However, trade's positive influence on economic development (0.05) ultimately pays off as economic development spurs democracy (0.24), which in turn enhances security rights (0.22).

Deconstructing Trade

However, the story does not end there. The trade openness variable is designed to measure the degree of liberalization of a country's trade policy. In order to capture this, the measure necessarily takes into account both imports and exports. The benefit of this variable is that it yields an overall picture of a country's trade liberalization. The cost is that it masks the differences, to the extent that there are any, in the effects of imports and exports. Thus, we conduct two subsequent analyses, examining the impact of each of the components of trade on both subsistence and security rights independently.

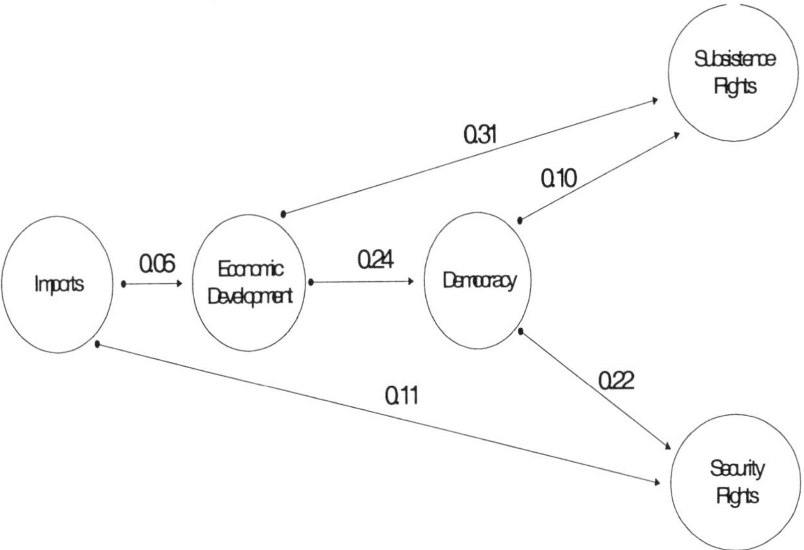

The coefficients used above are standardized by calculating the following: (sdx1/sdy) * b1. These coefficients allow us to compare their effects across models.

Figure 5.4 Imports

Figure 5.4 depicts the impact of imports on economic development, democracy, subsistence rights and security rights. As indicated in the figure, imports alone have a positive effect on economic development (0.06). This economic development, as in the trade openness model, enhances democracy (0.24), which further improves both security (0.22) and subsistence rights (0.10). Contrary to the trade openness model, imports have no significant direct effect on subsistence rights. Rather, the impact of imports on subsistence rights appears largely indirect, due to the resulting improvement in economic development (0.31). In addition to the indirect relationship, imports further appear to affect security rights directly, as the results indicate that higher levels of imports facilitate improved security rights (0.11).

Similarly, we can consider the impact of exports alone (Figure 5.5). Consistent with our other measures of trade, countries with higher levels of exports experience increases in economic development (0.05). The influence of economic development appears to affect human rights both directly and indirectly. It directly increases subsistence rights (0.31), as well as improving levels of democracy (0.24), which further improves subsistence rights (0.10). In addition, the level of exports has an independent effect on subsistence rights (0.07). Since the level of imports does not exhibit a direct effect on subsistence rights (recall Figure 5.3), we conclude that the direct effect of trade openness on subsistence rights is the specific result of increased exports. Thus, simply advocating general trade liberalization fails to take into account the specific influence of exports. Pursuing trade liberalization policies may lead a country to simply increase their current strategy, which may not place an emphasis on exports.

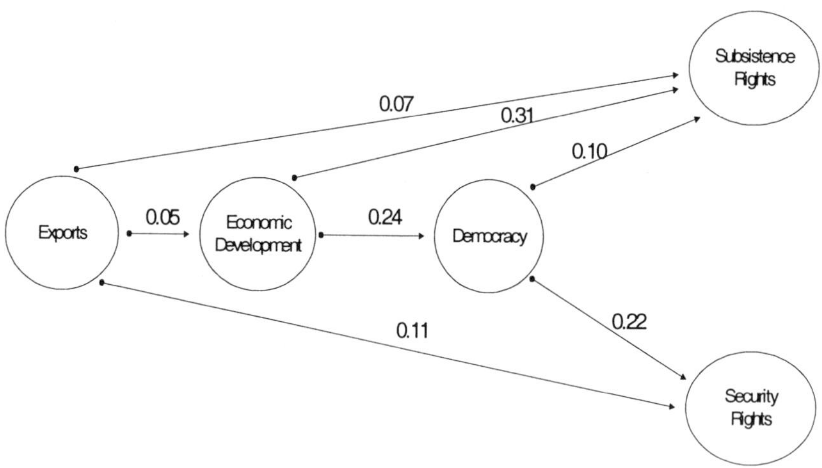

The coefficients used above are standardized by calculating the following: (sdx1/sdy) * b1. These coefficients allow us to compare their effects across models.

Figure 5.5 Exports

There is no substantial difference in the behaviour of exports and imports in relation to security rights. Increases in exports further tend to elicit direct improvements in security rights (0.11). As with imports, exports appear to indirectly affect security rights via economic development, which improves democracy. In sum, a country that has increases in trade, be it by import, exports or overall trade openness, is less likely to experience torture, political arrests, disappearances or other personal integrity violations.

Discussion and Conclusion

In this analysis, we attempt to untangle the theoretical relationship between trade and human rights. Specifically, we find evidence that lends credence to the liberal perspective. The use of path analyses helps to further explain the inchoate relationship between trade and human rights. Empirical research in human rights typically ignores indirect relationships among variables. Path analysis allows us to identify and quantify these indirect effects as well as the direct ones.

Overall, these findings suggest some important implications for the study of human rights. Our results support the liberal argument that increases in trade lead to improvements in economic development, which facilitates democracy and human rights. Most importantly, we find that the impact of trade on human rights is likely to be underestimated if one solely examines direct effects, when, in fact, there are significant indirect relationships as well.

Two general patterns develop. First, from a holistic approach, not all factors influence human rights in a uniform, consistent manner. Our findings support previous findings that trade has a direct impact on both security (Harrelson-Stephens and Callaway, 2003) and subsistence rights (Milner, 2002). However, as suspected, trade openness masks many of the nuances of trade. That is, exports and imports may indeed have distinct effects. While all of our trade measures influence economic development in a similar manner, exports and imports have different relationships with democracy and human rights. For example, imports show no appreciable direct influence on subsistence rights, whereas exports do. Moreover, as the bivariate results indicate, imports may actually impede democracy, while exports have a positive, though not significant, relationship with democracy. Thus, we conclude that exports may be more important than imports in achieving higher levels of democracy as well as greater respect for human rights.

The second general pattern indicates that economic development serves as an additional conduit for trade to influence human rights. Each measure of trade positively influences economic development, which, in turn, directly impacts subsistence rights. Thus, economic development is one of the most important influences on a state's realization of basic human needs. However, the economic boost does little to directly alter a regime's treatment of the political opposition. In our model of developing states, greater wealth does not equate to less state repression. The only tangible benefit to security rights from economic development is through its positive influence on democracy. While democratic states enjoy higher levels of subsistence and security rights, there is no evidence that trade directly influences this relationship. Thus, we are left with a causal pattern that suggests that trade enhances economic development, which facilitates improvements in democracy, which is conducive to the realization of human rights.

Finally, our results allow policymakers to specify trade policies aimed at economic development as well as human rights. In spite of the arguments presented by both critics and activists alike, trade does bear fruit for the developing world. The boost to economic development alone suggests that states should pursue open trade policies in order to improve the level of wealth among its citizenry. Wealth still leads to democracy and both are conducive to the realization of basic human needs and security rights. We find that a variety of human rights concerns are assuaged by increases in trade. In general, trade's influence on human rights reveals a bright prospect for the future.

Notes

1 For example, a recent edition of *The Economist* (18 August 2001) highlighted the movement of some NGOs, such as Amnesty International, toward an emphasis on subsistence rights. This would mark a significant change in the direction and work of many activists and organizations from focusing on personal integrity and political rights to the issues of economic and social injustice. These organizations are starting to question whether the immediate needs of adequate living standards to combat poverty, malnutrition and disease are necessary in order for citizens to fully enjoy civil and political rights.

2 The literature is replete with theoretical discussion regarding the viability of the compatibility argument, that is that economic development and democracy are related to one another. The core debate rests on the causal arrow. Thus, there is also literature that contends that democracy stimulates economic growth. Feng (1996), in a study on sub-Sahara Africa, suggests that while there is evidence that democracy is conducive to economic development, there is a feedback mechanism. In other words, economic development does lead to higher levels of democratization.

3 See also Poe and Tate (1994); Gibney and Dalton (1996). For ease of interpretation, our scale is inverted from the original political terror scale so that we measure improvements in human rights practices, rather than human rights abuse.

4 This data is currently available at http://www.psci.unt.edu/ihrsc/poetate.htm

5 See Moon (1991); Milner (1998); Callaway (2001) for the explanation of how the PQLI index is derived.

6 We gather original data from the 2001 World Development Indictors on CD-Rom and recalculate the variable utilizing the derivation by Heston and Summers (1994). This allows for more recent years of data to be included in the sample.

7 For complete explanations regarding the control variables, see Mitchell and McCormick (1988); Henderson (1991); Poe and Tate (1994); Moon (1991). A correlation matrix revealed that there are no meaningful correlations between the independent variables in each model.

8 We utilize a pooled cross-sectional time-series (PCTS) design in Stata 6.0, which allows us to examine effects across both space and time (Stimson, 1985). However, time-series data is prone to autocorrelation and heteroscedasticity, which violate

assumptions of ordinary least squares regression and may bias the results of the significance tests. Thus, we use robust standard errors to control for possible heteroscedasticity and a first order auto-regressive component to deal with the autocorrelation (Beck and Katz, 1995, 1996; Achen, 2000).

9 We concentrate on the variables dealing with the impact of trade. The results for each model are displayed in Appendix A.5.2.

10 Examining the bivariate relationship suggests that trade openness and the level of democracy are negatively correlated (Pearson's correlation = -0.05, $p < 0.05$). However, the effect of trade on democracy in a country becomes negligible once other control variables are included. When we look at bivariate statistics of exports and imports separately, only the relationship between imports and the level of democracy is statistically significant (-0.10, $p < 0.05$). Given that the relationship with exports is positive, although not statistically significant, suggests that it is imports that are driving the negative relationship between trade openness and democracy. Countries that rely on imports rather than developing their own domestic manufacturing and products for exports may be at higher risk for polity disruption and/or democratic development. In such polities, the lack of internal economic development, which necessitates the importation of finished goods, suggests that the state also lacks an emerging middle class, which is conducive to democratization.

11 One consistent result from the empirical analysis, the effect of British colonial influence, is worth noting. In the subsistence rights model, the variable capturing the legacy of the British is negative and statistically significant. According to the results, states that were colonized by the British have less respect for basic human needs. This finding seems inconsistent with the results from the democracy model where a history of British rule led to improved levels of democracy. One plausible explanation rests with the idea that the British were able to instil political norms, at least at the elite level, but did little to provide guidance in how to accommodate or to insure the realization of basic human needs for the masses.

References

Achen, C. (2000), 'Why Lagged Dependent Variables Can Suppress the Explanatory Power of Other Independent Variables', paper presented for the annual meeting of the Political Methodological Section of the American Political Science Association.

Beck, N. and Katz, J. (1995), 'What to do (and not to do) with Time-Series Cross-Section Data', *American Political Science Review,* Vol. 89(3), pp. 634-47.

Beck, N. and Katz, J. (1996), 'Nuisance vs. Substance: Specifying and Estimating Time-Series Cross-Section Models', *Political Analysis*, Vol. 6(1), pp. 1-34.

Burkhart, R.E. and Lewis-Beck, M.S. (1994), 'Comparative Democracy: The Economic Development Thesis', *American Political Science Review*, Vol. 88(4), pp. 903-10.

Callaway, R.L. (2001), 'Is the Road to Hell Paved with Good Intentions? The Effect of U.S. Foreign Assistance and Economic Policy on Human Rights', PhD Dissertation, University of North Texas.

Carleton, D. and Stohl, M. (1985), 'The Foreign Policy of Human Rights: Rhetoric and Reality from Jimmy Carter and Ronald Reagan', *Human Rights Quarterly,* Vol. 7(2), pp. 205-29.

Chomsky, N. and Herman, E.S. (1979), *The Political Economy of Human Rights Series, Vol 1: The Washington Connection and Third World Fascism,*. Boston, MA, Sound End.

Cingranelli, D.L. and Pasquarello, T.E. (1985), 'Human Rights Practices and the U.S. Distribution of Foreign Aid to Latin American Countries', *American Journal of Political Science,* Vol. 29(3), pp. 539-63.

Dixon, W. (1984), 'Trade Concentration, Economic Growth, and the Provision Of Basic Human Needs', *Social Science Quarterly,* Vol. 65(3), pp. 761-4.

Dos Santos, T. (1970), 'The Structure of Dependence', *American Economic Review,* Vol. 60(2), pp. 231-6.

Feng, Y. (1996), 'Democracy and Growth: the sub-Saharan African Case, 1960-1992', *The Review of Black Political Economy,* Vol. 25(1), pp. 95-126.

Frank, A.G. (1966), 'The Development of Underdevelopment', *Monthly Review,* Vol. 18(4), pp. 17-31.

Frank, A.G. (1979), *Dependent Accumulation and Underdevelopment*, New York, Monthly Review Press.

Fukuyama, F. (1989), 'The End of History', *The National Interest,* Vol. 16(Summer), pp. 3-4.

Gastil, R. (1980), *Freedom in the World Political Rights and Civil Liberties,1980,* Cambridge, MA, Harvard University Press.

Gibney, M. and Dalton, M. (1996), 'The Political Terror Scale', in D. Cingranelli (ed), *Human Rights and Developing Countries*, Greenwich, CT, JAI Press, pp. 73 -84.

Harrelson-Stephens, J. and Callaway, R.L. (2003), 'Does Trade Openness Promote Security Rights in Developing Countries? Examining the Liberal Perspective', *International Interactions,* Vol. 29(2), pp. 143-58.

Helliwell, J.F. (1994), 'Empirical Linkages Between Democracy and Growth', *British Journal of Political Science,* Vol. 24(2), pp. 225-48.

Henderson, C. (1991), 'Conditions Affecting the Use of Political Repression', *Journal of Conflict Resolution,* Vol. 35(1), pp. 120-42.

Heston, A. and Summers, R. (1994), The Penn World Table (Mark 5.6).

Homer-Dixon, T.F. (1999), *Environment, Scarcity, and Violence,* Princeton, NJ, Princeton University Press.

Jaggers, K. and Gurr, T.R. (1996). POLITY III: Regime Change and Political Authority, 1800-1994. [computer file] (Study #6695). 2nd ICPSR version. Boulder, CO: Keith Jaggers/College Park, MD: Ted Robert Gurr [producers], 1995. Ann Arbor, MI: Inter-University Consortium for Political and Social Research [distributor], 1996.

Kentor, J. (2001), 'The Long Term Effects of Globalization on Income Inequality, Population Growth, and Economic Development', *Social Problems,* Vol. 48(4), pp. 435-456.

Keohane, R.O. and Nye, J.S. (1989), *Power and Interdependence*, Boston, MA, Scott, Foresman and Company.

Keohane, R.O. and Nye, J.S. (2000), 'Globalization: What's New? What's Not (And so What?)', *Foreign Policy*, Vol. 118(Spring), pp. 104-19.

Krain, M. (1997), 'State-sponsored Mass Murder: The Onset and Severity of Genocides and Politicides', *The Journal of Conflict Resolution,* Vol. 41(3), pp. 331-60.

Leary, V. (1998), 'Globalization and Human Rights', in J. Symonides (ed), *Human Rights: New Dimensions and Challenges*, Dartmouth, Ashgate Publishing.

Leblang, D. and Bernhard, W. (2002), 'Democratic Processes, Political Risk, and Foreign Exchange Markets', *American Journal of Political Science,* Vol. 46(2), pp. 316-34.

Lipset, S.M. (1959), 'Some Social Requisites of Democracy: Economic Development and Political Legitimacy', *American Political Science Review*, Vol. 53(1), pp. 69-105.

Londregan, J.B. and Poole, K.T. (1996), 'Does High Income Promote Democracy?', *World Politics,* Vol. 49(1), pp. 1-30.

McNitt, A.D. (1986), 'Measuring Human Rights: Problems and Possibilities', *Policy Studies Journal,* Vol. 15(1), pp. 71-83.

Meyer, W. H. (1998), *Human Rights and International Political Economy in Third World Nations: Multinational Corporations, Foreign Aid, and Repression*, Westport, CT, Praeger Publishers.

Milner, W.T. (1998), 'Progress or Decline? International Political Economy and Basic Human Rights', unpublished Ph.D. dissertation, University of North Texas, Denton, TX.

Milner, W.T. (2002), 'Economic Globalization and Rights: An Empirical Analysis', in A. Brysk (ed.) *Globalization and Human Rights*, University of California Press, Berkeley and Los Angeles, pp. 77-97.

Mitchell, N. J. and McCormick; J.M. (1988), 'Economic and Political Explanations of Human Rights Violations', *World Politics*, Vol. 40(4), pp. 476-98.

Moon, B. (1991), *The Political Economy of Basic Human Needs*, Ithaca, NY, Cornell University Press.

Morris, M.D. (1979), *Measuring the Condition of the World's Poor: The Physical Quality of Life Index,* New York, Pergamon.

Morris, M.D. (1996), 'Measuring the Condition of the World's Poor: The Physical Quality of Life Index, 1960-1990', Providence, RI, Thomas J. Watson, Jr. Institute for International Studies Working Paper (#23/24).

Pease, K. S. (2000), *International Organizations: Perspectives on Governance in the Twenty-First Century,* New Jersey, Prentice Hall.

Poe, S.C. and Tate, C.N. (1994), 'Repression of Human Rights to Personal Integrity in the 1980s: A Global Analysis', *American Political Science Review,* Vol. 88(4), pp. 853-72.

Prebisch, R. (1950), *The Economic Development of Latin America and Its Principal Problem,* New York, United Nations.

Regan, P.M. (1995), 'U.S. Economic and Political Repression: An Empirical Evaluation of U.S. Foreign Policy', *Political Research Quarterly,* Vol. 48(3), pp. 613-28.

Richards, D.L., Gelleny, R.D., and Sacko, D.H. (2001), 'Money with a Mean Streak? Foreign Economic Penetration and Government Respect for Human Rights in Developing Countries', *International Studies Quarterly,* Vol. 45(2), pp. 219-39.

Stimson, J.A. (1985), 'Regression in Time and Space: A Statistical Essay', *American Journal of Political Science,* Vol. 29(4), pp. 914-47.

Appendix

Table A.5.1 Control variables for the three models

Variable Name, Measurement	Previous Research	Hypothesized Direction
British Influence [b c] 0 = No 1 = Yes	Mitchell and McCormick, 1988; Moon, 1991; Poe and Tate, 1994	Positive in Democracy Two-Tailed Test in PQLI
Civil War [b c] 0 = No; 1 = Yes Singer and Small, 1994	Poe and Tate, 1994; Milner, 1998	Negative in both
Democracy [c] Polity III Jaggers and Gurr, 1996	Moon and Dixon, 1985; Moon, 1991; Poe and Tate, 1994; Mitchell and McCormick, 1988	Positive
Economic Standing [c] Per Capita GNP	Mitchell and McCormick, 1988; Moon, 1991; Poe and Tate, 1994	Positive
International War [b c] 0 = No; 1 = Yes Singer and Small, 1994	Poe and Tate, 1994; Milner, 1998	Negative in both
Leftist Regime [c]	Mitchell and McCormick, 1988; Moon, 1991; Poe and Tate, 1994	Two-Tailed Test
Literacy [a] World Development Indicators	Bairoch, 1975; Felipe and Resende, 1996; Lin, 1997	Positive
Military Expenditures [a b] Military expense/GNP World Development Indicators	Benoit, 1973; Rosh, 1986; Moon and Dixon, 1985; Moon, 1991; Felice, 1998	Negative in both

Military Regime [c]	McKinlay and Cohen, 1975, 1976; Moon, 1991	Negative
Population Change [b] Level [c]	Mitchell and McCormick, 1988; Henderson, 1991, 1993; Poe and Tate, 1994	Negative in both
State Religion [c] Presence of Muslim/Buddhist 0 = No; 1 = Yes	Park, 1987; Moon 1991	Negative for Muslim Positive for Buddhist
Urbanization [a] % urban World Development Indicators	Bairoch, 1975; Midlarsky, 1992	Positive

[a] Economic Development Model
[b] Democracy Model
[c] Subsistence Rights Model

Table A.5.2 Economic development

	Openness	Imports	Exports
Trade	0.022*	0.322*	0.356*
	(0.001)	(0.082)	(0.133)
Education	-0.001	-0.001	-0.001
	(0.001)	(0.001)	(0.001)
Urbanization	0.056*	0.057*	0.056*
	(0.007)	(0.004)	(0.007)
Military Spending	-0.004	-0.004	-0.003
	(0.004)	(0.004)	(0.004)
Constant	-1.072*	-1.078*	-1.001*
	(0.217)	(0.217)	(0.215)
N	1542	1542	1542
χ^2	87.47	90.13	78.98
Prob > χ^2	0.000	0.000	0.000

Note: Figures in parentheses are panel-corrected standard errors; * $p < 0.05$

Table A.5.3 Democracy

	Openness	Imports	Exports
Trade	-0.002	-0.469	0.243
	(0.004)	(0.530)	(0.758)
British Influence	1.069*	1.100*	1.021*
	(0.408)	(0.408)	(0.405)
Military Spending	-0.046*	-0.045*	-0.047*
	(0.018)	(0.018)	(0.018)
Population Growth	-0.000	-0.000	-0.000
	(0.000)	(0.000)	(0.000)
Economic Growth	0.555*	0.555*	0.547*
	(0.097)	(0.096)	(0.098)
Civil War	0.011	0.017	0.023
	(0.192)	(0.193)	(0.193)
International War	0.016	0.018	0.027
	(0.219)	(0.220)	(0.219)
Constant	2.713*	2.787*	2.548*
	(0.419)	(0.402)	(0.414)
N	1489	1489	1489
χ^2	42.58	43.57	42.46
Prob > χ^2	0.000	0.000	0.000

Note: Figures in parentheses are panel-corrected standard errors; * $p < 0.05$

Table A.5.4 Subsistence and security

	Subsistence			Security		
	Openness	Imports	Exports	Openness	Imports	Exports
Trade	0.011*	-0.037	5.801*	0.002*	0.247*	0.542*
	(0.099)	(1.086)	(1.472)	(0.001)	(0.099)	(0.144)
Economic Growth	3.271*	3.250*	3.195*	0.011	0.013	0.009
	(0.463)	(0.455)	(0.463)	(0.018)	(0.018)	(0.018)
Democracy	0.453*	0.440*	0.442*	0.059*	0.059*	0.059*
	(0.099)	(0.097)	(0.097)	(0.009)	(0.009)	(0.009)
Civil War	-0.089	-0.100	0.056	-0.918*	-0.926*	-0.912*
	(0.791)	(0.789)	(0.775)	(0.126)	(0.127)	(0.126)
International War	-0.539	-0.556	-0.463	-0.305*	-0.313*	-0.292*
	(0.550)	(0.541)	(0.540)	(0.114)	(0.114)	(0.115)
Population	0.521*	0.338	0.689*	-0.246	-0.250*	-0.251*
	(0.550)	(0.287)	(0.285)	(0.026)	(0.027)	(0.025)
British Influence	-4.767*	-4.582*	-4.867*			
	(1.564)	(1.612)	(1.540)			
Leftist Regime	-1.106	-0.923	-1.234			
	(1.119)	(1.125)	(1.084)			
Military Regime	-2.421*	-2.397*	-2.283*			
	(0.848)	(0.842)	(0.831)			
Muslim	-7.737*	-7.521*	-7.684*			
	(1.458)	(1.453)	(1.464)			
Buddhist	14.383*	14.705*	14.021*			
	(1.815)	(1.823)	(1.830)			
Constant	50.817*	54.501*	47.276*			
	(4.677)	(4.734)	(4.864)			
N	1458	1458	1458	1623	1623	1623
χ^2	339.62	326.33	350.52	319.30	316.03	325.77
Prob > χ^2	0.000	0.000	0.000	0.000	0.000	0.000

Note: Figures in parentheses are panel-corrected standard errors; * $p < 0.05$

Chapter 6

Providing Subsistence Rights: Do States Make a Difference?

Wesley T. Milner, David Leblang, Steven C. Poe and Kara Smith

Introduction

One of the most amazing developments in world politics over the last the last fifty years has been the emergence of an international human rights regime. Affirming that all individuals have dignity and worth, human rights are an evolving effort to improve conditions for those who continue to be deprived of these values.

Ever since the first research of Lars Schoultz (Schoultz, 1981), now over twenty years ago, qualitative and quantitative social scientists, seeking general explanations of human rights-related phenomena, have attempted to come to an understanding of two related issues. The first is whether human rights make a difference in determining foreign policy outputs (e.g., Stohl, Carleton and Johnson, 1984; Cingranelli and Pasquarello, 1985; Apodaca and Stohl, 1999). The second is whether human rights violations themselves can be explained (e.g., Henderson, 1991).

Researchers have occasionally conducted analyses seeking to explain diverse categories of rights (e.g., physical integrity, political, economic, subsistence) in the same study (e.g., Meyer, 1998; Heinisch, 1998; Smith, Bolyard and Ippolito, 1999). Rarely, however, have they attempted to empirically identify the nature of the relationships between various kinds of rights. Much work has been done on the normative, theoretic connections between rights, however. Shue (1980) and Donnelly (1989, 2002), among others, make persuasive theoretical arguments that there is a set of core human rights that are normatively related and even indivisible from one another. Yet we know very little about whether these rights actually 'go together' in the real world. Some thinkers cite concerns that sometimes they do not. For example, Donnelly (1989) makes an argument that in the real world 'trade-offs' exist, whereby states have paid for higher achievement of subsistence rights by purposefully abusing political rights. As yet, though, the possibility that these trade-offs exist has not been fully investigated with quantitative methodologies. If we are to grasp the complexities that make up the human rights paradigm, we must gain a greater understanding of these relationships and potential tradeoffs.

The largest vein of research on the question of why human rights abuses occur has focused specifically on explaining cross-national variations in security rights; the rights to be free from torture, execution, imprisonment, or the violation of what has come to be known as integrity of the person or physical integrity rights (e.g., Mitchell and McCormick, 1988; Henderson, 1991, 1993; Poe and Tate, 1994; Poe, Tate and Keith, 1999). In a second area of focus, scholars have sought to explain cross-national variations in indicators that tap the degree to which political and civil liberties are enjoyed by citizens of countries around the world (Strouse and Claude, 1976; Park, 1987) or measures intended to capture the frequency of governments' sanctions that take them away (Ziegenhagen, 1986; Davenport, 1995, 1996a, 1996b). A third strand of literature has sought to explain why subsistence rights, or basic human needs, are protected in some countries and not in others (Moon and Dixon, 1985, 1992; Moon, 1991).

In this study we investigate the relationship between basic human needs, one of the three categories of rights that Shue (1980) argued were basic and two others he considered basic to reasonable level of human dignity: security rights and civil and political rights. We examine the effect of the provision of political rights (obviously closely related to democracy) on basic human needs but also focus on the uninvestigated issue of whether respect for personal security rights has an effect on the provision of basic human needs. Further, we incorporate substantial controls that we expect to yield theoretically interesting effects of their own. In order to gain a more complete picture of this specific aspect of human rights, we imbed these variables in a more comprehensive multivariate model of basic human needs. Further, this study provides one of the more robust tests of a model on basic human needs to date, as we will employ a pooled cross-sectional time series data set, consisting of cases taken from 118 less developed countries from 1980 to 1993.

Basic Human Needs and Trade-offs

International human rights documents, most notably the Universal Declaration of Human Rights (1948), establish in international law the right to a level of well-being sufficient for subsistence. Economists and political scientists have studied determinants of economic development and quality of life for many years, though for the most part without invoking the human rights framework (Scully, 1988; Leblang, 1996; Gwartney et al. 1997).[1] Only in few cases have basic human needs been examined in concert with other human rights (Toppen, 1996; Meyer, 1998; Heinisch, 1998; Milner, Poe and Leblang, 1999). For the most part, they have remained separate.

There is, however, a voluminous literature on the provision of basic human needs, the dependent variable of this study. We are concerned most with those that concentrate on the political aspects of basic human needs. One area of focus is on the Guns vs. Butter argument, where scholars have attempted to find if military spending, and other military related variables have an effect on provision of basic needs (e.g., Rosh, 1986). As Dixon and Moon (1987) and Moon (1991) suggest, the role of the military in the provision of basic human needs is a complex process.[2] Acting as a mediating mechanism, a military regime could have either positive or negative effects on a country's physical quality of life provision. First, the anti-democratic conservative nature of the military would tend to have a negative effect. Contrarily, the organizational efficiency inherent in these types of governments would potentially elevate the level of basic needs. Again from a positive standpoint, regimes under military control could be a modernizing force in social development. Finally, increases in defense spending as a result of a military-friendly government would likely divert scarce resources from the needy, thereby degrading overall physical quality of life. It is obvious here that further investigation is needed to account for the divergence of the effects of the military on subsistence rights.

Another set of studies examines whether institutional arrangements of government have any impact on the provision of these needs (e.g., Burkett, 1985; Spalding, 1985; Moon and Dixon, 1985; Moon, 1991). The findings of these investigations regarding the effects of democracy are relatively clear – more democratic countries are apt to enjoy superior provision of basic human needs once other factors are controlled. Countries with leftist governments are found to have a higher level of basic human needs performance than others.

In looking specifically at security rights (those pertaining to personal integrity), little research has been done on the direct relationship between their realization and basic human needs fulfillment; thus there are no well specified theories regarding what this relationship may look like. One might pose the argument that limited infringements on personal integrity rights are sometimes desirable for the overall security of the nation and for the basic human needs fulfillment of persons within the country. In some contexts, labour unions or other politically powerful groups might make political demands that are against the best interests of society as a whole. Donnelly (1989) presents some evidence that such trade-offs may have occurred in the South Korean case. Certainly dictators around the world have made claims of just this sort of compromise, whether they intended to increase needs fulfillment or not. If such trade-offs are common, then we might expect the relationship between repression and subsistence rights to be positive. That said, we expect that a different kind of trade-off is just as likely in the general case. Contradicting the above argument, we expect that personal integrity abuse will tend to subtract from the efforts that governments make to improve basic human needs fulfillment. It is quite possible that at times, in reaction to a threat, governments might view improved efforts at fulfilling needs and repression as two substitutable policy options. With limited resources at their disposal, any effort spent to increase repression is apt to take away from any effort to increase achievement of subsistence rights. Put in terms of the framework discussed by Poe in Chapter 2 of this volume, regimes might perceive that threats can be dealt with through repression or accommodation, but rarely will they do both. If that is the case, then the relationship between repression and needs fulfillment might be negative.

However, in the only quantitative test of this relationship we know of, Milner, Poe and Leblang (1999) found a positive relationship between these two kinds of rights, in simple bivariate analyses, indicating that these two kinds of rights tend to be realized together. Theoretically, countries that afford citizens greater personal integrity rights, allow those citizens to express their preferences and to make demands, which may result in greater subsistence rights also. As yet, though, this relationship has not been examined in the context of a multivariate model accounting for other possible determinants of human needs fulfillment. Constructing such a model in the present study will allow us to have greater confidence in our conclusions.

Framework of Analysis

Physical Quality of Life

In terms of basic human needs or physical quality of life, many would agree that these include unpolluted air and water, sufficient food, clothing and shelter and minimal public healthcare. For the generation that has addressed these complex issues of development, finding consensus on measuring physical quality of life has been illusory. Typically, scholars have relied on basic gross national product (in addition to its components and growth) because of its near universal availability and ease of use. While we will not rehearse the various shortcomings of this approach (see Hicks and Streeten, 1979; Morris, 1979; Milner, Poe and Leblang, 1999; Moon, 1991), there have been additional efforts (many funded by the United Nations) to combine individual indicators into composite indices. For numerous reasons such as lack of data/comparability and attempting to combine too many indicators, most of these indices have not been implemented by most scholars.[3]

The most widely used composite measure is that of Morris (1979) developed under the auspices of the Overseas Development Council. This 'Physical Quality of Life Index' (PQLI) is a composite of three indicators: infant mortality per thousand live births, life expectancy at age one and basic literacy as the proportion of the population who are at least fifteen years of age and literate. Ultimately, the overall PQLI composite is the unweighted arithmetic mean of these three indicators. The measure for life expectancy at age one (LE^1) considers 38 years as the 'worst' case scenario (since 1950) and 85 years as the 'best' performance.[4]

Infant mortality and life expectancy at age one arguably capture the combined effects of public health, nutrition, family environment and social relations. On the surface, it might appear that infant mortality and life expectancy measure the same things (i.e., health). In reality, they indicate different aspects of social performance. Looking at the historical pattern of the two, it becomes evident that the factors affecting changes in life expectancy at age one are not the same as those affecting infant mortality. An example of this has occurred countries since 1950 where mortality rates of persons over age one were typically falling, while infant mortality rates refused to decline. Infant mortality rates eventually came down, but in a separate and later occurrence. The sources of survival improvements (whether nutrition, environment, medicine, etc.) did not impact each age group in the same manner or at the same rate. Even during the 1990s, countries that have similar life expectancies do not always have the same infant mortality rates and *vice versa* (Morris, 1979, p.35).

Infant mortality reflects social conditions inside the home, especially the well-being of women. Life expectancy at age one indicates conditions in the external environment. The indicator for literacy indicates the potential for development and ability of the underclass to gain the advantages and responsibilities of this development. As Morris (1979, p.35) correctly argues, literacy is a superior measure to school enrollment or numbers of classrooms or instructors. These are only indicators of inputs and do not guarantee any improved results or at best indicate the educational benefits going typically to elite groups. Indeed, the basic literacy component not only measures gains to the very poor but can also record literacy gains obtained through informal as well as formal processes.[5]

Much of the criticism of the PQLI centers around the basic weighting scheme of placing equal emphasis on infant mortality, life expectancy and literacy (Hicks and Streeten, 1979; Larson and Wolford, 1979; Bayless and Bayless, 1982; Goldstein, 1985). The primary objection is that there is no theoretical basis for assigning equal weights to the components. Morris (1979, pp. 47-9) forcefully argues that since there is no overriding theoretical justification for treating any one indicator as more important than another, we must employ equal weights.[6] In an effort to be as comprehensive as possible, we analyze both the PQLI, as used by Morris (1979) and Moon (1991), as well as the three individual components of the index. By doing so we hope to determine if the covariates influence the various elements of PQLI differently.

Independent Variables

Security rights Integrity of the person rights or security rights include execution, torture, forced disappearance and imprisonment/detention of persons, either arbitrarily or for their political and/or religious beliefs. Though defining these rights is rather straightforward, measuring their provision is more challenging. Notwithstanding the substantial work utilizing the events-based approach,[7] we are persuaded by the arguments surrounding the standards-based approach (e.g., Lopez and Stohl, 1992). The measure we employ is the five point Political Terror Scale, or PTS (Gibney and Dalton, 1996), which was created from the annually published human rights reports of Amnesty International.[8] They are coded so that a '1' represents a country where these rights are not seriously abused, while the highest score, '5,' is assigned to countries with the worst human rights disasters. Consistent with the idea that these kinds of rights fulfillment go together, and that if there are trade-offs it is between repression and accommodation, we hypothesize a negative relationship between personal integrity abuse and needs fulfillment. That is, as personal integrity abuse increases, needs fulfillment will decrease, once other factors are accounted for (Milner, Poe and Leblang, 1999).

Political rights/democracy The rationale for expecting greater physical quality of life guarantees as a result of greater democracy (or political rights) is that these rights give citizens the ability to remove regimes that do not perform well in this respect. Also, the civil liberties usually associated with democracies (such as freedom of speech, press, assembly, etc.) enable citizens and opposition groups to publicize the failures of a particular regime. These freedoms could also result in publicity of human needs failures that could lead to further pressure on a domestic government from other governments, the U.N. and other international organizations.

Supporting the conclusion that democracy and political rights affect basic human needs performance are the findings of several scholars that democracies are better equipped to provide for basic human needs. Similar to the reasoning with personal integrity rights, countries that allow for effective participation of citizens tend to better accommodate the demands of those citizens, which would therefore result in greater realization of subsistence rights. Moon and Dixon (1985), Rosh (1986), Spalding (1986) and Moon (1991) find that political democracy is associated with higher levels of basic needs satisfaction, even when controlling for wealth (i.e., GNP). These conclusions are bolstered by the fact that the authors utilize different measures of democracy to define and measure democracy.

The researcher is faced with many choices when facing measurement of political rights. For our purposes, we focus our measurement on the concept of 'democracy'. Well-known scholars such as Lipset (1963, p.27), Dahl (1956, pp. 67-90), Downs (1957, pp.23-4) and Lenski (1966, p.319) have proposed definitions that emphasize elections and political liberties which should expand political efficacy. We accept the definition of Schmitter and Karl (1996, p.50) who argue that democracy is 'system of governance in which rulers are held accountable for their actions in the public realm by citizens, acting indirectly through competition and co-operation of their elected representative.'

The measure that most closely fits our definitional and practical means is Jaggers and Gurr's Polity democracy measure, which covers 161 nations from 1946 through 1994. Jaggers and Gurr (1995, pp.471-2) argue that there are three essential, interdependent components of democracy in the context of Western liberal philosophy. First, institutions and procedures must be present where individuals can voice their preferences about alternative political policies and leaders. Second, it is vital that there be adequate constraints on the power of the executive. Finally, the state must guarantee civil liberties (e.g., freedom from slavery/servitude, torture, arbitrary arrest and imprisonment, inhuman punishment). Operationally, their indicator of democracy is drawn from codings of the openness and competitiveness of executive recruitment, the competitiveness of political participation and the level constraints of the chief executive.[9]

Military regimes Drawing from McKinlay and Cohan (1975) and Madani (1992), we define military regimes as those in which the armed forces (army, navy or air force) obtain power as a result of a coup, a military official serves as the chief executive and the government maintains power for at least six months.[10] Further, the category includes a few 'mixed regimes' in which a civilian acts as main executive surrounded by military personnel in the cabinet or a military leader who selects a civilian to head the government but retains ultimate power from the background. Dixon and Moon (1987) examine both military expenditures and regime type and find that military control has negligible effects at best on PQLI performance.[11]

Wealth Intuitively, one might expect that increased wealth in a country would result in a higher physical quality of life. Typically, wealth or economic development is measured with per capita gross national product (GNP) or gross domestic product (GDP) variables. In keeping with conventional wisdom, a number of studies show that economic development has a strong, positive impact on basic human needs fulfillment. For example, Park (1987) in his study finds that economic development is the strongest predictor of improved basic needs achievement. While their emphasis is on military expenditures, Rosh (1986) and Moon and Dixon (1985) also conclude that per capita GNP is closely associated with basic needs fulfillment.[12]

However, high levels of GNP or GDP are not always considered synonymous with the fulfillment of physical quality of life. This occurs in large part because the predominant measures fail to take into account inequality. This could occur in a country where overall per capita GDP is high but a majority of the citizens still live in poverty. Further, Goldstein (1985) and Rosh (1986) question whether the conventional wisdom of a linear relationship holds universally, especially at the higher levels of GNP. In terms of measurement, we follow a number of authors (e.g., Moon, 1991, and sources cited therein) in using the log of gross national product per capita for level of economic development.[13]

Leftist government We refer to leftist regimes as those governed by a socialist party or coalition that does not allow effective electoral competition with nonsocialist opposition (Poe and Tate, 1994, p.858). From a theoretical and rhetorical perspective, socialist parties espouse a commitment to the welfare of the working class and the poor. Whether this is indeed the case is in dispute. Looking at physical quality of life, Moon's (1991) findings do support the hypothesis linking leftist norms to superior performance in the provision of basic human needs. While state socialist nations that commit to the wholesale alteration of a domestic political economy provide superior basic needs, social democratic or populist forms of leftist ideology have virtually no effect. Our study, which utilizes a more specific definition and longer period, will hopefully shed more light on this controversy.

Internal or external war A number of studies argue that participation in international conflict (Stohl, 1975, 1976; Rasler, 1986; Poe and Tate, 1994) and civil conflict (Nieburg, 1969; Tilly, 1978; Skocpol, 1979; Poe and Tate, 1994) have a deleterious effect on human rights. It stands to reason that a country involved in either an international or domestic war would also be less able to provide adequate physical quality of life to its citizens. Notwithstanding other influences, this appears to happening in contemporary central African countries (e.g., Angola, Namibia, Zimbabwe, Rwanda, and Uganda) involved in the conflict in the Democratic Republic of the Congo (formerly Zaire). To operationalize both international war and civil war, we utilize the measures proposed by Small and Singer (1982). The first defines a country as being involved in an interstate war if 1) there were a total of a thousand or more battle deaths suffered by all of the participants in the conflict; or 2) the particular country suffered at least a hundred fatalities or had a thousand or more personnel taking part in the hostilities (pp. 50, 55). The second scale categorizing civil conflicts stipulates two criteria. The first criterion for an actual civil war would demand that the regime in power be *directly* involved in the conflict. Also, there must be a viable resistance where either both sides must be 'organized for violent conflict' or 'the weaker side, although initially unprepared [must be] able to inflict upon the stronger opponents at least five percent of the number of fatalities it sustains' (p.215). Countries that are participants in either type of war as identified by the definitions of Singer and Small will be coded '1' for a particular country-year. Others will be coded '0'.

Population density It has been argued that the larger a nation's population and population growth rate, the greater its government's tendency to violate basic human rights (Henderson, 1993; Poe and Tate, 1994).[14] Henderson (1993, p.324) emphasizes the stress put on all aspects of society as 'individuals and groups compete for every conceivable good. The extent of scarcity varies from country to country, [but] in the more hard-pressed countries, burgeoning demands will keep governments off-balance.' Further, as population increases this may tend to counter the benefits of any economic growth that may be present. Increasing population exacerbates the already difficult problem of ethnic conflict, 'as when an increase in the size of an ethnic group leads to a demand for a larger share of society's political and economic rewards' (Henderson 1993, p.324). This may also exacerbate efforts to provide basic human needs. Thus, as a first measure of population density, we use a standard measure of that concept, number of persons per square kilometer of land. The greater the number of persons per square kilometer, the more difficulty we expect that a country will have in achieving human needs.

Another dimension of the population density problem goes further to consider an aspect of geography overlooked by the other measure – whether the land is of good quality. Thus we also wish to consider a measure that captures the total amount of arable land available for human use/consumption. We include a measure of arable land (measured in hectares) divided by total population to give an indication of the ability of government agents to provide the services necessary for physical quality of life. Our expectation is that countries with greater per capita hectares of arable land will have less success in achieving subsistence rights, once other factors are controlled.

Data and Analysis

Sample and Methodology

As stated above, our sample is comprised of 114 non-OECD countries over the period 1980-1993. We focus primarily on developing states because of the relative lack of variability among industrialized states. We include all countries for which data on the independent and dependent variables are available. Some simple summary statistics, relating to both our independent and dependent variables, are presented in Table 6.1.

Table 6.1 Descriptive statistics

Variable	Mean	Std. Dev.	Min	Max
Physical Quality of Life	60.738	19.052	14.2	94
Life Expectancy	52.784	17.104	7.13	83.73
Infant Mortality	69.196	17.960	15.6	97.7
Literacy	59.903	25.112	5	99
Leftist Government	.161	.368	0	1
Per Capita GNP (log)	6.776	1.173	3.970	10.350
Arable Land (hectacres per capita)	.264	.181	.0003	.889
Population Density	120.303	423.193	1.502	4711.147
British Colonial Heritage	.369	.482	0	1
Personal Integrity Rights	2.811	1.080	1	5
Internal or External War	.085	.280	0	1
Military Government	.345	.475	0	1
Political Rights	3.391	1.936	1	7

Correlations (statistical significance in parentheses)

	PQLI	Literacy	Infant Mortality	Life Expectancy
PQLI	1.000			
Literacy	0.948 0.000	1.000		
Infant Mortality	0.948 0.000	0.823 0.000	1.000	
Life Expectancy	0.941 0.000	0.811 0.000	0.892 0.000	1.000

We are observing performance in physical quality of life and its components over time and across countries. As such, our interest in cross-national and cross-temporal variation necessitates the use of appropriate statistical techniques to deal with the problems of autocorrelated and heteroscedastic disturbances. We therefore utilize the procedure outlined in Beck and Katz (1995, 1996).[15] The model can be summarized as follows:

Subsistence $Rights_{tj}$ = a + B_1 Physical Integrity Rights + B_2 Political $Rights_{tj}$ + B_3 Military $Regime_{tj}$ + B_4 $Wealth_{tj}$ + B_5 Leftist $Government_{tj}$ + B_6 Internal/External War_{tj} + B_7 Population $Density_{tj}$ + B_8 Arable $Land_{tj}$ + B_9 British Colonial $Experience_{tj}$ + ε_{tj}

Empirical Results

Table 6.2 reports the results of our empirical analysis. The physical quality of life index is the dependent variable in column one and the components that make up PQLI are the dependent variables in columns two (life expectancy), three (infant mortality) and four (literacy).

We begin by examining the determinants of physical quality of life in column one of Table 6.2. In terms of overall goodness of fit, the π^2 indicates that the overall model is statistically significant. Individually, however, the coefficients for leftist government, arable land, personal integrity rights and internal/external conflict are not significantly different from zero. Due to the fact that prior research has shown that physical integrity rights are themselves a function of internal/external conflict and regime ideology (e.g., Poe and Tate, 1994; Poe, Tate and Keith, 1999), we performed joint significant tests (not reported here). Those results indicated that our findings are not compromised by any relationship between physical integrity rights and conflict.

Most of the variables in column one that are statistically significant are in the expected direction. The results indicate that political rights, as measured with the Polity III democracy score, are a statistically significant determinant of PQLI, but that physical integrity rights are not. The results also indicate a very strong substantive and statistically significant positive effect of wealth (as measured by the log of per capita gross national product) on physical quality of life. This result squares with the findings of prior research (e.g., Dixon and Moon, 1987; Moon, 1993; Moon and Dixon 1993) and indicates that richer countries tend to have populations with higher scores on the PQLI index. The results in column one also support prior research that examines the effect of British colonial heritage and the existence of a military government. We find that former British colonies tend to have lower physical quality of life as do those countries with military governments. This may be a result of fallout from previous British rule that resulted in somewhat exploitive economies and trade-offs between economic development and inequality.

Interestingly, the one significant statistic that indicates a relationship in an unexpected direction is that for population density. As population density increases, so does physical quality of life. We should indicate that this result does not go away if we drop the statistically insignificant variable measuring arable land from the model in column one.

Turning our attention to the components of physical quality of life, we note that the π^2 statistic and the R^2 are similar in columns two, three and four to that presented in column one. Recall (see the bottom panel of Table 6.1) that the correlations between PQLI, literacy, life expectancy and infant mortality are all over 0.80. Thus, the similarity across values for R^2 is not surprising. The purpose of

Table 6.2 Determinants of physical quality of life

Variable	PQLI	Life Expectancy	Infant Mortality	Literacy
Constant	10.49*	-4.80	8.72*	9.66*
	(3.62)	(3.11)	(4.12)	4.75)
Physical Integrity Abuse	0.06	0.16	0.08	0.30
	(0.15)	(0.21)	(0.24)	(0.22)
Political Rights	0.81*	0.99*	0.93*	1.19*
	(0.16)	(0.19)	(0.28)	(0.22)
Military Government	-1.67*	-2.38*	-2.56*	-1.86*
	(0.59)	(0.76)	(0.84)	(0.78)
Per Capita GNP (log)	7.38*	8.54*	8.58*	6.61*
	(0.50)	(0.39)	(0.54)	(0.63)
Leftist Government	1.49	2.82*	1.84	1.72
	(1.13)	(1.34)	(1.54)	(1.32)
Internal/External War	-0.99	-0.38	0.09	-0.60
	(0.72)	(0.97)	(0.97)	(0.81)
Population Density	0.004*	0.002*	0.003*	0.005*
	(0.001)	(0.001)	(0.001)	(0.001)
Arable Land	-3.26	-8.30*	-0.58	2.72
(hectacres per capita)	(3.18)	(2.56)	(3.46)	(5.00)
British Colonial	-2.26*	-3.36*	-0.17	0.11
	(1.12)	(1.10)	(1.39)	(1.86)
R^2	0.90	0.90	0.91	0.82
π^2	492.51	863.40	507.44	295.62
Prob > π^2	0.000	0.000	0.000	0.000

Figures in parentheses are heteroscedasticity-corrected robust standard errors,
* $p \leq .05$; ** $p \leq .01$; *** $p \leq .001$

breaking down the physical quality of life index into component parts is to see if the independent variables identified in this research, and prior studies influence the components differently than the overall index. An examination of Table 6.2 identifies two interesting findings. First, the effects of leftist governments and arable land on life expectancy are both statistically significant although in opposite directions. Leftist governments tend to increase life expectancy, *ceteris paribus,* perhaps because medical care is more widely available to all. Though the coefficients are in the expected direction, they do not reach statistical significance with any of the other components of PQLI. Additionally, contrary to our hypothesis, countries with more arable land tend to have lower life expectancy, perhaps indicating that countries with larger geographic size tend to have greater difficulty in delivering services. The second interesting finding from Table 6.2 is that British colonial heritage does not have a statistically significant effect on infant mortality or on literacy. Evidently the effect on the overall PQLI index was due to a relationship between British colonial ties and life expectancy at age one.

Exhibiting rather stable, statistically significant effects across all of the analyses are logged per capita GNP, military government and political rights. However, physical integrity rights seem to have little effect on PQLI. The coefficient of this variable in each analysis is positive, indicating that greater abuse is actually associated with greater needs fulfillment, as we would expect if human rights trade-offs were being made. However, in three of the four cases the coefficients were rather small, and far from being statistically significant. The coefficient obtained in the analysis explaining variations in literacy is a bit stronger, but still statistically insignificant at conventional levels.

Summary and Conclusions

Numerous interesting and useful findings have resulted from this study. Consistent with other studies on basic human needs, we found economic development, military government and population density to be consistent in explaining basic human needs fulfillment, regardless of the dependent variable that was used. Exercising effects on at least one of the components of PQLI, but not on others were leftist government, arable land, and British colonial heritage. Interestingly, participation in war did not appear to affect basic human needs fulfillment in our sample.

Our main purpose in conducting this study, though, was to investigate the relationships between various kinds of rights, once other factors are controlled. In this study we have attempted to isolate the effects of political rights and personal integrity rights on basic human needs. Political rights were found to have a positive impact on needs fulfillment, as we expected. Perhaps most intriguing, though, is what we did not find. These analyses yielded no evidence supporting the hypothesis that countries that allow greater physical integrity abuse tend to better realize subsistence rights. This contradicts our past research on the relationship between these different kinds of rights (Milner, Poe and Leblang, 1999), which tended to show that they are compatible and perhaps even mutually reinforcing. In this study we perform more sophisticated multivariate analyses than we did in our first pass at that issue, and these findings tell a somewhat different story. Democracy and the provision of political rights lead to better achievement in terms of subsistence rights, perhaps because people are allowed to take part in the political system, voicing their demands for the conditions necessary to lead longer, healthier lives. However, once democracy, wealth and other factors are included in the model, personal integrity rights do not reinforce and encourage subsistence rights. Thus we conclude that our previous findings were spurious, occurring as a result of variance shared with determinants, such as wealth and democratic governance that basic human needs and physical integrity have in common. Though statistically insignificant the direction of the coefficients would indicate that countries high on personal integrity abuse actually have slightly better performance on basic human needs in our sample, once other factors are controlled.

At very least we have found that not all human rights are mutually reinforcing. Future analyses should examine whether governments attempt 'trade-offs' between various kinds of rights, and whether such attempted trade-offs are ever successful.

Notes

1 For an exception see Spalding (1985).

2 While numerous scholars have highlighted the negative aspects of the military (e.g., Bienen, 1971; Wolpin, 1981), others have argued for positive outcomes from military rule (Levy, 1966; Wolpin, 1981).

3 A notable exception is the Human Development Index, which is the most recent measurement offered by the United Nations. It combines indicators of national income, life expectancy and educational attainment. Although it is an improvement over some previous attempts, it however presents some shortcomings. These include only measuring human development since 1990 and mixing ends and means.

4 See Morris (1996, p.7) and Morris (1979, p.45) for details of the PQLI formula.

5 In constructing his index, Morris (1979, pp. 30-4) lays out six criteria that all composite measures should meet: 1) they should not assume that there is only one pattern of development; 2) they should avoid standards that reflect the values of specific societies; 3) they should measure results, not inputs; 4) they should be able to reflect the distribution of social results; 5) they should be simple to construct and easy to comprehend; and 6) it should lend itself to international comparison. The PQLI indeed meets all of these criteria.

6 Moon (1991, p.27) echoes this position and stresses that reweighting the components in various plausible alternatives produces measures with a Spearman rank order correlation consistently over .98. This level of intercorrelation is well above that usually considered sufficient to warrant a composite index.

7 The events approach involves coding cases of repressive events from newspaper accounts. Typically, the number of these events is summed for a particular period (a month or year) and the number of events is considered a measure of repression. Some difficulties with this approach as a means to measure levels of human rights violation (e.g., Western bias) have been identified (e.g., Poe and Tate, 1994).

8 Following the lead of Poe and Tate (1994), missing cases are filled in using similar codings gained from the U.S. State Department Reports.

9 Jaggers and Gurr (1995) provide a solid comparison of Polity with some of the most utilized constructs of democracy. Further, Munck and Verkuilen (2002) identify difficulties in the various indices and prescriptions for areas of improvement. We use the Polity III version of this data, which was the most recently available at the time when this research was originally undertaken.

10 This measure was also used by Poe and Tate (1994), in their examination of personal integrity rights violations.

11 It must be noted that their results only reflect the period from 1970-1975.

12 While ultimately arriving at this conclusion, Rosh (1986) warns that the relationship is expected to be greatly reduced if research is concentrated on developing countries rather than the entire world.

13 While GNP is considered the traditional and most popular approach, there have been several alternatives offered (including energy consumption, Henderson, 1991) and a number of basic human needs measures. The primary difficulty in employing measures such as energy consumption is that accurate data do not exist for many of the years and countries that are included in this study. The basic needs measures obviously would be problematic in that our dependent variable (PQLI) utilizes components of these indices. The log is employed to overcome the skewed distribution of income that would otherwise hamper the statistical assumptions.

14 Henderson (1993) finds that population pressures, as evidenced by population growth rate, are related to integrity of the person violations by governments. On the other hand, population size itself demonstrated little or no affect on government repression. The results from Poe and Tate's (1994) study, however, indicate that population size has a positive impact on human rights abuse while population growth has no statistical effect on repression.

15 Beck and Katz advocate the use of ordinary least squares and suggest a number of ways to correct the standard errors. The variant of their approach we adopt uses Prais-Winsten regression to estimate the parameters and corrects the standard errors for unequal variation across panels (countries). To account for the fact that physical quality of life and its components do not change very quickly over time, we specify that the error term is first-order autocorrelated. Our sample is comprised of 114 countries over the period 1980-1993. An unbalanced panel produced a total of 1431 observations.

References

Apodaca, C. and Stohl, M. (1999), 'United States Human Rights Policy and Foreign Assistance', *International Studies Quarterly*, Vol. 43(1), pp. 185-98.

Bayless, M. and Bayless, S. (1982), 'Current Quality of Life Indicators: Some Theoretical and Methodological Concerns', *American Journal of Economics and Sociology*, Vol. 41, pp. 421-37.

Bienen, H. (ed.), (1971), *The Military and Modernization*, Chicago, Aldine.

Beck, N. and Katz, J. (1995), 'What to Do (and not to do) With Time-Series Cross-Section Data', *American Political Science Review*, Vol. 89(3), pp. 634-47.

Cingranelli, D.L., and Pasquarello, T.E. (1985), 'Human Rights Practices and the Distribution of US Foreign Aid to Latin American Countries', *American Journal of Political Science*, Vol. 29(3), pp. 539-63.

Dahl, R.A. (1956), *A Preface to Democratic Theory*, Chicago, University of Chicago Press.

Davenport, C. (1995), 'Multi-Dimensional Threat Perception and State Repression: An Inquiry Into Why States Apply Negative Sanctions', *American Journal of Political Science*, Vol. 39(3), pp. 683-713.

Davenport, C. (1996a), 'The Weight of the Past: Exploring Lagged Determinants of Political Repression', *Political Research Quarterly*, Vol. 49(June), pp. 377-403.

Davenport, C. (1996b), 'Constitutional Promises and Repressive Reality: A Cross-National Time Series Investigation of Why Political and Civil Liberties are Suppressed', *Journal of Politics*, Vol. 58(3), pp. 627-54.

Dixon. W.J. and Moon, B.E. (1987), 'The Military Burden and Basic Human Needs', *Journal of Conflict Resolution*, Vol. 30(4), pp. 660-84.

Donnelly, J. (1989), *Universal Human Rights in Theory and Practice*, Ithaca, NY, Cornell University Press.

Gibney, M. and Dalton, M. (1996), 'The Political Terror Scale', In *Human Rights and Developing Countries*, in David Cingranelli, (ed.), Greenwich, CT, JAI Press, pp. 73-84.

Goldstein, J. (1985), 'Basic Human Needs: The Plateau Curve', *World Development*, Vol. 13, pp. 595-609.

Gwartney, J., Lawson, R., and Block, W. (1997), *Economic Freedom of the World: 1975-1995*, Vancouver, The Fraser Institute.

Heinisch, R. (1998), 'The Economic Nature of Basic Human Rights: Economic Explanations of Cross-National Variations in Governmental Basic Human Rights Performance', *Peace and Change*, Vol. 23, pp. 333-72.

Henderson, C. (1991), 'Conditions Affecting the Use of Political Repression', *Journal of Conflict Resolution*, Vol. 35(1), pp. 120-42.

Henderson, C. (1993), 'Population Pressures and Political Repression', *Social Science Quarterly*, Vol. 74(2), pp. 322-33.

Hicks, N. and Streeten, P. (1979), 'Indicators of Development: The Search for a Basic Needs Yardstick', *World Development*, Vol. 7, pp. 567-80.

Jaggers, K. and Gurr, T.R. (1995), 'Tracking Democracy's Third Wave with the Polity III Data', *Journal of Peace Research*, Vol. 32(4), pp. 469-82.

Leblang, D. (1996), 'Property Rights, Democracy, and Economic Growth', *Political Research Quarterly*, Vol. 49(1), pp. 5-25.

Lenski, G. (1966), *Power and Privilege*, New York, McGraw-Hill.

Lipset, S.M. (1963), *Political Man*, Garden City, Anchor Books.

Lopez, G.A. and Stohl, M. (1992), 'Problems of Concept and Measurement in the Study of Human Rights', in. T.B. Jabine and R.P. Claude (eds.), *Human Rights and Statistics: Getting the Record Straight*, Philadelphia: University of Pennsylvania Press.

Madani, H. (1992), *Socioeconomic Development and Military Policy Consequences of Third World Military and Civilian Regimes 1965-1985*, unpublished Ph.D. dissertation, University of North Texas.

McCormick, J.M. and Mitchell., N.J. (1988), 'Is U.S. Aid Really Linked to Human Rights in Latin America?' *American Journal of Political Science*, Vol. 32(1), pp. 231-9.

McKinlay, R.D. and Cohen, A.S. (1975), 'A Comparative Analysis of the Political and Economic Performance of Military and Civilian Regimes', *Comparative Politics*, Vol. 8(1), pp. 1-30.

Meyer, W.H. (1998), *Human Rights and International Political Economy in Third World Nations*, Westport, CT, Praeger.

Milner, W.T., Poe, S.C. and Leblang, D. (1999), 'Security Rights, Subsistence Rights and Liberties: A Theoretical Survey of the Empirical Landscape', *Human Rights Quarterly*, Vol. 21(2), pp. 403-43.

Mitchell, N.J. and McCormick, J.N. (1988), 'Economic and Political Explanations of Human Rights Violations', *World Politics*, Vol. 40(4), pp. 476-98.

Moon, B. (1991), *The Political Economy of Basic Human Needs*, Ithaca, NY, Cornell University Press.

Moon, B. and Dixon, W. (1985), 'Politics, the State, and Basic Human Needs: A Cross-National Study', *American Journal of Political Science*, Vol. 29(4), pp. 661-94.

Moon, B.E. and Dixon, W.J. (1992), 'Basic Needs and Growth-Welfare Trade-Offs', *International Studies Quarterly*, Vol. 36(2), pp. 191-212.

Morris, M.D. (1979), *Measuring the Condition of the World's Poor: The Physical Quality of Life Index*, New York, Pergamon.

Nieburg, H.L. (1969), *Political Violence: The Behavioral Process*, New York, St. Martin's Press.

Park, H.S. (1987), 'Correlates of Human Rights: Global Tendencies', *Human Rights Quarterly*, Vol. 9, pp. 405-13.

Poe, S.C. and Tate, C.N. (1994), 'Repression of Human Rights to Personal Integrity in the 1980s: A Global Analysis', *American Political Science Review*, Vol. 88(4), pp. 853-72.

Poe, S.C., Tate, C.N., and Keith, L. (1999), 'Repression of the Human Right to Personal Integrity Revisited: A Global Crossnational Study Covering the Years 1976-1993', *International Studies Quarterly*, Vol. 43(2), pp. 291-315.

Rasler, K. (1986), 'War, Accommodation, and Violence in the United States, 1980-1970', *American Political Science Review*, Vol. 80(3), pp. 921-45.

Rosh, R. (1986), 'The Impact of Third World Defense Burdens on Basic Human Needs', *Policy Studies Journal*, Vol. 15, pp. 135-46.

Schoultz, L. (1981), 'U.S. Foreign Policy and Human Rights Violations in Latin America: A Comparative Analysis of Foreign Aid Distributions', *Comparative Politics*, Vol. 13(2), p.149-170.

Scully, G. (1988), 'The Institutional Framework and Economic Growth', J*ournal of Political Economy*, Vol. 96(3), pp. 652-62.

Shue, H. (1980), *Basic Rights: Subsistence, Affluence, and U.S. Foreign Policy,* Princeton, N.J., Princeton University Press.

Skocpol, T. (1979), *States and Social Revolutions: A Comparative Analysis of France, Russia, and China*, London, Cambridge University Press.

Small, M., and Singer, J.D. (1982), *Resort to Arms: International and Civil Wars, 1816-1980*, Beverly Hills, CA, Sage.

Spalding, N.L. (1985), 'Providing for Economic Human Rights: The Case of the Third World', *Policy Studies Journal*, Vol. 15, pp. 123-34.

Stohl, M. (1975), 'War and Domestic Political Violence: The Case of the United States, 1890-1970', *Journal of Conflict Resolution*, Vol. 19(3), pp. 379-416.

Stohl, M. (1976), *War and Domestic Political Violence: The American Capacity for Repression and Reaction*, Beverly Hills, CA, Sage.

Stohl, M., Carleton, D., and Johnson, S. (1984), 'Human Rights and U.S. Foreign Assistance from Nixon to Carter', *Journal of Peace Research*, Vol. 21(3), pp. 215-33.

Stohl, M., Carleton, D., and Johnson, S. (1984), 'Human Rights and U.S. Foreign Assistance from Nixon to Carter', *Journal of Peace Research*, Vol. 21(3), pp. 215-33.

Strouse, J.C. and Claude, R.P. (1976), 'Empirical Comparative Rights Research: Some Preliminary Tests of Development Hypotheses', in R.P. Claude (ed.), *Comparative Human Rights*, Baltimore, MD, Johns Hopkins University Press.

Tilly, C. (1978), *From Mobilization to Revolution*, Reading, MA, Addison-Wesley.

Toppen, J.J. (1996), 'Development and Human Rights: An Alternative Analysis', *Peace and Change*, Vol. 21, pp. 318-37.

Vanhanen, T. (1990), *The Process of Democratization: A Comparative Study of 147 States, 1980-88*, New York, Crane Russak.

Wolpin. M. (1986), 'State Terrorism and Repression in the Third World: Parameters and Prospects', in G.A. Lopez and M. Stohl (eds.), *Government Violence and Repression: An Agenda for Research*, Westport, CT, Greenwood Press.

Ziegenhagen, E.A. (1986), *The Regulation of Political Conflict*, New York, Praeger.

Chapter 7

Human Rights and Structural Adjustment: The Importance of Selection

M. Rodwan Abouharb and David L. Cingranelli[1]

Introduction

The World Bank, along with the International Monetary Fund (IMF), plays an important role in providing external capital for developing countries. Thus, it is not surprising that there has been much controversy over the lending practices of both of these international financial institutions. Most of the controversy has been centred upon the fairness of the structural adjustment conditions and the effects of these conditions on economic development and on the human rights practices of loan recipients (Sadasivam, 1997). In this work, the factors that increased or decreased the probability of a country's government receiving a structural adjustment loan (SAL) from either the World Bank or the IMF in the period from 1981 to 1993 are identified. The governments of 161 'significant' countries of the world are included in the analysis. The results are important for those who wish to assess the impact of structural adjustment loans on the human rights practices of recipients because one must determine whether it was the conditions imposed by the Bank or the IMF or the pre-existing situation that accounted for the impacts.

The results of our study indicate that states having a higher probability of receiving a World Bank or IMF loan were poorer, had larger populations and had higher levels of government respect for workers' rights. The World Bank also was less likely to give a loan to a country involved in interstate conflict. While Przeworski and Vreeland (2000) had found that the IMF preferred to give loans to more authoritarian states, we found that the IMF was slightly more likely to give loans to democratic states. It was also biased against giving loans to countries that had experienced recent economic growth. These findings provide evidence that both international financial institutions may be placing a higher priority on 'good governance' factors when making loan decisions (Kaufman et al., 2003).

Structural Adjustment Loans

The missions of the World Bank and the IMF, though still distinct, have increasingly overlapped. Today, the World Bank's core mission remains the promotion of economic growth and the eradication of poverty in less developed countries. At the same time, the Bank has also been involved in a number of 'bail-out' packages that have had the effect of providing liquidity support to countries in crisis. These 'bail-out' packages have similar objectives to those of the IMF. The core mission of IMF continues to be to maintain the stability of the monetary system and of the world economy in general. Like the World Bank, the Fund too has evolved over time. Through its Enhanced Structural Adjustment Facility (ESAF) program, the IMF provides assistance to countries in transition from socialism to capitalism and to less developed countries (Stiglitz, 1999). This programme of the IMF, and others like it, brings its mission closer to that of the World Bank.

There are somewhat different eligibility criteria for IMF and World Bank loans. Przeworski and Vreeland (2000) note that in order for states to be eligible for IMF loans, they must contribute a quota amount to the Fund that is proportional to the size of that country's economy. Loans or 'repurchases' of less than 25 per cent of the country's quota do not require agreement with the IMF. Larger repurchases require an agreement with the IMF. According to IMF policies, a balance of payments deficit or a foreign reserves crisis is the prerequisite for signing an IMF agreement (Przeworski and Vreeland, 2000). As of 2000, there were 182 eligible member countries. In comparison, World Bank eligibility is decidedly more opaque. The World Bank provides structures to offer finance to the poorest countries with the worst credit ratings through the International Development Association and to wealthier countries that have better credit rating through the International Bank for Reconstruction and Development (World Bank, 2002a). Wealthier countries pay a higher rate of interest and have a shorter loan repayment period. Though previous research on the impact of SALs has focused almost exclusively on the IMF, there is no reason to believe that the impact of certain World Bank loans would be any different. There is also no reason to expect that the loan selection criteria for SALs for the World Bank and IMF would be different.

Structural adjustment conditions required by the Bank and IMF are intended to encourage recipient governments to adopt what World Bank and IMF staff refer to as 'good governance' policies. Thomas Friedman refers to this set of good governance policies as 'the Golden Straightjacket':

> To fit into the Golden Straightjacket a country must either adopt, or be seen as moving toward, the following golden rules: making the private sector the primary engine of its economic growth, maintaining a low rate of inflation and price stability, shrinking the size of its state bureaucracy, maintaining as close to a balanced budget as possible, if not a surplus, eliminating and lowering tariffs on imported goods, removing restrictions on foreign investment, getting rid of quotas and domestic monopolies, increasing exports, privatizing state-owned industries and utilities,

> deregulating capital markets, making its currency convertible, opening its industries, stock and bond markets to direct foreign ownership and investment, deregulating its economy to promote as much domestic competition as possible, [and] eliminating government corruption, subsidies and kickbacks as much as possible (2000, p.105).

There is evidence that, in addition to Friedman's list, the multilateral banks are increasingly interested in encouraging more democracy and better human rights practices among their loan recipients (Kaufman et al., 2003). While exact structural adjustment measures insisted upon by the World Bank and IMF tend to differ on a case by case basis, common steps include reductions of social spending for such things as education, food subsidies, health services, income subsidies and housing and reductions in public employment (Franklin, 1997). All of these steps might reduce the level of government respect for certain economic and other internationally recognized human rights in recipient countries.

Notwithstanding this danger, the governments of less developed countries have little choice but to turn to the IMF and World Bank for the capital they need for development. Without the seal of approval of the IMF and the World Bank, it is difficult for a developing country to raise external capital from any sources. Traditionally, the World Bank is reluctant to lend money unless the IMF certifies that the country in question has a solid macro-economic framework. According to Stiglitz (1999), then speaking for the World Bank, this provision is well intentioned. Bank experience has shown that governments that cannot manage their overall economy do not do a good job managing foreign aid. Thus, it is not surprising that the US government and private banks are less willing to provide grants and loans unless the IMF and World Bank are willing to extend international credit as well (Pion-Berlin, 1984).

Which governments receive World Bank and IMF loans is decided by the Bank's Board of Directors. The World Bank and IMF use a weighted voting system for determining which loans are approved and which are denied. The weights assigned are roughly in proportion to the share of the Bank's development funds contributed by each of the member governments. For the last 25 years, the United States, Japan and Germany have accounted for more than half of all funds contributed (Banks and Muller, 2002), so it is reasonable to assume that the preferences of their country representatives have dominated the preferences of other members of the Bank's Board of Directors. World Bank and IMF representatives protest against any allegations that their lending policies are motivated by political considerations, but the internal decisionmaking process of the World Bank and IMF privileges the ideological perspectives of some governments over others, allows for logrolling and vote trading and in all other respects provides fertile ground for what, in any other context, would be called 'politics'.

The stated goal of the Bank is to promote economic growth and to reduce poverty in less developed countries (World Bank, 1992, 2002a). Through its public policy statements, the Bank has announced some of its loan selection rules. The code of practices by which the Bank operates recommends that the Bank give preference to applicants that have a capitalist ideology, have not nationalized private industry without providing fair compensation to the owners, are not able to borrow on the private market and are creditworthy (Van De Laar, 1980). These criteria created an unabashed bias against making loans to communist countries, though some (formerly) communist countries, including Yugoslavia and Romania, did receive them. The publicly stated criteria are also ambiguous enough to provide the Bank's Board of Directors considerable discretion. Terms such as 'capitalist ideology' and 'creditworthy' must be defined and applied to specific applicants. It is also likely that many governments that are not able to borrow on the private market are not creditworthy either. The Board's role then must also involve deciding how to reconcile these criteria.

Previous Research

As explained by Achen (1986), Heckman (1988), Przeworski and Vreeland (2000) and Vreeland (2002, 2003), issues of selection and randomization must be accounted for when assessing the impact of public policy. Collier (1991, p.114) nicely summarizes when he notes that one needs to 'disentangle' the impacts of the policy from any prior attributes that may also have an impact. Traditional single-stage models, like those used in previous large-N studies of the impact of IMF conditionality on human rights practices (Keith and Poe, 2000), implicitly assume a uni-directional causal relationship; that is, structural adjustment loans affect human rights practices. More likely, the relationship is simultaneous. Human rights practices affect the probability of loan receipt, while loans affect human rights practices, which, in turn, affect the subsequent probability of loan receipt. Thus, both SAL receipt and human rights practices are mutually dependent or endogenous variables. Application of a single-stage model to estimate these theoretical relationships will generate inconsistent parameter estimates (Gujarati, 1995). The methodological resolution to this conundrum is found in a variety of two-stage statistical models that disentangle the impact of these mutually dependent variables. This work estimates the first stage of that two-stage equation.

Examining the cases of IMF loans, Przeworski and Vreeland (2000) note that not all countries, which are eligible to receive loans, actually obtain them, in effect generating a non-random sample of cases. Thus variation in the independent variable will not help generate valid inferences about the potential effects of adjustment programs since the structure of countries which do and do not receive loans is non-random. The possibility of a non-random sample of cases means that researchers of the adjustment process must also deal with the potential problems of case selection in that there may be a connection between the non-random sample of countries that receive these loans and the effects attributed to the adjustment process. Studies that utilize a method that does not account for case selection where there are good theoretical reasons to suspect that it might be present can lead to biased parameter estimates and in some cases substantively change the nature of conclusions drawn (Przeworski and Vreeland, 2000; Vreeland, 2001).

Przeworski and Vreeland (2000) and later work by Vreeland (2002, 2003) model both the determinants and consequences of IMF programs on economic growth and labour. In comparison to most of the work concerning the impacts of IMF loans, they model the factors that change the probability of receiving any kind of IMF loan. Working from an economic perspective, their excellent work places an emphasis on the economics of potential loan recipients that make them more or less likely to sign an IMF program. There are indications that both the IMF and World Bank are not random in their choices of countries for receipt of SALs (World Bank, 1992, 2002a; Stiglitz, 2002). Indeed, according to IMF policies, a balance of payments deficit or a foreign reserves crisis is the prerequisite for signing an IMF agreement (Przeworski and Vreeland, 2000). If the Bank and Fund were random in their choice of loan recipient then the issue would be moot and we could have confidence in the existing studies, which compared recipient and non-recipient countries.

If one is interested in assessing the impact of World Bank SALs, then methods that compare countries that did and did not receive loans (e.g., Harrigan and Mosley, 1991) or engage in before and after assessments of a particular country (e.g., Sowa, 1993; McLaren, 1998), while improving our knowledge of the process still need to account for the crucial issues of selection and randomization. McLaren (1998), for example, studied the effects of IMF SALs on government respect for personal integrity rights in Peru, Argentina and Brazil between 1976 and 1993. She drew her conclusions based on the changes in respect for physical integrity rights subsequent to the award of a SAL over that time period. She concludes that there was a one or two-year lag, but that the SAL worsened human rights practices in Peru and Brazil, but improved them in Argentina (McLaren 1998, p.21). She also speculates that, while the short-term human rights impacts are variable, the long-term impacts of IMF SALs are likely to be negative for all recipients (McLaren, 1998, p.23). Her insights concerning lag times and potentially different short and long-term impacts are important, but her findings about the impacts of the SALs in those countries are suspect. We have no way of knowing whether the positive or negative impacts she attributes to SALs are the result of the SALs or because of the pre-existing situation in the country under examination. It is thus critical to determine the process that increases or reduces the probability of loan receipt before any research can make substantive claims concerning the impact of World Bank or IMF loans on the particular dependent variable of interest.

Even single-stage, large-N comparative studies, comparing cases where the intervention occurred with cases where it did not, controlling for other factors that might have affected the dependent variable of interest, are problematic. Keith and Poe (2000) for example, sought to evaluate the effects of getting an IMF SAL by comparing the human rights practices of governments with and without such loans, while controlling for other factors reliably associated with good or bad human rights practices of governments. Keith and Poe focused on a global sample of countries between 1981 and 1987, finding a weak short-term increase in the level of repression following the receipt of an IMF SAL.

Using cross-sectional analysis, Franklin's (1997) work reflects mixed findings with respect to arguments concerning the impact of conditionality. He finds little support for the argument that governments implementing IMF agreements are more likely to pre-empt dissent through repression, with only one of the three years he tests reflecting a statistically significant relationship between conditionality and pre-emptive repression. He also finds no support for arguments that IMF conditionality leads to protest, which generates repression. In comparison, he finds support for the argument that conditionality, when it limits the resources available to leaders, to placate potential opposition, increases the use of repression in two out of the three years examined in his study. However, generating valid inferences on the basis of variation in the independent variable is premised on the idea that variation in the independent variable will, in effect, produce a sample that is not systematically biased.

There have been some studies of the loan selection criteria used by the IMF, the World Bank and other regional multilateral development banks to determine which countries should receive SALs. A number of scholars have suggested that these banks essentially serve as instruments of US foreign policy. Forsythe (1987) wrote that, during the Reagan administration, the US representative voted for loans to right-wing allies and voted against loans to left-wing governments. On the other hand, US laws instruct its representatives on the boards of these banks to oppose loans to countries that have a pattern of serious human rights abuses, excepting loans for basic human needs.

There are also a number of more quantitative studies of loan recipients. Frey and Schneider (1986) conducted a study of 60 loan recipients in 1981 and 1982, examining the characteristics of countries most likely to receive the largest loans from the World Bank. Among the loan recipients, loans were bigger if the loan recipient showed a high degree of economic need (per capita income was low, the rate of inflation was high, external debt was high and past economic growth was poor). They received bigger loans from the IBRD if they were politically stable and they had a good 'capitalist climate.' Unfortunately, studies of the recipients of World Bank loans tell us nothing about loan selection criteria. Since Frey and Schneider (1986) only sought to answer questions about World Bank loan recipients, they tell us nothing about the selection rules of the Bank.

The most careful quantitative research on selection criteria has focused on the IMF and has given disproportionate attention to potential economic selection criteria (Joyce, 1992; Przeworski and Vreeland, 2000). Most recently, research on selection criteria has been conducted as part of a two-stage model to estimate the effects of IMF loans on economic growth (Przeworski and Vreeland, 2000). Previous research results have been divided on whether a balance of payments deficit is sufficient to explain agreements or not. Economic factors are part of the explanation, but the literature suggests that they do not provide a complete picture. Przeworski and Vreeland (2000) find, for example, that, controlling for economic loan selection criteria, democratic governments are less likely to get an IMF loan than authoritarian governments. More generally, there is a growing consensus that, besides economic selection criteria publicly acknowledged by the World Bank and the IMF, a variety of political, institutional and social characteristics of potential recipient governments also affects the probability of receiving a SAL (Forsythe, 1987; Joyce, 1992).

Besides economic and political selection rules, there is good reason to believe that the multilateral development banks prefer to give SALs to countries that are not involved in conflict. However, there has been little, if any, attention to how conflict proneness domestically or internationally affects the probability of getting a loan from either international financial institution. There is a strong theoretical basis to believe that if the Bank and IMF operate like other banks, they would view involvement in both domestic and international conflict as factors reducing the probability of prospective agreements being implemented and existing loans being repaid in a timely manner. Countries in conflict are a poor investment. If there is domestic unrest, a new government may be installed, and previous agreements made by the government, including those made with the World Bank, may not be honoured. Argentina is a good example where, during the 2000-2002 period, large-scale riots led to a revolving door of presidents and administrations, generating considerable uncertainty about the likelihood of IMF loan repayment. Similarly, if a potential recipient is involved in a war with another state, the governments of the warring parties may be conquered and replaced. Once again previous agreements might not be honoured by the new regime. Both these situations would lead us to believe that the Bank is less likely to loan to countries involved in domestic or international conflict.

There also is some suspicion that the Bank and the IMF prefer giving loans to governments that are more willing to repress workers' rights and personal integrity rights. Klak (1996), who studied the Caribbean basin with special emphasis on Jamaica, argues that structural adjustment conditions provide indirect incentives to limit workers' rights in order to be more competitive internationally. He notes the establishment of Export Processing Zones (EPZs), where international corporations are encouraged to invest for export purposes, which have long-term exemptions from taxes and duties. These EPZs are looked upon favourably by the World Bank (Klak, 1996, p.358). In an effort to make these EPZs as competitive as possible Klak notes (1996, p.358), the governments of developing countries attempt to keep wages and rental rates for industrial space low. Thus, labour loses out in order to make countries as attractive as possible to international investors. Pion-Berlin (1984), in his analysis of Argentina's relationship with the IMF from 1955-80, makes a more controversial argument that the IMF rewarded Argentina when its government was willing to repress organized labour in order to quell domestic protest against the implementation of liberal economic policies. In contrast, Nelson (2000) contends that the Bank has in fact had a long-standing commitment to maintaining labour standards, because Bank officials believe that such standards actually promote economic growth. This is the first large-N, comparative study to examine the effects of respect for workers' rights on the probability of obtaining a SAL from the World Bank or IMF.

Two studies have also asked whether the degree of protection of personal integrity rights affected the probability of receiving a SAL from a multilateral bank. On the basis of a bivariate analysis, Keith and Poe (2000) present evidence showing that countries with recent histories of serious human rights abuse were not excluded from receiving an IMF SAL. Going even further, they concluded that 'countries with extensive political imprisonment were actually more likely to receive loans than countries with better human rights practices' (Keith and Poe, 2000, p.285). Neumeyer's (2003) quantitative analysis of the distribution of grants and loans by regional multilateral development banks, as well as some United Nations agencies, concluded that there was no relationship between government respect for personal integrity human rights and the amount of aggregate multilateral aid received.

Hypotheses

Previous research suggests that there are four categories of factors – economic, political, conflict and human rights - that help determine the probability of receiving a SAL. Since both the IMF and the World Bank insist upon the imposition of structural adjustment conditions for loan recipients and since both use a similar weighted voting system for deciding upon loan applications, one would expect that the loan selection criteria of both institutions would be similar. Those possible selection rules are reflected in the hypotheses described in Table 7.1.

Research Design

This study uses a cross-national, annual time-series dataset comprised of all nations of the world having a population of at least 500,000 in 1981. The data span the time period from 1981 to 1993. Both the IMF and World Bank have given SALs to a number of more economically developed countries. During the 1981-93 period, the World Bank awarded SALs to countries with a GDP per capita as high as $13,478, and the IMF to countries with a GDP per capita as high as $11,290. For this reason, the analysis includes all countries in the world, not just less developed countries.

The analysis uses logit regressions, which allow estimation of an equation where the dependent variable takes on only two values. For example, the IMF and World Bank can decide to award a loan or not. Thus the dependent variable indicates either receipt or no receipt of a loan. Some countries in our sample received loans from both the IMF and the World Bank; others received a SAL from one, but not the other, and still others did not receive a SAL from either institution during the entire period covered by the study. Between 1981 and 1993, the IMF awarded 247 SALs to countries in our sample; the World Bank awarded 258.

As noted in Table 7.1, it is hypothesized that two types of human rights practices – respect for personal integrity rights and respect for workers' rights – by potential recipient governments might affect the selection process of the IMF or the World Bank awarding SALs. The human rights measure used in this analysis is the Mokken Scale developed by Cingranelli and Richards (1999) of four physical integrity rights - extrajudicial killings, disappearances, political imprisonment and torture.

Table 7.1 Hypotheses and data sources

Independent Variable	Probability of Loan Receipt	Indicator	Source
Economic			
Growth in GDP Per Capita	Reduces	% Change in GDP Per Capita Current U.S.$	World Bank: WDI
Larger Foreign Currency Reserves	Reduces	Average Government Foreign Reserves to reflect Monthly Imports.	World Bank: WDI
Higher Exchange Rate Value	Increases	Average Annual Official exchange rate Local Currency Unit per U.S.$	World Bank: WDI
Higher GDP Per Capita	Reduces	GDP Per Capita Current U.S.$	World Bank: WDI
Political			
Alliance With the United States	Increases	Correlates of War Alliance Variable	Gibler and Sarkees (2002)
Extent of Trade	Reduces	Trade % of GDP	World Bank: WDI
Higher Levels of Democracy	Reduces	Democracy-Autocracy Measure	POLITY IV
Larger Populations	Increases	Logged Midyear Country Population	U.S. Govt. Census: I.D.B
Conflict			
More Domestic Conflict	Reduces	Weighted Sum of Dom. Conflict: strikes, assassinations, guerrilla warfare, govt. crises, riots, revolutions, anti-govt demos	Banks (2000)
More External Conflict	Reduces	Ordinal Level of Interstate Conflict	Strand et. al (2002)
Human Rights			
More Respect for Human Rights	Increases	Index of Killing, Disappearances, Torture and Imprisonment	Cingranelli and Richards (1999a)
More Respect for Workers' Rights	Increases	0=Not protected by Govt; 1=Somewhat protected by Govt; 2=Protected by Govt.	Cingranelli (2002)

Information about the level of respect governments around the world provided for important workers' rights was taken form the U.S. State Department's annual *Country Reports on Human Rights Practices*. This report, published since 1974, includes analyses of workers' rights in each country's report. The workers' rights reported on are those that are defined in Section 502(a) of the Trade Act of 1974. These are freedom of association, the effective recognition of the right to collective bargaining, the elimination of all forms of forced or compulsory labour, the effective abolition of child labour and acceptable conditions of work with respect to minimum wages, hours of work and occupational safety and health. This list is much the same as the International Labour Organization's list of five core labour rights. The variable was coded on a three-point scale as follows. Workers' rights are:

1. not protected by the government;
2. somewhat protected by the government;
3. protected by the government.

Cingranelli (2002) provides a full description of the coding procedure.

Results

The results of the logit regression analysis are presented in Table 7.2. Although it was hypothesized that the loan selection criteria of the IMF and the World Bank would be the same, the results show some modest differences in the selection rules of both institutions. There is a core of three factors affecting the selection processes of both institutions in the same way. Both have a higher probability of awarding SALs to the governments of countries with relatively low gross domestic product per capita, relatively large populations and higher levels of respect for workers rights. In each case, the finding was as hypothesized.

The IMF was also less likely to loan to countries experiencing economic growth, in line with expectations. In contrast with expectations, the IMF was more likely to loan increasingly democratic countries, while the Bank was neither more nor less likely to loan to different kinds of regimes. In addition to the criteria noted above, the World Bank was also less likely to give SALs to the governments of countries involved in interstate conflict. In contrast, domestic and international unrest does not seem to play a role in the IMF's calculations.

Both institutions had a bias towards countries with lower gross domestic products per capita. There is some indication that the IMF chose to help countries with distressed economies, with respect to the finding concerning the change in GDP per capita. Other indicators of economic distress, including a low level of foreign currency reserves and overvalued exchange rates, were statistically insignificant.

Table 7.2 Logistic regression results of World Bank and IMF selection criteria, 1981-93

<table>
<tr><th>Independent Variables</th><th>Probability of A World Bank SAL 1981-1993</th><th>P>|z</th><th>Probability of An IMF SAL 1981-1993</th><th>P>|z</th></tr>
<tr><td>Economic</td><td></td><td></td><td></td><td></td></tr>
<tr><td>Positive Percent</td><td>-0.0005</td><td>0.08</td><td>-0.001</td><td>0.007**</td></tr>
<tr><td>Change GDP Per Capita</td><td>(0.0003)</td><td></td><td>(0.0003)</td><td></td></tr>
<tr><td>Average Foreign</td><td>-0.0568</td><td>0.056</td><td>-0.008</td><td></td></tr>
<tr><td>Currency Reserves</td><td>(0.036)</td><td></td><td>(0.033)</td><td>0.408</td></tr>
<tr><td>Exchange Rate</td><td>-0.0001</td><td>0.188</td><td>-0.001</td><td></td></tr>
<tr><td>Value</td><td>(0.0001)</td><td></td><td>(0.0002)</td><td>0.285</td></tr>
<tr><td>GDP Per Capita</td><td>-0.0002</td><td>0.000***</td><td>-0.0004</td><td>0.000***</td></tr>
<tr><td></td><td>(0.00003)</td><td></td><td>(0.00005)</td><td></td></tr>
<tr><td>Extent of Trade</td><td>-0.002</td><td>0.256</td><td>0.003</td><td></td></tr>
<tr><td></td><td>(0.003)</td><td></td><td>(0.003)</td><td>0.16</td></tr>
<tr><td>Political</td><td></td><td></td><td></td><td></td></tr>
<tr><td>Alliance With the</td><td>0.034</td><td>0.305</td><td>0.044</td><td>0.2775</td></tr>
<tr><td>United States</td><td>(0.068)</td><td></td><td>(0.075)</td><td></td></tr>
<tr><td>Level of</td><td>0.02</td><td>0.097</td><td>0.038</td><td></td></tr>
<tr><td>Democracy</td><td>(0.015)</td><td></td><td>(0.016)</td><td>0.01**</td></tr>
<tr><td>Larger Populations</td><td>0.284</td><td>0.001***</td><td>0.12</td><td></td></tr>
<tr><td></td><td>(0.072)</td><td></td><td>(0.069)</td><td>0.043*</td></tr>
<tr><td>Conflictual</td><td></td><td></td><td></td><td></td></tr>
<tr><td>More Domestic</td><td>-0.001</td><td>0.069</td><td>-0.0002</td><td></td></tr>
<tr><td>Conflict</td><td>(0.0004)</td><td></td><td>(0.0004)</td><td>0.324</td></tr>
<tr><td>More External</td><td>-0.586</td><td>0.04*</td><td>-0.02</td><td></td></tr>
<tr><td>Conflict</td><td>(0.333)</td><td></td><td>(0.251)</td><td>0.469</td></tr>
<tr><td>Human Rights</td><td></td><td></td><td></td><td></td></tr>
<tr><td>Level of Respect</td><td>0.012</td><td>0.393</td><td>-0.0325</td><td>0.262</td></tr>
<tr><td>for Personal Integrity Rights</td><td>(0.046)</td><td></td><td>(0.051)</td><td></td></tr>
<tr><td>Level of Respect</td><td>0.268</td><td>0.017*</td><td>0.235</td><td></td></tr>
<tr><td>for Workers Rights</td><td>(0.126)</td><td></td><td>(0.127)</td><td>0.032*</td></tr>
<tr><td>Constant</td><td>-5.282</td><td>0.000***</td><td>-2.827</td><td></td></tr>
<tr><td></td><td>(1.257)</td><td></td><td>(1.209)</td><td>0.01**</td></tr>
<tr><td>N</td><td>1167</td><td></td><td>1167</td><td></td></tr>
<tr><td>Pseudo R2</td><td>0.1223</td><td></td><td>0.1438</td><td></td></tr>
<tr><td>Pr. χ2</td><td></td><td>0.000***</td><td></td><td>0.000***</td></tr>
</table>

Standard errors in parentheses.
* p<0.05, **p<0.01, ***p<0 .001 One tailed test.

Neither institution favoured giving SALs to countries that had alliances with the United States. Both the IMF and the World Bank had a loan selection bias in favour of governments that respected the rights of workers; a finding that runs directly contrary to the hypothesis derived from dependency theory. Most importantly, given our interest in the human rights consequences of selection rules, neither institution showed a higher probability of awarding a SAL to the governments of countries having a relatively low level of respect for the physical integrity rights of their citizens.

Discussion

This study examined the loan selection criteria of the IMF and World Bank when negotiating structural adjustment loans. The main question was whether selection biases existed that might have ultimately affected conclusions about the impact of SALs on the human rights practices of loan recipients. This is one of only a few scientific studies to examine the IMF's loan selection criteria and the only one to examine the World Bank's selection rules.

Perhaps the most puzzling finding to emerge from this investigation was that democracies were not at a disadvantage when attempting to conclude SAL negotiations with the World Bank and that they actually had an advantage when negotiating with the IMF. This finding may indicate that the Putnam's (1988) two-level games theory, which suggests that the presence of domestic politics hamstrings democracies in their dealings with international institutions is not useful in the context of IMF and World Bank SAL negotiations. More likely, it indicates that the loan selection bias in favour of democracies by both the IMF and the Bank is so strong that it allows democracies to overcome their negotiation disadvantages. Przeworski and Vreeland (2000), who examined the selection bias of the IMF for or against democracies when making all loans, found a bias against democratic states. Our study does not cover exactly the same time period and uses a different measure of democracy, and the different results may be explained by these research design differences, but, at the very least, this relationship deserves more scrutiny.

Our results suggest that, in addition to the stated economic criteria of the World Bank and IMF, there are important political selection rules at work. Both institutions showed a bias towards providing SALs to the governments of countries with large populations, all other things being equal, the most important players in the international system, and both favoured governments that respected the rights of their workers. The World Bank also avoided providing SALs to the governments of countries involved in external conflicts, while the IMF was more likely to give loans to democratic governments. These findings indicate that future work on the selection criteria of the IMF and Bank should examine other domestic level characteristics of states that might increase or decrease the probability of receiving a structural adjustment loan.

One of the more interesting domestic level characteristics examined in this study was the level of respect for workers' rights in potential loan recipient states.

As noted above, the case study literature is full of stories suggesting that the IMF seeks out loan recipients willing to be tough, even repressive in the face of domestic protest against the implementation of liberal economic policies. Pion-Berlin (1984) cogently argued that Argentina, at several points in its history, increased its repression of labour, especially organized labour, in order to convince the IMF that it had the fortitude to implement economic liberalization policies. We found no evidence of lower levels of respect for workers' rights among the recipients of IMF loans in our world sample from 1981 to 1993. There was evidence that both institutions were actually more likely to give SALs to states, which have a higher level of respect for workers' rights, perhaps because these rights are viewed as more conducive to economic growth, a key policy aim of both the World Bank and IMF.

Although neither the IMF nor the World Bank had a higher probability of providing SALs to the governments of countries that showed little respect for the physical integrity rights of their citizens, the selection criteria uncovered in this analysis still should be accounted for when assessing the human rights effects of SALs on loan recipients. Some of the factors shown to positively affect either the World Bank or the IMF's decision to award a SAL – higher levels of democracy and less external conflict – are also factors that have been shown to be associated with higher levels of government respect for physical integrity rights. Other factors that increase the probability of receiving a SAL from either the IMF or World Bank - a lower level of gross domestic product per capita and a large population - have been shown to be associated with lower levels of respect for physical integrity rights.

While these substantive results are important, the main point we wish to make is about the appropriate research strategy for assessing the effects of SALs on loan recipients. While previous research has focused on the uni-directional effects of structural adjustment conditions on the human rights practices of loan recipients, the actual relationship between loan selection and human rights practices is mutually dependent. As shown here, some human rights practices, such as the level of government respect for workers' rights, affect the probability of loan receipt. Receiving the loans and implementing the structural adjustment conditions probably affects subsequent human rights practices, which, in turn, affect the subsequent probability of loan receipt. The process through which SALs affect the human rights practices of recipients has two stages, and the relationship between the two stages is mutually dependent.

Note

1 We would like to thank James Raymond Vreeland for his assistance and the sharing of his data. Any errors are entirely our own.

References

Achen, C.H. (1986), *The Statistical Analysis of Quasi Experiments,* University of California Press, Berkeley.

Banks, A. S. (2002), *Cross-national time-series data archive* [computer file], Computer Solutions Unlimited, Binghamton, New York.

Banks, A. S. and Muller, T. (Annual), *Political Handbook of the World*, Binghamton University, Binghamton, New York.

Cingranelli, D.L. (2002), 'Democratization, Economic Globalization, and Workers' Rights', in E.A. McMahon and T.A.P. Sinclair (eds), *Democratic Institutional Performance: Research and Policy Perspectives*, Westport, Praeger Press, pp. 139-58.

Cingranelli, D.L. and Richards, D.L. (1999), 'Measuring the Level, Pattern, and Sequence of Government Respect for Physical Integrity Rights', *International Studies Quarterly*, Vol. 43(2), pp. 407-18.

Collier, D. (1991), 'The Comparative Method: Two Decades of Change', in D. Rustow and K. Erickson (eds), *Comparative Political Dynamics*: *Global Research Perspectives,* New York, HarperCollins.

Forsythe, D. (1987), 'Congress and Human Rights in U.S. Foreign Policy: The Fate of General Legislation', *Human Rights Quarterly,* Vol. 9, pp. 391-411.

Franklin, J. (1997), 'IMF Conditionality, Threat Perception, and Political Repression: A Cross-National Analysis', *Comparative Political Studies,* Vol. 30, pp. 576-606.

Frey, B.S. and Schneider, F. (1986), 'Competing Models of International Lending Activity', *Journal of Development Economics,* Vol. 20, pp. 225-45.

Friedman, T.L. (2000), *The Lexus and the Olive Tree*, New York, Anchor Books.

Gujarati, D. (1995), *Basic Econometrics,* 3rd edition, New York, McGraw Hill.

Harrigan, J. and Mosley, P. (1991), 'Assessing the Impact of World Bank Structural Development Lending 1980-1987', *The Journal of Development Studies*, Vol. 27(3), pp. 63-94.

Heckman, J.J. (1988), 'The Microeconomic Evaluation of Social Programs and Economic Institutions', in *Chung-Hua Series of Lectures by Invited Eminent Economists*, No. 14, The Institute of Economics Academia Sinica, Taipei.

Joyce, J.P. (1992), 'The Economic Characteristics of IMF Program Countries,' *Economics Letters*, Vol. 38, pp. 237-42.

Kaufman, D., Kraay, A. and Mastruzzi, M. (2003), 'Governance Matters III: Governance Indicators for 1996-2002.'
Available from www.worldbank.org/wbi/governance/govdata2002/ Accessed 1 June 2003

Keith, L.C. and Poe, S.C. (2000), 'The United States, the IMF, and Human Rights', in D.F. Forsythe (ed.), *The United States and Human Rights,* University of Nebraska Press, Lincoln, Nebraska pp. 273-299.

Klak, T. (1996), 'Distributional Impacts of the "Free Zone" Component of Structural Adjustment: The Jamaican Experience', *Growth and Change*, Vol. 27 (Summer), pp. 352-87.

McLaren, L.M. (1998), 'The Effect of IMF Austerity Programs on Human Rights Violations: An Exploratory Analysis of Peru, Argentina, and Brazil', Paper presented at the 1998 Meeting of the Midwest Political Science Association.

Nelson, P. (2000), 'Whose civil society? Whose governance? Decision-making and practice in the new agenda at the Inter-American Development Bank and the World Bank', *Global Governance*, Vol. 6(4), pp. 405-31.

Neumeyer, E. (2003), 'The Determinants of Aid allocation by Regional Multilateral Banks and United Nations Agencies', *International Studies Quarterly,* Vol. 47(1), pp.101-22.

Pion-Berlin, D. (1984), 'The Political Economy of State Repression in Argentina', in M. Stohl and G.A. Lopez (eds), *The State as Terrorist: The Dynamics of Governmental Violence and Repression,* Westport, Connecticut, Greenwood Press, pp. 99-123.

POLITY IV. (2000), *POLITY IV,* Available from http://weber.ucsd.edu/~kgledits/Polity.html (Accessed 1 June 2003).

Putnam, R. D. (1988), 'Diplomacy and Domestic Politics: The Logic of Two-level Games', *International Organization,* Vol. 42(3), pp. 427-60.

Przeworski, A. and Vreeland, J.R. (2000), 'The Effects of IMF Programs on Economic Growth', *The Journal of Development Economics,* Vol. 62, pp. 385-421.

Sadasivam, B. (1997), 'The Impact of Structural Adjustment on Women: A Governance and Human Rights Agenda', *Human Rights Quarterly,* Vol. 19(3), pp. 630-55.

Sowa, N.K. (1993), 'Ghana', in A. Adepoju (ed.), *The Impact of Structural Adjustment on the Population of Africa',* United Nations Population Fund, Heinemann, New Hampshire, pp. 7-24.

Stiglitz, J.E. (1999), 'The World Bank at the Millennium', *Economic Journal,* Vol. 109(459), pp. 577-97.

Strand, H., Wilhelmsen, L. and Gleditsch, N.P. (2002), 'Armed Conflict Dataset Codebook', Version 1.1, 9 September, Available from http://www.prio.no/cwp/ArmedConflict/ Accessed 16 March 2003.

United States Census Bureau (2003), *International Data Base,* Available from http://www.census.gov/ipc/www/idbsprd.html, Accessed 16 March 2003.

Van De Laar, A. (1980), *The World Bank and the Poor,* Boston, Nijhof.

Vreeland, J.R. (2001), 'Institutional Determinants of IMF Agreements', Available from http://pantheon.yale.edu/~jrv9/Veto.pdf, Accessed 1 June 2003.

Vreeland, J.R. (2002), 'The Effect of IMF Programs on Labor', *World Development,* Vol. 30(1), pp. 121-39.

Vreeland, J.R. (2003), *The IMF and Economic Development,* Cambridge University Press.

World Bank (1992), The World Bank Operational Manual: Operational Directive Adjustment Lending Policy (OD 8.60), Available from http:wbln0018.worldbank.org/institutional/manuals/opmanual.nsf, Accessed 1 June 2003.

World Bank (2002a), 'Country Eligibility for Borrowing from the World Bank (IBRD/IDA)', Available from http://www.worldbank.org/about/organization/members/eligibility.htm, Accessed 1 June 2003.

World Bank (2002b), *World Development Indicators,* CD-ROM.

PART IV
LEGAL AND INSTITUTIONAL DETERMINANTS OF HUMAN RIGHTS

Introduction to Part IV

The fourth section of the volume addresses an increasingly important issue that has received little attention from the academic community. The two chapters investigate legal and institutional aspects of human rights. The call for institutionalizing both the provision of human rights and the punishment of their violations has grown over the past several decades. And making these issues more pressing is that members of the community of nations have increasingly found themselves setting up new governments in the aftermath of violent struggles. At the beginning of the twenty-first century the United Nations was faced with the task of building from scratch a new government in East Timor, after violence raged in that country destroying most of its infrastructure. As this book goes to press, the United States and Britain face a similar task in Iraq, after overthrowing the repressive government of Saddam Hussein. These events demand greater knowledge of the effects of various governing institutions and constitutions on human rights. Some scholars are responding by seeking instruments of law that can be used to uphold human rights standards in the affected areas.

Apart from institutionalizing the respect of human rights, the legal prosecution of perpetrators has also been further implemented over recent years. In 1995 the International Criminal Tribunal for Rwanda has been set up by the UN Security Council to prosecute serious violations of international humanitarian law during the genocide in 1994, and in 2002 the United Nations and Sierra Leone set up a special court for war crimes committed during the 10-year civil war. The chapters in the fourth section of this collection address these issues of legal and institutional determinants of human rights.

The contribution by Jim Meernik and Kimi King is one of the very first empirical studies to examine sentencing by International Criminal Tribunals. It represents an important innovation in the study of the punishment of human rights abuses. The authors investigate sentencing by the International Criminal Tribunals for the former Yugoslavia. The academic and legal communities have been divided over the question of whether there are some crimes against humanity that are more heinous than others, and whether other crimes must be punished more severely in order to provide redress to victims. Some have argued that crimes which exhibit bias against a people, such as genocide, deserve the harshest sanctions, while others have argued that it is the act itself – murder – that is most important, not the category of crime to which it belongs. Meernik and King find that judges make important distinctions between both the general categories of offences, as well as the specific types of crimes. This chapter concludes that the Tribunal judges punish bias crimes against people more harshly, but also make distinctions among the more specific types of offences, such as murder, torture and rape.

Linda Camp Keith analyzes in her chapter the linkage between constitutional provisions and the violation of human rights between 1973 and 1996. Over the past several decades we have seen the development of a nearly universal acceptance of the International Bill of Human Rights and a concomitant movement toward formally adopting these rights in written constitutions. Yet some human rights scholars remain sceptical of whether we can truly achieve the internationalization of human rights. Camp Keith investigates the effect of constitutional provisions, such as the provision for fair trial and formal judicial independence, in various regions of the world. This study is by far the most comprehensive examination of the effect of constitutions to date. The findings indicate that written constitutions do indeed make a difference in human rights practices. Most constitutional provisions have a stable impact across regions, but a few interesting regional variations arise. The results should be of interest to policy makers and those who are interested in 'engineering' constitutions to create greater respect for human dignity.

Chapter 8

Crimes and Punishments: How the International Criminal Tribunal for the Former Yugoslavia Distinguishes Among Massive Human Rights Violations

James D. Meernik and Kimi L. King

Introduction

The International Criminal Tribunal for the former Yugoslavia (ICTY), established under United Nations Security Council authority and the UN Charter Chapter VII, is supposed to bring to justice accused war criminals, further peace and reconciliation in the Balkans and to promote deterrence of future international crimes. Initially, critics disparaged the Tribunal as an attempt by the major powers to absolve themselves of responsibility for their inaction during the Balkan wars (see Holbrooke, 1998, p.190; Beigbeder, 1999, p.46; Bass, 2000, p.207; Robertson, 2000, p.286). Over time, however, the ICTY has gained custody of top ranking, indicted war criminals and completed numerous trials, and the discussion has shifted from questioning the Tribunal's creation to analyzing the judicial standards and procedures by which the ICTY carries out the UN mandate. How does the Tribunal provide justice to the victims of war crimes and genocide while ensuring that the accused are granted fair and impartial hearings?

Key to achieving this goal is the punishment meted out to persons proved guilty beyond a reasonable doubt. Tribunal judges must find a penalty that provides redress to the victims, is commensurate in some manner to the scope and nature of the crimes committed and also considers the individual circumstances of each defendant. The Tribunal judges are not allowed to impose the death penalty; nor can they impose a fine on the guilty party, although they can order restitution. The guilty are sentenced to some number of months in prison. In many respects these decisions are the most visible and important ones the ICTY makes for they signal the international community's attribution of blame and condemnation for some of the worst human rights atrocities committed since World War II. If these judgments are perceived as fair and consistent with international rules of law, it will further the Tribunal's other missions to restore peace and promote reconciliation in the region (Keller, 2001). Judgments viewed as biased or inconsistent applications of international law may well leave the injured communities in the former Yugoslavia still divided over the origins of their wars and may perpetuate the cycle of violence. The precedents established by the ICTY will also be critical as the international community establishes the first permanent international criminal tribunal, the International Criminal Court (ICC). As the ICC will be heavily relying upon the decisions of the ad hoc tribunals, there is a critical need for fair, clear and consistent judicial opinions regarding the punishment of war criminals.

Given the systemic and heinous nature of the atrocities committed during the conflicts in the former Yugoslavia, we must wonder how the judges find punishments that are both proportionate to the crimes committed and based on the unique circumstances of each convicted person. In particular, have the ICTY's sentences reflected the general type of offence of which an individual is found guilty, such as war crimes or genocide, or are the judges more concerned about providing punishment based upon the specific criminal acts committed, such as murder or rape? Furthermore, do the judges distinguish between categories of international crimes – war crimes[1], crimes against humanity and genocide – when rendering judgments? Because the ICTY Statute provides the judges with a great deal of discretion in their decision-making and because there are so few precedents regarding punishment for international crimes (because international criminal tribunals have been so rare in history), we must wonder how the judges determine punishment for such massive abuses of human rights.

We will argue that the general categories of crimes will prove more influential in sentencing than the specific criminal acts and that the judges have constructed a hierarchy of criminal offences. First, we believe that while the specific criminal acts will be predictive of sentencing decisions, the general categories of crimes will provide the judges with greater historical and legal precedent as well as a more efficient decision making methodology for punishing individuals. Second, there is reason to believe that genocide and crimes against humanity are considered especially atrocious and deserving of harsher sanctions than war crimes. These crimes involve widespread and intentional targeting of civilians and innocents outside an armed conflict. As such, they are fundamentally different and more heinous than war crimes that do not involve such actions (Danner, 2001).

In this chapter, we first discuss the relevant portions of the ICTY statute regarding prosecutable offences and judicial decision-making. We then analyze the impact of the general categories of crimes and the specific criminal offences on sentences handed down to date by the ICTY. Finally, we summarize the results and assess their meaning in light of the Tribunal's mission to 'do justice' for victims and the accused.

Categorizing Crimes in the ICTY's Statute

The ICTY, established in 1993, is authorized to investigate and prosecute specific violations of international laws occurring in the former Yugoslavia since 1991. The Tribunal is responsible for trying cases involving: 1) grave breaches of the Geneva conventions regarding the treatment of soldiers and civilians in wartime; 2) violations of the laws and customs of war; 3) genocide; and 4) crimes against humanity. The violations of human rights during the Balkan wars were political and systemic, as well as vicious and personal. Political and military leaders adopted and planned campaigns to remove or exterminate peoples and inspired thousands of agreeable bureaucrats and zealous foot soldiers to execute their orders. Sorting out the guilty from the not guilty, the willing from the unwilling and the truly evil from the merely terrible is a legally and morally dense task for the ICTY judges. They must judge acts that, had they been committed under 'ordinary circumstances' and tried in a domestic court, might all warrant life imprisonment. Yet, the judges have chosen not to treat all crimes alike and impose the same sentence on all the guilty. How is it that judges make these decisions? Which criteria do they use to differentiate among the many horrible violations when they sentence those found guilty?

To analyze the decision process, we must first explain the legal structure of the ICTY statute and the two parts of each offence category. Articles Two through Five of the ICTY Statute outline the crimes over which the ICTY has jurisdiction. Each article begins with the *chapeau,* or threshold test that contains the criteria that must characterize each specific violation and makes the crime an international rather than a domestic offence. Following the chapeau, each article lists the criminal acts that fall within the ambit of the general category. For example, Article Five addressing crimes against humanity requires that violations be 'committed in armed conflict, whether international or internal in character and directed against any civilian population'.[2] Article Five then enumerates various specific acts that constitute criminal offences, such as murder, deportation, rape and torture. Similarly, under Article Four, judges may find an accused guilty of genocide if his activity meets the rigorous definition – namely, 'acts committed with intent to destroy, in whole or in part, a national, ethnical, racial or religious group, as such'.[3] Genocidal acts include murder, rape and forcibly transferring children to another group, among other offences. There are analogous requirements relating to war crimes and grave breaches of the Geneva Conventions.

Comparatively less attention is given in the ICTY Statute to providing the judges with guidance about ascertaining guilt and assessing punishment (Chesterman, 2000) for these crimes. Critics have charged that the statute is vague and leaves too much room for discretion by the judges (Bolton, 2000). Humanitarian laws regarding intrastate conflicts have lagged substantially behind the development of violations committed within the context of war (Lippman, 1997, 1998) allowing judges broad discretion to 'fill the gaps' (Simonovic, 1999), perhaps to the detriment of individual defendants (Sherman, 1996).

Indeed, the judges do have broad discretion to decide what evidence and testimony to admit and assess and the probative value of such proof. They can admit hearsay, affidavits and anonymous testimony and then must assess the credibility and relevance of such information. The judges can also call their own witnesses and exhibits and interject questions to the prosecution or defence during the proceedings. In assessing punishment, the judges weigh:

> any aggravating circumstances; any mitigating circumstances including the substantial cooperation with the Prosecutor by the convicted person before or after conviction; the general practice regarding prison sentences in the courts of the former Yugoslavia[4]; the extent to which any penalty imposed by a court of any State on the convicted person for the same act has already been served.[5]

Thus, the judges have only the most skeletal framework to guide them in determining an appropriate prison sentence. Given the wide latitude the judges have in their deliberations, and especially punishment, some scholars have speculated that there are few, if any, discernible patterns in the sentences (Johnson, 1998; Keller, 2001). The inchoate state of international criminal law, evolving rules of procedure and evidence at the Tribunals and external political pressures on the judges to punish some defendants more or less harshly might lead to bias and a lack of coherence in the sentencing regime (Bolton, 2000). Even if the judges strive to provide consistency and fairness in their opinions, the development of an international equivalent to sentencing guidelines might well take a number of years to emerge (Murphy, 1999; Meron, 2000).

Still, the need for appropriate sentencing standards is critical to the efficiency and legitimacy of the ICTY for several reasons. First, defendants can petition to the Appeals Chamber to review judgments handed down by the Trial Chambers that should encourage convergence and uniformity among the sentences (Fleming, 2002). Second, the judges likely will want to articulate defensible sentencing criteria in the context of the emerging International Criminal Court, which will soon be functioning and relying upon the precedents established by the ICTY (Penrose, 2000; Caianiello and Illuminati, 2001). Third, its mandate is finite as the UN Security Council could terminate the ICTY at any time for financial, political or practical reasons.[6] The ICTY does not have the luxury of slowly developing precedents in international criminal law. Rather, the judges are likely to converge on sentencing norms to expedite their work and ensure a degree of consistency in their sentences (Mettraux, 2002). If the ICTY is to contribute to furthering peace and reconciliation in the former Yugoslavia, the punishment of the guilty must be as fair and impartial as possible. How then do we as scholars identify appropriate standards to be used for sentencing convicted war criminals?

We argue that the judges have developed, either explicitly or implicitly, sentencing criteria that will allow us to explain the severity of punishment meted out to the guilty. Contrary to others who have argued sentencing is unpredictable (Penrose, 2000; Keller, 2001), we argue that we should find substantial consistency in sentencing decisions. However, we believe that we will find greater consistency in sentences as the judges distinguish among the general categories of crimes – war crimes, crimes against humanity and genocide. Because these general categories of crimes entail substantially different types of circumstances, they are qualitatively different from one another and can be penalized as such. In contrast, we should find less consistency when we examine the effects of more specific criminal acts because there is greater variation among comparable domestic laws and because of the relatively greater difficulty involved in differentiating such crimes.

Distinguishing Among the General Categories of International Crimes

We argue that distinguishing among the broad categories of international crimes to determine punishment rests on well-grounded historical and legal arguments, and provides the most efficient, administrative rationale for sentencing the guilty. Those types of international offences that are historically associated with the most heinous of crimes, and whose proof requires evidence of intentional and systematic atrocities will be judged the most harshly in order to send strong signals to would-be perpetrators that such behaviour is not acceptable. Although the judges have acknowledged that '[b]y far the most important consideration, which may be regarded as the litmus test for the appropriate sentence, is the gravity of the offence',[7] their opinions are mixed as to the existence of a hierarchy of crimes. Some judges clearly perceive certain categories of crimes as deserving the most severe sanctions, while others have argued that the specific acts of the accused are more important for determining the length of the sentence.[8] Judges at the International Criminal Tribunal for Rwanda have stated on numerous occasions, however, that genocide is the most serious offence, but there has been a reluctance to create a hierarchy among the categories at the ICTY (Danner, 2001). While scholars have paid considerable attention to the differences between the doctrinal treatment of the different categories and underlying charges, there has been little theory-building about differences between the different classes of crimes.[9] For several reasons, we hypothesize that the crime of genocide will be punished most severely, followed by crimes against humanity and then the remaining two types of war crimes.

First, the chapeau of each article has a distinctive history and qualitatively different meaning (Chesterman, 2000; Meron, 2000). The grave breach provisions come from the Geneva Conventions of 1949 and subsequent protocols in the 1970s (Green, 1997-98). Article Three of the ICTY Statute pertaining to 'violations of the laws and customs of war' arises from The Hague Convention of 1907 and precedents established by the Nuremberg Tribunal. Together, they are mainly designed to protect civilians from unnecessary and especially cruel ravages of international and civil wars and to shield combatants from harm after they have laid down their arms (Fenrick, 1999). The crimes prohibited are generally less extensive in scope than crimes against humanity and genocide.

In contrast, crimes against humanity are committed in the context of a widespread or systematic attack against a civilian population – it is not necessary that the crimes be related to war. For this reason, a crime committed during a time of war will not necessarily be considered a war crime if it is not proximately related to the ongoing conflict. There is no international statute codifying crimes against humanity, and even the term itself is subject to varying interpretations (Van

Schaack, 2002). Its etymological history extends well before World War II, but it was at Nuremberg that the Nazis were first charged with crimes against humanity. On the other hand, 'The Convention on the Prevention and Punishment of Genocide' of 1948 came into force as international law after World War II to criminalize attempts to destroy entire groups of people. Genocide has been called the 'crime of all crimes' and 'ultimate crime against humanity' both because of the special intent and because of the scope and magnitude of the crime.[10] Crimes against humanity seem to fall somewhat uncomfortably between the international laws governing war crimes and genocide. In a sense, crimes against humanity serve as a catchall category for those actions that do not meet the legal requirements of genocide but involve widespread abuses of human rights, not necessarily connected with armed conflict. Therefore, we should find that punishment for crimes against humanity is greater than that for war crimes and less than the punishment for genocide.

Second, there is a critical distinction between crimes against humanity and genocide, whose victims are *peoples,* and war crimes committed in the course of conflict. The crime of genocide is characterized by an attempt to deliberately target or destroy an ethnic, racial or some other group of people who are not combatants, while crimes against humanity often (not always) involve persecution of civilians (Van Schaak, 1999; Schabas, 2001). Both are distinguishable by the scope and the intent of the criminal act (Meron, 2000). The victims are attacked, not because they are part of the war, but because they are a part of a targeted group. The loss for the community suffered when an organic part of their group is eliminated affects the whole body of a people in much same manner as the human body is harmed with the loss of a limb – the damage can never be repaired. Such crimes are so inhumane because humanity itself is under attack. Hence the international community has a direct stake in the outcome.

The intent is also a critical element of such crimes. Genocide requires the special intent to eliminate an entire group of people, while crimes against humanity may be characterized by persecution and bias toward a particular group of people (Mettraux, 2002). As in domestic law, where crimes motivated by prejudice may be punished more severely, ICTY judges may believe that the special intent of genocide and the persecutory element of some crimes against humanity warrant lengthier incarceration (see also Danner, 2001). War crimes, horrific though they may be, by definition lack these special elements of scope and intent that differentiate crimes against humanity to some extent and genocide to a much greater extent.

More importantly, beyond distinctions regarding the broad categories, there are important reasons to believe that judges are more likely to focus on the chapeau rather than the specific underlying charges. We believe that ICTY judges will behave consistent with theories about decision-making in situations where information is abundant (Fiske and Taylor, 1991). Such decision-makers typically establish decision rules to guide information processing (Steinbruner, 1974). Judges, like all decision-makers, are faced with voluminous evidentiary exhibits (numbering in the thousands in some cases), witness testimony from dozens of persons heard over months and months of a trial and multiple legal claims that must be resolved within a framework of international law that is relatively embryonic. While we believe that judges will make use of a variety of information in the sentences they hand down, when seeking to differentiate among crimes, utilization of general categories of such crimes is significantly more efficient for the judges when sentencing than constructing a hierarchy among specific criminal acts. If judges relied on the underlying charge, they might have to determine for each type of criminal action its placement on a scale of pain and suffering, compounded by the scope of the abuses, to assess the gravity of the offence. Would killing two people be viewed as more harmful than raping and torturing ten people? Is the plunder of private property worse than bombing a Muslim mosque? It would seem more rational for the judges to rely on the guidelines and criteria for assessing the fewer and more distinguishable broad categories of crimes rather than evaluate the multitudinous variety of specific offences when determining appropriate punishment.

As such, we believe that defendants found guilty by the ICTY will receive lengthier sentences if the crime is genocide or crimes against humanity and that these two broad categories are more important for determining sentences as compared to the underlying charge against the accused. To test this hypothesis, we rely on data from the ICTY website. The dependent variable, sentence length, measures the number of months of imprisonment mandated by the Trial Chambers in all cases to 1 May 2003.[11] Because the specific crimes for which individuals are found guilty vary by count in many, although not all cases, we have elected to use the specific punishment for each count on which an individual has been found guilty as the unit of analysis.[12] Of the 37 individuals who have either been tried before the ICTY or pled guilty, 35 have been found guilty in the Trial Chambers of one or more counts. Those 35 individuals found or pleading guilty were convicted on a total of 211 counts (out of a total 376 that have been charged), which represents the 'N' in our sample, or the number of sentences handed down by the judges. In this case our independent variables include one measure for instances in which an individual was found guilty of committing a war crime (either a grave breach or a violation of the laws and customs of war) and another variable for convictions of crimes against humanity (both of which are dummy variables). We elected to combine grave breaches and violations of the laws and customs of war into one variable because they have been considered together in other research (Danner, 2001) and because we have no *a priori* expectation that they would be treated differently by the ICTY judges. As a control variable we include a measure of the guilty party's level of political or military responsibility.[13] This variable ranges from '1' for low-level parties, primarily foot soldiers and concentration camp guards, '2' for those with local command authority in the military, or local political authority and '3' for individuals with regional or national military or political command responsibility. Because the data often contain multiple observations for each individual party, we use regression with robust standard errors to minimize problems associated with heteroscedasticity.

Table 8.1 General categories of crimes and sentence length, regression with robust standard errors

Sentence	Robust Coefficient	Standard Error	T	P Value
Crimes against Humanity	-146.87	26.07	-5.63	0.000
War Crimes	-128.06	21.90	-5.85	0.000
Level of Responsibility	61.06	15.72	3.88	0.000
Constant	295.13	47.12	6.26	0.000
N=211				
R^2=0.11				

The results are presented in Table 8.1. Genocide convictions are the reference category for the three discrete types of offences. In part, the impact of genocide convictions will be registered in the constant. In this case we see that the value of the intercept is quite large, indicating that such convictions are met with lengthy sentences. More interestingly, however, is that those convicted of crimes against humanity can expect lesser sentences than those convicted of genocide, while those found guilty of war crimes are typically sentenced to even fewer months in prison, *ceteris paribus*. Both coefficients are statistically significant and in the direction anticipated. These findings support the hypothesis that the judges punish those guilty of genocide the most severely, those convicted of crimes against humanity less severely and those guilty of war crimes the least severely of all. Even if the ICTY judges have yet to sort out whether a hierarchy of crimes and punishment should exist, the results indicate that it apparently does exist. Contrary to some scholars who argue that the ICTY has been incoherent in its sentencing process, we find that indeed the jurists may be determining sentences based on a view that crimes committed in the fog of war are not be worth punishing as heavily as attacks on humanity (Van Schaack, 1999; Mettraux, 2002). It may be that ICTY judges, like their domestic counterparts, resist the formulation of codified sentencing guidelines because they do not wish to tie their hands or prejudge cases. Nevertheless, most judges probably utilize some sort of ranking of the severity of crimes in their decision-making process. Consistent with our expectations, the results also indicate that prison sentences become lengthier as one progresses up the chain of command. For each unit increase in this variable, judges sentence the guilty to an additional 61 months. Those in the highest echelons of power are punished the most severely for they bear the greatest responsibility for the atrocities committed upon their orders.

Distinguishing Among Specific Criminal Acts

We next determine whether the specific criminal acts are relevant for sentencing purposes as compared to the broader category of crimes under the statute. To evaluate this, we identified almost 30 different types of acts for which individuals have been found guilty and sentenced. Most of these crimes are conceptually similar, however, and so we have chosen to create several broader types of offences for use in explaining punishment, regardless of the general category. These are: 1) property crimes generally involving looting or destruction of objects held by individuals or communities; 2) forcible movement or illegal use of groups of people, including ethnic cleansing, use of civilians as human shields, and slavery; 3) acts specifically characterized by the judges as persecution of a group of people; 4) acts of torture; 5) acts of sexual violence; 6) premeditated violence that results in death such as murder, extermination, and mass executions; and 7) illegal military acts such as sniping and causing unnecessary damage. We created binary variables for each of these crimes and used them along with a control variable for the individual's level of responsibility to predict punishment.

Table 8.2 Specific types of crimes and sentence length

Sentence	Robust Coefficient	Standard Error	T	P Value
Property Crime	103.64	50.58	2.05	0.042
Hostage Crime	-11.05	33.68	-0.33	0.743
Persecution	-18.52	32.93	-0.56	0.575
Torture	0.34	31.00	0.01	0.991
Rape	41.40	35.45	1.17	0.244
Death	144.85	31.69	4.57	0.000
Level of Responsibility	76.42	16.31	4.69	0.000
Constant	82.05	42.62	1.93	0.056

N=211
R^2=0.26

We present the results of the model using the first six variables described above in Table 8.2. The reference category is crimes involving military tactics and operations. Only two of the six specific criminal behaviour variables are statistically significant in predicting sentence length. Actions that result in the theft or destruction of property tend to increase sentence length by 103.6 months on average, while individuals who caused the death of others tend to receive an additional 144.8 months to their sentence. While the effect of the 'death' variable is to be expected since it may be the most severe or consequential violation of international law, the fact that the property crime variable was statistically significant, while other variables such as torture and rape were not, is somewhat troubling and adds to the criticism that the ICTY has not been aggressive enough in its sentencing (Keller, 2001). For example, the ICTY has trumpeted its role in prosecuting and punishing acts of sexual violence, but while judges have set landmark precedents in this area in cases involving sexual enslavement and equating rape with genocide (at the ICTR), those who commit such acts are not necessarily punished more severely. This is consistent with other feminist criticism that the ICTY has not gone far enough (Hoefgen, 1999). We examined a correlation matrix of all variables to determine if multicollinearity may be affecting the estimates, but found nothing that would cause us to doubt the validity of these results.

Perhaps it is the context in which individuals commit these specific crimes that is most important. For example, those individuals who commit acts of torture that are proven to be crimes against humanity may be punished more severely than those who commit such acts as a war crime. To investigate these possibilities we generated multiple interactive variables for the six specific crimes and the three general categories of offences. We were unable to use all the variables in one model because multicollinearity problems caused the statistical program to drop one variable out of the estimation. Property crimes have only been sentenced in the context of war crimes, and so we do not include these results because they simply replicate what we found in Table 8.2. Persecutions occur only in cases of crimes against humanity and so we did not perform analyses using those interactive variables.

First, we see that there is a slight difference in the manner in which murder is treated. When it falls under the crimes against humanity provision, sentences increase by 136.9 months on average, while murder as a war crime generally results in a sentence 129.8 months longer on average. There is a more marked difference between sexual violence when it is classified as a crime against humanity versus a war crime, although the coefficients are statistically insignificant. The coefficient for sexual assault as a crime against humanity is positive, while the coefficient for sexual assaults falling under the war crimes provision is negative (the use of genocide as the reference category may help account for the comparatively weak effects here). We find the same hierarchy in the context of torture crimes. Those acts that fall under the war crimes provision are punished more leniently than those that are classified as crimes against humanity. Finally, the taking of hostages or actions taken against populations is not likely to result in longer prison terms. As well, the distinction between crimes against humanity and war crimes is reversed here – the latter are punished more severely. With the exception of the last result, the estimates demonstrate that the judges punish each of the specific types of actions differently depending on which chapeau they come under. This further supports our argument that it is the distinction among the general categories of crimes that is most important in sentencing.

Table 8.3 Interactions between general categories and specific types of crimes and sentence length

	Robust Coefficient	Standard Error	T	P Value
Death/CAH	136.97	40.08	3.42	0.001
Death/WC	129.82	32.20	4.03	0.000
Crime against Humanity	-95.35	29.71	-3.21	0.002
War Crime	-101.69	32.59	-3.12	0.002
Level of Responsibility	77.53	15.30	5.07	0.000
Constant	189.54	49.21	3.85	0.000
N=211				
R^2=0.24				
Rape/CAH	14.63	30.43	0.48	0.631
Rape/WC	-18.65	39.81	-0.47	0.640
Crime against Humanity	-129.23	22.35	-5.78	0.000
War Crime	-145.77	26.97	-5.41	0.000
Level of Responsibility	61.13	15.78	3.87	0.000
Constant	295.20	48.15	6.13	0.000
N=211				
R^2=0.11				
Torture/CAH	-30.78	41.01	-0.75	0.454
Torture/WC	-77.65	27.80	-2.79	0.006
Crime against Humanity	-123.41	37.31	-3.31	0.001
War Crime	-117.40	38.00	-3.09	0.002
Level of Responsibility	55.30	16.49	3.35	0.001
Constant	305.57	55.13	5.54	0.000
N=211				
R^2=0.14				
Hostage/CAH	-55.66	20.77	-2.68	0.008
Hostage/WC	-63.68	46.83	-1.36	0.175
Crime against Humanity	-130.85	20.92	-6.25	0.000
War Crime	-146.52	25.13	-5.83	0.000
Level of Responsibility	64.57	15.65	4.13	0.000
Constant	296.44	46.49	6.38	0.000
N=211				
R^2=0.12				

CAH = Crimes against Humanity
WC = War Crimes

Discussion and Conclusions

We have sought to show that the judges at the International Criminal Tribunal for the former Yugoslavia have utilized sentencing norms to punish those who violated international human rights laws in the Balkans in the 1990s. We demonstrated that the judges especially distinguish among the general categories of international crimes. Those who committed genocide and crimes against humanity in the former Yugoslavia received the most severe punishment. Whether the guilty party committed murder, rape or torture, the judges almost always sentenced the individual to longer prison terms if the violation could be categorized as one of these bias crimes. The context of the criminal act within international law apparently is more influential in assessing punishment than the act itself. While confinement of the guilty may not satisfy the victims and their communities, it does represent international documentation and condemnation of these massive violations of human rights. Of particular importance is the judges' treatment of bias crimes. We had argued that offences such as crimes against humanity and especially genocide are deserving of the utmost condemnation because they are deliberate and systematic attacks on innocent civilians. That the judges distinguish among these categories of crimes to punish bias crimes more severely is critical in light of the previous culture of impunity. While none of the crimes committed in the former Yugoslavia should be considered minor, bias crimes have passed a critical threshold of gravity. Genocide and crimes against humanity have been defined both as international crimes and as assaults on peoples. In particular, the crime of genocide involves the attempt to destroy a group of people, thereby affecting not only those who are physically harmed, but the greater whole of those people whose existence has been imperilled. This 'crime of crimes' was considered so extraordinary that the international community passed the 'Convention on the Prevention and Punishment of Genocide'. The aim of prevention has never been realized, while the goal of punishment has only recently received any attention. Therefore, it is critical for the ICTY to enforce this aspect of the Genocide Convention and provide the most severe sanctions for those who commit this most egregious of crimes. While there is as yet no international convention on crimes against humanity, these offences have also too long been accepted as a regrettable but inevitable consequence of war or as falling within the domain of state sovereignty.

Why is it important for the judges at the ICTY to utilize sentencing norms? If sentences do not follow any consistent pattern, but instead appear to be in a state of continual evolution, dependent upon the composition of the Trial Chamber hearing the case or even subject to occasional political pressure, this damages the legitimacy of Tribunal (Meron, 2000). Such problems in turn may hurt local and international efforts at peace and reconciliation in the former Yugoslavia. As Danner (2001, p.441) writes: 'inconsistent sentencing practices decrease the overall legitimacy of the Tribunals' work and reinforce the views of critics who view the enforcement of international criminal law as fatally arbitrary'. Second, punishment that is not informed by transparent and clearly defined logic and goals does not send a clear message to would-be perpetrators elsewhere in the world.

One of the central goals of the ICTY's mandate from the United Nations is to promote deterrence, and key to this is the certainty of punishment. Third, with the establishment of the International Criminal Court the world has finally taken a decisive step toward ending this culture of impunity, and the decisions by the ICTY and ICTR will provide a wealth of important legal precedents. The development of fair and sound sentencing norms will greatly assist the judges of the International Criminal Court as they begin trying a complex diversity of cases arising from all corners of the globe. Lastly, inconsistent punishment is unfair to those most directly involved in the ICTY's cases – the victims and defendants. It violates the defendants' rights to a fair trial as guaranteed in the ICTY's statute, its Rules of Procedure and Evidence and the International Covenant on Civil and Political Rights. Inconsistent and/or inexplicable penalties may also arouse resentment among victims who have long waited for some sort of redress or acknowledgment of their suffering by the international community. That we find judges employing sentencing norms, even before half of their caseloads have been completed, we take as a good sign for international law and justice.

Notes

1 The descriptions of the crimes over which the ICTY has jurisdiction are available on its web site at http://www.un.org/icty/legaldoc/index.htm on 4 July 2003.

2 http://www.un.org/icty/basic/statut/stat2000.htm#1 on 4 July 2003.

3 http://www.un.org/icty/basic/statut/stat2000.htm#4 on 4 July 2003.

4 In fact, the ICTY has ruled that the general sentencing practices in the former Yugoslavia can only provide limited guidance (Prosecutor vs. Dragoljub Kunarac et al, Case No. IT-96-23, Trial Chamber Judgment, 22 February, 2001, paragraph 859).

5 http://www.un.org/icty/basic/rpe/IT32_rev21.htm#VISection5 on 4 July 2003.

6 The ICTY recognized this pressure to speed up its work in its 2001 Annual Report to the United Nations and implemented several reforms. See http://www.un.org/icty/rappannu-e/2001/index.htm on 4 July 2003.

7 The Prosecutor vs. Zejnil Delalic et al, Case No: IT-96-21, Trial Chamber Judgment, 16 November, 1998, paragraph 1225.

8 See, Prosecutor v. Dusko Tadic, Case No. IT-94-I, Trial Chamber Judgment, 14 July 1997, paragraph 73 on the former point, and Prosecutor vs. Tihomir Blaskic, Case No. IT-95-14, Trial Chamber Judgment, 3 March 2000, paragraph 801 on the latter point.

9 For doctrinal analyses of the four categories see Fenrick (1999), Van Schaak (1999), Green (1997-98), and Lippman (1997).

10 Attorney-General vs. Eichmann, 36 I.L.R. 5 (1961), *aff'd*, 36 I.L.R. 277 (Supreme Court of Israel 1962)

11 The sentences do not reflect months that may be subtracted for time spent in ICTY detention or custody elsewhere. Individuals may be given a sentence for each count on which they are found guilty, or one global sentence for all guilty convictions.

12 We do not incorporate changes made in sentences by the Appeals Chamber since the appeals process has not finished for most defendants. Therefore, such data would be incomplete and problematic to analyze.

13 Data on these variables is taken from the ICTY web site.

References

Bass, G.J. (2000), *Stay the Hand of Vengeance*, Princeton, NJ, Princeton University Press.

Beigbeder, Y. (1999), *Judging War Criminals*, New York, St. Martin's Press.

Bolton, J.R. (2000), 'War and the United States Military: Is There Really "Law" in International Affairs?' *Transnational Law & Contemporary Problems,* Vol. 10, pp. 1-19.

Caianiello, M. and Illuminati, G. (2001), 'From the International Criminal Tribunal for the Former Yugoslavia to the International Criminal Court', *North Carolina Journal of International Law & Commercial Regulation,* Vol. 26 pp. 407-55.

Chesterman, S. (2000), 'An Altogether Different Order: Defining the Elements of Crimes Against Humanity', *Duke Journal of Comparative & International Law,* Vol. 10, pp. 307-42.

Danner, A.M. (2001), 'Constructing a Hierarchy of Crimes in International Criminal Law Sentencing', *Virginia Law Review,* Vol. 87, pp. 415-501.

Fenrick, W.J. (1999), 'Should Crimes Against Humanity Replace War Crimes?' *Columbia Journal of Transnational Law,* Vol. 37, pp. 767-85.

Fiske, S.T. and Taylor, S.E. (1991), (2nd ed.), *Social Cognition,* New York, McGraw Hill.

Fleming, M.C. (2002), 'Appellate Review in the International Criminal Tribunals', 37 *Texas International Law Journal,* Vol. 37, pp. 111-55.

Green, L.C. (1997-98), 'Grave Breaches or Crimes Against Humanity?' *U.S. Air Force Academy Journal of Legal Studies,* Vol. 8, pp. 19-30.

Hoefgen, A.M. (1999), 'There Will Be No Justice Unless Women are Part of That Justice: Rape in Bosnia, the ICTY and "Gender Sensitive" Prosecution,' *Wisconsin Womens' Law Journal,* Vol. 14, pp. 155-179.

Holbrooke, R. (1998), *To End a War,* New York, Random House.

Keller, A.N. (2001), 'Punishment for Violations of International Criminal Law: An Analysis of Sentencing at the ICTY and ICTR', *Indiana International & Comparative Law Review* Vol. 12, pp. 53-74.

Johnson, S.T. (1998), 'On the Road to Disaster: The Rights of the Accused and the International Criminal Tribunal for the Former Yugoslavia', *International Legal* Perspectives, Vol. 10, pp. 111-92.

Lippman, M. (1998), 'The Convention on the Prevention and Punishment of the Crime of Genocide: Fifty Years Later', *Arizona Journal of International and Comparative Law,* Vol. 15, pp. 415-514.

Lippman, M. (1997), 'Crimes Against Humanity', *Third World Law Journal*, Vol. 17, pp. 171-273.

Meron, T. (2000), 'The Humanization of Humanitarian Law', *American Journal of International Law,* Vol. 94(2), pp. 239-78.

Mettraux, G. (2002), 'Crimes Against Humanity in the Jurisprudence of the International Criminal Tribunals for the Former Yugoslavia and for Rwanda', *Harvard International Law Journal,* Vol. 43, pp. 237-316.

Murphy, J.F. (1999), 'Civil Liability for the Commission of International Crimes as an Alternative to Criminal Prosecution,' *Harvard Human Rights Journal,* Vol. 12, pp. 1-56.

Penrose, M.M. (2000), 'Lest We Fail: The Importance of Enforcement in International Criminal Law', *American University International Law Review,* Vol. 15, pp. 321-94.

Robertson, G. (2000), *Crimes Against Humanity*, The New Press, New York.

Schabas, W.A. (2001), 'Was Genocide Committed In Bosnia and Herzegovina? First Judgments of the International Criminal Tribunal for the Former Yugoslavia', *Fordham International Law Journal,* Vol. 25, pp. 23-53.

Sherman, A. (1996), 'Sympathy for the Devil: Examining A Defendant's Right to Confront Before the International War Crimes Tribunal', *Emory International Law Review,* Vol. 10, pp. 833-78.

Simonovic, I. (1999), 'The Role of the ICTY in the Development of International Criminal Adjudication', *Fordham International Law Journal,* Vol. 23, pp. 440-59.

Steinbruner, J. (1974), *The Cybernetic Theory of Decision*, Princeton, New Jersey, Princeton University Press.

Van Schaack, B. (1999), 'The Definition of Crimes Against Humanity: Resolving the Incoherence', *Columbia Journal of Transnational Law*, Vol.. 37, pp. 787-850.

Chapter 9

National Constitutions and Human Rights Protection: Regional Differences and Colonial Influences

Linda Camp Keith

Introduction

The unmistakable wave of constitutional writing across the globe in the last decades has led to substantial academic debate over whether these newly promulgated constitutions, and their bills of right in particular, have made a difference in regard to states' human rights practices (see Siegan, 1994; Finer et al., 1995; Ludwikowski, 1996). Sceptics have been particularly doubtful about European-rooted constitutionalism taking hold in non-European regions. Political scientists have begun to explore this important question empirically through systematic data collection and analysis. While the effects of constitutional provisions may be less than constitutional scholars would hope for, recent studies have found that some constitutional provisions do make a difference in human rights behaviour, and the studies have demonstrated that their collective impact is rather substantial (Davenport, 1996; Keith, 2002a, 2002b). Thus far, the analysis has not sought to answer the secondary question of whether constitutional provisions for human rights work consistently across all world regions. This question is linked to the ongoing normative debate of whether international human rights are universal or whether they are culturally limited products of Western individualism. For those of us who seek to find ways to improve human rights practices, the more important question is whether national constitutions are a viable path to achieve this goal in all countries or in only a limited set. This chapter seeks to empirically test this question. I examine the impact of three types of constitutional provisions on personal integrity rights: 1) provisions for specific individual freedoms; 2) provisions for an independent judiciary that are believed to be necessary for implementation of these constitutional protections; and 3) states of emergency provisions, which arguably will curb a regime's proclivity toward human rights abuses.

Constitutionalism beyond Europe

Numerous scholars question whether constitutionalism will function fully in regions outside of Europe (and European-settled countries). The primary argument is that the Western values, which focus on individualism, run counter to traditional values that are strongly embedded in communal societies. Huntington (1993), for example, argues, 'Western ideas of individualism, liberalism, constitutionalism, human rights, equality, liberty, the rule of law, democracy.... often have little resonance in Islamic, Confucian, Japanese, Hindu, Buddhist, or Orthodox cultures' (p.40). Moderne (1990) echoes some of these concerns, noting that no concept of the person exists in traditional African society where it is the community that defines the person. He asserts that individual rights, such as freedom of thought or opinion, are irrelevant to African politics because they are designed to ensure fairness in an atomized society and a competitive non-consensual political system, which is alien in the African context. Moderne argues that in most African states developing a strong national identity and viable economy has been the major preoccupation, not judicial review and individual rights. Hutchful (1993) expands this argument, adding that constitutionalism's focus on individual legal rights and on negative rights instead of positive rights is offensive to the ideological agenda of African nationalism.

Still, other scholars such as Ibhawoh (2000) counter these arguments, noting that Asian and African cultures are not monolithic and that 'so-called traditional societies – whether in Asia, Africa, or Europe – were not culturally static but were eclectic, dynamic, and subject to significant alteration' (p.841). Davis (1998) also disagrees with the relativist argument, particularly the assertion that human rights practices of the West are 'unsuited to Asian soil and to the particular cultural and historical conditions of the East' (p.109). He argues that scholars have tended to over-mystify culture and overuse generalized stereotypes and that the relativist arguments fail to appreciate the rich values discourse of the East Asian region and that the relativist arguments are tautological and overly deterministic because they fail to appreciate the roles of both human agency and institutions to the transformative processes of cultural discourse. These arguments recognize the potential role that the process of constitution making and subsequent creation of democratic institutions could play in the ongoing transformative process of cultures.

Manasian (1998) specifically challenges Huntington's assumption that there is a single set of western, Islamic or Asian cultural values. He, too, notes that none of these cultures are monolithic, and that each of these cultures has elements within them that are hostile to human rights and elements that are supportive of human rights. He argues that international human rights are not exclusively Western but rather are based on 'values widely shared across many cultures: respect for the sacredness of life and for human dignity, tolerance of differences, and desire for liberty, order, fairness, and stability' (p.10). Ibhawoh (2000) agrees and concludes that the polarized debate over the universality of human rights seems to have given way in recent years to a broad consensus that there is indeed 'a core set of human rights to which all humanity aspires' (pp. 838, 843).

Even if we can discount somewhat the relativist's scepticism about constitutionalism, several other concerns remain that suggest caution in our expectations for these formal documents' universal effectiveness in curbing state human rights abuse, particularly in less economically developed and post-colonial states. Scholars such as Daima (1998) argue that democracy and liberalism both require much time and money, which are a dire scarcity in most African countries. Boron's (1993) concerns are similar; he notes that constitutions in Latin American countries have successfully imitated U.S. constitutions but that the countries were missing the necessary social and economic structures to support actual constitutionalism. Both scholars suggest that constitutionalism has been a fraud or convenient cover for the elite and the powerful to pursue their own goals.

Much of the scepticism about the universality of constitutionalism relates directly to colonialism and its enduring legacy, particularly in Africa, which experienced the most recent and widespread colonialism. Many of the constitutions in post-colonial states were imposed upon the states by the departing colonial powers, therefore lacking the legitimacy of public consensus. Mutua (2001) notes that despite Kenya's liberal constitution, 'the post-colonial state was autocratic at its inception because it wholly inherited the laws, culture, and practices of the colonial states' (p.97). Welch (1984) concurs, suggesting that colonialism created states that were antithetical to self-government and it set up an authoritarian framework for local administration. Hutchful (1993) posits that colonial rule 'delegitimated or submerged traditional linking mechanisms of African society and instead established a political discourse only available to a small minority and that the political selection mechanisms similarly excluded large strata of population' (p.218). Rusk (1986) explores the issue further and argues that colonial modes of production were instrumental in the formation of a privileged comprador class whose interests were more linked to the international system of trade than to indigenous interests. He argues that when a system of privilege within a developing nation was challenged by the masses, the ruling elite, lacking sufficient economic or political resources to deal with the discontent, inevitably turned to repression to deal with this challenge. Thus, colonialism not only set up a system of exclusion, but also established a pattern of state repression as a tool to deal with popular dissent.

The arguments asserting colonialism's damaging legacy in stifling liberal democracy are substantial. And some of the assertions of the cultural limits of liberal constitutionalism are difficult to dismiss, despite the strong counter-arguments made by internationalists. Ultimately, it remains an empirical question whether, despite these inauspicious conditions, constitutionalism can work in non-Western regions. This chapter attempts to answer that question in regard to the human right to personal integrity.

State Abuse of the Human Right to Personal Integrity

The human right to personal integrity is the right not to be imprisoned, tortured, killed or made to disappear, either arbitrarily or because of your political affiliations or convictions. While the components of this right are not inclusive of all international rights, they represent the types of rights abuse that are considered to be the most 'egregious and severe crimes against humanity' (Poe and Tate, 1994, p.854). And more importantly, these core rights are those that would have to be fulfilled in order for the provision of the other rights to be meaningful. The measure of state abuse of personal integrity rights used here are those originally developed by Michael Stohl and several others (Stohl et al., 1984). The measures are currently maintained by Mark Gibney (see http://www.unca.edu/~mgibney/), and have been expanded to greater geographical and temporal coverage by Steven C. Poe and his collaborators (Poe and Tate, 1994; Poe et al., 1999). Each measure consists of a rating scale that ranges from 1 to 5, with 1 assigned to states with the lowest, and 5 to states with the highest, levels of personal integrity abuse. Poe and his co-authors have identified several factors that have consistently demonstrated an impact on the state personal integrity abuse: the level of political democracy, international and civil wars, organized violent and non-violent rebellion and population size (Poe and Tate, 1994; Poe et al., 1999). Other factors have produced somewhat less consistent but nevertheless substantive impacts: economic development, leftist regimes, British cultural heritage and military regimes.

Constitutional Provisions and Personal Integrity Abuse

The analysis presented in this chapter seeks to examine the effects of twenty constitutional provisions. I coded the presence of ten fundamental constitutional rights and liberties in the text of the constitutions of the world's nations for each year in the period from 1976 to 1996. The freedoms and rights I coded include the freedoms of speech, association, assembly, press and religion, the right to strike, the writ of *habeas corpus*, a public trial, a fair trial and ban against torture or cruel and usual punishment.[1] I coded for the presence of nine provisions of judicial independence: guaranteed terms of office, finality of judicial decisions, exclusive judicial authority, ban of exceptional or military courts, fiscal autonomy, separation of powers, enumerated qualifications, judicial review and hierarchical system.[2] I coded for the presence of four states of emergency provisions: legislative declaration requirements, duration limits, ban against dissolving the legislature and a non-derogable rights list.[3] In the following analysis I test the effects of each of the twenty constitutional provisions while controlling for the major factors affecting state terror, described fully in Poe et al. (1999).

Empirical Analysis

Regional Models

First, I examine the effects from a purely regional perspective, based on geographic location, with the exception of European-settled countries such as the United States, Canada and Australia. The countries are divided into five regional groups: 1) Europe and European-settled countries; 2) Latin America and the Caribbean; 3) South and East Asia; 4) North Africa and Middle East and 5) sub-Saharan Africa. Table 9.1 reports these results. The results from the analysis with European and European-settled countries are reported in the first column. Here we do not find as strong an impact from the constitutional provisions as optimists would expect – only five of the constitutional provisions are statistically significant at an acceptable level. The four freedoms index produces the effect we would expect, but our level of confidence in the results would be marginal.[4] The addition of a single one of these four freedoms, if explicitly provided for, would improve the human rights score by approximately one-tenth point and the explicit provision of all four freedoms would improve the score by one-quarter point. Constitutional provision for fair and public trial improves a country's score by approximately one-fifth to one-quarter point, if adopted fully. The provisions for judicial independence and states of emergency perform poorly. Only the ban against exceptional courts is statistically significant and its impact is quite small. Only the provision for legislative declaration of states of emergency produces a statistically significant (but small) impact. Based on these results, we would expect that if a country adopted each of these constitutional provisions *simultaneously,* they would see an improvement in their human rights score of one full level.

In the second column we can see that despite the cultural relativist argument that Western constitutionalism runs counter to Asian values, the provisions actually work *best* in this region. Nine of the provisions produce the expected effects and achieve a level of statistical significance that allows us to accept these results with confidence. Three of the individual freedoms (freedom of press, right to strike and fair trial) produce strong effects: an Asian country that goes from no constitutional provisions to fully providing for these provisions could improve its human rights score by up to 0.68. It is interesting to note that only in this region does freedom of press achieve statistical significance.[5] The elements of formal judicial independence perform much better in the Asian countries than in other regions, except Latin America and the Caribbean. Four provisions are statistically significant: provisions for exclusive judicial authority, banning exceptional courts, separation of power and enumerated qualifications for judges. The effects of these provisions are not as strong individually as the individual freedoms but when the expected effects of a one-unit change in each provision are combined, the impact is exactly one point on the scale. The two statistically significant states of emergency provisions, legislative declaration and limited duration also produce large effects. As in previous studies the duration provision is problematic in that it is *harmful* to human rights – suggesting that a constitutional clause that sets a time limit on states of emergency and requires states to renew their declarations may have the

Table 9.1 The impact of constitutional provisions on state terror (1977-96), analysis by region

	Europe and European Settled	South and East Asia	Latin America and Caribbean	North Africa, Near and Middle East	Sub-Saharan Africa
Lagged State Terror	0.36 (0.04)****	0.56 (0.06)****	0.43 (0.06)****	0.45 (0.07)****	0.53 (0.05)****
Individual Rights and Freedoms					
Four Freedoms Index	-0.03 (0.02)	0.08 (0.03)	-0.04 (0.04)	0.17 (0.12)	0.01 (0.02)
Freedom of Press	0.17 (0.06)	-0.18 (0.12)*	-0.13 (0.13)	0.27 (0.21)	0.07 (0.09)
Right to Strike	0.19 (0.08)	-0.42 (0.21)**	-0.12 (0.14)	-0.42 (0.33)*	0.01 (0.09)
Habeas Corpus	0.07 (0.03)	-0.02 (0.08)	0.12 (0.15)	0.51 (0.33)	-0.02 (0.07)
Public Trial	-0.12 (0.03)****	0.04 (0.10)	-0.21 (0.08)***	-0.90 (0.33)***	0.12 (0.10)
Fair Trial	-0.08 (0.04)**	-0.34 (0.10)****	-0.29 (0.23)*	-2.77 (1.99)*	-0.15 (0.06)***
Torture	0.04 (0.03)	-0.04 (0.18)	0.10 (0.09)	-0.22 (0.25)	-0.01 (0.05)
Judicial Independence					
Guaranteed Terms	-0.02 (0.11)	0.26 (0.18)	-0.32 (0.23)*	-0.19 (0.41)	0.04 (0.09)
Decisions Final	-0.03 (0.06)	0.01 (0.07)	-0.26 (0.09)***	-0.17 (0.17)	0.11 (0.09)
Exclusive Authority	-0.05 (0.06)	-0.20 (0.09)**	-0.31 (0.16)**	0.67 (1.00)	-0.02 (0.10)
No Exceptional Courts	-0.09 (0.06)**	-0.21 (0.09)****	-0.44 (0.27)**	0.05 (0.30)	0.02 (0.08)
Fiscal Autonomy	0.01 (0.05)	0.03 (0.12)	0.06 (0.12)	-0.52 (0.96)	0.09 (0.15)
Separation of Powers	-0.02 (0.08)	-0.34 (0.20)**	-0.41 (0.20)**	0.97 (0.63)	-0.03 (0.08)
Enumerated Qualifications	0.09 (0.04)	-0.25 (0.10) ***	0.15 (0.17)	-0.31 (0.39)	0.05 (0.09)
Judicial Review	0.08 (0.04)	0.23 (0.11)	0.21 (0.25)	-0.02 (0.19)	-0.04 (0.05)
Hierarchical System	0.09 (0.08)	0.10 (0.13)	0.44 (0.21)	0.25 (0.37)	0.04 (0.08)

States of Emergency					
Legislative Declaration	-0.07 (0.02)***	-0.13 (0.06)***	0.13 (0.06)	-0.23 (0.23)	-0.10 (0.03)*
Limited Duration⁺	-0.01 (0.04)	0.23 (0.06) ****	0.26 (0.10)***	-0.00 (0.12)	-0.11 (0.04)***
Cannot Dissolve Legislature	0.08 (0.05)	0.28 (0.09)	0.20 (0.15)	-0.21 (0.10)**	-0.01 (0.05)
Non-Derogable Rights⁺	0.02 (0.06)	-0.01 (0.21)	-0.19 (0.17)	-0.38 (0.29) *	0.25 (0.25)
Control Variables					
Civil War	0.94 (0.31)***	0.29 (0.11)***	0.54 (0.14)****	0.47 (0.15)***	0.62 (0.12)****
International War	0.12 (0.14)	-0.02 (0.18)	0.11 (0.20)	0.19 (0.10)**	0.36 (0.15)***
Democracy	-0.07 (0.02)****	-0.03 (0.01)**	-0.03 (0.02)**	-0.06 (0.02)***	-0.01 (0.01)
Military Control	0.15 (0.23)	0.07 (0.12)	0.32 (0.14)***	-0.09 (0.12)	0.04 (0.06)
Leftist Regime⁺	0.36 (0.14)***	0.15 (0.15)	-0.43 (0.31)	0.10 (0.16)	-0.15 (0.09)*
Economic Development	-0.01 (0.00)	-0.01 (0.00)	-0.08 (0.04)***	0.00 (0.01)	0.03 (0.04)
Population	0.05 (0.01)****	0.07 (0.03)***	0.32 (0.07)****	0.11 (0.07)*	0.13 (0.02)****
Constant	-0.63 (0.25)***	-0.05 (0.42)	-3.06 (1.08)***	-0.15 (0.97)	-0.78 (0.27)****
N	647	432	432	356	751
R^2	0.76	0.78	0.72	0.77	0.59
χ^2 p > 0.0001 for all 5 models					

Main entries are unstandardized OLS coefficients, generated using STATA 6.0. Robust standard errors are in parentheses.
⁺= two-tailed test ****= $p < 0.001$ ***= $p < 0.01$ ** = $p < 0.05$ *= $p < 0.10$

unintended consequence of *encouraging* the extension of states of emergency. The combined impact of a South or East Asian country adopting even the minimal level of the nine provisions simultaneously would be an improvement in their human rights score by two full levels on the five-point scale. Clearly, these results run counter to Huntington's admonition that Western ideas of constitutionalism, liberalism, and rule of law have little resonance in Eastern cultures.

The results of the analysis for the Latin American and Caribbean countries also run counter to scholars' scepticism that these countries would lack the requisite social and economic structure to support constitutionalism. Eight of the constitutional provisions produce the expected effects and achieve an acceptable level of statistical significance. The adoption of provisions for fair and public trials would reduce the human rights abuse scores in the region by almost one point on the five-point scale. The constitutional provisions for judicial independence perform best in this set of countries. These results run counter to the observations made by Latin American specialists, who worry about the politicalization of the judiciary (Prillaman, 2000) and who argue that the judiciary has been but a docile agent of the executive (Boron, 1993; Fruhling, 1993). Five of the nine judicial provisions produce the expected effect at an acceptable level of confidence: guaranteed terms of office, finality of judicial decisions, exclusive judicial authority, banning exceptional courts and separation of power. The effect of the provision against exceptional courts is quite important in this region, as the practice of trying civilians in special or military courts has been quite prevalent. For example, in the 1980s 95 per cent of all Chilean criminal cases were tried in military courts (O'Keefe, 1989). And in Colombia the secret court system created for drug and terrorism cases denies the accused such rights as a pre-trial hearing and a public trial, and it allows for secret witnesses against the accused; these courts have been used to punish student protestors, peasants and critics of the regime as terrorists. The effect of a maximum change in regard to this provision would produce a decrease in the state terror score almost equivalent to a full point on the five-point scale. Only one of the states of emergency provisions is statistically significant: the limited duration provision, which produces a harmful effect not surprising in this region, given the record of perpetual states of emergency in countries such as Peru and Uruguay. We find that if these countries adopted the minimal level of these eight provisions simultaneously their human rights score could be expected to improve by about two levels on our scale.

The constitutional provisions do not perform as well in the countries of North Africa, Near and Middle East. Only five of the constitutional provisions are statistically significant – three of the individual freedoms, the two trial provisions, the right to strike and two of the states of emergency clauses. Scholars such as Allain and O'Shea (2002) have noted that even though large numbers of the Muslim states of North Africa and Middle Eastern states have joined international human rights conventions, they have placed reservations on their signature that have subordinated their legal obligations to the dictates of Shari 'a law (p.91). Other scholars, such as El Naiem (1984), have argued that human rights can be compatible with Shari 'a, but his prognosis was not promising. Additionally, most of these states have only limited constitutional provision for human rights. And, as

Allain and O'Shea note, many of these states such as Egypt and Algeria have further reduced their human rights obligations through declaration of states of emergencies, and they suspect that through these declarations, the states 'may have effectively suspended the right to liberty and security of the person, rights related to treatment in prison, mass expulsion of aliens, right to a fair trial, right to privacy, and freedoms of expression, assembly, and association, among others' (p.94). Given Allain and O'Shea's concerns about states of emergency in this region, it is encouraging that the adoption of two of the constitutional provisions for states of emergency appears to improve human rights protection: the provision that bans dissolving the legislature during a state of emergency and the provision that lists the rights that cannot be derogated during such an emergency. Here the constitutional list of derogable rights works as intended in this set of countries and increases the probability for respect of personal integrity rights as the ICJ and ILA have argued it would. Even though the number of effective provisions is small in this region, when they are present their impact is large, producing a combined impact equal to three points in the five-point scale.

The cultural relativist argument finds the strongest support in sub-Saharan Africa, where no provisions of judicial independence are statistically significant and only three constitutional provisions appear to be important: the provisions for fair trials, legislative declaration of state of emergency and limited duration of states of emergency. In this region the limit on the duration of states of emergency has the effect the international legal community had expected. The combined contemporaneous impact of a sub-Saharan country adopting fully the three significant provisions is quite small compared to the other regional sets of countries; it would produce a change of only half a level in the five-point scale.

While the sub-Saharan Africa countries have adopted human rights in much greater detail in their constitutions than their northern counterparts, the provisions appear to have little effect on actual human rights behaviour. This result is consistent with Allain and O'Shea's (2002) conclusion that in southern African states the sad reality is that the constitutions are simply rhetoric. As I noted before, none of the provisions for judicial independence have an impact on the protection of human rights. This regional result is consistent with the observations of Mutua (2001) in regard to particular case of Kenya, where despite its constitutional provisions for judicial independence, the judiciary has evaded its constitutional responsibility to protect individual rights and instead has served as an agency of the executive. Okoth-Ogendo's (1993) observations suggest that this result is directly linked to Africa's colonial past, in which the judiciary served as *administrators* of the coercive colonial order. I examine this question next.

Colonial Experience Model

Welch (1984) argues that the shape of states largely is a consequence of colonialism, and much of the scholarly scepticism about the effectiveness of Western constitutionalism is grounded in concerns about the damaging legacy of colonialism, especially in Africa. Colonial experience clearly shaped the types of executive systems newly independent nations adopted, as well as the types of legal systems adopted in post-colonial states (see Nwabueze, 1973; Moderne, 1990). Therefore, an analysis that divides countries on the basis of their colonial experience seems to offer an additional opportunity to understand the nexus between constitutionalism and human rights. I examine in three separate analyses, states that were colonized either by 1) Great Britain; 2) France or 3) the Iberian Peninsula countries (Spain and Portugal).[6] The constitutional model was then tested on each of these three subsets of countries. These results are reported in Table 9.2.[7]

Table 9.2 The impact of constitutional provisions on state terror (1977-96), analysis by colonial experience

	British Colonies	French Colonies	Iberian Colonies
Lagged State Terror	0.60 (0.05)***	0.59 (0.05)***	0.62 (0.05)***
Individual Rights and Freedoms			
Four Freedoms Index	-0.02 (0.02)	0.001 (0.03)	-0.02 (0.02)
Freedom of Press	0.05 (0.05)	0.03 (0.08)	0.09 (0.09)
Right to Strike	0.04 (0.15)	-0.08 (0.12)	0.09 (0.08)
Habeas Corpus	-0.04 (0.05)	-0.02 (0.09)	0.20 (0.07)
Public Trial	0.03 (0.05)	-0.12 (0.10)*	-0.09 (0.06)**
Fair Trial	-0.12 (0.07)**	-0.16 (0.07)***	-0.14 (0.12)***
Torture	0.07 (0.05)	0.13 (0.08)	-0.05 (0.07)
Judicial Independence			
Guaranteed Terms	-0.12 (0.08)**	0.05 (0.08)	-0.25 (0.20)*
Decisions Final	-0.03 (0.06)	-0.06 (0.10)	0.15 (0.13)
Exclusive Authority	-0.04 (0.08)	0.01 (0.10)	-0.26 (0.14)**
No Exceptional Courts	-0.05 (0.06)	0.16 (0.14)	-0.09 (0.07)*
Fiscal Autonomy	0.11 (0.07)	0.16 (0.25)	0.24 (0.14)
Separation of Powers	-0.02 (0.07)	0.06 (0.10)	0.28 (0.16)
Enumerated Qualifications	-0.04 (0.06)	-0.26 (0.16)**	-0.06 (0.17)
Judicial Review	0.08 (0.08)	-0.13 (0.10)*	-0.11 (0.12)
Hierarchical System	0.11 (0.07)	0.16 (0.10)	0.26 (0.15)
States of Emergency			
Legislative Declaration	0.04 (0.04)	-0.07 (0.03)***	-0.06 (0.04)**
Limited Duration +	0.10 (0.04)***	-0.12 (0.00)***	0.12 (0.06)**
Cannot Dissolve Legislature	0.02 (0.07)	0.03 (0.06)	-0.03 (0.09)
Non-Derogable Rights+	0.01 (0.12)	0.29 (0.23)	0.04 (0.12)

Control Variables			
Civil War	0.58 (0.12)***	0.35 (0.15)**	0.42 (0.10)***
International War	0.13 (0.13)	0.22 (0.11)**	0.05 (0.13)
Democracy	-0.04 (0.01)***	-0.01 (0.02)	-0.06 (0.01)***
Military Control	-.018 (0.06)	0.09 (0.08)	-0.08 (0.10)
Leftist Regime+	0.07 (0.14)	-0.15 (0.10)	-0.25 (0.10)**
Economic Development	-0.02 (0.01)***	0.03 (0.05)	-0.03 (0.01)***
Population	0.11 (0.02)***	0.05 (0.03)*	0.10 (0.05)***
Constant	-0.49 (0.23)***	0.31 (0.52)	-0.53 (0.64)
N	859	586	490
R^2	0.73	0.57	0.75
χ^2 p > 00001 for all 3 models			

Main entries are unstandardized OLS coefficients, generated using STATA 6.0. Robust standard errors are in parentheses.

+ The two-tailed test was used for the statistical significance. The one-tailed test was used for all the other variables.

****= p < 0.001 *** = p < 0.01 ** = p < 0.05 **= p < 0.10.

Contrary to expectations, formal constitutional provisions appear to have the least effect in former British colonies, where only three of the twenty provisions are statistically significant: provision for fair trials, guaranteed terms of office and the duration clause. From these results we would expect that countries fully adopting provision for fair trials or fully adopting the provision for guaranteed terms of office for the judiciary could improve their human rights score by one-tenth to one-quarter point on the five-point scale. Again, here the state of emergency duration clause is disturbing in that it *increases* the likelihood of a higher human rights abuse score.

The constitutional provisions perform best in the former Iberian colonies. Seven of the twenty constitutional provisions are found to produce significant effects: fair and public trials. Three of the provisions for judicial independence also appear to be statistically significant: guaranteed terms, exclusive judicial authority and the ban against exceptional courts. Formal judicial independence performs best in former Iberian colonies, casting some doubt on the scepticism of some Latin American specialists that we discussed previously. Once again, the provision for legislative declaration of states of emergencies improves states human rights scores while the duration clause harms them. Cumulatively, the analysis leads us to expect that if a former Iberian colony were to adopt fully these six constitutional provisions they would see a contemporaneous improvement in the human rights score of one and one-third levels in the five-point scale.

In former French colonies, the constitutional provisions do not perform as well as in the former Iberian colonies but they do perform much better in the former British colonies. Six of the twenty provisions are found to be statistically significant: fair and public trials, enumerated qualifications, judicial review, legislative declaration and limited duration of the state of emergency. Cumulatively, the analysis leads us to expect that if a former French colony were to adopt fully these six constitutional provisions they would see a contemporaneous improvement in the human rights score of 1.40, close to one and a half levels in the five-point scale. [8]

The impact of the judicial review provision in this set of countries is quite interesting because in all previous analyses this variable had consistently produced a coefficient that was positive rather than negative. While we have been reluctant to engage in post hoc explanations, these previous results had suggested that the power of judicial review could be used to facilitate or legitimize an abusive regime's behaviour. It is only within the former French colonies that this constitutional provision makes a difference. This result runs counter to concerns by African specialist Moderne (1990), who argues that judicial review, and judicial independence in general, is weaker in Francophone Africa than Anglophone Africa.

There is another striking difference between the three sets of countries in regard to one of the control measures – political democracy, as measured by the Polity index, an eleven-point scale that captures the competitiveness of political participation, the competitiveness of executive recruitment, the openness of executive recruitment and constraint on chief executive. The level of political democracy has been found to be one of the strongest factors related to personal integrity rights, but in this analysis the democracy measure has no impact on the human rights score in states that share a French colonial influence. The mean score on level of political democracy for these states was 1.66; the scores for the other two sets of countries were twice as large (3.82 in former British colonies and 3.94 in former Iberian colonies). These results suggest the need for further study of the differences in the political system of these countries. It may be that the presidential systems, which the former French colonies were more likely to have adopted, constrain the executive less than the Westminster system that influenced the former British colonies (see Nwabueze, 1973). The differences could also be related to the colonial power's influence on the type of legal system adopted by the independent state – with British colonies more likely to adopt common law systems and Iberian and French colonies more likely to adopt Dutch-Roman civil code. Nwabueze draws a link between the British common law, where most executive power has to be conferred by the legislature, leaving the executive no inherent discretionary power to act against citizens, and the French presidential system, which give the executive considerable areas of rule-making power that is independent of legislature (p.35). These differences suggest that the French system would be more likely to facilitate an executive's dictatorial actions. However, Nwabueze (1973) also observed other key differences between the constitutions of Anglophone and Francophone African states. He noted that Francophone constitutions were shorter and simpler, leaving many aspects to organic law and that they had only limited provision for human rights. Moderne (1990) also expects that constitutionalism and judicial independence will be less prevalent in Francophone than Anglophone Africa. He believes the Francophone states have had less exposure to U.S.

constitutionalism and that the 'dual link of common language and French metropolitan training enjoyed by a majority of Francophone African elites' has influenced the new states' judicial models (p.335).

Next, I performed a limited test of Nwabueze's hypotheses to gain additional insight into the above results. I returned to the sub-Saharan set of countries, which had performed rather poorly on the regional constitutional analysis, and separated out the Anglophone from the Francophone countries for analysis. The results are reported in Table 9.3. Counter to Nwabueze's expectations, the constitutional provisions perform about the same in Francophone and Anglophone Africa. Four constitutional provisions appear to be important in both sets of states and the effects are approximately equal: in Anglophone Africa we would expect to see an improvement of 1.95 were a state to adopt fully the constitutional provisions that benefit human rights and in Francophone Africa we would expect to see a combined effect of 1.96. While separating out the Anglophone and Francophone countries does not definitively settle the question of whether the British colonial experience of African countries left these countries better able to protect or provide human rights, it does provide some evidence that this expectation might not be valid.

Table 9.3 The impact of constitutional provisions on state terror (1977-96), sub-Saharan Africa: Anglophone versus Francophone

	Full sub-Saharan Africa	Anglophone SSA Only	Francophone SSA Only
Lagged State Terror	0.53 (0.05)****	0.40 (0.07)****	0.48 (0.06)****
Individual Rights and Freedoms			
Four Freedoms Index	0.01 (0.02)	-0.03 (0.09)	-0.06 (0.07)
Freedom of Press	0.07 (0.09)	-0.56 (0.25)***	0.30 (0.20)
Right to Strike	0.01 (0.09)	-0.21 (0.38)	-0.12 (0.16)
Habeas Corpus	-0.02 (0.07)	-0.36 (0.30)	0.05 (0.18)
Public Trial	0.12 (0.10)	0.18 (0.20)	0.08 (0.19)
Fair Trial	-0.15 (0.06)***	0.29 (0.20)	-0.42 (0.17)***
Torture	-0.01 (0.05)	-0.28 (0.26)	-0.07 (0.13)
Judicial Independence			
Guaranteed Terms	0.04 (0.09)	-0.53 (0.29)***	0.24 (0.18)
Decisions Final	0.11 (0.09)	0.16 (0.22)	0.15 (0.23)
Exclusive Authority	-0.02 (0.10)	-0.04 (0.26)	0.01 (0.18)
No Exceptional Courts	0.02 (0.08)	0.26 (0.24)	0.51 (0.17)
Fiscal Autonomy	0.09 (0.15)	0.29 (0.33)	0.41 (1.2)
Separation of Powers	-0.03 (0.08)	-0.21 (0.26)	0.35 (0.14)

Enumerated Qualifications	0.05 (0.09)	0.08 (0.23)	-0.02 (0.21)
Judicial Review	-0.04 (0.05)	0.20 (0.14)	-0.70 (0.18)****
Hierarchical System	0.04 (0.08)	0.21 (0.23)	0.24 (0.15)
States of Emergency			
Legislative Declaration	-0.07 (0.02)***	-0.10 (0.08)*	-0.18 (0.07)***
Limited Duration +	-0.01 (0.04)	0.09 (0.11)	-0.19 (0.07)****
Cannot Dissolve Legislature	0.08 (0.05)	0.55 (0.17)	0.01 (0.11)
Non-Derogable Rights+	0.02 (0.06)	1.24 (0.37)****	0.26 (1.1)
Control Variables			
Civil War	0.62 (0.12)****	0.69 (0.16)****	0.44 (0.26)**
International War	0.36 (0.15)***	------------	0.03 (0.20)
Democracy	-0.01 (0.01)	-0.03 (0.02)****	0.01 (0.02)
Military Control	0.04 (0.06)	0.18 (0.14)*	0.25 (0.11)****
Leftist Regime +	-0.15 (0.09)*	------------	0.01 (0.12)
Economic Development	0.03 (0.04)	0.06 (0.06)	0.05 (0.07)
Population	0.13 (0.02)****	0.30 (0.05)****	0.14 (0.06)****
Constant	-0.78 (0.27)****	-2.90 (0.63)****	-0.99 (0.91)
N	751	316	402
R^2	0.59	0.69	0.57
χ^2 p > 00001 for all 3 models			

*Main entries are unstandardized OLS coefficients, generated using STATA 6.0.
Robust standard errors are in parentheses.
+ = two-tailed test ****= p < 0.001 ***= p < 0.01 **= p < 0.05 *= p < 0.10.

Summary and Implications

This chapter has attempted to address the question of whether liberal models of constitutionalism work across all regions in protecting against the state abuse of personal integrity or whether they are limited in their cultural relevance. My analysis found that constitutional provisions do play an important role in protecting against this form of abuse, but the level of impact and the type of provision varied somewhat across regions and across colonial experience. The constitutional provisions for fair and public trials are clearly the most universally applicable provisions in protecting personal integrity rights. The individual freedoms, such as expression, press and assembly do in fact seem to be culturally limited, at least in their relevance to personal integrity abuse. The four freedoms index was only important in Western Europe and European-settled countries. The link between formal judicial independence and state terror seems to be the most tenuous. The provisions are not important in the countries of North Africa and the Near and Middle East region or sub-Saharan Africa. It is only in Latin American and Caribbean countries (and in former Iberian colonies) that numerous indicators of formal judicial independence make a substantive difference. It should be kept in mind that this study only looks at formal judicial independence, as outlined in national constitutions. It may be that the promised independence is not actually realized in state practice. One perplexing result is the lack of a role for judicial review in the protection of human rights, with the exception of former French colonies. This power has been one of the more strongly argued links to the protection of individuals against arbitrary government power. And, yet, the analyses suggest that the provision for this power actually *harms* human rights. The ban against trying civilians in exceptional or military courts is by far the most consistently important provision in decreasing the probability of state repression of human rights. This finding is insightful, given the current debate in the United States over the president's executive order that appears to call for just such courts in the aftermath of 11 September.

States of emergency, another prevalent threat to human rights today, are not easily dealt with in formal constitutions because of unintended, but perhaps not unexpected, consequences. Some provisions, intended to protect against abuse, actually have the opposite effect. The duration provision continues to be the most consistently problematic clause in this regard; the analyses clearly suggest that regimes are taking advantage of such clause to perpetuate states of emergency and concomitantly to limit human rights. The most important constitutional provision for a state of emergency is a clause that puts the declaration firmly in the legislature's hands rather than the executive, thus providing a significant check against a potentially abusive executive. These results do suggest that we should be cautious in promoting these provisions as a check against abuse during times of emergency.

While this study makes an important first attempt to answer significant questions about the effect of constitutionalism on actual human rights behaviour in non-Western countries, there are limitations to the study – which perhaps can be dealt with in future research. One of the most important links for future studies to examine further is the nexus between executive constraints and human rights, especially in regard to the independence of the legislature during times of internal crisis. It may be that the legislature provides a much more important check on an abusive executive than the judiciary. We should explore more the provisions that foster such independence and specifically examine the effect of different types of executive systems, especially in newly independent states. Additionally, scholars need to move beyond the exploration of formal judicial independence to the much more daunting task of examining the actual independence of the judiciary. The role of judicial review also remains a ripe area for future research, as well. We need to examine differences between review by constitutional courts, which may operate outside the regular court system, and review by the traditional judiciary. Ultimately, we need to assess empirically whether courts use this power to protect individuals from arbitrary government power or whether courts use this power to legitimize or even facilitate the abuses of the state.

Ultimately, if our goal is not only to understand, but to improve state human rights practices, this study suggests that we must not only pursue paths that are most applicable to the global body of countries, but we should also examine the paths that may be more appropriate for a particular region or specific set of countries, which share similar experiences and influences. And if we are fortunate and do our job well, it may be that our exploration of particular paths, will eventually lead us back to a more generalizable theory.

Notes

1 Each freedom or protection was coded: 2 = explicitly guaranteed or mentioned in the constitution; 1 = explicitly guaranteed or mentioned in the constitution but with (an) exception(s) or qualification(s), such as a public interest clause; or 0 = not mentioned in the constitution

2 Each provision was coded as follows: 1) Guaranteed Terms. The constitution guarantees terms of office, regardless of whether judges are appointed or elected, and restricts removal of judges. 2) Decisions Final. The decisions of judges are not subject to any revision outside any appeals procedures provided by law. 3) Exclusive Authority. The courts have exclusive authority to decide on their own competence, as defined by law -- their decisions are made without any restrictions, improper influences, inducements, pressures, threats or interference, direct or indirect, from any quarter or for any reason. 4) No Exceptional (or Military) Courts. The courts have jurisdiction over all issues of a judicial nature and civilians are tried by ordinary courts or tribunals, not military or exceptional courts. 5) Fiscal Autonomy. The courts are fiscally autonomous. The salaries of their judges and/or their annual budgets are protected from reduction by the other branches. 6) Separation of Powers. The courts are housed in a separate branch from the executive and legislative powers. 7) Enumerated Qualifications. The selection and career advancement of judges are based on merit qualifications, e.g., integrity, ability and efficiency. 8) Judicial Review. Courts exercise judicial or constitutional review of legislative and executive branches. 9) Hierarchical System. Courts are structured in multiple layers with the highest level court exercising final control/review of lower court decisions. The presence in the constitutions of each of these components of judicial independence and effectiveness was coded as follows: 2 = constitution provides for it fully and explicitly, 1 = constitution provides for it somewhat or provides for it vaguely, but not fully, 0 = constitution does not provide for it. In addition, two variables were coded -1 for the presence of provisions that specifically designed to counter judicial independence and effectiveness: No exceptional courts (4 above) was coded -1 for constitutions that specifically allowed civilians to be tried in military courts or explicitly allowed the formation of exceptional courts, and judicial review was coded -1 for constitutions that gave the power of constitutional review to another branch of government such as the executive or the legislature.

3 Both International Commission of Jurists (ICJ) the International Law Association's (ILA) Paris Minimum Standards (Section A) (reported in Chowdhury, 1989) suggest that constitutions contain several specific clauses to deal with states of emergency or national crises. These indicators represent their suggestions. However, there has been

some debate over states of emergency clause. Numerous observations suggests that regimes may use the clauses as a rationalization to abuse human rights, often curbing rights well beyond that which the constitutional provisions would allow. Particularly, the constitutional list of individual freedoms and rights that may not be derogated during an emergency may imply that at least some other rights may justifiably be denied because of the special circumstances. The implication that some rights may be denied during an emergency may provide regimes with a cover of legitimacy that facilitates their denial of human rights, even those that are non-derogable. And provisions that set a time limit on states of emergency and require states to renew their declarations may have the unintended consequence of encouraging the extension of states of emergency. We have consistently found evidence to support these two fears (Keith, 1999; Keith et al., 2001).

4 $P < 0.11$.

5 This result is not too surprising in that Asia ranks number two when comparing in the average regional scores for the provision for freedom of press. On average Asian countries score 0.61 on a scale from 0 to 2, second only to European-settled countries' mean score of 0.75. Other regions have substantially less formal commitment to freedom of press.

6 I do not examine the former colonies of other states, such as the Netherlands or Prussia because of the small N value, which makes statistical analysis unreliable. In the dataset there are 52 former British colonies, 28 former French colonies, and 25 former Iberian colonies. The three sets of former colonies varied somewhat in their mean human rights abuse score. Former British colonies earned a mean of 2.48 for this time period. The former French colonies' mean score was somewhat higher at 2.67, and the former Iberian colonies earned the highest abuse score, a mean of 3.0.

7 I also tried to test the three types of colonial experience as dummy variables designating countries that had British, French, or Iberian colonial experiences. However, this was not possible due to high correlation.

8 To get a better estimate of the explanatory power added by the addition of the constitutional variables to the three colonial models, I ran Wald tests to test the joint significance of the constitutional provisions. The addition of the provisions is statistically significant across all three models. In former French colonies the F score was 1.61 (p of 0.05); in the former British colonies F score was 2.47 (p of 0.0005); and in the former Iberian colonies the F score was 2.04 (p of 0.006).

References

Allain, J. and O'Shea, A. (2002), 'African Disunity: Comparing Human Rights Law and Practice of North and South African States', *Human Rights Quarterly*, Vol. 24(1), pp. 86-125.

Boron, A.A. (1993), 'Latin America: Constitutionalism and the Political Traditions of Liberalism and Socialism.' in D. Greenberg et al. (eds.), *Constitutionalism and Democracy: Transition in the Contemporary World*, New York, Oxford University Press.

Chowdhury, S.R. (1989), *Rule of Law in a State of Emergency*, New York, St. Martin's Press.

Daima, A. (1998), 'Challenges for Emerging African Democracies', *Peace Review*, Vol. 10, pp. 57-64.

Davenport, C, (1996), '"Constitutional Promises" and Repressive Reality: A Cross-National Time-Series Investigation of Why Political and Civil Liberties are Suppressed', *Journal of Politics*, Vol. 58(3), pp. 627-54.

Davis, M.C. (1998), 'Constitutionalism and Political Culture: The Debate over Human Rights and Asian Values', *Harvard Human Rights Journal*, Vol. 11, pp. 109-47.

Finer, S.E, Bogdanor, V. and Rudden, B. (1995), *Comparing Constitutions*, Oxford, Clarendon Press.

Frühling, H.E. (1993), 'Human Rights in Constitutional Order and in Political Practice in Latin America', in D. Greenberg et al., (eds.), *Constitutionalism and Democracy: Transition in the Contemporary World*, New York, Oxford University Press.

Huntington, S.P. (1993), 'The Clash of Civilizations?' *Foreign Affairs*, Vol. 72(3), pp. 22-49.

Hutchful, E. (1993), 'Reconstructing Political Space: Militarism and Constitutionalism in Africa', in D. Greenberg et al. (eds.), *Constitutionalism and Democracy: Transition in the Contemporary World*, New York, Oxford University Press.

Ibhawoh, B. (2000), 'Between Culture and Constitution: Evaluating the Cultural Legitimacy of Human Rights in the African State', *Human Rights Quarterly*, Vol. 22(3), pp. 838-60.

Keith, L.C. (1999), 'The United Nations International Covenant on Civil and Political Rights: Does it Make a Difference in Human Rights Behavior?' *Journal of Peace Research*, Vol. 36(1), pp. 95-118.

Keith, L.C. (2002a), 'Constitutional Provisions for Individual Human Rights (1976-1996): Are They More than Mere "Window Dressing"?' *Political Research Quarterly*, Vol. 55, pp. 111-43.

Keith, L.C. (2002b), 'International Principles for Formal Judicial Independence: Trends in National Constitutions and Their Impact (1976 to 1996)', *Judicature*, Vol. 85, pp. 194-200.

Keith, L.C., Tate, C.N. and Poe, S.C. (2001), 'Constitutional Protections, Judicial Independence and State Repression of Personal Integrity: Is the Law a Mere Parchment Barrier to Human Rights Abuse?' Paper presented at the Southwestern Political Science Association Annual Meeting, Ft. Worth, Texas, 15-18 March 2001.

Ludwikowski, R.R. (1996), *Constitution-making in the Region of Former Soviet Dominance*, Durham, NC, Duke University Press.

Manasian, D. (1998), 'Human Rights Law: Controversies and Culture', *Economist*, Vol. 349, pp. S8-S10.

Moderne, F. (1990), 'Human Rights and Postcolonial Constitutions in Sub-Saharan Africa', in L. Henkin and A.J. Rosenthal (eds.), *Constitutionalism and Rights: the Influence of the United States Constitution Abroad*, New York, Columbia University Press.

Mutua, M. (2001), 'Justice Under Siege: The Rule of Law and Judicial Subservience in Kenya', *Human Rights Quarterly*, Vol. 23(1), pp. 96-118.

Naiem, E. and Admed, A. (1984), 'A Modern Approach to Human Rights in Islam: Foundations and Implications for Africa', in Welch and R.I. Meltzer (eds), *Human Rights and Development in Africa*, Albany, State University of New York Press.

Nwabueze, B.O. (1973), *Constitutionalism in the Emergent States*, Rutherford, NJ, Fairleigh Dickinson University Press.

O'Keefe, T.A. (1989), 'The Use of the Military Justice System to Try Civilians in Chile', *New York State Bar Journal*, Vol. 61, pp. 43-7.

Okoth-Ogenco, H.W.O. (1993), 'Constitutions without Constitutionalism: Reflections on an African Paradox', in Douglas Greenberg et al. (eds.), *Constitutionalism and Democracy: Transition in the Contemporary World*, New York, Oxford University Press.

Poe, S.C. and Tate, C.N. (1994), 'Repression of Human Rights and Personal Integrity in the 1980s: A Global Analysis', *American Political Science Review*, Vol. 88(4), pp. 853-72.

Poe, S.C., Tate, C.N., and Keith, L.C. (1999), 'Repression of Human Rights to Personal Integrity Revisited: A Global Cross-National Study Covering the Years 1976-1993', *International Studies Quarterly*, Vol. 43(2), pp. 291-313.

Prillaman, W. (2000), *The Judiciary and Democratic Decay in Latin America: Declining Confidence In The Rule Of Law*, Westport, CT, Praeger.

Rusk, J. (1986), 'Structures of Neo-Colonialism: The African Context of Human Rights', *Africa Today*, Vol. 33(4), pp. 71-6.

Siegan, B. (1994), *Drafting a Constitution for a Nation or Republic Emerging into Freedom*, Fairfax, VA, George Mason University Press.

Stohl, M., Carleton, D., and Johnson, S. (1984), 'Human Rights and U.S. Foreign Assistance: From Nixon to Carter', *Journal of Peace Research*, Vol. 21(3), pp. 215-26.

United Nations High Commissioner for Human Rights (1993), *Vienna Declaration And Programme Of Action* http://www.unhchr.ch/huridocda/huridoca.nsf/(Symbol)/A.CONF.157.23.En?OpenDocument.

Welch, C.E. (1984), *Human Rights and Development in Africa*, Albany, NY, State University of New York Press, pp. 75-89.

PART V
NEW DIRECTIONS IN THE RESEARCH ON HUMAN RIGHTS VIOLATIONS

Introduction to Part V

The final section asks where we go from here and what new avenues need to be explored to alleviate human suffering at the hands of governments. It introduces new approaches and new areas to the research on human rights. It contains analyses of conditions that facilitate human rights violations, as well as inquiries into how human rights violations by the state influence the behaviour of domestic opposition in the form of protest and dissent. The last section also addresses a new issue on how human rights are violated and what the structural and individual mechanisms behind such violations are. The first chapter by Chris Lee et al. addresses the role of ethnicity and the chapter by Sabine Carey focuses on the link between protest and repression. The last two chapters address two unique questions about the dynamics behind coercion. They ask, firstly, what the characteristics of organizations are that are behind the human rights violations, and how different organizational structures influence the nature of human rights violations, and secondly, what transforms ordinary people into gross human rights violators and what characterizes this process.

Chris Lee et al. explore the impact of the ethnic composition of a country on the extent to which the government violates human rights. Scholars have found that the ethnic composition of a country affects its foreign policy behaviour (Davis and Moore, 1997; Saideman, 2000), and the literature on ethnic conflict proposes that it has an effect on violence (Muller and Seligson, 1987). More recently, scholars have reported that ethnic civil wars can be distinguished empirically from non-ethnic civil wars and that the former last longer and are more violent (Ellingsen, 2000; Sambanis, 2001). Lee et al. analyze the impact of the ethnic composition of a country on state violations of human rights using a global database ranging from 1976 to 1993, presenting the most comprehensive examination of the effects of ethnic composition on human rights to date.

Research on the conditions that may lead to human rights violations has largely concentrated on structural factors, such as economic development and regime type. However, it is not merely the structure of political regimes and the environment that influence governments' decision to repress, but also the behaviour of the population, such as the display of dissent and protest against the rulers. The chapter by Sabine Carey analyzes how different types of domestic protest influence state repression, using data from Latin America and sub-Saharan Africa between 1977 and 1994. It offers a new approach to the study of domestic dissent and state repression by differentiating between five types of dissent and employing a statistical tool that allows for non-linear relationships between the different forms of dissent and repression. Carey distinguishes between peaceful anti-government demonstrations, strikes, violent riots, guerrilla warfare and large-scale rebellion. The results suggest that governments group these five different protest activities into two broad categories. They appear to distinguish between acts of protest that are either non-violent or spontaneous and activities that are violent and require a certain level of organization of the dissidents. The second category of protest activities seems to trigger harsher and more violent state responses than the first one. Putting this finding into the concept of the

Strength/Threat ratio as discussed in the chapter by Poe in this volume, guerrilla warfare and revolutionary revolts are particularly threatening for the government in power and thus lead to greater repression.

The last two chapters offer different perspectives on the study of human rights violations by looking inside the 'black box' of the nation-state, to concentrate on the organization and individuals that are behind the violations. Pablo Policzer focuses on the characteristics of organizations and Alette Smeulers on the individuals that carry out human rights violations. Policzer's study is based on the argument that state-sponsored coercion does not appear in a vacuum but has to be organized. The main question is how different types of organizations affect the intensity and types of human rights violations perpetrated by them. This is based on the assumption that the ways in which states organize coercion shape how coercion is carried out. Organizations are characterized according to their structures and procedures for internal and external monitoring. The study develops a new framework to analyze four distinct consequences for the way in which coercion is carried out: targeting, intensity, regime stability and the likelihood of bringing perpetrators to justice. Examples are drawn from four authoritarian regimes in Chile, Argentina, East Germany and South Africa.

Policzer's chapter presents a new framework to describe the various ways states organize coercion. Similar to this one, Smeulers addresses the road to repression from a new perspective as well. It turns the focus of the previous chapter from the organization to the individual and the group. This qualitative study analyzes how ordinary people are transformed into human rights violators. She identifies certain phases that people usually go through before they become human rights violators and commit crimes of obedience as part of state-sponsored repression. The chapter tests various theories on psychological and social-psychological mechanisms, analyzing ego-documents, such as trial statements, interviews, diaries, autobiographies, letters and other oral or written statements made by the perpetrators themselves. However, it goes beyond testing existing theories. It develops a theoretical model about individual and collective defence mechanisms and the techniques used by individuals and groups to justify their acts and live with this experience. Smeulers distinguishes a specific set of phases of the transformation process that turns ordinary people into gross human rights violators. This especially provocative study puts the perpetrators of gross human rights violations in the centre of the analysis and develops theories, mechanisms and processes to outline and explain this transformation.

References

Davis, D.R. and Moore, W.H. (1997), 'Ties that Bind? Domestic and International Conflict Behavior in Zaire', *Comparative Political Studies*, Vol. 31, pp. 45-71.

Ellingsen, T. (2000), 'Colorful Community or Ethnic Witches' Brew? Multiethnicity and Domestic Conflict During and After the Cold War', *Journal of Conflict Resolution*, Vol. 44, pp. 228-49.

Muller, E.N. and Seligson, M.A. (1987), 'Inequality and Insurgency', *American Political Science Review*, Vol. 81, pp. 425-52.

Saideman, S. (2000), *The Ties That Divide: Ethnic Politics, Foreign & International Conflict*, New York, Columbia University Press.

Sambanis, N. (2001), 'Do Ethnic and Nonethnic Civil Wars Have the Same Causes?' *Journal of Conflict Resolution*, Vol. 45, pp. 259-82.

Chapter 10

Ethnicity and Repression: The Ethnic Composition of Countries and Human Rights Violations

Chris Lee, Ronny Lindström, Will H. Moore and Kürşad Turan[1]

Introduction

This study explores the impact of the ethnic composition of society on the violation of human rights in that country. Scholars have found that the ethnic composition of society has an impact on the foreign policy behaviour of countries (Davis and Moore, 1997; Saideman, 2000), on the level of political violence in countries (Muller and Seligson, 1987), on rebellion (Hibbs, 1973) and civil wars (Ellingsen, 2000; Sambanis, 2001). Further, Walker and Poe (2002) explore the impact of ethnic diversity on the provision of a variety of human rights. They find limited support for the proposition that ethnic diversity reduces the provision of human rights. We build on these previous studies and ask whether the ethnic composition of society has an impact on the extent to which governments observe the human rights of their citizens.

Why anticipate that the ethnic composition of society might influence provision of human rights? We tie together the work of three of the authors of this study, among others, to make a case. First, government coercion tends to be responsive to dissident threats: protest and rebellion from the population. Second, ethnic groups have a mobilization advantage over economic – or politically – based groups. Thus, ethnic minority groups are especially likely to mobilize and engage in protest. Third, democratization ties governments' hands with respect to coercion, thus creating more space for protest. Ethnic groups should have a mobilization advantage and thus be more likely to mobilize during democratization. If governments indeed find protest and rebellion threatening, then societies with large ethnic minority groups and societies transitioning to democracy should experience greater levels of human rights violations. We sketch these arguments, and the literatures on which they draw, below.

The study proceeds in five sections. In the following section we briefly review the literature on the link between the ethnic composition of countries and protest and rebellion. This is followed by a discussion of the determinants of the propensity of governments to respond to threats with coercion. We discuss the impact of democratization on ethnic mobilization and government response in section three. In the fourth section we describe our research design and the data we use to measure our concepts. We present our findings in a fifth section and then conclude with a discussion of the implications of our study.

Ethnic Composition of Countries and Violence

An ethnic group may be defined as

> a segment of a larger society whose members are thought, by themselves and/or others, to have a common origin and to share important segments of a common culture and who, in addition, participate in shared activities in which the common origin and culture are significant ingredients (Yinger, 1985, p.159).

This definition includes two important characteristics of Gellner's version (1983, p.7): a shared culture and the recognition by self and others of group membership. Horowitz (1985, pp.17-8) provides us with an inclusive concept of ethnicity: 'Ethnic groups are defined by ascriptive differences, whether the indicium is colour, appearance, language, religion, some other indicator of common origin, or some combination thereof.' Our definition is a combination of Gellner (1983) and Horowitz (1985): we define ethnic groups on the basis of ascriptive differences that the members of the group and others see as salient to their identity.

Today, a large portion of the over 190 existing countries consist of more than one ethnic group. Writing in the 1980s, Connor (1983, p.374) found that only fifteen of the world's states were homogenous nation states. That select group included Iceland, the two Koreas, Portugal and Japan.[2] Perhaps more importantly, back then the largest ethnic group was a majority in only 31 per cent of the existing countries (Connor 1983, p.375). There is little reason to believe that the countries of the world have become substantially more homogenized in the last 20 years.

It is also true that since the end of World War II, at least one half of the world's countries have experienced significant ethnic conflict and 80 per cent of deaths from political violence have been internal to nation states (Williams, 1994, p.50). Clearly every domestic political conflict is not caused by ethnicity, but as Gurr (1993) reports, between 1950 and 1989 non-violent protest[3] by ethnic minorities went up by 230 per cent; violent protest by ethnic minority groups rose by 420 per cent; and rebellion[4] by ethnic minority groups increased by 360 per cent. So most nation states have ethnically heterogeneous societies and a non-trivial amount of protest and rebellion one observes in the world is undertaken on behalf of ethnic minority groups.

Among multiple identities possessed by people, ethnicity is one of the most salient and thus serves as a potential mobilization cleavage.[5] Lindström (1996) builds on this contention by drawing on Olson (1965) and Tilly (1978) and argues that ethnic groups mobilize more easily and effectively than other societal actors. He begins with Olson's claim that collective action arises more easily when a group is small and homogenous: since individuals are recognizable inside the smallest units, free riding is more difficult among ethnic groups than among other segments of society because sanctions are easier to administer and psychological factors are more likely to come into play. Thus, although ethnicity in itself does not lead to mobilization, pre-existing networks among ethnic groups provide a link between ethnicity and the capacity to mobilize for conflict behaviour.

Lindström (1996) tests his hypotheses using Phase II of Gurr's (1993) Minorities at Risk data[6] and finds support for the contention that ethnicity is positively correlated with mobilization for conflict through the concepts of homogeneity and pre-existence of group networks. We thus have some reason to anticipate that the ethnic composition of society may have an impact on the extent to which a society experiences protest: if grievances are relatively constant across many groups in a given society, then one would expect ethnic groups to more readily mobilize than other types of groups. In the next section we build on that insight by considering the extent to which governments respond to threats.

Determinants of Human Rights Violations: An Argument

To properly determine whether ethnic structures have an impact on human rights requires that we include other factors that are also expected to affect the extent to which a government respects human rights. Because we use statistical analyses to evaluate the claims about ethnic structure, we must first construct a baseline statistical model of human rights violations. To be useful, statistical models must be grounded in argument or theory. Here we present the arguments we use to specify our baseline statistical model of human rights violations.

The argument is similar to the one advanced by Davenport, Moore, and Poe (2003) in a study on refugee flows. Davenport et al. contend that refugees respond to three major sources of threat in their environment: dissident violence, government coercion and the violent interaction of dissidents and governments. Following Poe and Tate (1994) and Poe, Tate and Keith (1999), we argue that governments are more likely to engage in repression and violate the physical rights to integrity of the person when they perceive dissident activities as threatening.

Various authors (e.g., Gurr, 1986; Gartner and Regan, 1996; Poe, Tate and Lanier, 2000) recognize a link between threat perception and the use of repression. The basic premise is that the use or attempted use of coercion shows that a regime anticipates danger, and that the greater the magnitude of force used by dissidents, the higher the state's perception of threat. Davenport's (1995) cross-national study of government coercion is built on the idea that regimes respond to domestic threats with repression, and his results suggest that governments respond to the perceived threat of multiple dimensions of dissident activity. Furthermore, he finds that the degree to which the government is democratic significantly changes the relationship patterns between political conflict and repressive behaviour. King (1998) and Lee (2001) test Davenport's model using time-series data from several Latin American cases and find substantial support for the multidimensional threat perception hypothesis: several of the dimensions were relevant in each case. We build on this basic insight and contend that dissident protest activities and violence influence the state's decision to engage in human rights violations.

Another factor that we expect to have an effect on the extent to which countries violate the right to physical integrity of the person is civil war. We conceptualize civil wars as events where both the government and a dissident group are actively engaged in armed struggle with one another. Dissident groups largely begin with guerrilla tactics, but in some cases professional soldiers may break away from the army and fight for the dissidents. Recent research (and events such as those in the former Yugoslavia, Colombia, Sierra Leone, etc.) suggest that both sides may spend more time attacking unarmed civilians than one another (Kalyvas, 2000), but as long as both the government and at least one dissident group are actively engaged in sustained armed conflict with one another, we consider it a civil war. And we expect this type of armed conflict to have an independent effect – beyond dissident protest and violence – on human rights violations.

We expect the government to decrease its respect for human rights during a civil war because it is mobilizing its citizens in the context of being threatened. Both governments and populations tend to respond to security threats by restricting liberties and expanding the judicial power of the executive. Further, while some counter-insurgent doctrines emphasize the importance of the rule of law when fighting insurgents (e.g., Thompson, 1966), other counter-insurgent doctrine explicitly justifies human rights violations as a means to secure victory (Pion-Berlin, 1989). Supporting our argument, research by Henderson (1991) and Mitchell and McCormick (1988), among others, shows that civil wars increase human rights violations.

The next concept that we anticipate to have an impact on the violation of human rights is international war. The argument is much the same here as it was for civil war: governments have a broad tendency to both restrict freedom and liberty and to expand the executive's judicial power when mobilizing for war. Supporting our argument, Stohl (1975) and Rasler (1976) report that in the United States the level of government coercion tended to rise during periods when the US was at war, and Poe and his colleagues (1994, 1999) show that international wars increase the level of human rights violations throughout the world.

The above concepts are behavioural: they focus on the behaviour of one or more groups in society. The main factor we examine in this study is structural: the ethnic composition of society. Yet, it is not the only structural factor that is likely to have an impact. In the next section we discuss democratization as a transition process that may well affect the extent to which a government observes human rights.

Transitions to Democracy

Davenport (1999), Davenport and Armstrong (2002) and Henderson (1991), among others, find that the extent to which a government's institutions are democratic influences the extent to which that government engages in repression or violates human rights. In her study of civil violence, Ellingsen (2000) reported that regime type had a larger effect on violence than did ethnic structure. These findings suggest that the institutional structure of the regime is an important characteristic to consider.

Turan (2002) studies recent transitions to democracy and describes two parallel processes taking place. On the one hand, opposition groups compete with the former regime in forming the new institutional framework of the new system. During this bargaining process the state faces a dilemma: accommodation or repression. With repression the democratization attempt comes to an end and is likely to be followed by violence when ethnic groups refuse to surrender the rights they have already obtained.[7]

Accommodation creates an equally problematic situation. When the first wave of demands is accommodated, a second and more extreme wave is likely to follow. During the second process, Turan (2002) argues that ethnic groups and their leaders compete with each other for better positioning in the new system. With new institutions shaping up, they want to maximize their power or, at the very least, they try not to fall too far behind other groups. This security dilemma is explained by Saideman et al. (2002, p.106) 'the ethnic security dilemma starts with the idea that the government of any state is the greatest potential threat to any group inside its boundaries… Groups may fear that others control the government and may use its resources… against them'.

Contrary to these arguments, Cingranelli and Richards (1999), Scarritt and McMillan (2000) and Zanger (2000) have found that democratization has a positive impact on governments' human rights behaviour. This is likely to be due to the government's limited ability to repress once democratic rules are adopted. Yet, Turan (2002) found that democratizations are followed by increasing levels of protest and rebellion by ethnic groups. Because ethnic violence is a result of the state and the ethnic group responding to each other's actions, these results imply that post-democratization violence is initiated by group policies, in which case a democratizing government's human rights violations are due to a lack of better methods to deal with the crisis. We thus anticipate that democratization will be associated with greater levels of rights violations while democracy (or regime type) will have a negative association with rights violations.

To summarize, the combined arguments of Lindström (1996), Lee (2001), and Turan (2002) suggest that countries with ethnic divisions should violate human rights at higher levels than more homogenous countries: governments respond to threats; countries with ethnic divisions are more likely to experience mobilization than those without, and that probability rises with more groups who might mobilize; and democratization processes raise the likelihood that all groups – including ethnic minorities – will engage in protest and rebellion.

Research Design and Data

The arguments raised above suggest that dissident violence, government coercion, the violent interaction of governments and dissidents, international war, regime type, democratization and the ethnic composition of society will each have an independent impact on, and ethnic composition and democratization will have a joint impact on, the extent to which a government respects the physical integrity rights of its citizens.

To include as large a group of countries as possible we collected data on all countries with a population over one million people. That limit is a practical constraint: few large data sets in political science collect data on countries with less than one million people. Our results should then hold for countries that have a population larger than one million people. Our sample is similarly constrained by the availability of data on our variables. As such, our study is based on the years from 1976 to 1993 and includes between 114 and 158 countries.

In the interest of space, we have placed the technical discussion of operational indicators on the website associated with this volume. Most of our indicators are widely used, and we simply identify the source of the data in Table 10.1. Readers interested in more detail will find it on the web document.

Table 10.1 Operational indicators

Variable	*Data for Measure*
Physical Integrity of Person	Five point Political Terror Scale.
Ethnic Composition of Society	Three different measures: Largest minority as a % of total pop; 2nd largest minority as a % of total pop; # of groups in society.
Linguistic Composition of Society	Three different measures: Largest minority as a % of total pop; 2nd largest minority as a % of total pop; # of groups in society.
Religious Composition of Society	Three different measures: Largest minority as a % of total pop; 2nd largest minority as a % of total pop; # of groups in society.
Frequency of Dissent	Numbers of protests and armed attacks; from Banks' Cross Polity.
Presence of Violence	Dummy variable coded 1 when at least one armed attack or riot recorded in Banks' Cross Polity.
Variety of Dissent	The frequency of event categories with at least one event; from Bank's Cross Polity.

Deviation from Normal Dissent	Dummy variable coded positive when level of dissent exceeds the average level for that country; from Banks' Cross Polity.
Civil War	Correlates of War Civil and Extrasystemic wars.
Ethnic Civil Wars	Sambanis' Ethnic Civil War data.
International War	Correlates of War International War data.
Institutional Regime Type	1=democracy, 2=autocracy, 3=anocracy; from Polity IV.
Democratization	Three measures: dummy coded 1 when a +4 or higher change occurs in democracy scale, the level change in democracy from preceding year, and a counter measuring the number of years since the last change in democracy; from Polity IV.
Democratization and Ethnic Composition	The product of the democratization dummy and the ethnic composition measures.
Bureaucratic Inertia	Previous year's value on the Political Terror Scale.

Findings

The results are reported in Table 10.2, which contains coefficient estimates from our statistical analyses. Those readers who are not interested in the technical details can ignore Table 10.2 in favour of the description provided here.[8]

There are five models reported in Table 10.2, the first of which we consider a baseline model: it contains the measures of the concepts described in the section above (dissident violence, civil war, international war and regime type). The results support most of our arguments. Unlike Davenport, we find that only one of the variables has an impact on violations of the right to physical integrity: the absence/presence of dissident violence. The effect of violence is small: a country with violence will, on average, experience one tenth of a point more human rights violations on the five point scale. Both civil war and international war increase the average level of violations a country will experience: civil war produces a four tenths of a point higher level of violations, international war produces a three tenths of a point higher level of violations. Further, the type of regime also has an impact: an autocratic regime will, on average, violate rights at a level eight hundredths of a point greater than a democracy, and an anocratic regime[9] will, on average, violate rights at a level eight hundredths of a point greater than an autocracy.

Table 10.2 Regression results

Variables	Model 1	Model 2	Model 3	Model 4	Model 5
Constant	0.53***	0.50***	0.83**	1.05**	0.48*
	(0.06)	(0.06)	(0.25)	(0.30)	(0.24)
PTS_{t-1}	0.71***	0.72***	0.67***	0.66***	0.66***
	(0.02)	(0.02)	(0.03)	(0.03)	(0.03)
Frequency	-0.00	-0.00	0.00	0.00	-0.00
	(0.01)	(0.00)	(0.01)	(0.00)	(0.00)
Violence	0.08**	0.10*	0.13**	0.10*	0.17**
	(0.05)	(0.05)	(0.06)	(0.06)	(0.06)
Variety	0.03	0.02	0.04	0.03	0.04
	(0.03)	(0.03)	(0.03)	(0.03)	(0.03)
Deviance	0.05	0.07	-0.03	-0.02	-0.05
	(0.05)	(0.05)	(0.05)	(0.06)	(0.05)
Civil War	0.51***	--	0.42***	0.43***	0.43***
	(0.03)		(0.07)	(0.07)	(0.08)
Ethnic Civil War	--	0.33***	--	--	--
		(0.06)			
Non-ethnic Civil War	--	0.35***	--	--	--
		(0.07)			
International War	0.24**	0.27**	0.31**	0.28**	0.27*
	(0.12)	(0.13)	(0.13)	(0.12)	(0.16)
Polity	0.11**	0.12**	0.07**	0.10**	0.08**
	(0.03)	(0.03)	(0.03)	(0.03)	(0.03)
Democratization	-0.11	-0.12	-0.12	-0.07	-0.20
	(0.09)	(0.09)	(0.12)	(0.14)	(0.14)
Time since	0.01	0.01	0.01	0.00	0.01
Democratization	(0.01)	(0.01)	(0.01)	(0.01)	(0.01)
Change in Democracy	0.00	0.00	-0.00	-0.00	0.01
Score	(0.01)	(0.01)	(0.01)	(0.01)	(0.01)
1st Ethnic Group	--	--	-0.00	--	--
			(0.00)		
2nd Ethnic Group	--	--	-0.00	--	--
			(0.00)		
# of Ethnic Groups	--	--	0.01	--	--
			(0.02)		
1st Religious Group	--	--	--	-0.00	--
				(0.00)	

2nd Religious Group	--	--	--	-0.00 (0.00)	--
# of Religious Groups	--	--	--	-0.07** (0.04)	--
1st Linguistic Group	--	--	--	--	0.00 (0.00)
2nd Linguistic Group	--	--	--	--	0.00 (0.00)
# of Linguistic Groups	--	--	--	--	0.02 (0.02)
Ethnic Interaction[a]	--	--	0.00 (0.00)	--	--
Religious Interaction[b]	--	--	--	0.00 (0.00)	--
Linguistic Interaction[c]	--	--	--	--	0.00 (0.00)
F	283.75	212.09	163.69	153.79	145.58
R^2	0.64	0.64	0.64	0.62	0.65
# of Cases	1966	1966	1568	1594	1344
# of Countries	158	158	135	129	114

a An interaction term created from democratization change and the population ratio of the second largest ethnic group to country population.

b An interaction term created from democratization change and the population ratio of the second largest religious group to country population.

c An interaction term created from democratization change and the population ratio of the second largest linguistic group to country population.

* indicates the level of statistical significance at p<0.1, ** at p<0.05 and ***at p<0.001.

These effects are small in size, and one reason they are is that we included the previous year's score on the political terror scale (PTS) in the model. We did so in part for statistical reasons, but also because it allows us to examine the argument that countries tend to follow standard procedures. The value of that estimate is 0.67, which suggests that governments have a strong tendency to continue to do what they have done in the past.[10] Because we include this term in the model, and it is so strong, the other variables (dissident violence, civil war, international war and regime type) have less to explain. That helps to explain why the size of the other estimates is so small (i.e., tenths and hundredths of a point on a five point scale). The way to think about those results, then, is that they are the impact of the variables given that the government will largely maintain its past level of rights violations.

The second model includes the two measures of civil war: ethnic civil wars and non-ethnic civil wars. We include these variables to test for the possibility that countries that experience an ethnic civil war will have higher levels of rights violations than countries that have a civil war, but one that is not fought over ethnic divisions. The question is whether the estimates are the same or different. It turns out that the estimates are effectively the same, and a formal statistical test indicates that we can rule out the hypothesis that they are different. The implication is that ethnic civil wars are associated with the same level of human rights violations as non-ethnic civil wars. Our first test indicates that the ethnic composition of society does not have an impact on violations of the right to the physical integrity of the person.

The third model includes the three measures of the ethnic composition of society: the percentage of the population comprised by the largest ethnic group in society, the second largest group in society and the number of ethnic groups in society. The variables from the baseline model are essentially unchanged, but not one of the ethnic variables has an impact on the violation of physical integrity rights.[11] As noted above, because we included the previous year's PTS score, there is not much variance left to explain. To probe that issue, we re-estimated the model without the previous year's PTS score, but this did not change the findings for the three ethnic composition variables (results not shown): they do not have an impact. This finding implies that, on average, the ethnic structure of society does not affect the extent to which governments violate personal integrity rights. This was also the only model where our interaction term displayed significant results. The intensity of the democratic transition the country experiences, combined with the proportional size of the second largest ethnic group, has a significant and positive effect on human rights violations. This finding supports our argument that following a major political change a large ethnic group will be perceived as a threat by the state, leading it to use repression in order to prevent a potential challenge.

The fourth model uses the three religious variables to measure the ethnic composition of society: the size of the largest and second largest religious group and the number of religious groups. These findings also fail to support the argument that the ethnic (more specifically, religious) composition of society affects the observation of human rights: neither of the size of population variables has an impact,[12] and the number of religious groups has a small negative impact on rights violations. That is, a society with 11 religious groups will, on average, have a seven tenths of a point *lower* level of violations on the five point scale than a society with one religious group. So the more religious groups there are in society, the lower will be the rights violations. This is the opposite of what was anticipated.

The fifth model includes the three measures of the linguistic composition of society: the percentage of the population comprised by the largest linguistic group in society, the second largest group in society and the number of linguistic groups in society. Linguistic structure also fails to have an impact: not one of the variables has a statistically discernible effect. Again, the baseline variables have essentially the same effect as they do in all of the other models. Linguistic differences are, on average, not associated with human rights violations.

Aside from the interactive effect noted above, the democratization variables failed to produce significant results in any of our models. Neither a recent democratization, nor a drastic regime change appears to affect the government's human rights behaviour. This goes against previously cited work that related democratization to an improvement of human rights (Cingranelli and Richards, 1999; Scarritt and McMillan, 2000). There may be a perfectly reasonable explanation for these results. It is possible to argue that once democratic norms start to take root, human rights violations cease to be an available policy option for these governments. A young democracy may not have all the necessary institutions in place to achieve an improvement on its human rights record, but it would definitely lack some of the repressive institutions it used for human rights violations.

To summarize, then, we have found that while our baseline model performs well, the ethnic composition of society variables do not have an effect on the extent to which government's violate the physical integrity rights of the person of their citizens: only the largest ethnic group and largest religious group measures had an impact and these only when we used the US State Department PTS variable. The other variables that had an impact were robust: their effects were consistent and strong across multiple specifications and samples.

More specifically, the structural variable that had an impact was the type of regime; the other variables code the behaviour of both the government and dissidents and the government and other countries. This suggests that while the ethnic composition of society may have other effects on violent conflict in society, it does not appear to have a direct effect on the violation of human rights.

Conclusion

Our results are somewhat at odds with some results reported elsewhere in the literature. With respect to ethnic structure and human rights, our findings are consistent with Walker and Poe (2002), who conclude that there is only limited support for the proposition that ethnic fractionalization has a negative impact on human rights. Most of their findings failed to support the proposition, though they did report a linear negative relationship between ethnic fractionalization and physical quality of life indicators, which is a different dimension of human rights than examined here. With respect to democratization and human rights, Davenport (1999), Scarritt and McMillan (2000), and Zanger (2001) report a negative relationship between democratization and government coercion/physical integrity rights abuses. We took exception to the conventional wisdom and expected to find a positive relationship, mediated by the ethnic composition of society. We found no relationship, thus failing to find evidence to support arguments advanced by others or the argument advanced here.

Given that summary, it seems useful to suggest that our analysis of the ethnic composition of society on human rights violations is, in some sense, incomplete. Other studies have found that factors such as former colonial ties, the ideological orientation of the society (Poe and Tate, 1994; Poe, Tate and Keith, 1999), provisions in constitutions (Davenport 1996), elections (Davenport, 1997), population growth (Henderson, 1991), foreign aid (Cingranelli and Pasquarello, 1985; Blanton, 2000) and foreign economic penetration (Richards, Gelleny and Sacko, 2002) have an impact on respect for human rights. We do not control for such factors in our study, and it is possible that were we to do so, one (or more) of the relationships we reported might change. Future studies may want to probe such relationships.

In addition, we do not model what are almost surely reciprocal relations among some of these variables. Lindström and Moore (1995) and Gurr and Moore (1997) have shown that protest/rebellion and coercion are interconnected and that when one models them this way, one can uncover somewhat different relationships. The argument behind such a finding is simply that the level of dissident violence in a society is (partly) determined by the level of government repression in that society. Francisco (1995, 1996) and Carey (2002) study the reciprocal relations between dissent and repression across regime types and show that the behaviour of both dissidents and governments is mutually constituted. We, like others studying human rights violations, have modeled it as unidirectional phenomenon. But future work would do well to follow the lead of these studies to try to model the interactions between human rights violations and dissent.

The results presented here are, thus, provisional rather than definitive. That said, the baseline model findings are remarkably consistent across different groups of countries: data availability caused us to estimate parameters using as many as 158 countries and as few as 114 countries. Yet, the estimates reported in Table 10.2 are very similar in each column. This suggests that the relationships are strong. Thus, while we cannot rule out that some of the results might change in the face of a more sophisticated, reciprocal model, we have good reason to anticipate that most of the relationships will stand much as reported here.

Turning our attention away from research technicalities toward human rights, the tragedy is that there is a great deal of variance to be explained. If there is a positive note to take away from this study it is this: ethnically diverse societies are just as likely as ethnically homogenous societies to experience a positive or negative human rights environment. Some scholars have argued that ethnic partition is the best way to solve ethnic conflicts (e.g., Kauffman, 1996; Mearsheimer and Van Evera, 1999). Our results do not speak directly to that issue, but they are somewhat related, and they suggest that the ethnic composition of societies does *not* have a general (or inevitable) negative effect on human rights provision. Violence and mobilization for war most assuredly erode human rights provision, but the ethnic, religious, and linguistic composition of societies does not. As Moore (2002) has argued, warnings with respect to ethnic divisions can become self-fulfilling prophecy: we will do well to ground analyses of such phenomena in evidence.

Notes

1 The authors wish to thank Sabine Carey and Steve Poe for helpful comments on a previous draft. Dr. Lindström's contribution to this chapter has been written outside of his professional work with UNFPA and the context of this article does not in any way represent the views of the organization. Additional information about the operationalization of the indicators, see http://www.psci.unt.edu/ihrsc/careypoe.htm.

2 Japan has a small Korean minority, showing that even the countries we consider homogenous do not always consist of one ethnic group.

3 Gurr (1993, p.93) defines protest as acts aiming at 'persuading or intimidating officials to change their policies toward the group' by mobilizing support on behalf of reform. Any violence used by protesters is sporadic and unplanned.

4 Gurr (1993, p.93) distinguishes rebellion from protest by its more fundamental goals, its strategy of mobilization of coercive power, and its systematic and planned use of violence.

5 Ethnicity is, of course, but one identity. As we explain below, we believe it is an important identity with respect to understanding political mobilization, but it is certainly not the only type of category over which people mobilize. We nevertheless restrict our attention to ethnicity in this study.

6 Minorities at Risk dataset contains information on 233 ethnic, or communal, groups that have at one time or another since 1945 showed some signs of political activity

7 Ethnic groups are not the only ones that are likely to mobilize. However, as we argued above, ethnic minority groups are likely to mobilize, and we focus our attention on those groups because that is the focus of our study.

8 The results are based on ordinary least squares (OLS) regression. The data are arrayed in what is known as a pooled time-series cross-section format. This format raises two technical difficulties known as autocorrelation and (panel) heteroskedasticity. The standard solutions to those problems were not available in this study due to missing data which gave us a non-square data matrix. Rather than 1) exclude cases that were missing data; or 2) interpolate missing data; we chose to use OLS regression with robust standard errors (to ameliorate heteroskedasticity) and a lagged dependent variable (to address autocorrelation). A replication data set will be available at the third author's web site, and interested scholars may want to replicate the results using different techniques. One might also want to consider using an ordered logit model rather than OLS regression.

9 Anocracies are countries that have a score less than 6 on both the DEMOC and the AUTOC scales in the Polity data.

10 If the estimate was 1.0 then governments would, on average, do exactly what they did the year before – there would be very little change in the extent to which countries violate physical integrity rights over time.

11 The largest ethnic group has a negative impact, as hypothesized, when we use the State Department PTS variable.

12 Again, the largest ethnic group has a negative impact, as hypothesized, when we use the State Department PTS variable.

References

Blanton, S.L. (2000), 'Promoting Human Rights and Democracy in the Developing World: U.S. Rhetoric versus U.S. Arms Exports', *American Journal of Political Science*, Vol. 44(1), pp. 123-31.

Carey, S.C. (2002), 'The Dynamic Relationship Between Protest, Repression, and Political Regimes', paper presented at the annual meeting of the American Political Science Association, Boston.

Cingranelli, D.L. and Pasquarello, T. (1985), 'Human Rights Practices and US Distribution of Foreign Aid in Latin America', *American Journal of Political Science*, Vol. 29(3), pp. 539-63.

Cingranelli, D.L. and Richards, D.L. (1999), 'Respect for Human Rights after the End of the Cold War', *Journal of Peace Research*, Vol. 36(5), pp. 511-34.

Connor, W. (1983), 'Beyond Reason: The Nature of the Ethnonational Bond', *Ethnic and Racial Studies*, Vol. 16, pp. 373-89.

Davenport, C.A. (1995), 'Multi-Dimensional Threat Perception and State Repression: An Inquiry into Why States apply Negative Sanctions', *American Journal of Political Science*, Vol. 39(3), pp. 683-713.

Davenport, C.A. (1996), 'Constitutional Promises and Repressive Reality: A Cross-National Time-Series Investigation', *Journal of Politics*, Vol. 58(3), pp. 627-54.

Davenport, C.A. (1997), 'From Ballots to Bullets: National Elections and State Uses of Political Repression', *Electoral Studies*, Vol. 16(4), pp. 517-40.

Davenport, C. (1999), 'Human Rights and the Democratic Proposition', *Journal of Conflict Resolution*, Vol. 43(1), pp. 92-116.

Davenport, C. and Armstrong, D. (2002), 'Democracies Love Me, They Love Me Not: Exploring the Relationship between Human Rights and Democracy in the Third Wave', University of Maryland, unpublished manuscript.

Davenport, C, Moore, W.H. and Poe, S.C. (2003), 'Sometimes You Just Have to Leave: Domestic Threats and Forced Migration, 1964-1989', *International Interactions*, Vol.29, pp. 27-55.

Davis, D.R. and Moore, W.H. (1997), 'Ties that Bind? Domestic and International Conflict Behavior in Zaire', *Comparative Political Studies*, Vol. 31, pp. 45-71.

Ellingsen, T. (2000), 'Colorful Community or Ethnic Witches' Brew? Multiethnicity and Domestic Conflict During and After the Cold War', *Journal of Conflict Resolution*, Vol. 44(2), pp. 228-49.

Francisco, R.A. (1995), 'The Relationship between Coercion and Protest: An Empirical Analysis in Three Coercive States', *Journal of Conflict Resolution*, Vol. 39(2), pp. 263-82.

Francisco, R.A. (1996), 'Coercion and Protest: An Empirical Test in Two Democratic States', *American Journal of Political Science*, Vol. 40(4), pp. 1179-1204.

Gartner, S.S. and Regan, P.M. (1996), 'Threat and Repression: The Non-Linear Relationship between Government and Opposition Violence', *Journal of Peace Research*, Vol. 33(3), pp. 273-87.

Gellner, E. (1983), *Nations and Nationalism*, Ithaca, NY, Cornell University Press.

Gurr, T. (1986), 'The Political Origins of State Violence and Terror: A Theoretical Analysis', in *Governmental Violence and Repression: An Agenda for Research,* New York, Greenwood Press.

Gurr, T. (1993), *Minorities at Risk: A Global View of Ethnopolitical Conflicts*, Washington DC, United States Institute for Peace.

Gurr, T.R and Moore, W.H. (1997), 'Ethnopolitical Rebellion: A Cross-sectional Analysis of the 1980s with Risk Assessments for the 1990s', *American Journal of Political Science*, Vol. 41(4), pp. 1079-103.

Henderson, C. (1991), 'Conditions Affecting the Use of Political Repression', *Journal of Conflict Resolution*, Vol. 35(1), pp. 120-42.

Hibbs, D. (1973), *Mass Political Violence*, New York, Wiley.

Horowitz, D.L. (1985), *Ethnic Groups in Conflict*, Berkeley, CA, University of California Press.

Kalyvas, S.N. (2000), 'The Logic of Violence in Civil War: Theory and Preliminary Results', Estudio/Working Paper 2000/151, Madrid, Juan March Institute.

Kaufmann, C. (1996), 'Possible and Impossible Solutions to Ethnic Civil Wars', *International Security*, Vol. 20(4), pp. 136-75.

King, J.C. (1998), 'Repression, Domestic Threat and Interactions in Argentina and Chile', *Journal of Political and Military Sociology*, Vol. 26, pp. 1-27.

Lee, C. (2001), 'Protest and Repression in Latin America: A Synthetic Model', unpublished Ph.D. dissertation, Riverside, CA, University of California.

Lindström, R. (1996), 'Private Goods and Collective Action: Overcoming the "Large N" Problem in Ethnic Conflict', unpublished Ph.D. dissertation, Riverside, CA, University of California.

Lindström, R. and Moore, W.H. (1995), 'Deprived, Rational or Both? "Why Minorities Rebel" Revisited', *Journal of Political and Military Sociology*, Vol. 23, pp. 167-90.

Mearsheimer, J.J. and Van Evera, S. (1999), 'Redraw the Map, Stop the Killing', *The New York Times*, 19 April.

Mitchell, N.J. and McCormick, J.N. (1988), 'Economic and Political Explanations of Human Rights Violations', *World Politics*, Vol. 40(4), pp. 476-98.

Moore, W.H. (2002), 'Ethnic Minorities and Foreign Policy', *SAIS Review*, Vol.22(2), pp. 77-92.

Muller, E.N. and Seligson, M.A. (1987), 'Inequality and Insurgency', *American Political Science Review*, Vol. 81(2), pp. 425-52.

Olson, M. (1965), *The Logic of Collective Action; Public Goods and the Theory of Groups*, Cambridge, Harvard University Press.

Pion-Berlin, D. (1989), *The Ideology of State Terror*, Boulder, Colorado, Lynne Rienner.

Poe, S.C. and Tate, N.C. (1994), 'Repression of Rights to Personal Integrity to the 1980s: A Global Analysis', *American Political Science Review*, Vol. 88(4), pp. 853-72.

Poe, S.C., Tate, C.N. and Keith, L.C. (1999), 'Measuring the Level, Pattern, and Sequence of Government Respect for Physical Integrity Rights', *International Studies Quarterly*, Vol. 43(2), pp. 407-18.

Poe, S.C., Tate, C.N., Keith, L.C., and Lanier, D. (2000), 'Domestic Threats to Regimes' Rule and Their Abuse of Human Rights Across Time', in C. Davenport (ed.), *Paths to State Repression: Human Rights and Contentious Politics in Comparative Perspective*, Boulder, Colorado, Rowman and Littlefield, pp. 27-70.

Rasler, K.A. (1976), 'War, Accommodation, and Violence in the United States, 1890-1970', *American Political Science Review*, Vol. 80(3), pp. 921-45.

Richards, D.L., Gelleny, R.D., and Sacko, D.H. (2001), 'Money with a Mean Streak? Foreign Economic Penetration and Government Respect for Human Rights in Developing Countries', *International Studies Quarterly*, Vol. 45(2), pp. 219-39.

Saideman, S. (2000), *The Ties That Divide: Ethnic Politics, Foreign & International Conflict*, New York, Columbia University Press.

Saideman, S.M., Lanoue, D.J., Campenni, M., and Stanton, S. (2002), 'Democratization and Political Institutions: A Pooled Time-Series Analysis, 1985-1998', *Comparative Political Studies*, Vol. 35(1), pp. 103-29.

Sambanis, N. (2001), 'Do Ethnic and Nonethnic Civil Wars Have the Same Causes?' *Journal of Conflict Resolution*, Vol. 45(3), pp. 259-82.

Scarritt, J.R. and McMillan, S. (2000), 'Protest, Democratization and Human Rights in Africa,' in C. Davenport (ed.), *Paths to State Repression: Human Rights Violations and Contentious Politics*, pp. 195-216.

Stohl, M. (1975), 'War and Domestic Political Violence: The Case of the United States, 1890-1970', *Journal of Conflict Resolution*, Vol. 19, pp. 379-416.

Thompson, R.G.K. (1966), *Defeating Communist Insurgency: The Lessons of Malaya and Vietnam*, New York, Praeger.

Tilly, C. (1978), *From Mobilization to Revolution*, Reading, Massachusetts, Addison Wesley.

Turan, K. (2002), 'Ethnic Violence and Democratization: Can Democratization Reduce Ethnic Violence?' Paper presented at the annual meeting of the International Studies Association, New Orleans.

Walker, S. and Poe, S.C. (2002), 'Does Cultural Diversity Affect Countries' Respect for Human Rights?' *Human Rights Quarterly*, Vol. 24(1), pp. 237-63.

Williams, Jr., R.M. (1994), 'The Sociology of Ethnic Conflicts: Comparative International Perspective', *Annual Review of Sociology*, Vol. 20, pp. 49-79.

Yinger, J.M. (1985), 'Ethnicity', *Annual Review of Sociology*, Vol. 11, pp. 151-80.

Zanger, S.C. (2000), 'A Global Analysis of the Effect of Political Regimes Changes on Life Integrity Violations', *Journal of Peace Research*, Vol. 37(2), pp. 213-233.

Chapter 11

Domestic Threat and Repression: An Analysis of State Responses to Different Forms of Dissent

Sabine C. Carey

Introduction

In this volume, Poe argues that an increase in threat creates a situation of alarm in which states respond by trying to decrease the threat or to increase the strength of their regime. To do this they may choose from a variety of substitutable policy choices, but often they choose to lower the threat through repression. There is a considerable body of literature that analyzes how political regimes react to domestic protest as a form of threat (e.g., Gurr and Lichbach, 1986; Gupta, Singh et al., 1993; Davenport, 1995). Some studies distinguish between violent and non-violent protest (Gupta, Singh et al., 1993; Moore, 2000), whereas most aggregate different forms of dissent into one measure of protest. This chapter offers a new approach to the study of domestic dissent and state repression. It differentiates between five types of dissent and uses a statistical tool that allows us to find non-linear relationships between the different forms of dissent and repression. It distinguishes between peaceful anti-government demonstrations, strikes, violent riots, guerrilla warfare and large-scale rebellion.

The idea that governments' reactions to dissent are not uniform is not a new one. In his book on domestic mobilization and revolutions, Tilly argues that '[g]overnments respond selectively to different sorts of groups, and to different sorts of actions' (Tilly, 1978, p.106). This study empirically tests how governments use repression when faced with different types of protest activities that vary in intensity, organization and objective. Different protest activities pose different types of threat for the government. For example, the coup attempts in the Ivory Coast during the autumn in 2002 triggered a different kind of government response than riots in the Eastern part of the Democratic Republic of Congo did, demonstrations of the opposition party in Zimbabwe or the guerrilla warfare in Colombia. I analyze how different types of protest affected repression in 60 African and Latin American countries between the late 1970s and the late 1990s.

Davenport (1995) lists four different dimensions of threat to which governments might respond. These are: frequency of events, presence of violence, strategic variety and deviation from the norm. The presence of violence might substantially alter the response of the state, since violent dissent poses a greater threat than non-violent forms of dissent. Additionally, when faced with violent protest, the use of repression might be perceived as being legitimate and it would therefore be easier to justify it to the domestic and international community. He also suggests that if dissidents use only one form of protest and do not employ a large variety of dissent activities, the perceived threat is relatively low. And finally, he makes the argument that if protest activities fall within a cultural norm, the government is less likely to feel threatened by the conflict and will therefore be less likely to use force as a tool to increase its strength. Analyzing 53 countries between 1948 and 1982, he finds that governments increase sanctions when faced with a higher number of dissident activities, but also when different forms of protest are employed and when the activities lie outside the norms of interaction in that country. These findings suggest that governments take more than one aspect of domestic threat into the calculation of their response.

Gartner and Regan (1996) propose that the government's response to protest depends on the demands made by dissidents. Their study of 18 Latin American countries between 1977 and 1986 does not support the argument of the Strength/Threat ratio, which expects that the larger the threat, the more repressive the response of the government will be. Instead their results suggest that as the demand of the dissidents increases, governments react with more restraint. Similarly, governments appear to overreact to relatively low demands of the rebels with violent coercion.

This study intends to shed more light on the use of repression as a response to dissident behaviour by distinguishing between different types of protest activities. In the following, I introduce my model of domestic threat in the form of dissent and state coercion. Then I discuss the data and the results obtained from the empirical analysis. I conclude with some suggestions for further research that seeks to explain variations in human rights violations.

Repressive Response to Domestic Dissent

As mentioned in the beginning, I distinguish between five different forms of domestic dissent. These are demonstrations, strikes, riots, guerrilla warfare and revolutions. They differ in the amount of people involved, the level of organization, the level of violence and the nature of their objectives. Before discussing the impact of these types of protest on repression, the following section delineates the concepts by outlining their main characteristics.

Defining Dissent

Anti-government demonstrations are defined as peaceful gatherings, protesting against the government and/or against certain government policies. The amount of people involved might vary, but the crucial characteristic is that these are peaceful activities. The objectives of a demonstration range from being relatively narrow, such as lowering taxes, for example, to more general, such as demanding new elections to dispose of the incumbent government. General strikes are also defined as non-violent forms of dissent, but at least 1,000 people have to participate in the activity to qualify as a strike. Again, the objectives of strikes might vary, but the amount of organization involved is higher than that for demonstrations. Riots are defined as spontaneous and violent activities. The level of organization required for riots is low, which might decrease the threat perceived by the government. However, it is a violent display of protest, which might trigger a particularly harsh response. Guerrilla warfare is defined as violent dissent displayed by organized groups. The main differences between riots and guerrilla warfare are the level of organization and the amount of people involved, which are both higher in the case of guerrilla warfare. And finally, revolutions are defined as large-scale, organized and violent forms of events that are aimed at '[a]ny illegal or forced change in the top government elite' (Banks, 2000). They do not only refer to a successful overthrow of a government, but also include unsuccessful attempts, as well as rebellious activities aimed at gaining independence from the central government. Therefore, the objectives, the level of organization and participation form a particularly threatening mixture for the ruling elite.

Responding with Repression

The different types of protest activities pose different kinds of threats and costs to the government. Tilly argues that:

> the extent to which a given collective action by a given group is subject to repression, toleration, or facilitation is mainly a function of two factors: (1) the scale of the action, (2) the power of the group. The larger the scale of the action, the more likely its repression; the more powerful the group, the less likely its repression' (Tilly, 1978, p.115).

The categories applied in this chapter do not entirely overlap with Tilly's characteristics, but they are related to each other. Non-violent activities probably pose a similar level of threat to the government as small-scale actions, and violent activities are likely to pose a similar threat as large-scale actions do. The level of organization can be compared to the power that the group holds. Low levels of organization correspond to less power and high levels of organization to more power. This would suggest that demonstrations (non-violent and low level of organization) are least likely to trigger repression, whereas guerrilla warfare (violent and high level of organization) and revolutions (violent, high level of organization and overthrow of the government as policy goal) are expected to lead to state repression.

The levels of organization and violence are likely to affect the calculations of governments in different ways. Both characteristics of protest activities influence governments' cost-benefit calculations and both elements increase the costs of repression. However, the expected utility, or expected success rate, of repression is likely to differ between protest activities depending on their level of organization. If a government is faced with several highly organized dissent activities, such as guerrilla warfare or revolutions, the expected success rate of repression diminishes. This is based on the assumption that highly organized activities are more difficult to set off and end than spontaneous activities, whether they are violent or not. Therefore, following Davenport's study on multi-dimensional threat perception (1995), I expect that not only the type of activity, but also its frequency influences the government's response. In the following, I discuss how the state is expected to respond to different types of dissent.

Demonstrations Demonstrations pose a relatively low level of threat since they are both non-violent and do usually not require a strong network or organization of dissidents. Therefore, even if they occur several times, governments are expected to respond with relatively low levels of repression. The costs of repression as a response to non-violent demonstrations could be very high. Repression might trigger international condemnations as well as increased frustration and dissent among the population due to the perceived low legitimacy of such a response.

Strikes Strikes are seen as more threatening than demonstrations since they involve a larger number of people and often require more organization and hence commitment from at least some dissidents. Therefore, I expect the state's response to strikes to be more coercive than in the case of demonstrations. As strikes become more frequent, the government might still refrain from further increasing its use of coercion. The rationale behind this is that the costs of a further increase in repression when faced with several strikes would outweigh the potential benefits since this could lead to the escalation of the violent behaviour of the dissidents. Since strikes are, by definition, gatherings of at least 1,000 people, the 'safety in numbers' might trigger the escalation and turn the non-violent display of discontent into a violent form of protest, which the government is keen to avoid. Why would the government use force against strikes at all? The government is expected to view the use of some form of repression as necessary in order to deal with strikes, but the level of repression is unlikely to be increased when faced with a larger number of strikes. This is due to the increased risk attached to the use of more severe and violent forms of repression since extensive coercion as a response to a non-violent display of protest is likely to be interpreted as disproportionately harsh, and as such might trigger further resistance from the population.

Riots Riots are violent and spontaneous displays of dissent. Due to their violent nature, governments are expected to respond with repression, even if faced with only one riot in a given year. As riots become more frequent, governments are expected to further tighten their grip. Since riots are by definition not based on well-organized networks, the government can expect to crush the riots eventually. Therefore, the expected utility of repression when confronted with riots is very high.

Guerrilla warfare Guerrilla warfare also poses a violent threat, but it involves a higher level of participation and organization than spontaneous riots. Therefore, the threat of such protest activities is very high. But as such events become more frequent, the cost-benefit calculation of a repressive response changes. The government might at first increase its strength in the form of repression, but as the attacks become more frequent the costs are likely to outweigh the benefits. It might then opt for accommodating the dissidents rather than accelerating repression even further.

Gartner and Regan (1996) investigate the impact of opposition violence on state repression in 18 Latin American countries from 1977 to 1986. Their findings suggest that 'as the nature of the threat posed by an opposition group moves from minor to extreme, the marginal increment of government repression decreases' (Gartner and Regan, 1996, p.273). The same rationale applies to the argument made above. Since the level of repression as a response to guerrilla warfare is already relatively high, the benefits from a further increase in coercion diminish. Similarly, in a study of repression and dissent in Peru and Sri Lanka between 1955 and 1991, Moore (2000) finds that if repression is high, states react to dissent with less repressive and more cooperative behaviour.

In the case of guerrilla warfare, governments already use a substantial amount of repression in an attempt to deter the threat, but without signs of success the costs are expected to quickly outweigh the benefits, decelerating state coercion. The reason why this behaviour differs from that taken by governments when they are faced with riots is because the perceived probability of eventually overwhelming riots, which are spontaneous outbursts of violent dissent, is expected to be higher than the probability of crushing attacks from guerrilla groups.

Revolutions The last scenario is the response to revolutions. Revolutions are both violent and based on an organized group of dissent, similar to guerrilla warfare, but revolutions have the specific aim to overthrow the government. Therefore, the threat to the government is extremely high and the initial response is expected to be very violent. However, the opportunity costs of further repression in the face of additional large-scale rebellion is even higher than in the case of guerrilla warfare, which is why repression is expected to decline when confronted with numerous such attacks. For example, leaders often leave the country or disappear from the national stage when faced with sustained revolutionary activities instead of concentrating on preparing several counter-attacks. Table 11.1 summarizes how repression is expected to be used as a response to the different types of protest activities.

Table 11.1 Summary of hypotheses

Protest activity	Expected effect on repression
Demonstrations	Low; independent of frequency
Strikes	Low; Independent of frequency

Riots	Medium-high; Increasing with higher frequency of activity
Guerrilla Warfare	High; Declining with higher frequency of activity
Revolutions	Very high; Declining with higher frequency activity

Willingness and Opportunity

Various studies have pointed out that domestic protest is only one among other factors that influence repression (Gupta, Singh et al., 1993; Davenport, 1995; Krain, 1997). Gupta, Singh and Sprague (1993) argue that the reason for the lack of consensus on the relationship between government coercion and dissident behaviour lies in the neglect of the overall political, socio-economic and international context. Similarly, Poe argues in this volume that the Strength/Threat ratio is also influenced by the opportunity and the willingness of the regime to use violence against its citizens. The nature of the political regime plays a particularly important role in that context. Political regimes are 'rules and basic political resource allocations according to which actors exercise authority by imposing and enforcing collective decisions on a bounded constituency' (Kitschelt, 1992, p.1028). They lay the ground rules for political governance and power allocation. Political regimes define the boundaries within which the government can legitimately use force. Therefore, the nature of political regimes is likely to influence the calculations of particular governments whether or not to use repression against their citizens.

Empirical studies on the relationship between democratic institution and repression have consistently found that democracies are associated with lower levels of state coercion (Mitchell and McCormick, 1988; Poe and Tate, 1994; Poe, Tate et al., 1999). I hypothesize that the more democratic a regime, the less repressive will be the government, *ceteris paribus*, since democratic norms and institutions are expected to provide non-violent channels for conflict settlement.

In addition to regime type, I include a measure of regime durability to investigate the impact of young and unconsolidated regimes on state coercion. The authority patterns in young regimes are usually not (yet) firmly established and accepted as the 'rules of the game.' When faced with dissent, the threat perception of a younger regime is likely to be greater than that of an established regime. Therefore, I expect that the older a regime is, the lower is the level of repression. The ruling elites have either found a way to deal with opponents, for example via democratic institutions, or they might have eliminated them and injected enough fear into potential dissidents so that the level of repression can be kept relatively low.

And finally, the analysis accounts for the impact of various socio-economic factors that have previously been found to influence state repression. These are lagged repression, the level of economic development, involvement in international war and population size. In line with previous research, lagged repression is expected to increase state coercion due to bureaucratic inertia and the self-perpetuating effect of the repressive apparatus. Economic development is expected to decrease repression (Mitchell and McCormick, 1988; Poe and Tate, 1994; Zanger, 2000). Economically stronger countries are less likely to feel threatened than economically weak countries and, therefore, they are less likely to use repression as a policy instrument (see also Davenport, 1995). Similar to economic development, population size has widely been used in research of human rights violations, finding a positive relationship between population size and repression (Henderson, 1991, 1993; Poe, Tate et al., 1999; Zanger, 2000). Apart from the fact that in a country with more people, more people can be repressed, a larger population is expected to place 'stress on national resources and [to bring] the threat of environmental deterioration, further reducing available resources' (Poe and Tate, 1994, p.857). Therefore, in countries with a large population, the resources are potentially limited and the government feels more threatened and hence is more likely to use repression. And finally, international war has been argued to pose a significant threat for governments, affecting their behaviour towards their own population and increasing repressive actions (Gurr, 1986; Poe and Tate, 1994). I also include a dummy variable for African countries to account for differences in the nature of repression between Latin America and Africa.

Data and Analysis

To empirically investigate the arguments made above, I analyze 42 countries from sub-Saharan Africa and 18 countries from Latin America between 1976 and 1993. Studies on protest and repression that implement cross-sectional analysis have often pooled the largest number of countries for which data were available (Muller and Weede, 1994; Poe and Tate, 1994; Davenport, 1995). I concentrate my analysis on countries from Latin America and sub-Saharan Africa. The Latin American countries share many characteristics, such as history, culture and societal characteristics, which might influence the relationship between dissent and state repression. Also, the African countries share many characteristics that are not controlled for in the analysis. Countries on both continents had similar experiences with authoritarian regimes and democratization. Including countries from Eastern Europe or Asia, or even developed Western democracies would have reduced the applicability and precision of the results due to the very different patterns of domestic conflict in these countries. Therefore, I follow the approach of restricting my analysis to more homogeneous set of cases (Aflatooni and Allen, 1991; Gartner and Regan, 1996; Swaminathan, 1999). As mentioned above I include a dummy variable for the African countries to control for systematic differences between countries from Africa and Latin America.

To measure repression, I use the Political Terror Scale (PTS). This is a standard-based measure based on categories developed by Gastil (1980), used in various chapters in this book. It codes yearly country reports issued by Amnesty

International and the US State Department. It assigns a value from one to five to each country in each year based on the occurrence of arbitrary imprisonment, torture, disappearances and extra-judicial killings. Level 1 indicates that life integrity violations are generally absent. For example, Botswana and Mauritius are coded as Level 1 of the Political Terror Scale throughout most of the observed time period. Level 2 indicates that there is limited political imprisonment but that state violence is rare. Examples include Panama and Cameroon during most of the 1980s. Level 3 stands for a country where people are frequently imprisoned for political reasons and where state violence in the form of torture and extrajudicial executions are common. Mexico and the Sudan fell in this category until the mid-1980s. Level 4 is assigned to countries where state violence is part of common life but is targeted mainly at political opponents, as in Angola during the late 1980s. And finally, Level 5 refers to a country that suffers from indiscriminate and large-scale state violence. Examples are Argentina and Uganda during the late 1970s. In general, state coercion between 1977 and 1993 was more violent in Latin America than in Africa. For my statistical analysis I use the data based on the Amnesty International Reports and for the years in which a country was not covered by this report, I took the score coded from the U.S. State Department Country Reports.

The data measuring the protest activities are taken from the Cross-National Time-Series Archive by Arthur Banks (2000). Each protest activity (anti-government demonstration, strike, riot, guerrilla warfare and revolution) is measured with a yearly count variable, counting the number of times such an event has occurred. Table 11.2 shows the maximum and the mean of the different protest activities in Africa and Latin America.[1] It highlights that dissent was more common in Latin America, in particular demonstrations and strikes.

Table 11.2 Frequencies of protest activities

	Maximum		Mean	
	Africa	Latin America	Africa	Latin America
Demonstrations	6	15	0.17	0.89
Strikes	4	6	0.04	0.51
Riots	7	7	0.18	0.36
Guerrilla warfare	3	3	0.14	0.29
Revolutions	3	2	0.28	0.24

To measure regime type, I use the Polity variable from the Polity IV dataset (Marshall and Jaggers, 2001). It ranges from minus 10 (autocratic regimes) to plus 10 (democratic regimes) and measures institutional characteristics. Regime duration is also taken from the Polity IV dataset and counts the number of years since the last regime change. This variable ranges from zero to 93 years with a mean of 14.6 years. Economic development is measured as logged GNP per capita, the variable capturing population size is also used in its logged form due to the skewed distribution. Both variables are taken from the World Bank Development Indicators. The involvement in international war is measured with a dummy variable, coded as one for those country-years during which the country was involved in an international war and zero for all other country-years. These data are based on Singer and Small (Singer and Small, 1994).

Since the dependent variable, state repression, is measured on an ordinal scale, I use ordered probit models to analyze variances in repression. This model, introduced to the social sciences by McKelvey and Zavoina (1975), is based on a measurement model in which a latent variable is mapped onto an observed variable.[2] I estimate the following three models, where the star * at the dependent variable represents the unobserved underlying variables.

$$\text{Repression}^*_{tj} = \beta_1 \text{Repression}_{(t-1)j} + \beta_2 \text{Demonstrations}_{tj} + \beta_3 \text{Strikes}_{tj} + \beta_4 \text{Guerrilla Warfare}_{tj} + \beta_5 \text{Revolutions}_{tj} + \beta_6 \text{Polity}_{tj} + \beta_7 \text{Polity Durability}_{tj} + \beta_8 \text{International War}_{tj} + \beta_9 \text{logged GNP per capita}_{tj} + \beta_{10} \text{logged Population Size}_{tj} + \beta_{11} \text{Africa}_{tj} + \varepsilon_{tj}$$

Due to high correlation between demonstrations and riots, I analyze the impact of riots by replacing the variable measuring demonstrations with the one measuring riots. The results of the ordered probit analysis are shown in Table 11.3. The overall fit of the models is very good as indicated by the chi^2 statistic, which is statistically significant at the level of $p < 0.000$.

All control variables display the hypothesized effect, with the exception of international war, which is statistically significant but has a negative effect.[3] Repression at time t-1 leads to an increase in repression at time t with approximately 0.95 probability. Similarly, economic development in the form of GNP per capita decreases the probability of repression, whereas larger populations increase it. The polity coefficient is negative and statistically significant, indicating that more democratic regimes display a lower probability of repression. These results confirm previous findings of empirical studies on state coercion. Polity duration does not appear to influence the probability of repression in sub-Saharan Africa and Latin America during the late 1970s and early 1990s. The age of a regime does not seem to have a substantial impact on the probability of repression being used as a policy tool.

All protest activities increase the probability of repression and are statistically significant with the exception of demonstrations and strikes. Both forms of dissent are expected to trigger a certain level of state coercion, but this response is hypothesized to be independent of the number of protest activities confronting the government. This might explain why an increase in the number of strikes or demonstrations does not affect the probability of repression.

Table 11.3 Results from ordered probit analysis

	Model 1 with demonstrations Coefficient		Model 2 with riots Coefficient	
Repression$_{t-1}$	0.958***	(0.052)[c]	0.963***	(0.052)
Demonstrations	0.031	(0.035)		(0.035)
Strikes	0.014	(0.068)	0.005	(0.067)
Riots			0.084*	(0.049)
Guerrilla warfare	0.508***	(0.105)	0.503***	(0.105)
Revolutions	0.365***	(0.081)	0.361***	(0.081)
Polity	-0.038***	(0.007)	-0.038***	(0.007)
Polity duration	-0.003	(0.002)	-0.003	(0.002)
International war	-0.402**	(0.171)	-0.391**	(0.172)
GNP per capita[a]	-0.129**	(0.056)	-0.133**	(0.056)
Population size[a]	0.195***	(0.032)	0.185***	(0.032)
Africa	-0.636***	(0.125)	-0.650***	(0.124)
τ_1[b]	2.301	(0.636)	1.452	(0.807)
τ_2	4.379	(0.643)	3.600	(0.811)
τ_3	5.948	(0.656)	5.167	(0.825)
τ_4	7.323	(0.667)	6.396	(0.837)
N	980		981	
LR ch^2	978.24		979.47	
Prob > chi^2	0.000		0.000	

a The natural log was taken due to skewed distribution.
b These figures indicate the calculated cut-off points of the unobserved dependent variable.
c Standard errors in parentheses.
* indicates the level of statistical significance at $p < 0.1$, ** at $p < 0.05$ and *** at $p < 0.001$.

The Probability of Repression

In the following, I present the results in a more intuitive way by simulating quantities of interest based on the models presented in Table 11.3 (King et al., 2000; Tomz, Wittenberg et al. 2001).[4] Table 11.4 shows the probabilities of the different levels of the Political Terror Scale in an 'average' African and Latin American country. This means that average values were assigned to the variables measuring repression$_{t-1}$, polity, polity duration, logged GNP per capita and logged population size, without any protest activities and no involvement in an international war.[5] The simulations show that in an African country, mostly non-violent forms of state coercion (PTS Level 2) are most likely with 50.5 per cent (±4.8 per cent), but some violence with extensive political imprisonment (PTS Level 3) occurs with a probability of 42.1 per cent (±4.5 per cent).[6] In an average

Latin American country, however, violent state coercion (PTS Level 3) is by far the most likely form of repression with the probability of 55.3 per cent (±4.5 per cent). Non-violent coercion (PTS Level 2) occurs with 28.4 per cent (±6.8 per cent) probability. In Latin America and sub-Saharan Africa neither the absence of any repression nor widespread state terror are very likely.

The question is whether these probabilities change as the government faces different forms of dissent. Table 11.5 lists the simulated changes in the predicted probabilities of repression when the frequency of a particular protest activity changes from zero to the maximum frequency, as shown in Table 11.2 above.[7] In general, when a country experiences a high number of protest activities, the probability of non-violent levels of coercion decreases and the probability of torture and political killings increases. Due to space limitations, the standard errors of the probability changes are not shown. But where the confidence intervals were small enough to include only positive or only negative changes, the figures are put in italics. Only changes in guerrilla warfare, revolutions and regime type, indicated by the Polity variable, lead to changes in the predicted probability. For example, if a country in Africa experiences an increase in the guerrilla warfare measure from none to three (the maximum) in a particular year, political imprisonment without state violence becomes 42.4 per cent (±10 per cent) less likely, whereas widespread torture and killings of political opponents become 33.1 per cent (±15 per cent) more likely.

It is interesting to note that when a country moves from being very autocratic to very democratic, corresponding to a change from minimum to maximum in the Polity variable, the probability of no state repression increases only slightly, namely by 5.5 per cent in Africa and only 1.5 per cent in Latin America. This might be due to the relative absence of the respect of life integrity rights in the dataset. At the same time, limited state coercion (Level 3 on the Political Terror Scale) becomes more and violent coercion less likely, both in Africa and Latin America. Note that when a country moves from most autocratic to most democratic, in Africa limited violent repression becomes 22.2 per cent (±8.2 per cent) less likely but only 10.4 per cent (±6.6 per cent) less likely in Latin America.

In general, state responses to demonstrations and riots are very similar to each other, as are the responses to guerrilla warfare and revolutions. This suggests that governments group protest activities into two broad categories. One category consists of activities where violence is either absent, as in the case of demonstration, or sporadic and uncoordinated, as in the case of riots. The other category contains organized and violent attacks, as identified with guerrilla warfare or revolutions. Plotting the predicted probabilities of the different levels of the Political Terror Scale for increasing numbers of the various protest activities, both for Latin America and Africa, suggests the following.[8] As the numbers of demonstrations or riots in Africa increase, the probability of repression at the PTS Level 2 (limited political imprisonment) decreases from around 50 per cent for one demonstration/riot down to approximately 25 per cent for six or more demonstrations/riots per year. This downward trend, however, is accompanied by increasing confidence intervals as the number of protest activities increase.

Table 11.4 The probability of repression

	Pr(PTS=1)[a]		Pr(PTS=2)		Pr(PTS=3)		Pr(PTS=4)		Pr(PTS=5)	
	Africa	LA[b]	Africa	LA	Africa	LA	Africa	LA	Africa	LA
Mean	0.023	0.004	0.505	0.284	0.421	0.553	0.050	0.150	0.001	0.009
Std. Err.	0.005	0.022	0.024	0.161	0.022	0.091	0.008	0.098	0.001	0.018

Table 11.5 Changes in the probability of repression

Min->Max	ΔPr(PTS=1)[a]		ΔPr(PTS=2)		ΔPr(PTS=3)		ΔPr(PTS=4)		ΔPr(PTS=5)	
	Africa	LA[b]	Africa	LA	Africa	LA	Africa	LA	Africa	LA
Demonstrations	-0.008	-0.001	-0.156	-0.105	0.066	-0.049	0.087	0.121	0.011	0.035
Strikes	0.004	0.001	-0.034	-0.013	0.007	-0.023	0.021	0.028	0.002	0.007
Riots[c]	-0.015	-0.003	-0.197	-0.143	0.106	-0.038	0.097	0.149	0.009	0.036
Guerrilla Warf.	*-0.022*	*-0.004*	*-0.424*	*-0.261*	0.039	*-0.267*	*0.331*	*0.334*	*0.076*	*0.198*
Revolutions	*-0.021*	*-0.004*	*-0.343*	*-0.228*	*0.122*	*-0.137*	*0.213*	*0.275*	*0.029*	*0.094*
Polity	*0.055*	*0.015*	*0.237*	*0.254*	*-0.222*	*-0.104*	*-0.066*	*-0.148*	*-0.003*	*-0.016*

The figures in *italics* indicate that the 95 per cent confidence interval does not include a zero probability.

[a] PTS=1 indicates no life integrity violations, PTS=2 limited political imprisonment, violence being rare, PTS=3 extensive political imprisonment, state violence being common, PTS=4 state violence part of common life, targeting political opponents and PTS=5 indiscriminate and large-scale state violence

[b] Latin America

[c] These results are based on Model 2, in which demonstrations have been replaced with riots

The probability of the PTS Level 3 (political imprisonment, limited violence) first increases from about 31 per cent to almost 60 per cent, but then declines as demonstrations occur more than five times a year. In the case of riots, the probability of some violent repression appears to level off at about 40 per cent. The probability of the widespread repression (PTS Level 4) continuously increases from about zero to 20 per cent, as demonstrations or riots become more frequent. Concerning guerrilla warfare and revolutions, it appears that only two such events are needed for limited state violence to become the most likely form of repression. The probability of widespread state violence (PTS Level 4) increases to about 0.35 but with rather large confidence intervals.

Figures 11.1 and 11.2 show these developments by plotting the probabilities of PTS Levels 3 and 4 during an increase in demonstrations for both an average African and Latin American country. The x-axis refers to the number of demonstrations per year, the y-axis shows the predicted probabilities. The lines show the predicted mean probability, based on 1,000 simulations. The vertical bars indicate the 95 per cent confidence intervals of the predicted probabilities.

In Africa, the most likely state response is limited violence (PTS Level 3). Limited repression is likely to occur with about 40 per cent probability, independent of the number of demonstrations. In Latin America, extensive state violence appears to be slightly more likely than in Africa at around 15 per cent and the confidence intervals widen as demonstrations occur more often. These two figures support the argument that the frequency of demonstrations does not alter the state's response.

Figures 11.3 and 11.4 plot the predicted probabilities for increasing numbers of guerrilla activities. In general, the figures suggest that if a government is faced with more guerrilla attacks, it becomes more likely that it employs widespread violence and repression in order to minimise the threat. If there are only one or two attacks, state repression appears to be targeted at a much smaller selection of the population. Figure 11.3 suggests that if a government in Africa is confronted with three or more guerrilla activities a year, extensive imprisonment (PTS Level 3) is almost as likely as violent repression (PTS Level 4) because the confidence intervals start to overlap at this point. Governments in Latin America appear to use harsher responses when faced with just over one guerrilla activity, reacting with repression to such dissident activities. These figures seem to falsify the hypothesis that repression declines as guerrilla warfare becomes more frequent.

Gupta et al. (1993) and Davenport (1995) point out that regime type shapes governments' reaction to activities of dissent. Gupta et al. analyze the response of coercion to protest demonstrations and deaths from domestic group violence in 24 countries between 1960 and 1980. They find a positive linear relationship in democracies, which means that more protest triggers harsher responses from the government. In non-democracies, however, their results suggest that there is an inverted U-shaped relationship, meaning that coercion is low under low and high levels of protest and high under medium levels of protest. I could not detect such stark differences between the responses of democratic and non-democratic regimes. However, the response was consistently less violent in democracies compared to non-democracies.

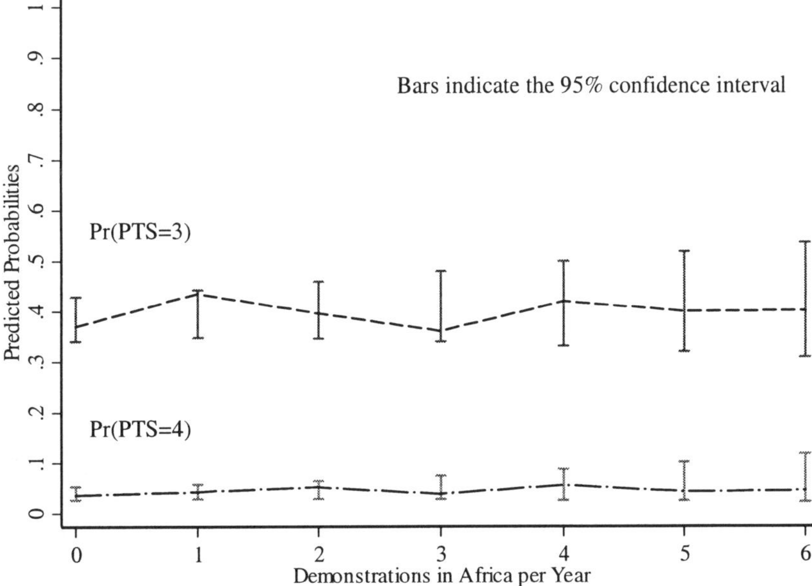

Figure 11.1 Probability of repression responding to demonstrations in Africa

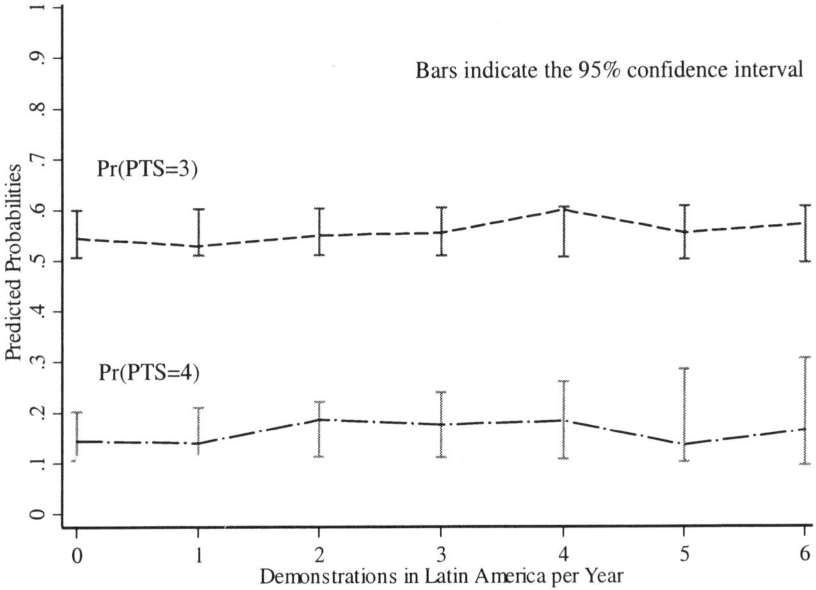

Figure 11.2 Probability of repression responding to demonstrations in Latin America

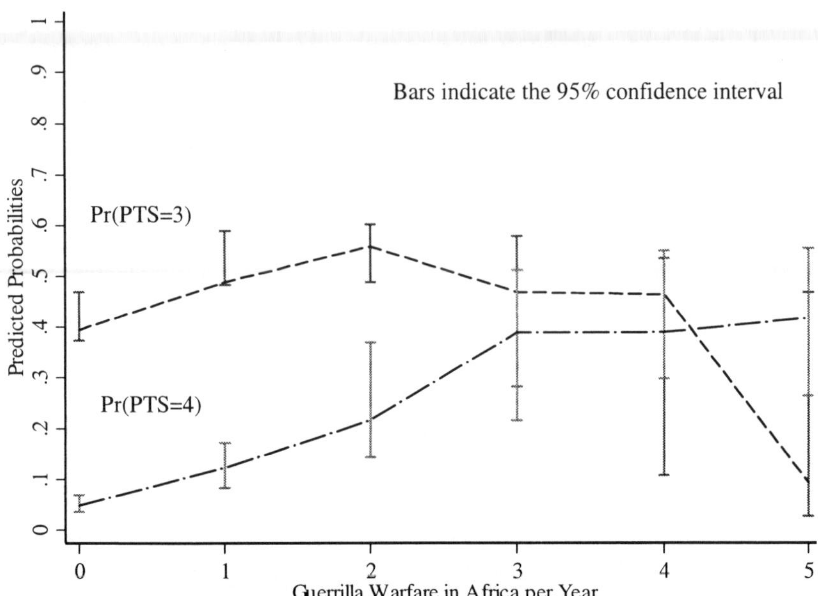

Figure 11.3 Probability of repression responding to guerrilla warfare in Africa

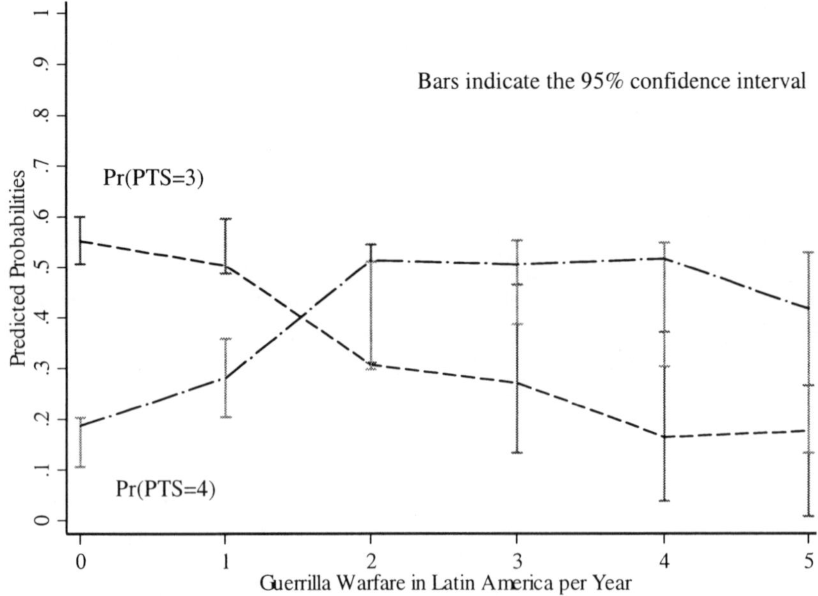

Figure 11.4 Probability of repression responding to guerrilla warfare in Latin America

Conclusion

This study set out to analyze governments' responses, in the form of repression, to different types of protest activities. It analyzed the probability of different levels of repression as a response to peaceful anti-government demonstrations, strikes, riots, guerrilla warfare and revolutions in 60 countries from Africa and Latin America between the late 1970s and early 1990s. The results suggest that governments group these five different protest activities into two broad categories. They appear to distinguish between acts of protest that are either non-violent or spontaneous on the one side and activities that are violent and require a certain level of organization of the dissidents on the other. The second category of protest activities seems to trigger harsher and more violent state responses than the first one.

Putting this finding into the concept of the Strength/Threat ratio as discussed by Poe in this volume, the answer for the governments' reactions seems intuitive. Guerrilla warfare and revolutionary revolts are particularly threatening for governments in power for at least four reasons. First, both types of dissent require a relatively strong and well-established network of oppositional forces. This means that they have overcome the rebel's dilemma of collective action (Lichbach 1998) and are therefore in a good position to mobilize further dissent, indicating a long-term threat to the governing elite. Second, both protest activities also require the participation of a large number of people. Again, this increases the probability of further dissent as argued by micromobilization theory, bandwagon models and threshold models (Opp, 1989; Chong, 1991; Rasler, 1996). These approaches argue that once you have mobilized a certain number of people, the mobilization of additional dissidents becomes less difficult. Whereas the first point mentioned above relates to the organizational structures that are in place and facilitate further recruitment, this argument hints at the mobilizing power of personal commitment. The third reason is that revolutions and guerrilla attacks are highly violent forms of dissent, hence posing a particularly acute threat to the government. And finally, guerrilla warfare and revolutions usually have a much more fundamental policy goal, namely substantially changing the structure of the political regime. Again, this attacks the heart of governments' existence and is therefore seen as particularly dangerous and threatening. The combination of these factors explains the harsh reaction of governments to the display of these types of dissent.

Unfortunately, no clear conclusions can be drawn about the behaviour of governments as these events become more frequent. This is due to the high level of uncertainty in predicting levels of repression for more than two to three such activities. The figures indicate that the simulated confidence intervals of the predicted probabilities become larger when guerrilla warfare is modelled as occurring several times a year. The larger confidence intervals are mainly due to the fact that this type of dissent occurs, at most, only a few times a year.

The study showed that government behaviour in Africa and Latin America largely resembled each other. It would be an interesting task for future research to extend the analysis to countries in Eastern Europe and Asia, for example, to test whether these are global patterns. Two limitations of this research are both the temporal and spatial level of aggregation. As more detailed data become available, researchers need to tackle the question of how, and under what conditions, domestic dissent spreads across a country. Similarly, with data that are coded over smaller time intervals we ought to investigate both nature of government responses as well as their timing. This would allow us to build a better understanding of the dynamics of state repression.

Notes

1 The minimum is zero for all variables and is not shown in the table.

2 For a detailed discussion of ordered probit, see Long, J. S. (1997).

3 One explanation for the unexpected finding that countries, which are involved in an inter-state war, are less likely to violate the life integrity rights of their citizens, could be that variety of opposition activities, which might increase during international conflict and eventually lead to repression, are already accounted for. This might cancel out the positive effect of international war, which is usually found in quantitative human rights research.

4 The results are based on 1000 simulations from Model 1, which excluded the variable measuring riots due to its high collinearity with demonstrations. The simulations with riots instead of demonstrations are almost identical. and are therefore not displayed.

5 This means that Repression at time t-1 was set at 2.76, Polity at –2.89, Polity Duration at 14.58 years, logged GNP per capita at 6.32 and logged Population Size at 15.57.

6 The percentages in parentheses show the 95 per cent confidence interval.

7 The results only refer to the contemporaneous effects. The over-time impact of the variables measuring protest activities is likely to be higher but is included in the effect of the lagged dependent variable.

8 The graphs can be obtained from the author upon request.

References

Aflatooni, A. and Allen, M.P. (1991), 'Government Sanctions and Collective Political Protest in Periphery and Semi-Periphery States: A Time-Series Analysis', *Journal of Political and Military Sociology*, Vol. 19(1), pp. 29-45.

Banks, A. (2000), Cross-national Time-series Database. [machine-readable data file] / Cross-National Time-Series Data Archive, Binghamton, New York. Cross-National Time-Series Data Archive [distributor].

Chong, D. (1991), *Collective Action and the Civil Rights Movement*, Chicago and London, The University of Chicago Press.

Davenport, C. (1995), 'Multi-Dimensional Threat Perception and State Repression: An Inquiry into why States apply Negative Sanctions', *American Journal of Political Science*, Vol. 39(3), pp. 683-713.

Gartner, S.S. and Regan, P.M. (1996), 'Threat and Repression: The Non-Linear Relationship between Government and Opposition Violence', *Journal of Peace Research*, Vol. 33(3), pp. 273-87.

Gastil, R. (1980), *Freedom in the World: Political Rights and Civil Liberties*, Westport, CT, Greenwood.

Greene, W.H. (2000), *Econometric Analysis*, New York, Prentice-Hall.

Gupta, D.K., Singh, H. and Sprague, T. (1993), 'Government Coercion of Dissidents', *Journal of Conflict Resolution*, Vol. 37(2), pp. 301-39.

Gurr, T.R. (1986), 'Persisting Patterns of Repression and Rebellion: Foundations for a General Theory of Political Coercion', in M. Karns (ed.), *Persistent Patterns and Emergent Structures in a Waning Century*, New York, Praeger, pp. 149-68.

Gurr, T.R. and Lichbach, M.I. (1986), 'Forecasting international Conflict: A Competitive Evaluation of Empirical Theories', *Comparative Political Studies*, Vol. 19(1), pp. 3-38.

Henderson, C.W. (1991), 'Conditions Affecting the Use of Political Repression', *Journal of Conflict Resolution*, Vol. 35(1), pp. 120-42.

Henderson, C.W. (1993), 'Population Pressures and Political Repression', *Social Science Quarterly*, Vol. 74(2), pp. 322-33.

King, G., Tomz, M. and Wittenberg, J. (2001), 'Making the Most of Statistical Analyses: Improving Interpretation and Presentation', *American Journal of Political Science*, Vol. 44(2), pp. 347-61.

Kitschelt, H. (1992), 'Political Regime Change: Structure and Process-driven Explanations', *American Political Science Review*, Vol. 86(4), pp. 1028-34.

Krain, M. (1997), 'State-Sponsored Mass Murder: the Onset and Severity of Genocides and Politicides', *Journal of Conflict Resolution*, Vol. 41(3), pp. 331-60.

Lichbach, M.I. (1998), *The Rebel's Dilemma*, Michigan, University of Michigan Press.

Long, J.S. (1997), *Regression Models for Categorical and Limited Dependent Variables*. London, Sage.

Marshall, M.G. and Jaggers, K. (2001), Polity IV Project: Political Regime Characteristics and Transitions, 1800-1999. The Polity IV dataset, http://www.bsos.umd.edu/cidcm/inscr/polity/index.htm.

Mason, D. and Krane, D. (1989), 'The Political Economy of Death Squads: Toward a Theory of the Impact of State-Sanctioned Terror', *International Studies Quarterly* Vol. 33(2), pp. 175-98.

McKelvey, R.D. and Zavoina, W. (1975), 'A Statistical Model for the Analysis of Ordinal Level Dependent Variables', *Journal of Mathematical Sociology*, Vol. 4, pp. 103-20.

Mitchell, N.J. and McCormick, J.M. (1988), 'Economic and Political Explanations of Human Rights Violations', *World Politics*, Vol. 40(4), pp. 476-98.

Moore, W.H. (2000), 'The Repression of Dissent: A Substitution Model of Government Coercion', *Journal of Conflict Resolution*, Vol. 44(1), pp. 107-27.

Muller, E.N. and Weede, E. (1994), 'Theories of Rebellion: Relative Deprivation and Power Contention', *Rationality and Society*, Vol. 6(1), pp. 40-57.

Opp, K.-D. (1989), *The Rationality of Political Protest*, Boulder, CO, Westview Press.

Poe, S.C. and Tate, C.N. (1994), 'Repression of Human Rights and Personal Integrity in the 1980s: A Global Analysis', *American Political Science Review*, Vol. 88(4), pp. 853-72.

Poe, S.C., Tate, C.N. and Keith, L.C. (1999), 'Repression of the Human Right to Personal Integrity Revisited: A Global Cross-National Study covering the Years 1976-1993', *International Studies Quarterly*, Vol. 43(2), pp. 291-313.

Rasler, K.A. (1996), 'Concessions, Repression, and Political Protest in the Iranian Revolution', *American Sociological Review*, Vol. 61(1), pp. 132-52.

Singer, J.D. and Small, M. (1994), Correlates of War Project: International and Civil War Data, 1816-1992 (ICPSR 9905), Ann Arbor, MI: Inter-University Consortium for Political and Social Research.

Swaminathan, S. (1999), 'Time, Power, and Democratic Transitions', *Journal of Conflict Resolution*, Vol. 43(2), pp. 178-91.

Tilly, C. (1978), *From Mobilization to Revolution*, New York, McGraw-Hill.

Tomz, M., Wittenberg, J. and King, G. (2001), CLARIFY: Software for Interpreting and Presenting Statistical Results. Cambridge, MA, Harvard University, http://gking.harvard.edu/.

Zanger, S.C. (2000), 'The Global Analysis of the Effect of Political Regime Changes on Life Integrity Violations, 1977-93', *Journal of Peace Research* Vol. 37(2), pp. 213-33.

Chapter 12

How Organizations Shape Human Rights Violations

Pablo Policzer

Introduction

People in a wide variety of coercive organizations commit human rights violations. In some places, perpetrators operate in highly bureaucratized, hierarchical police and military forces, over which rulers maintain tight central control. In others, perpetrators are a more varied and decentralized set of agents, such as independent task forces or death squads, operating with a great deal of autonomy and little direct oversight. In some cases, perpetrators are agents of an executive that monopolizes power by repressing all alternative sources of power in the other branches of government as well as in society at large. In others, at least some forms of independent power sources outside the executive are tolerated. Do these differences in the structure of coercive organizations shape broad patterns of human rights violations, and if so how?

This chapter argues that there is a discrete set of possible organizational alternatives within which agents can operate. These alternatives can be measured according to varying levels of how principals monitor the behaviour of their agents. Different monitoring levels and combinations have various trade-offs and consequences, which have profound consequences for broad patterns of human rights violations such as the number and selection of victims.

The following section presents a new framework to analyze organizational forms, based on how leaders obtain information on their agents' behaviour. I then use this framework to analyze how three different authoritarian regimes organized coercion: Chile, Argentina and East Germany. A subsequent section compares these cases according to two important consequences of coercion, namely targeting and intensity. Finally, the conclusion summarizes the analysis and discusses directions for further research.

Institutions and Information

Nowhere do rulers rule alone. All complex human activity requires some sort of organization to coordinate different people. A fundamental aspect of running any organization is monitoring the performance of agents on the ground. Leaders (or principals) normally lack constant direct oversight over agents. It is not possible for them to know one hundred per cent of their agents' operations one hundred per cent of the time. As a result, they need to rely on other ways to gather information on them. Internal monitoring (IM) is one available option. It refers to information gathered from within the principal's same organization. Agents can report on their own activities, or rulers can rely on specialized monitors to track the behaviour of their agents.

Internal monitoring is higher where agents and monitors provide the principal with regular and detailed briefings on operations, and lower where these reports are ad hoc, patchy or non-existent. A centralized information clearinghouse indicates a higher level of internal monitoring than an organization where information is dispersed, and consequently more difficult to track down. Also, internal monitoring is higher when the ratio of monitors to agents is high (when many monitors are overseeing few agents) than when it is low. If principals display a great deal of trust in their agents, this is likely to indicate a higher level of internal monitoring than when no such trust exists. A high degree of intra- and inter-branch coordination is also more likely with high internal monitoring. Low internal monitoring is more likely to result in poor coordination, delays and lack of accurate and timely information to the relevant parties. And last, a high degree of corruption and coercion for personal ends (such as extortion) indicates low internal monitoring, as agents pursue their personal goals over those of the organization. The reverse (low corruption indicates high internal monitoring) is also a useful indicator.

The second information-gathering mechanism is external monitoring (EM). This involves information that comes from sources outside the direct control of the leader or ruler.

External monitoring is likely to be higher where independent human rights agencies are present and where their rights are respected than where they may be present but repressed, or not present at all. The same is true of an independent media's reporting on legal and political issues. External monitoring is higher where the media is free and effective than where it is either not free, not effective or both. The degree of independent legislative oversight over the executive's use of coercion is also an important indicator of external monitoring. Regular standing committees indicate a higher degree of external monitoring than more ad hoc or non-existent oversight. By extension, external monitoring is also higher where the courts are effective and have full jurisdiction over all relevant aspects of the executive's coercive activities than where jurisdiction is partial, ineffective or both. Another indicator is the presence of an interlocutor or ombudsman for outside groups. Organizations that make this link to outsiders available on a full-time basis have higher external monitoring than those where interlocutors operate only on an ad hoc basis, or do not exist at all. Also, external monitoring is higher where outsiders have regular access to prisoners than where this access is ad hoc or non-existent. The degree of trust that principals have in monitors' reports is also a useful indicator. Higher trust indicates higher external monitoring, and *vice versa.* Finally, external monitoring is higher where freedom of information legislation permits broad access by outsiders to the executive's activities than where this access is ad hoc or non-existent.

Internal and external monitoring are not mutually exclusive. It is possible to have different combinations of the two. Indeed, many organizations and regimes rely on such combinations, and these might change over time. Plotting degrees of internal and external monitoring along vertical and horizontal axes yields a readily identifiable typology to analyze the organization of coercion across different cases.

Cases with high internal monitoring and low external monitoring are those where the top executive leadership is likely to have a great deal of information on the operations of coercive agents, but this information is not available outside the executive. I have labelled this space 'bureaucratic coercion' to denote the monopolization of information at the top of the leadership hierarchy and the fact that here a complex organization is likely to gather and process information. Many dictatorships, including the USSR, Nazi Germany or the German Democratic Republic (see below), would fall into this category.

By contrast, cases that score low on both axes – 'blind coercion' – are those where neither the leadership nor any other group or institution is likely to be very informed about the activities of the coercive agents. There is unlikely to be much of a formal organization in this sphere. If there is one, it is likely to be ineffective. As a result, where information on agents is available, it is at best patchy and ad hoc. Agents in this case operate with neither internal supervision nor the expectation of accountability to outside groups. State coercion in places such as Argentina during the dictatorship of 1976-1982 (see below), or present-day Sierra Leone would be examples of blind coercion.

The diametrical opposite of this is 'transparent coercion,' where the principal and other institutions and groups are likely to have a great deal of information about the operations of the coercive agents. Information here comes not just from one organization, but from many. Coercion takes place in a fishbowl: where a large number of actors and institutions have a great deal of access to and ability to collect information on all aspects of the organization's coercive activities, from the principal's policies to his agent's actions. Places such as the UK or Canada are examples of transparent coercion.

Finally, in cases that score high on external monitoring and low on internal monitoring, information on coercive agents is likely to be widely available to different groups, but not particularly deep. No one is likely to know very much about the details of the operations themselves, given that there is little or no direct oversight. Indeed, the leaders in this case may deliberately not want to exercise very much oversight, for example if their agents are carrying out controversial missions, or ones likely to carry a high political cost. The leader's mechanism to check whether the operations have achieved the desired results in these cases is to learn about their agents only from outsiders' reports, for example in the media. Information on the outcomes of coercion – such as the number and type of people killed – is likely to be readily available. More detailed information, however (such as the identities of the agents, or their precise modus operandi), is likely to be much harder to obtain. Indeed, coercive agents and external monitoring sources are likely to engage in a type of game: where the former try to hide their actions and the latter try to find out what happened. I have therefore labelled this 'hide and seek coercion'. An example of this is the squads that the Spanish government organized in the 1980s to crack down on the Basque terrorist group ETA. The government gave these groups wide latitude with minimal reporting requirements, but they operated in the context of a liberal democratic regime with institutions such as a free press and independent judiciary. Figure 12.1 illustrates the possibilities:

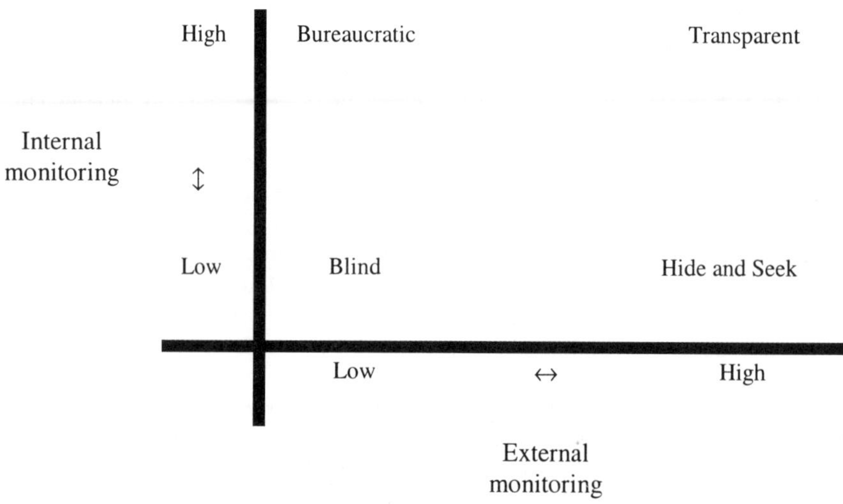

Figure 12.1 Types of coercion

There are costs and benefits to the different types of organizations. For example, bureaucratic coercion presents obvious advantages. With high internal monitoring, leaders are likely to trust their agents. An organization in this space acts with a unity of purpose. Agents are likely to follow orders and transgressions are likely to be reported (and punished). There is a low level of corruption, and a high ability to coordinate activities within the organization's branches or with other institutions. Moreover, because of the low level of external monitoring, a ruler in this kind of organization will not have to worry about independent power centres either inside or outside the state.

However, there are also costs to bureaucratic coercion. The principal ones are expense and risk. A large amount of resources is required to build and maintain a complex organization, which not all leaders may be able to raise. Moreover, creating a complex organization of this kind may expose a leader to the risk of having its members gain in power and turn against him. Any leader or ruler will want to evaluate whether, all things being equal, the benefits of creating such an organization outweigh the costs.

Transparent coercion offers a different set of trade-offs. Because organizations that monopolize information are likely to be more powerful than those that do not, in transparent coercion the costs of creating a too powerful bureaucracy may be mitigated by the increased external monitoring capacities of independent groups, organizations and institutions in society. On the other hand, in transparent coercion there may be too much information on coercive agents' activities, resulting in overload and confusion. In addition, because transparent coercion requires respecting independent organizations, leaders will necessarily face more constraints in their actions. Leaders who already operate in this area (for example in a democratic system that respects independent courts, press and other independent monitors) may simply assume these costs as a given and not question them. However, a ruler or leader who wants to maximize his own power and minimize the power of other institutions either inside or outside the state would likely try to avoid moving in this direction. With low external monitoring, rulers do not have to negotiate the limits of their coercive agencies with other independent institutions.

Blind coercion, with minimal internal and external monitoring, yields diametrically opposite sorts of trade-offs. Here, leaders do not need to accept limitations on their power from external sources, but they are also unlikely to receive very much information on their agents' operations from *any* source, internal or external. This sort of deliberate ignorance may be useful for leaders who do not want to know what their agents are doing, especially if they are carrying out politically sensitive operations. Indeed, most coercive operations (anything from detentions to killings) arguably fall into this category. Not knowing may be a good option for rulers who do not want to bear the costs of the 'dirty work' their agents may be doing.

All things being equal, there are less likely to be strong incentives in blind coercion for coercion to be carried out in secret or to be applied selectively. (The reason is that agents are likely to have greater incentives to hide their actions as the effectiveness of external monitors grows. More effective external monitoring is also likely to impose costs on broad-based repression and lead to the application of coercion in a much more narrowly-targeted manner.) Leaders who want to operate in this area to reap the benefits of plausible deniability will likely have to take special measures to ensure that coercion is applied more secretly and in a more targeted manner than would otherwise be the case.

In blind coercion moreover, there are likely to be more difficulties in coordinating inter- and even intra-branch activities. This may be a severe disadvantage for those rulers or leaders for whom such coordination may be important. In addition, the likelihood that agents will deviate from their organization's task and engage in corruption and coercion for their own purpose is extremely high in blind coercion. With neither internal nor external monitoring as a check, it is hard to imagine how leaders may effectively be able to prevent this, or even to know much about it.

In hide and seek coercion, a ruler may deliberately want to have no direct internal knowledge of the details of his agents' operations, such as exactly who is doing what, how or when. Only vague, general orders might be given, and the leader may be interested only in whether or not the task is done, e.g. whether the intended targets are arrested or killed. Moreover, this can be provided reasonably effectively by external monitors' reports, for example in the media. However, even though hide and seek coercion provides a leader with more checks (through available external monitoring reports), coordination of agents and agencies in this case may remain as difficult as in blind coercion.[1]

Comparisons

We can apply this framework to analyze how coercion is organized in a variety of cases. As indicated in the introduction, I focus mainly on state coercion in three authoritarian regimes: Chile, Argentina and East Germany.

Chile

The Chilean military regime (1973-1990) underwent a series of profound transformations in how it organized its coercive institutions. During the first several months after the coup, all four branches of the armed forces practised all aspects of coercion, from taking prisoners to carrying out summary executions, although the army and *Carabineros* carried out the bulk of these tasks. This early period was by far the most violent in terms of the sheer numbers of victims of the military's repression. Roughly half of all the deaths that occurred during the military regime took place in 1973. This period also witnessed about a third of all detentions and anywhere from a quarter to three-fifths of all tortures. The victims included people from a wide range of political backgrounds, from the left to the centre, to those without political affiliation and even including some who had been opponents of the Allende government. This was by far the broadest range targeted during the course of the regime (Comisión Nacional de Verdad y Reconciliación, 1991; Padilla Ballesteros, 1995: pp.45-66). Although many prisoners were held (and killed) in secret, most were kept in highly public places like the country's main sporting stadiums and hastily improvised concentration camps.

Notwithstanding the level of violence and the speed with which the military took control, the measured levels of internal monitoring during this time were surprisingly low. There were few established procedures and there was a great deal of variation in the application of coercion. Some local commanders took a harder line than others did. In some places commanders imposed strict discipline, while in others (especially in more remote regions) local police and soldiers were less constrained and could enact personal revenge. There was no doubt a great deal of reporting, and the Junta appears to have had a reasonably good idea of broad patterns such as the number of prisoners and casualties. But the great variation in the administration of coercion during this time suggests that reporting on many aspects of coercion was patchy, ad hoc and in many cases unreliable.

Also, during this period each service essentially carried out its own internal monitoring, but there was no specialized overarching monitor for all the services. The principal clearinghouse for information about prisoners was the *Servicio Nacional de Detenidos* (SENDET). But there are several reasons why the SENDET failed to act as a comprehensive clearinghouse. The most important is that it only dealt with the status of prisoners, and coercion did not amount simply to holding prisoners. The SENDET could provide no information on the scores of victims who, for example, had been rounded up and summarily executed. (In many rural areas, for example, local commanders permitted such summary operations.) Also, the SENDET lacked the power to carry out independent investigations. It depended essentially on self-reports by the different branches on how many prisoners they held and on what their status was.

With respect to coordination of activities, the four branches had acted in unison to overthrow the Allende government and, notwithstanding their deep internal divisions and confusions, were coordinating their actions to run the government. But it is difficult to isolate a single coercive modus operandi during this time that applied to all branches.

The military issued '*bandos*,' official public announcements with the character of edicts, with lists of names of people it was looking for. In many cases, these persons presented themselves to *Carabineros* or army bases voluntarily. Sometimes they were released but oftentimes they were detained on the spot. The country's two main police forces, *Carabineros de Chile* and *Investigaciones de Chile*,[2] also carried out searches, for instance within the shantytowns of Santiago, once the victim's identity and whereabouts had been established.

Sometimes *Carabineros* would act in coordination with the other branches of the armed forces, such as the army and the air force, to carry out more massive search and detention raids in particular *poblaciones*, for instance to search for supposed weapons caches. Typically, all the men would be rounded up and detained in a local field or guarded compound, a smaller group within this would be selected and carried to a military or police centre, where they would be kept for several hours or even days. During this time there would be questioning, rough beatings and tortures. The majority of these prisoners were subsequently released, and the remainder would be either detained or taken to isolated spots, usually on the outskirts of Santiago, and executed. The bodies would usually be taken to the morgues, or in some cases hastily dumped in fields, ditches or even in Santiago's Mapocho River (Comisión Nacional de Verdad y Reconciliación, 1991, p.38, pp. 109-11).

Moreover, as suggested earlier, in many cases coercion was not carried out strictly for the political purposes dictated by the Junta. While there is little evidence of personal corruption, in parts of the countryside especially, many summary executions were carried out in revenge for local disputes. When agents acted in their own interests, the problems in the coordination and monitoring mechanisms did not prevent actions that were contrary to the interests of the principal.

With respect to external monitoring, the opposition press was shut, Congress was disbanded, and there were no freedom of information laws through which outsiders could request details about the Executive's operations. Nevertheless, some sources of external monitoring remained. While the military summarily executed some prisoners, it permitted family members and representatives of organizations such as the ICRC to monitor the condition of others, especially those held in the large stadiums.

Even though the judiciary was allowed to remain independent by the military, it failed to pose much of a challenge to the Junta's exercise of power with regard to coercion. The Junta also moved to deliberately constrain the judiciary's jurisdiction with regard to coercion, by imposing restrictions on civilian courts and expanding the jurisdiction of military courts.

Some of the limitations on the judiciary were self-imposed;[3] some were imposed by the new regime itself as it sought to implement coercion with a maximum degree of discretion. But for these reasons, with respect to judicial jurisdiction the level of external monitoring was low.

One of the few tools available to the opposition was the *recursos de amparo*, which is roughly equivalent to the writ of habeas corpus. Even though the courts rejected the overwhelming majority of these, as opposition lawyers systematically presented increasing numbers of these, they gradually began to accumulate a large database of information on the regime's coercive activities. Information gathered on the coercive operations served as an important nexus for the opposition to mobilize resources against the regime. Organizations as varied as Amnesty International and the Organization of American States used this information as the basis for numerous reports on human rights violations in the country. While these reports posed problems for the regime, which denounced them as Communist propaganda, there is no evidence that the principals (the Junta) had any direct confidence in their validity during this time.

Taking all these criteria into account, we can surmise that there was a moderate amount of internal monitoring during the first several months after the coup, and a relatively low level of external monitoring. By early 1974, the regime reorganized its coercive apparatus, bringing it under tighter central control under a single new agency, the *Dirección de Inteligencia Nacional* (DINA), which operated until 1977. The DINA was given broad powers not only to carry out its own operations, but also to oversee those of the other branches of the military and the police. Under the DINA, coercion was applied more consistently according to the regime's goals. Fewer people were targeted and assassinations were carried out in a much more strategically secretive manner. The DINA carried out hundreds of 'disappearances,' which permitted the regime to claim plausible deniability for the human rights violations.

I argue elsewhere that the regime created the DINA to bring order to the relatively chaotic coercion during the first months after the coup (Policzer, 2001, 2002). Essentially, the DINA promised to organize coercion more efficiently and provide the regime with 'plausible deniability,' through the new practice of disappearances. Stated in different terms, the regime expected an increase in internal monitoring, the organizational prerequisite that would permit its powerful new secret police to administer coercion more efficiently and secretly. In return, the Junta gave the DINA unprecedented powers, including the ability to make arrests without restriction, to monitor the rest of the state's activities and to establish operations abroad.

Whatever the regime or the DINA may have intended, however, my research shows that the actual measured levels of internal monitoring rose only marginally under the DINA.[4] The DINA became an information clearinghouse on coercion for a regime that had previously lacked this function (Policzer, 2001). Indeed, the DINA was known to have kept extensive records on others, with informants throughout various state agencies and elsewhere. The people the DINA watched ranged from opposition individuals and groups to members of the regime itself, according to the Chilean National Commission on Truth and Reconciliation.[5]

A second shift in the organization of coercion took place from 1977 to 1978. In 1977 the regime replaced the DINA with a different institution, the *Central Nacional de Informaciones* (CNI). At first the DINA team also led the CNI. But in 1978 this team fell from power, restrictions on civil liberties were relaxed and the CNI adopted a new modus operandi. It came under tighter central control and worked under stricter civilian supervision inside the regime.

Internal monitoring increased noticeably after 1978, as the regime imposed greater constraints on the CNI and supervised its activities more closely. For example, instead of reporting directly to the President, as the DINA had done, the CNI reported to a civilian Minister of Interior.

More surprisingly, the levels of external monitoring also increased sharply after this time. New human rights organizations joined the Church-based groups in monitoring coercion,[6] and in some cases established unprecedented information-sharing networks with the CNI. The regime and the opposition shared knowledge about prisoners' fates and coordinated actions prior to protests and demonstrations. And finally, coercive agents operated under somewhat increased judicial restrictions.[7]

Even though the DINA had amassed a great deal of power and had become the most feared institution in the country, it failed to achieve substantially higher levels of internal monitoring. Conflicts remained between the DINA and other coercive agencies (especially inside the air force), which undermined regime cohesion. Moreover, as the DINA ran increasingly amok, unconstrained by any other power inside the regime, it also failed to deliver on the promise of plausible deniability. These factors made it easier for reformists within the regime to press for its removal, and for Pinochet (who had been the DINA's prime advocate and beneficiary inside the Junta) to agree to its removal.

Argentina

Coercion during the military dictatorship in Argentina (1976-1983) was most similar to Chile before the DINA, but far closer to pure blind coercion. First, external monitoring was lower than at any period in Chile. When the military took power in 1976, unlike Chile where the judiciary remained at least nominally independent, it took complete control of all three branches of the state. There was no interlocutor to outside groups, and outsiders had no access to prisoners. There was a comparatively far weaker independent media than Chile,[8] and there were no freedom of information laws to speak of. There were several human rights organizations, some of which, such as the *Asamblea Permanente de Derechos Humanos* (APDH), existed for a long time. These organizations provided a measure of external monitoring, but far less so than in Chile. First, they lacked the protection of the Argentine Church, which supported the dictatorship. And second, they made less use of the *recurso de amparo* as a strategy for challenging the state's detentions, and consequently they developed far less comprehensive archives. There is no indication that the principals inside the regime trusted these organizations' reports. On the contrary, the human rights groups operated under constant threat of harassment, detention or closure.

Internal monitoring levels were also very low. The Argentine dictatorship oversaw a hydra-headed repressive apparatus with shadowy connections to a highly decentralized network of different military and paramilitary organizations. The roots of this lie in the fact that there is no clearly dominant branch within the Argentine armed forces.[9] Unlike countries such as Chile or Brazil, where the army has unquestioned predominance over the other branches, in Argentina the navy is a serious rival for power against the army. As a result and likely in order to avoid a severe power struggle among the different branches, when they took power the army, navy and air force divided the country into geographically separate areas over which each branch enjoyed virtually complete control (Stepan, 1988, p.25).[10] Moreover, although the Junta set the broad outlines of repression, in practice there was a great deal of autonomy within and inside each branch over which enemies to target and in which ways. Brysk writes that:

> each service, each military zone, each concentration camp, and even each task force had considerable latitude in deciding whom to detain, whether and how much to torture them, whether to officially, release, or execute them, and how to dispose of their children and property. ... As one who was a political prisoner at the time (and subsequently, a Peronist legislator) put it: 'In those days, the country was feudalised; there were guys decorated by the First Corps, kidnapped in the Second, killed by the Third, and vindicated by the Fifth' (Brysk, 1994, p.39).[11]

This kind of organizational decentralization was also believed to be a fundamental strategy of counter-insurgency: the fight against an enemy decentralized in clandestine cells was thought to require similar kinds of organization. The Junta relied extensively on highly autonomous task forces (*grupos de tarea*) within the armed forces to carry out detentions, tortures and assassinations. Paramilitary groups such as the Triple A had begun operations before the coup, but the military replaced the activities of the Triple A with its own task forces, often groups of five to fifteen members from the military, the police and civilian groups who operated in secret (McSherry, 1997, p.93). As a result of the wide discretion given to radically decentralized agents both within the military and outside groups, there was very low information available to principals on the details of agents' operations, and coordination among the different institutions and organizations, as Brysk notes, was often poor.

There was also no equivalent to the DINA or CNI as an information clearinghouse. The closest institution that could have served this function in Argentina was the State Intelligence Service (*Servicio de Inteligencia del Estado*, or SIDE). But this institution lacked the power and scope to systematically monitor all coercive agencies. Moreover, the SIDE had been created under the Perón government, which meant that it lacked prestige and legitimacy in some sectors of the military (Stepan, 1988, pp.24-25) and was relatively ineffective as a clearinghouse. At most, each branch monitored its own divisions and in particular its own intelligence agencies (Pion-Berlin, 1989, pp.102-4). As a result, the ratio of monitors also reflected low internal monitoring.

The degree of trust principals had over agents is hard to gauge in any military institution that is prone to secrecy, but this is even more problematic in Argentina because of the relatively unspecialized manner in which coercion was organized. Each branch of the armed forces took part in repression and all branches rotated their agents to ensure a pact of silence by widespread guilt (Brysk, 1994, p.39; Roniger and Sznajder, 1999, pp.20-1). A chilling account of this rotation is provided by Horacio Verbitsky's interview of (Ret.) Captain Francisco Scilingo. Scilingo took part in missions to kill opponents by throwing them from a plane, alive and drugged, into the open ocean. His was the first public confession of this practice. He stated that the majority of the Navy took part in the flights, and that this rotation was a deliberate policy, a kind of 'communion,' something 'that had to be done'. He notes, 'The whole country had been on rotation. Maybe one guy might have been able to avoid it, but only rarely (*en forma anecdótica*). It was not one little group: it was the entire Navy [that took part]' (Verbitsky, 1995, pp.31-2). This kind of rotation among the agents of coercion can thus serve the purpose of accentuating the differences between the agents and the victims, by preventing any possible formation of affective bonds and by emphasizing the differences between 'us' and 'them'.[12] It also serves to build loyalty and to make crimes difficult to prosecute, by ensuring that everyone's hands are dirty.[13] I have taken this as an indicator of basic mistrust by principals in their agents.

And last, corruption was far more common in Argentina than Chile. For example, taking possession of a victim's property was often an important incentive for agents to take part in repression.[14]

This pattern of organizing coercion remained remarkably stable during the dictatorship. Why were there no shifts? Shifts in the direction of external monitoring are inherently problematic for authoritarian regimes. Accepting legitimate independent actors involves restrictions on the powers and scope of the government. It would take a severe crisis to force the government to consider trading off limitations on its power for increased accountability of its coercive institutions. In Argentina, the Junta might have responded to rising popular discontent by shifting to external monitoring, but chose instead to attempt to divert attention away from these problems by stirring up nationalist sentiment through the invasion of the Malvinas/Falkland Islands. The staggering defeat, if the military regime had somehow managed to survive, would likely have prompted calls for political reform and opening: external monitoring under different guises. Instead, external monitoring was imposed de facto with the collapse of the military regime and the transition to a democracy with a separation of powers and respect for basic rights and liberties. Had the war been fought (and lost) earlier, the shift might also have happened earlier.

Somewhat more puzzling is why the Argentine generals did increase internal monitoring. The explanation for this is most likely rooted in the decision at the time of the coup to radically divide power among the three branches of the armed forces. (This division was far more severe than anything attempted in Chile.) This initial division made it extremely difficult to later create a single all-powerful coordinating or overseeing institution. Any such attempts would have faced the hurdle of inter-service competition for control of a new agency of obvious political importance (Stepan, 1988, pp. 24-5).

East Germany

The new East German state was formally declared in November 1949, and the Socialist Unity Party of Germany (SED, or *Sozialistische Einheistpartei Deutschlands*) imposed a strictly Stalinist model of social and political control, which had emerged in the post-war years. East Germany was a case of almost pure bureaucratic coercion. There was no external monitoring to speak of. A *Politbüro* and a *Zentralkomitee* (ZK) were established by the cadre of party executives to ensure political control and to allow Moscow supervision of its new satellite. A new Ministry of Security (MfS) was created in February 1950. This State Security Service (*Staatssicherheit* or *Stasi*), aimed to centralize control over coercion and intelligence throughout the country. The coercive apparatus was crucial to the party's control.

The failure of the *Stasi* to predict a serious uprising in 1953 led to the fall of its head, Ernst Wollweber, who had neither Moscow's nor the SED's confidence (Fulbrook, 1995, pp.33-4; Childs and Popplewell, 1996, pp.54-65).[15] Wollweber was replaced by Erich Mielke, a Moscow-educated long-time KPD member and admirer of Felix Dzerzhinskii (the founder of the Soviet Union's *Cheka*).[16] Mielke remained in charge of the *Stasi* until the break-up of the GDR[17] and imposed a hierarchical '*Chekist*' structure on the agency (Childs and Popplewell, 1996, p.81). Under his command, especially given his deep Soviet ties, the *Stasi* established extremely close relationships with the KGB in the Soviet Union.

Mielke also used his position to turn the *Stasi* into the leading coercive institution, especially after the 1960s. It became more powerful than any other coercive force, reporting on all agents and operations. Also, the functions of domestic and foreign intelligence were not carried out by separate and independent agencies (as, for instance, in the US or the UK), but by different branches of the *Stasi*. And, particularly through a rapidly growing and massive file system on the GDR's citizens, the *Stasi* acted as the crucial vetting mechanism for career advancement and for keeping social control (Rosenzweig and Le Forestier, 1992).

The *Stasi* under Mielke was crucial to Moscow's control over the GDR. In 1970, Mielke's support was instrumental in removing GDR President Ulbricht from the top leadership of the SED, after Moscow felt that Ulbricht had established too close a relationship with West Germany's Willy Brandt under the sway of the latter's '*Ostpolitik*' (Childs, 1966; Fulbrook, 1995, p.36; Koehler, 1999, pp.65-75).[18] His lieutenant, Erich Honecker, who remained in power until 1989, replaced Ulbricht. Under Honecker, Mielke continued to expand the size and reach of the *Stasi*, turning it into the premiere coercive institution in the country (Childs, 1983, 1985).

There were two kinds of agents who worked for the *Stasi*: officers and informants. The former were full-time employees directly employed by the *Stasi*. The number of full-time officials had grown from 52,700 in 1973 to 81,500 in 1981, to roughly 100,000 by the time of the breakdown, including some 11,000 MfS special guard regiments. This represented roughly one MfS agent per 165 inhabitants in 1989. By contrast, official statistics showed one medical practitioner per 450 inhabitants in 1988 (Childs and Popplewell, 1996, p.82).

The number of informers (IM or *Inoffizielle Mitarbeiter*)[19] was far larger, and had grown especially in the 1970s. Conservative estimates are that by the mid-1990s there were some 174,000 IMs (Childs and Popplewell, 1996, pp.82-6; Garton Ash, 1997, p.84; Koehler, 1999, p.8). By this measure, in a country of 16 million, this meant that one out of every 50 people had a connection with the *Stasi*.[20]

The *Stasi* was thus the antithesis of a small and highly specialized institution. As these figures suggest, the level of specialization was very low as regards IMs, and somewhat higher as regards the full-time employees. The *Stasi*'s broad reach was crucial to establishing control over the population. Not only were its agents literally everywhere, but also cooperation with the *Stasi* had a corrupting effect on the population (Rosenberg, 1991, 1995).

Like Argentina, there was very little variation in this pattern of organizing coercion after the *Stasi* under Mielke established its predominance in the 1960s. Fundamental change came only after 1989, when the collapse of the Berlin Wall led to the end of the GDR altogether.

Consequences

The second section (Institutions and Information) discussed the different trade-offs in organizing coercion. All things being equal, lower levels of internal monitoring are likely to result in more intra- and inter-organizational coordination problems and a higher likelihood that agents will deviate from their assigned task. Although rulers (principals) are less likely to have accurate information and hence direct control over agents' actions without high internal monitoring, there may be times when rulers want to simply let their agents loose to do as they may. Higher levels of internal monitoring, by contrast, give the principal more precise information on his agents and hence more direct control. While this has obvious advantages, it means more work, such as hiring and training a staff, writing reports and so forth. It can also make the principal more accountable for his agents' actions or more dependent on (and hence vulnerable to) any specialized internal monitor.

Low levels of external monitoring are likely to give coercive institutions maximum freedom from independent outside observers, with the attendant benefits of high discretion. Principals and agents may find it desirable to operate with this freedom, but on the other hand, more actors providing oversight means more available information and hence more feedback channels.

We can use the Chilean case along with Argentina and East Germany to make comparisons according to the trade-offs and consequences of different organizational types. For example, the more discretion agents on the ground have to apply coercion, the more likely their actions are to deviate from their principal's policies or from the strictures of outside observers, such as the courts or groups in society at large. The more discretion agents have, and the freer they are from outside oversight, the more differences there are likely to be among different agents' application of coercion, and hence the more broadly targeted this coercion is likely to be.

Our cases support this prediction. Coercion was targeted very imprecisely (and hence broadly) in Chile in 1973, and targeting became more precise and narrower as both internal and external monitoring increased. In East Germany, coercion was targeted very precisely to specific individuals that the SED deemed enemies, though the *Stasi*'s reach meant that virtually the entire population was the object of its snooping. With respect to Argentina, targeting was probably narrower than might be expected given quasi-blind coercion. Coercion was not applied to broad sectors of the population but rather targeted to specific sectors of the opposition. One explanation is that Argentina was not a pure case of blind coercion, but rather had some degree of internal monitoring. Another may be a learning effect from neighbouring countries such as Chile, which by the time the Argentine generals came to power had adopted a far more targeted (and secretive) modus operandi.

Another consequence of the organization of coercion is the sheer number of people killed. All things being equal, it follows that as agents have more discretion (less internal monitoring), and less oversight from outside sources (external monitoring), there are likely to be more victims. Again, our cases support this prediction. Argentina, the closest to pure blind coercion, had the highest number of victims, while in East Germany, with the highest level of internal monitoring, there were relatively few victims.[21] In Chile, the number of victims dropped as the levels of internal and external monitoring increased.

Conclusion

Several lessons can be drawn from this analysis. First, coercion has to be organized. Rulers can choose how to do so in various ways, but their choices are constrained by the trade-offs involved among a limited set of organizational options.

Second, how coercion is organized has concrete consequences on various aspects of coercion, including its intensity, targeting and secrecy. All of these factors also have consequences for regime stability and the likelihood of bringing perpetrators of human rights violations to justice.

Third, the framework presented here can be used to describe, compare and analyze different coercive organizations. I have taken a tentative first step by analyzing state coercion in three authoritarian regimes. But just about every element presented here can and should be disaggregated further and more systematically. Many more large- and small-N case studies are needed to make the analysis of the consequences of various organizational types more robust. We can disaggregate even further across time (more organizational shifts), space (more cases), institution (different police and military organizations) and so forth.

Fourth, we may also further disaggregate the relative weight and importance of various monitoring options. It is likely that not all of the criteria I have used carry the same weight across different times and places. For example, access to prisoners may be a relatively minor aspect of external monitoring, and there may be good reasons for giving different criteria different weights. Moreover, in some places information clearinghouses or legislative oversight may be far more significant than in others.

And finally, beyond these technical methodological questions, we should not lose sight of the larger goals of such an undertaking. A more systematic analysis of coercion is not simply a basis for better understanding the problems of governance that shape the conditions and contexts in which human rights violations take place. It is also a tool to better design and control coercive institutions themselves. This is an urgent task given the durability and pervasiveness of regimes whose coercive institutions are under the control of tyrants. As we gain knowledge and experience in how to do this, we can adjust internal and external monitoring to make coercive institutions better reflect our best democratic hopes.

Notes

1 High levels of internal monitoring are generally more likely under hierarchically organized institutions, such as formal bureaucracies, than more loosely organized networks, but not always. It is possible for a formal bureaucratic hierarchy to be poor at internal monitoring. And it is also possible for networks to be very good at gathering information on their various members' activities.

2 Both institutions operate throughout the country, often with considerable overlap, even though they are sharply distinct. *Carabineros* is a uniformed police force, while *Investigaciones* is a civilian police force and has always been under the control of the Ministry of Interior (Frühling, Portales and Varas, 1982; Maldonado, 1990; Mery Figueroa, 1996).

3 Hilbink argues that the judiciary's rigid hierarchy and its 'extreme legalism' contributed to its capitulation to the new regime (Hilbink, 1999).

4 External monitoring, by contrast, decreased marginally. Because disappearances became the DINA's signature practice, outsiders had far less access to prisoners and found no interlocutor inside the regime.

5 The DINA spied on top civilian supporters of the regime because its director, Colonel Manuel Contreras, believed that they had failed to build a solid base of support for the regime and hence could not really be trusted (Guzmán Errázuriz, 1992; Huneeus, 2000).

6 The largest and most important of the new organizations was the Chilean Human Rights Commission (*Comisión Chilena de Derechos Humanos*, CChDH), created in 1978. It was led by high-profile political leaders and received support especially from various international organizations. A series of other groups would continue to appear throughout the 1980s (Frühling, 1984, 1986; Orellana and Hutchison, 1991, p.103). Although these groups often suffered severe restrictions, their appearance was a major departure with respect to the previous period.

7 This was a result of the Amnesty Decree of 1978. While the decree provided a blanket amnesty for state crimes committed between 1973 and 1978, it also opened the door to a new legal and political space, in which the regime would operate *without* the benefit of an amnesty. Although the regime successfully cajoled most judges into turning a blind eye to human rights violations after 1978, some judges made use of the new opportunities presented by the new legal space to challenge the regime – in some cases successfully – over its human rights violations (Policzer, 2001).

8 The sole exception was the English language paper, the *Buenos Aires Herald*.

9 By contrast, the Chilean army is unquestionably the dominant branch within the armed forces. Pinochet, as head of the army and the armed forces at the time of the coup, was also named head of the Junta. This appointment was a recognition of his de facto status as *primus inter pares* among the Junta members, even though, unlike the heads of the navy and air force, he had joined the coup plots only at the last minute.

10 In Chile, only the army and *Carabineros* had an organizational reach that extended throughout the country. The navy and air force took and held prisoners in their respective regiments and bases, but their reach was limited by the fact that they simply have far fewer bases. The navy, however, was essentially given control over the city of Valparaíso, the most important port and the centre of navy operations.

11 Brysk quotes Moncalvillo and Fernández (Moncalvillo and Fernández, 1985, pp.29-33).

12 Al Capone hired a variety of out-of-town assassins to ensure the hired gun would feel he was killing one of 'them' rather than one of 'us' (Diamond, 1992, p.298).

13 See also Rosenberg (1991).

14 The most notorious difference between Chile and Argentina in this regard was the Argentine practice of keeping the babies of detained expectant mothers. The search for these children, many of whom were brought up by military officers' families, has been championed by the Grandmothers of Plaza de Mayo (*Las Abuelas*).

15 'Despite all the SED's efforts to depict the upheaval as a fascist putsch or the work of West German provocateurs,' Maier observes, 'the movement revealed how alien and dependent on a continuing Soviet presence the regime remained. Until the disappearance of the GDR, the uprising remained an anxious memory; as their authority evaporated in 1989, Politbüro members repeatedly asked whether unrest had become as serious as it had been in 1953' (Maier, 1997, p.15).

16 On Dzerzhinskii and the Cheka, in English, see Leggett (Leggett, 1981).

17 Which makes him (one of) the most durable intelligence chief(s) in history.

18 Koehler points out that in the Soviet system the secret police is a powerful kingmaker, and that 'No Soviet leader had ever been removed from office without the active support of the secret police' (Koehler, 1999, p.71). But in East Germany the fragility of the state contributed to an especially strong leverage by Moscow, through the secret police, over the SED leadership. Mielke was crucial to this. Koehler argues that Mielke was a master at switching personal allegiances, and that he was not loyal to a particular person per se, but rather to the joint KGB/*Stasi* goal of building and cementing Communist power (Koehler, 1999, p.72).

19 In 1968 the MfS changed the classification of its informers. Previously referred to as *Geheime Informatoren* (GI or secret informants), the new title became *Inoffizielle Mitarbeiter* (IM or unofficial colleagues, or collaborators). Mielke intended this shift as a way to ease the psychological burden of informing and to allow the number of informants to increase (Childs and Popplewell, 1996, p.83).

20 Garton Ash adds: 'Allow just one dependent per person, and you're up to one in twenty-five' (Garton Ash, 1997, p.84).

21 Strictly in terms of people killed. In terms of number of people affected by coercion, East Germany was undoubtedly the highest, given the *Stasi*'s reach.

References

Brysk, A. (1994), *The Politics of Human Rights in Argentina: Protest, Change, and Democratization*, Stanford, CA, Stanford University Press.

Childs, D. (1966), *From Schumacher to Brandt: the story of German socialism, 1945-1965* (1st ed.), Oxford, New York, Pergamon Press.

Childs, D. (1983), *The GDR: Moscow's German Ally*, Boston, MA, G. Allen & Unwin.

Childs, D. (1985), *Honecker's Germany*, Boston, MA, Allen & Unwin.

Childs, D. and Popplewell, R.J. (1996), *The Stasi: The East German Intelligence and Security Service*, New York, NY, New York University Press.

Comisión Nacional de Verdad y Reconciliación. (1991), *Informe Rettig: Informe de la Comisión Nacional de Verdad y Reconciliación*, Santiago, Chile, La Nación & Ediciones Ornitorrinco.

Diamond, J.M. (1992), *The Third Chimpanzee: The Evolution and Future of the Human Animal*, New York, HarperCollins.

Frühling, H. (1984), 'Repressive Policies and Legal Dissent in Authoritarian Regimes: Chile 1973-1981', *International Journal of Sociology of Law*, Vol. 12, pp. 351-74.

Frühling, H. (1986), *Represión política y defensa de los derechos humanos* (1st ed.). Santiago, Chile, Programa de Derechos Humanos Academia de Humanismo Cristiano Centros de Estudios Sociales Ediciones Chile y América.

Frühling, H., Portales, C. and Varas, A. (1982), *Estado y fuerzas armadas*, Santiago, Chile, Facultad Latinoamericana de Ciencias Sociales.

Fulbrook, M. (1995), *Anatomy of a Dictatorship: Inside the GDR, 1949-1989*, Oxford, Oxford University Press.

Garton Ash, T. (1997), *The File: A Personal History*, New York, Random House.

Guzmán Errázuriz, J. (1992), *Escritos personales* (1st ed.), Santiago, Chile, Zig-Zag.

Hilbink, E. C. (1999), *Legalism against Democracy: The Political Role of the Judiciary in Chile, 1964-94,* unpublished Ph.D. dissertation, University of California, San Diego.

Huneeus, C. (2000), 'Technocrats and Politicians in an Authoritarian Regime. The "ODEPLAN Boys" and the "Gremialistas" in Pinochet's Chile', *Journal of Latin American Studies*, Vol. 32(2), pp. 461-501.

Koehler, J. O. (1999), *Stasi: The Untold Story of the East German Secret Police*, Boulder, CO, Westview Press.

Leggett, G. (1981), *The Cheka: Lenin's Political Police, The All-Russian Extraordinary Commission for Combating Counter-Revolution and Sabotage, December 1917 to February 1922*, Oxford, Oxford University Press.

Maier, C. S. (1997), *Dissolution: The Crisis of Communism and the End of East Germany*, Princeton, NJ, Princeton University Press.

Maldonado, C. (1990), Los Carabineros de Chile: Historia de una Policía Militarizada Ibero-Americana, *Nordic Journal of Latin American Studies*, 20(3), pp. 3-31.

Mery Figueroa, N. (1996) *Policía de Investigaciones de Chile: discurso del Director General de la Policía de Investigaciones de Chile, Don Nelson Mery Figueroa, en el 63o aniversario de la Institución*. Santiago, Chile.

Moncalvillo, M. and Fernández, A. (1985), *La renovación fundacional*, Buenos Aires.

Orellana, P. and Hutchison, E.Q. (1991), *El Movimiento de Derechos Humanos en Chile 1973-1990*. Santiago, Chile, Centro de Estudios Políticos Latinoamericanos Simón Bolívar.

Padilla Ballesteros, E. (1995), *La Memoria y el Olvido: Detenidos Desaparecidos en Chile*, Santiago, Chile, Ediciones Orígenes.

Pion-Berlin, D. (1989), *The Ideology of State Terror: Economic Doctrine and Political Repression in Argentina and Peru*, Boulder, CO, Lyne Rienner Publishers.

Policzer, P. (2001), *Organizing Coercion in Authoritarian Chile*, unpublished Ph.D. Dissertation, Massachussetts Institute of Technology.

Policzer, P. (2002), 'Reorganizing Repression: From the DINA to the CNI in Authoritarian Chile', San Francisco, CA, 116th Annual Meeting of the American Historical Association.

Roniger, L. and Sznajder, M. (1999), *The Legacy of Human-Rights Violations in the Southern Cone: Argentina, Chile, and Uruguay*, Oxford, Oxford University Press.

Rosenberg, T. (1991), *Children of Cain: Violence and the Violent in Latin America*, New York, Wm. Morrow.

Rosenzweig, L. and Le Forestier, Y. (1992), *L'empire des mouchards: les dossiers de la STASI*, Paris, J. Bertoin.

Stepan, A. (1988), *Rethinking Military Politics*, Princeton, NJ, Princeton University Press.

Chapter 13

What Transforms Ordinary People into Gross Human Rights Violators?

Alette Smeulers

Introduction

Pictures of the huge piles of bodies found after the liberation of the Nazi-Germany death camps make us shiver with horror. Witness accounts of former South-American torture victims fill us with disgust. Yet, even more chilling than learning about these horrendous crimes and gross human rights violations, which sadly enough are no isolated incidents in history, is becoming aware of the fact that the actual perpetrators of these crimes are ordinary people. Research has shown that these people do not significantly differ from people like you and me. Nothing has been found that would lead us to conclude that the perpetrators are intrinsically more aggressive or sadistic than other people, nor can we conclude that all ordinary people have sadistic character traits, which are present but hidden, waiting for an appropriate outlet. These perpetrators who commit these crimes do not torture, maim or kill for their own pleasure but they commit their crimes on behalf of the state and because they get the orders to do so.[1] How can this be explained, keeping in mind that under ordinary circumstances ordinary and average people would be revolted by such atrocious crimes?

This paper focuses on the transformation process that turns ordinary people into gross human rights violators. It aims to show that ordinary and natural reactions of ordinary and average people to very specific circumstances almost inevitably result in turning these people into perpetrators of gross human rights violations. Within this transformation process we should distinguish between three different phases and one decisive moment. The three phases are, in chronological order: the preparation phase, the initiation phase and the habituation phase. On the borderline between the initiation phase and the habituation phase there is the all-decisive moment that is right after when the perpetrator has committed his first crime. His reaction to this first crime is crucial.[2] The one-time perpetrator either comes to his senses and quits, or he starts to rationalize and justify his action in order to avoid the almost unbearable feelings of guilt and thus unwittingly paves the way for many more crimes. I will explain the dynamics surrounding the perpetrator during the all-decisive moment. In addition, I explain why and how some perpetrators find a way to quit and include a section on how perpetrators look back. One of the main research methods used is to test the existing theories by analyzing so-called ego-documents of perpetrators, I have tried, whenever appropriate, to include typical illustrative quotes.

The Underlying Assumptions

The starting point and underlying assumption of this study is that: 1) most perpetrators or gross human rights violators (GHRV-ors) are ordinary people; and 2) within specific circumstances all ordinary people can become gross human rights violators. The aim of this research is not to prove these underlying assumptions but to merely postulate them. Although some scholars have cast doubt on this thesis (e.g., Goldhagen, 1996), I feel no need to reopen this debate because in my eyes many other scholars have already sufficiently proven the thesis that most perpetrators are ordinary people (e.g., Lifton, 1986; Staub, 1989; Kelman and Hamilton, 1989; Crelinsten and Schmid, 1993). The second premise is an outcome of, on the one hand, two laboratory experiments which gave a good insight into how easily ordinary people are transformed into perpetrators and, on the other, the outcome of an intensive study on a Greek torture school. In the infamous 'obedience to authority' experiment, Milgram (1969) showed that the majority of people (65 per cent) are prepared and willing to give their fellow human beings an electric shock of 450 volts if demanded to do so by a perceived authority. Zimbardo's (1974) prison experiment showed that the environment is an extremely important determinant in explaining the causes of gross human rights violations. Apart from these laboratory experiments many studies on the causes of gross human rights violations show that perpetrators often find themselves in extremely compelling circumstances, in which they believe themselves to have no choice but to torture, maim or kill. One of the most chilling accounts of such circumstances has been given by Haritos-Fatouras (1986), who conducted an intensive research on a torture school during the Greek colonels' regime (1967-1974) and concluded that given the appropriate training almost anyone can become a torturer.[3] These conclusions and the assumptions 1) and 2) are to be seen as the underlying premise and starting point of this study.

Delineation of the Subject of Analysis

This study focuses on the perpetrator as gross human rights violator; that is to say, perpetrators who commit gross human rights violations such as torture, maiming and killing on behalf of the state and/or state authorities. Perpetrators, therefore, commit these crimes *because* they received the explicit order to do so, or do so on the basis of an implied order or policy which has made it unmistakably clear to them that they are expected to torture, maim or kill. Leaders responsible for many GHRV, like Hitler and Idi Amin for example, are excluded from the study because they personify the ultimate authority in their state and therefore cannot be said to have committed these crimes out of obedience. The main focus is on people who actually commit the gross human rights violations, mainly the torturers, executioners, camp and prison guards and members of special squads or units who carry out special orders that include either of these crimes. The focus is less on the superiors, associates and accessories, but they are not excluded from the research. Bystanders generally play an important and sometimes decisive role when it comes to gross human rights violations; however, they too will, for practical reasons, be excluded from this research.[4] Ordinary criminals and terrorists are also excluded from this study.[5]

The Transformation Process

The Preparation Phase

Most perpetrators are members of some kind of militaristic unit. This can be the police, army, prison guards, special or elite force, special units, secret services and similar groups. Practically all these units are characterized by various typical organizational features. Most importantly they have a very clear and strict order and hierarchy in which the position of each individual is clearly marked by a specific rank. The tasks and duties of each rank are clearly specified and all play their own role in the continuous chain of command. All ranks are obliged to obey the orders of their superiors, that is, to either pass them on or to carry them out as expected. Within this chain of command obedience, discipline and loyalty are demanded. The idea is that the leaders (this can be, for example, a president, but also a general, a chief police inspector or a chief prison guard) determine the policy and that all others carry out this policy without questioning it. Within this system the responsibility for the choices made on a policy level are purely for the leaders, all others merely follow orders and their only task is to carry them out. Hoess, commander of Auschwitz wrote the following typical statement in his memoirs:

> Whether the reasons behind the extermination of the Jews were necessary or not was something on which I could not allow myself to form an opinion (Hoess, 1959, p.162).

Another typical feature is that within these organizations individuals are de-individualized. Recruits are often not known by names, but by rank and number. They all wear uniforms indicating their rank and often even have the same haircut. There is little room for the recruits to show their individual personalities. These organizations often stand apart from the outside world and form a closed secret world of their own. They have a special basis, which is closed to the public. Within this world a different set of rules and morals apply. Outsiders are kept away and in some organizations many things are secret. From within the compound of the organization it is sometimes very difficult for the recruits to get in touch with the outside world. For a certain period of time recruits are often not allowed to call home or to receive letters. This, combined with the fact that sometimes they may not even listen to the radio, watch television and read newspapers, will make recruits completely dependent on their superiors for information about the outside world. This dependency, with no possibility of any cross-checking, makes them more prone to believe what they are told.

Recruits of these organizations generally go through a militaristic training period during which they often must endure an exhausting physical training program. They learn the special skills they need, they learn the rules, morals and values of the organization and they are taught what their respective roles are and how they should behave. In other words: the recruits are disciplined and learn to obey without questioning the orders, learn to be loyal and to think and act in line with the outlined policy.

> You must understand … I was a soldier. Like you. I had orders to follow. … The order came from the Führer himself. … There was nothing to be done (Eichmann quoted by Malkin and Stein, 1960, pp. 231-2).

On the one hand, this phase is nothing out of the ordinary and many people, especially those who have gone through military service, will recognize these features. On the other hand, we should be aware that even an ordinary military training changes people and makes many of them more prone to obey orders, as they have been trained to refrain from questioning orders. Recruits who have gone through such an ordinary training period are probably not aware of the fact that they have accepted a different kind of moral attitude. Within the organization they feel absolved from responsibility for their own actions and behaviour and the consequences thereof. Their only duty is to carry out the orders and they are held accountable towards their superiors for their success or failure in doing so. Although ordinary military training alone is not a sufficient condition to turn ordinary people into perpetrators, important and necessary preconditions have thus already been fulfilled: recruits feel a strong pressure to obey orders and they feel primarily responsible towards their superiors, instead of taking responsibility for their own actions.[6] Without the recruits being aware of this, an important moral restraint to commit torture, maim or kill a fellow human being has thus already been reduced.

Many perpetrators, however, have not only undergone ordinary military training but have subsequently undergone special training. This training differs from an ordinary military training in the sense that the training is more extreme. The training method is harsher and continuous threats, insults, humiliation, emotional and physical violence, such as beating the recruits. Recruits are extremely disciplined by the trainers and unquestioning obedience is demanded of them. The difference from ordinary military training is that the orders that are given are often extreme, senseless, absurd or cruel. A suitable (and horrifying) example of such a senseless and cruel order comes from a South-American torture school in which the recruits were obliged to take a pet at the beginning of their training period and were told to look after their pet well. Because of the harsh training and the inability to contact family or friends, many recruits naturally bonded with their pets. The superiors stimulated this bonding. At the end of the training period the recruits were told that they would only pass their exams if they successfully pass the ultimate test. This ultimate test was to fulfil the order to kill their own pet.

A continuous atmosphere of violence and fear often characterizes these special training programs. Recruits within such a training program or school completely lose control of their own fate and life becomes unpredictable. The only way to survive during such a course is to do as you are told in order to avoid punishment, further insults and humiliation, physical violence and sometimes even torture. The designers of the courses aim to stimulate the survival instincts of their recruits and thus turn them into obedient soldiers by making it clear to them that the only way out is to succeed in the program. Almost all soldiers who have gone through such a harsh and inhumane training program no longer think for themselves, no longer question orders but merely follow orders, all orders. Petrou, a Greek torturer and former recruit of the torture school, said:

> They changed us into instruments. People without a will of our own. Who obey. .... You were trained not to think (Amnesty International video, *Your Neighbour's Son*).

The extreme circumstances and terror used changes people. They get used to violence, become brutalized, get used to a different set of norms and values and learn not to question any order. They have learned to do as they are told. These recruits will not like an order to torture, maim or kill a fellow human being, but they will definitely feel obliged and compelled to carry it out, despite all moral and emotional restraints they might still feel. During the training period they have learned to disregard these feelings, and the fear that if they disobey they themselves will be severely punished, tortured or killed, plays an important role. Although most recruits will carry out their orders to torture or kill by now, many training schools, especially torture schools, do not leave it here but even go one step further and make their recruits go through an initiation phase.

The Initiation Phase

The process of accustoming recruits to violence is continued during the initiation phase, but in a more deliberate way. Movies on torture sessions are shown, for example, or recruits are given sessions on torture techniques. The most characteristic feature of this phase, however, is their very gradual involvement in the actual crimes that are committed. Their active involvement is enlarged on a step-by-step basis. In the Greek torture school (1967-1974), for example, recruits were not suddenly ordered to torture a so-called subversive but were ordered to guard the prisoners and bring them food first. The second step was to bring prisoners to the torture chamber and to take them back to their cells after the torture sessions. Thus they got used to seeing the prisoners after they had been beaten and tortured. They became accustomed to seeing them bleeding, wounded and in pain. A third step was to bring something into the room where the prisoners would be tortured. Hence they witnessed but did not yet participate in torture. A fourth step was to order them to make notes during torture sessions. A fifth step was to very slightly increase their role, e.g., having them to hold the victim for a moment in between the application of various torture techniques. During these steps the recruits' roles would be extremely minor, but in the meantime they would get used to torture and seeing people being tortured. At the same time it would become clear to them that if they themselves would not do as they were told, their fates would not be much different from that of the alleged subversives. The result of such an initiation is twofold. Firstly, the threat to be tortured themselves is enforced on them in this implied manner. Secondly, the recruits will get the idea that the prisoners will be tortured anyway, whether they will take part in it or not and that torture is nothing out of the ordinary. In this phase recruits are prepared for the choice they are about to make (follow the order to torture, maim or kill or not) and are given the strong impression that there is only one rational choice with little costs and many benefits.

This phase ends when the recruit is asked to actively assist during a torture session for the first time. After a long preparation and initiation period this is the most decisive moment. The recruit who follows the order to torture, kill or maim will cross an important line and will become a perpetrator. The dynamics of this moment are described in the next section. One remark should be made beforehand though. Not all recruits will go through such a phase, not even all future perpetrators will go through an imposed and deliberate initiation phase. Some will go through a kind of spontaneous initiation, for example when fighting in a war. The mere fact of being there and fighting in a frontline, for example, *can make* such an impression on the recruit that he is prepared to carry out every order or even turns (temporarily) crazy.[7] Examples hereof are the American soldiers who took part in the My Lai massacre during the Vietnam War, in which hundreds of innocent civilians were killed and executed. Many of them were so traumatized by their war experiences that under the given circumstances they no longer needed another initiation phase to overcome natural feelings of disgust or moral inhibitions. In this situation an ordinary military training, traumatizing experiences, an extremely stressing situation (they had expected to face enemy soldiers) and an order to kill was enough to set them off. An American soldier remembers:

> That day in My Lai, I was personally responsible for killing about 25 people. Personally. Men, women. From shooting them, to cutting their throats, scalping them, to … cutting off their hands and cutting out their tongue. I did it. I just went. My mind just went. And I was not the only one that did it. A lot of other people did it. I just killed. Once I started the … training, the whole programming part of killing, it just came out. … It just came. I did not know I had it in me … I had no feelings or no emotions or no nothing. No directions. I just killed (Bilton and Sim, 1992, p.7).

The First Time: Crossing a Line

After these prior phases many recruits will feel compelled to follow orders. The (implied) pressure from the environment and the fear from within will be too strong and most recruits will not be able, and would not dare, to resist and disobey the order. They have been taught to obey, to refrain from asking any questions and to push aside all possible inner doubts on the legitimacy and morality of the order. The fear of being punished severely, tortured or even killed themselves is no longer visible because these threats are no longer explicit, but during the training period the impregnation of this threat was so strong that it still functions for a long time after the actual training. When the order comes, they will thus follow it and for the first time will commit a GHRV and, for the first time, will cross an important and morally decisive borderline.

Evidence suggests, however, that despite the whole training program, which is designed to brutalize the recruits, to get them used to violence and to see and experience torture as something ordinary, all of them experience revulsion the first time they actually commit one of these crimes. They still, as ordinary people would, feel empathy for their victims and are horrified by the things they feel compelled to do to them.[8] They do not disobey, however, simply because they, unlike ordinary people who have not gone through the training program, no longer have the means to resist. A South-American torturer comments:

> I do know that there was plenty of torture. The first time I witnessed it, the victim was a girl. I was shocked. She was very young, middle class; she was blond. I had never seen anything like that before (Harper's, 1985, p. 15-7).

Once a recruit has crossed the line he has become a perpetrator, but whether he will commit many more crimes will depend on how he deals with this particular situation. On the one hand, the perpetrator had felt compelled to commit his crime, but on the other hand he is revolted by his own actions and knows that he has crossed a line: instinctively the perpetrator will feel and experience that what he has done is wrong. There are two possible reactions to this: either the perpetrator consciously acknowledges that he was wrong and decides for himself that despite all the pressure and the consequences he will refuse to carry out any comparable order in the future. This is an option, but it is not an easy one. By disobeying the next order most perpetrators will put their own lives in peril. Given the climate of fear that has surrounded them earlier, most recruits lack the moral courage to stand up at this point. Despite this fact, some object and still manage to survive, like this executioner from Reserve Police Battalion 101 did:

> Because I was already very upset from the cruel treatment of the Jews during the clearing of the town and was completely in turmoil, I shot too high. The entire back of my Jew was torn off and the brain exposed. Parts of the skull flew into Sergeant Steinmetz's face. This was grounds for me, after returning to the truck, to go to the First Sergeant and ask for my release. I had become so sick that I simply could not continue anymore. I was then relieved by the First Sergeant (Browning, 1992, p.66).

It must be said, however, that very few first-time perpetrators were given comparable chances to quit without being threatened, tortured or killed. It must be emphasized that some manage nevertheless, although with severe costs for them. At My Lai one of the soldiers who wanted to get out shot himself in the foot purposely, in the hope of being relieved of his duties.

The other, much more likely, reaction is to rationalize and justify the crime. This reaction is more likely because the environment will support this reaction: the recruits, as shown above, have been trained not to take the consequences of their actions into account. They are trained to leave moral questions regarding the legitimacy of their orders and behaviours to their superiors. This attitude will often be further reinforced by their superiors who will comfort their recruits by telling them that they have done the right thing and by praising them for being brave and courageous. They will imply that the feelings of horror are natural but that they are the true heroes because they are the ones to carry out the dirty job. If you feel horrible about what you have done, you welcome these words and bond with those in similar positions and together believe in what you are told. A member of the SS testifies:

> We were Germans best and hardest. Every single one of us dedicated himself to others. What held us together was an alliance of comradeship. Not even the bond of marriage can be stronger. Comradeship is everything. It gave us the mental and physical strength to do what others were too weak to do (Staub, 1989, p.130).

Besides, the ideology upheld by their organization will definitively support their efforts to rationalize and justify the crimes they have committed. According to the prevailing ideology (whether this is nationalism, patriotism, communism or fascism) the crime will not be defined as a crime but as a necessary means to achieve certain ultimate goals. The execution of the Jews was said to be necessary to achieve a better society or the elimination of all political opponents was said to be necessary for the survival of the country, for example.

However, an even more important and compelling reason why this reaction is more likely is because it is a natural reaction. By finding excuses for his crime, by rationalizing and justifying it, the perpetrator can absolve himself of guilt and of any blame, which is exactly what ordinary people instinctively do when they have done something wrong. By doing so, the perpetrator can avoid acknowledging the fact that he has committed an atrocious crime and has crossed a line which is not supposed to be crossed. Naturally and instinctively inner psychological defence mechanisms protect the perpetrator from feeling guilty, for example:

> I thought that I could master the situation and that without me the Jews were not going to escape their fate anyway... (Browning, 1992, p.72).

Once the perpetrator starts to rationalize or justify his crime he has passed a point of no return. Because the rationalization and justification will make him push aside his revulsion, he will not have enough means to disobey the next order. The most important barriers and restraints to torture, maim or kill have thus successfully been overcome by his natural reaction to absolve himself of any blame. During the next phase, which is labelled 'habituation and routinization', the rationalizations, justifications and other defence mechanisms will continue their immense but natural task to chase all feelings of guilt away. It is almost impossible to stop this process. It is hardly possible for an ordinary human being to accept and acknowledge full responsibility for an atrocious crime such as torture without finding excuses, which justify the crime or at least justify his own behaviour. While all natural and environmental forces push the one-time perpetrator towards justification of his behaviour, doing so and giving in to these justifications is the all-decisive and crucial moment in which the one-time perpetrator will unconsciously but inevitably decide his fate. The justification for his first crime will inevitably pave the way for a second crime and the one-time perpetrator passes a point from which a return is almost impossible. The reason for that can be found in the fact that if a perpetrator has not acknowledged his guilt after his first offence, it will be even harder to accept this after he has committed a second and third crime. Acknowledging guilt becomes almost impossible after he has committed many more crimes. The pressure to find excuses becomes stronger after each and every crime and finally will overcome all feelings of empathy, remorse and guilt.

Habituation and Routinization

During this phase many natural defence mechanisms besides rationalization and justification are active in order to keep the feelings of remorse, guilt and empathy away. Many perpetrators, for example, convince themselves that they do not really have any control and that it would not have made a difference if they had stood up and refused to carry out the order. Stangl, commander at Treblinka, said:

> If I had sacrificed myself, if I had made public what I felt and had died ... it would have made no difference. Not an iota. It would all have gone on just the same, as if it and I had never happened (Sereny, 1994, p.231).

Many perpetrators use evasion in order to avoid having to acknowledge what truly is happening. They block out their emotions, they dissociate themselves from their acts, they minimize their own roles, they avoid thinking or talking about it or they simply deny the reality of what they are really doing. They argue that they were trapped, not guilty and could not have done otherwise. Some start to blame the victim: it is his fault, he was in the wrong place at the wrong time. Perpetrators often start to create their own worlds in which they define the things around them in order to soothe their conscience. They create their own distorted realities. One executioner of Reserve Police Battalion 101 made the murdering of innocent children sound like mercy killings:

> I made an effort, and it was possible for me to shoot only children by the hand. My neighbour then shot the mother and I shot the child that belonged to her, because I reasoned with myself that after all without its mother the child could not live any longer (Browning, 1992, p.73).

This distorted logic works even if the perpetrator is aware of the fact that he actually fools himself rather than others. The perpetrator quoted above, for example, was very aware of what he was doing: 'It was supposed to be, so to speak, soothing to my conscience to release children unable to live without their mothers' (Browning, 1992, p.73). Perpetrators believe what they want to believe. The use of euphemisms is notorious. Torture, maiming and killing are never called by their real names. Torture techniques have names which sound innocent like 'parrot peach', 'submarino' and 'tea party'. These names seem to take away the awful reality they try to hide and conceal. Euphemisms reinforce the distorted realities perpetrators have created for themselves and in which they desperately want to believe.

Massive gross human rights violations are sometimes extremely well organized, such as the highly bureaucratized organization of the genocide of the Jews, gypsies and others deemed 'unworthy of life' in Nazi Germany. In this situation there is a clear hierarchical and functional division of labour, which creates a distance between the perpetrators and final consequences and outcome of their collective activity. Those higher up in the chain of command have no direct personal experience and sometimes do not even have knowledge of the final aims. Those lower in rank play a minor role and realize that they are merely a small cog in a machine. By fragmentizing the process of violence like this, the natural tendencies of the perpetrators to deny their own responsibility and accountability are reinforced. Within this system moral responsibility is substituted by a clear hierarchical and technical responsibility. Morality and responsibility are reduced to doing one's own job well.

> I must admit that this gassing set my mind at rest, for the mass extermination of the Jews was to start soon and now we had a procedure. I always shuddered at the prospect of carrying out extermination by shooting, when I thought of the vast numbers concerned, and of the women and children. I was relieved to think that the victims too would be spared all these bloodbaths and that the victims too would be spared suffering until their last moment came (Hoess, 1959, p.165).

Perpetrators dehumanise their victims. They call them names and look upon them as evil or inferior up to a point that ordinary moral norms no longer apply to them. This makes it easier to torture, maim or kill them. The treatment of the victims is often such that it is difficult for the victims to uphold their dignity. For example, if practically starved to death and not having opportunities to relieve themselves, they will start fighting over a scrap of bread and will dirty themselves. This will reinforce the contempt perpetrators have for their victims. Stangl explained:

> It has nothing to do with hate. They were weak: they allowed everything to happen – to be done to them. They were people with whom there was no common ground, no possibility of communication – that is how contempt is born. I could never understand how they could give in as they did (Sereny, 1994, p.233).

Lifton (1987) focused his research on the Nazi doctors and tried to understand how doctors who are meant to heal people, came to not only be involved but even played a crucial role in the killing process. According to Lifton, the Nazi doctors lived in two worlds, the ordinary world in which they were caring doctors, loving husbands and fathers and sociable types and in which ordinary human morality applied. However, they also lived in another world, the world of Auschwitz, in which completely different moral values applied and where they were prepared to participate in the killing process and conduct cruel medical experiments. The internal process of dual worlds made it possible for them to psychologically separate these two worlds and to clearly separate the different and often completely contradictory roles they played in each world. Thanks to this process of doubling they avoided the application of ordinary moral values and their role as healing doctors to their deathly work in the camps.

All these forces, which work upon the perpetrator from outside and from within, finally allows the perpetrator to get used to his job, so that he no longer views it as something out of the ordinary and gives it very little thought. Kelman and Hamilton (1989) referred to this process as routinization. To maim, torture and kill becomes a job, not much different from any other job, despite the revulsion they felt at the beginning. A Nazi doctor recalled:

> When you see a selection for the first time – I'm not talking only about myself. I'm talking about the most hardened SS people … you … how children and women are selected. Then you are so shocked … that it just cannot be described. And after a few weeks one can be accustomed to it. And that cannot be explained to anybody (Lifton, 1987, p.197).

Once the perpetrator has come to this point, he is prepared to commit the most gruesome crimes on his victims. His natural reaction of revulsion after he committed his first crime and his empathetic feelings for the victims are successfully overcome. The perpetrator uses all the excuses he can find for what he has done and out of pure self-preservation finally starts to believe in them. Due to the compelling circumstances he felt he could not evade and due to natural defence mechanisms, which started to work within him, ordinary men are thus successfully transformed into perpetrators prepared to do whatever is asked of them. Staub (1989, p.79) called the process, which transforms ordinary people into perpetrators 'a continuum of destructiveness': 'Once perpetrators begin to harm people, the resulting psychological changes make greater harm-doing possible.' There are some perpetrators, however, who along the way suddenly start realizing what is going on.

Turning Point and Exit

Some perpetrators simply reach a point where they can take no more and quit. They have had enough. This, however, is not very likely to happen if the perpetrators have already progressed on the continuum of destructiveness. In certain extraordinary circumstances though, it might happen early in this process. Browning (1992), for example, describes how several perpetrators from Reserve Police Battalion 101 quit. After a while the killings made them feel too uncomfortable, and they opted out. What was extraordinary in this situation was that the commander of Reserve Police Battalion 101 had, prior to the killing, given the recruits a chance to quit.

A more likely turning point is when the two worlds in which a perpetrator lives suddenly clash, and he can no longer uphold his dual role. This can happen when a perpetrator gets the order to torture, maim or kill a victim whom he knows, who comes from the same region as he does, or who strongly resembles a family member or friend. An Indonesian torturer, for example, suddenly recognized the man brought into the room about to be tortured. It was the doctor who had looked after him and his family when he was a child. He was immediately filled with many good memories of this man who had so often cured him from an illness. He was not able to torture this man and suddenly realized what had been going on all the time. He decided to quit the job and flee. Another example of a clash of these two worlds is when a perpetrator's girlfriend, wife, family or friends become aware of what his job really is and starts asking questions about it. Perpetrators often do not, and may not, reveal their jobs to anyone outside the organization. Their wives and family members will obviously know that they are working within the police or army but it is often easy to conceal what their exact job is. Sometimes the wives become aware of the fact that their husbands torture, maim or kill people and start asking questions about this work.

Many perpetrators who reach such a turning point will not be able to quit the job. They often are thought to 'know too much' and as a result of their refusal to act in their defined roles, they may be distrusted. If they are in the army they are not allowed to leave. The fear of what might happen to them if they quit may be enormous. They, more than anyone else, know what happens to people who have views different from those which have been prescribed. Fleeing the country is often the only possibility, and it will depend very much on the situation whether a flight would be successful.

In the next section I give some attention to how perpetrators look back on their crimes. This is not a phase in the transformation from ordinary man to perpetrator but it does give a good insight into how perpetrators feel about their crimes and into what led them to commit them.

Reflection

The way in which perpetrators look back differs from individual to individual. Many still believe that what they have done was completely justified. They strongly argue that they did the right thing, that it was necessary to maim, torture and kill in order to achieve a higher cause or to protect their home country. The strong need to still soothe their conscience will probably prevent many former perpetrators from ever acknowledging that they were wrong and that they have committed atrocious crimes. Many perpetrators hold on to their ideology out of pure self-preservation because they would not be able to handle the feelings of guilt and shame if they saw the truth as it is, like this Nazi doctor:

> I was able to perfect an absolutely new method of sterilization … [which] would be of great use today in certain cases (Lifton, 1987, p.277).

Others acknowledge that torture, maiming and killing are wrong but refuse to accept accountability for the crimes. They keep telling others and themselves that they had no choice, that they were given orders and that they could not have done otherwise. They keep saying that they were forced to act the way they did and they blame everyone else (superiors, victims, bystanders). Out of pure self-preservation they keep convincing themselves that they are not to blame, that they were mere instruments, that they were, and still are, innocent.

A third group tries to avoid all memories; they do everything in order to escape a confrontation with the past. Some go so far as to deny what happened and what they have done and strongly try to believe in their own denial. Not all who try to chase the past away are successful in doing so, however. Hurting memories, bad dreams and even nightmares haunt many perpetrators.

> I often have night-mares. I dream of the captain and the people I have killed. Look, I dress in black now, because of all that has happened. I feel guilty, but I can not get the people I have killed back to life (Member of a death squad).

Some feel depressed and ashamed. They feel rancour and repentance. For some these feelings, memories and depressions get so strong that they become ill or suffer from a post-traumatic stress disorder. The shield these perpetrators had built suddenly breaks down and the defence mechanisms no longer work effectively. They now have to accept and acknowledge the truth and that hurts. Not all manage to cope with the truth and are prone to insanity or suicide. The story of Varnado Simpson, one of the American soldiers who took part in the My Lai massacre, as described by Bilton and Sim (1992), shows what happens to ordinary people who have committed GHRV and who start to realize what they have done. Simpson is described by his doctors as being 'extremely fearful, and somewhat paranoid'. Nightmares became so frequent that he was afraid to go to sleep. His situation deteriorated when, nine years after My Lai, his ten-year-old son was accidentally killed by a bullet:

> I was in the house. And I came out and picked him up. But he was already dead … he was dying. He died in my arms. And when I looked at him, his face was like the same face of the child that I had killed. And I said: this is the punishment for me killing the people that I killed (Bilton and Sim, 1992, p.6).

The post-traumatic stress disorder from which he suffered became chronic and severe. Doctors remember that any discussion or activation of his memories from Vietnam created such extreme discomfort that he simply could not tolerate it. Bilton and Sim (1992) go on to describe how he lives in a small house with barred windows and drawn curtains and with his doors locked. His hands and legs shaking, his body shuddering and a bottle of pills on the table: 'for pain'. He attempted to commit suicide three times, but failed. He says he cannot remember and does not want to remember, but Bilton and Sim conclude that the truth is that he never forgets and that remembering has become a compulsion. Only very few perpetrators have the guts to face the truth, but even fewer have the strength to face it.

Conclusion

Most GHRV are committed by ordinary people who find themselves in very specific and in extremely compelling situations in which they do not find the means to resist and disobey an order to torture, maim or kill. Sadly enough the most natural reaction to the revulsion they feel about what they have done is to start to rationalize and justify their behaviour. Ordinary people start doing this because the revulsion and guilt would otherwise be more than they can face. Natural defence mechanisms protect us from these feelings through a natural tendency to self-preservation. These defence mechanisms, however, at the same time pave the path for more crimes up to a point where all feelings of empathy, revulsion and guilt will have been overcome and the transformation process is completed. Ordinary people have thus been turned into perpetrators who are prepared to carry out any order, no matter how cruel and horrifying. The chilling conclusion, therefore, is to agree with Vernado Simpson, participant in the My Lai massacre, who said: 'It can happen to anyone.' Not under all circumstances, not under ordinary circumstances, but under certain specific circumstances it can happen to anyone.

Notes

1 Arendt (1964) called this the banality of evil.
2 When I refer to the perpetrator I use the male form but everything I write applies equally to women.
3 See also Amnesty International (1977).
4 See for a study on the role of bystanders Grünfeld (2000).
5 For further information about the database used to conduct this study, please contact the author.
6 Kelman and Hamilton (1989) called this process authorization.
7 The words 'can make' are used and have been emphasized as it is important to notice that the war or front line experience in itself is not by definition sufficient to replace an initiation phase and makes soldiers prone to commit GHRV. Whether or not such experiences are sufficient depends on the surrounding circumstances and the prior experiences of the individual soldiers.
8 In all quotes I studied, I have found no single exception.

References

Amnesty International (1977), *Torture in Greece - the first torturers' trial 1975*, London, Amnesty International Publications.
Amnesty International (1982), *Your Neighbour's Son*, Ebbe Preistler, film/televisions aps.
Arendt, H. (1964), *Eichmann in Jerusalem*, London, Penguin Books.
Bilton, M. and Sim, K. (1992), *Four Hours in My Lai*, London, Viking.
Browning, C. (1992), *Ordinary Men. Reserve Police Battalion 101 and the Final Solution in Poland*, New York, Aaron Asher Books.

Crelinsten, R.D. and Schmid, A.P. (eds.) (1993), *The Politics of Pain*, Leiden, COMT.

Goldhagen, D.J. (1996), *Hitler's Willing Executioners – ordinary Germans and the Holocaust*, New York, Alfred A. Knopf.

Grünfeld, F. (2000), 'The Role of Bystanders in Human Rights Violations', in F. Coomans et al. (eds.), *Rendering Justice to the Vulnerable*, The Hague, Kluwer Law International.

Haritos-Fatouras, M. (1988), 'The Official Torturer: A learning model for obedience to the authority of violence', *Journal of Applied Social Psychology*, 1988, pp. 1107-20.

Harper's, (1985), *Confessions of a State Terrorist*, pp. 15-7.

Hoess, R. (1959), *Commandant of Auschwitz*, New York, World.

Kelman, H.C. and Hamilton, V.L. (1989), *Crimes of Obedience*, New Haven, Yale University Press.

Lifton, R.J. (1986), *Nazi Doctors: Medical killing and the psychology of genocide*, New York, Basic Books.

Malkin, P.Z. and Stein, H. (1960), *Eichmann in My Hands*, New York, Warner Books.

Milgram, S. (1969), *Obedience to Authority*, New York, Harper Torchbooks.

Sereny, G. (1994), *Into that Darkness: From mercy killing to mass murder*, New York, McGraw-Hill.

Smeulers, A. (1996), 'Auschwitz and the Holocaust through the Eyes of the Perpetrators', *Driemaandelijks tijdschrift van de stichting Auschwitz*, Vol. 50, pp. 23-55.

Staub, E. (1989), *The Roots of Evil*, Cambridge, Cambridge University Press.

Zimbardo, P.G., Haney, C., Curtis Banks, W., Jaffe, D. (1974), 'The Psychology of Imprisonment: Privation, power, and pathology', in R. Zick (ed.), *Doing unto Others*, London, Englewood Cliffs.

PART VI
CONCLUSION

Chapter 14

The Quest for Human Dignity: The Journey Continues

Sabine C. Carey and Steven C. Poe

Introduction

In our introduction to this volume we stated that during the last two decades there has been a proliferation of social scientific scholarly research on human rights. This book has brought together new research, applying the rules of social science to some of the most pressing topics on human rights. Chapters in this volume analyzed, for example, the link between foreign policy and human rights, addressed the linkage between trade and subsistence rights and investigated the use of legal institutions to prevent human rights abuses and to prosecute perpetrators. The motivation behind these and other contributions was to conduct research as if people really matter, to focus on people and their suffering. In this final chapter, we evaluate how the preceding contributions contributed to furthering our understanding of human suffering, with the ultimate goal being to reduce and prevent future anguish. We conclude by highlighting some of the questions that remain unanswered, in the hope that those in the growing community of human rights scholars will address them in their efforts to further the quest for human dignity.

Our Scholarly Deeds: An Assessment

We argued in our first chapter that the goal of research on human rights should be threefold. First, research in this area should help us to understand why human rights abuses occur. Second, it should enable us to make useful prescriptions for political practitioners, who could use that knowledge to design and implement policy choices that would allow people to enjoy greater dignity, at home and abroad. And third, it should allow for an informed and reliable assessment of future risks of human rights abuses that can be instituted in the future. Clearly, pursuing the first goal, understanding human rights violations, should facilitate achieving the other two goals. Considering each of the chapters, we now ask whether these studies made progress toward the goals that we set forth. And if so, how far did they travel?

Let us begin by briefly addressing the contributions of the chapters in the order in which they appeared. Chapter 2 by Steven Poe developed a theoretical framework to explain why human rights are violated. His goal was to integrate often contradictory and seemingly unrelated findings from the existing empirical literature on this topic. Using a decision-making model developed by Most and Starr (1989), Poe argued that governments' major aim is to maintain or increase their strength relative to their perceived threats. Repression, then, is seen as one option that can be used to increase governments' strength and to decrease various real or potential threats. He showed how previous findings, which were often based on rather narrow theoretical arguments, can be combined in a more parsimonious model, which can be used to help us understand some of the puzzling findings that have arisen in the quantitative literature on human rights.

His study provides an important contribution to our understanding of human rights violations because it enables us to think of such abuses within a single framework by painting one overall picture of why the basic rights of people are violated. But perhaps more importantly, it highlights the need for looking at the big picture: ideally, we should not investigate the impact of certain variables on the respect for human rights in isolation, but take into account how various factors interact and how certain *sets* of factors might influence the Strength/Threat ratio, and therefore affect the risk of repression. Arguably this could be a particularly important contribution for policy makers who are more apt to use strength and threat as a heuristic device for organizing their thoughts on the causes of repression, than to read and retain all of the various findings that have arisen in the repression literature to date. The parsimony of this model is certainly a strength, but clearly further empirical scrutiny is needed before we can confidently recommend it to government, NGO or IGO decision makers.

The second part of the book evaluated the links between foreign policy and human rights. The chapter by Bethany Barratt sheds light on how human rights do, or do not, influence the distribution of UK foreign aid, whereas Dawn Miller's contribution evaluates the effect of arms transfers on the human rights records in the recipient countries. Barratt's study suggests that countries with less respect for the life integrity rights of their citizens are less likely to be included in the aid programme of Great Britain. But for the developing countries that are among the recipients of UK foreign aid, human rights records do not appear to affect the amounts of aid they receive, once they are included in the pool of aid recipients. Instead, trade links seem to play a more important role in determining the amount of aid that is allocated to recipient countries.

Miller analyzed the consequences of arms transfers on the respect for human rights in the receiving countries. To date there has been very little research on the link between the trade of arms and its effect on the living conditions of people in the importing countries. It is the first study that examines the impact of the arms trade on a range of different human rights, analyzing the consequences of arms transfers for personal integrity rights, such as the right to be free from torture and political imprisonment, political and civil rights, such as the rights to free and fair elections and to open public discussion, and on subsistence rights, such as the right to an adequate standard of living. Her results show that arms transfers affect these different categories of human rights in different ways. While arms transfers do not seem to have a damaging effect on subsistence rights, they appear to decrease respect for personal integrity rights, as well as for political and civil rights. Thus, this study illustrated what foreign policy critics have long argued: such policies often can have unintended consequences, which have a derogatory effect on the human dignity of people around the world. As a result of these contributions, Miller's chapter is an important step in gaining a better understanding of the linkage between militarization and the achievement of human rights.

The third part of this volume focused more closely on subsistence rights. Rhonda Callaway and Julie Harrelson-Stephens examined multiple channels by which trade influences both security and subsistence rights. They subjected the arguments of both liberal and radical theories pertaining to the relationship between trade and development to systematic empirical analysis. The results suggest that trade fosters economic development, which in turn strengthens democracy and ultimately leads to the improvement of the respect of basic subsistence rights. Their study expands our understanding of the relationship between trade and human rights. It highlights the empirical finding that the impact on human right is not uniform across different aspects of trade. Exports appear to play a more important role in strengthening the respect for human rights than imports. Their study draws attention to the need for further disaggregation of trade in order to gain a better understanding of how different facets of trade influence human development and human rights, particularly in developing countries.

Wesley Milner et al. also focus on development and the provision of subsistence rights. This chapter addressed the questions of trade-offs between different types of human rights. Their empirical analysis did not support the notion of a trade-off between rights. Instead, political rights seem to strengthen the respect and provision of subsistence rights. Although personal integrity rights are not found to reinforce subsistence rights, they do not appear to have a negative effect on subsistence rights and development. This chapter extends our understanding of the relationship between various categories of human rights, but its findings should also be useful for human rights advocates who sometimes have had to confront government leaders' assertions that they must limit some human rights in order to make progress in the provision of other rights. This study provided no evidence that such trade-offs are necessary. But at the same time, and perhaps equally important, they show that while some of the various kinds of rights are strongly and positively correlated (that is, there is a tendency for them to be realized together), a country that performs well on one class of rights does not automatically mean that its performance on other kinds of rights will be equally good.[1]

Continuing on the journey towards understanding how human rights affect the behaviour of international actors, Rodwan Abouharb and David Cingranelli investigated the adjustment lending of the World Bank and the IMF. It is the first study that analyzes factors influencing the financial assistance from both institutions. They did not find support for the argument made by some critics that the lending institutions favour authoritarian regimes over democracies in their allocation of adjustment loans. Instead, the findings indicate that the World Bank and IMF are more likely to give loans to countries that are poor, that have large populations and those that have a good record of respecting workers' rights. The empirical record indicated that these institutions do, at least to some extent, consider issues pertaining to human dignity when loan monies are allocated. This chapter highlights the need to subject the human rights records of international actors, both governmental and non-governmental, to systematic empirical scrutiny.

The fourth part of this volume concentrated on the institutionalization of human rights. James Meernik and Kimi King approached the issue of human rights from a different angle than the aforementioned contributions. When evaluating the effect of certain behaviours and actions on human rights, researchers have traditionally focused on governments as the main actors. Instead, this study analyzed how international institutions deal with those who are charged with committing such violations. It is one of the first studies to systematically scrutinize the sentencing of an international criminal tribunal.

Their findings show that the tribunal dealing with the former Yugoslavia punished systematic human rights violations, such as genocide and crimes against humanity, with greater severity than specific types of crimes, such as murder or rape, that cannot be classified as being connected with those more serious types of crimes. The finding that there are consistent and just patterns in sentencing, related to the seriousness of the crime, is important and quite relevant to real world politics. Establishing the existence of such patterns in sentencing would seem to be one of the first vital steps toward establishing the legitimacy and fairness of such tribunals.

The chapter by Linda Camp Keith also extends our knowledge of human rights and their abuses and has important implications for political practitioners. Analyzing the linkage between constitutional provisions and the respect for human rights in various regions of the world, her findings highlight the need to compare the protection of human rights across culturally and geographically different areas. This is particularly important in an age when human rights experts are lobbying and in some cases offering advice directly to countries around the world that are in the process of adopting new constitutions or modifying existing ones. Human rights practitioners should take note of the main finding of the Keith study, that when it comes to drafting constitutions that protect internationally recognized human rights standards, 'one size doesn't fit all.'

The four chapters in the fifth part of this volume addressed new directions in the research on human rights violations by focusing on issues that have received very little scholarly attention. Chris Lee et al. investigated how the ethnic composition of a country affects its respect for personal integrity rights. There has been an increased interest in comparing characteristics of ethnic civil wars to non-ethnic civil wars in recent years (Ellingsen, 2000; Sambanis, 2001), but there has been very little research into how ethnic structures of a country influence its human rights records.[2] These researchers analyzed three aspects of the ethnic composition of a country, the size and number of ethnic groups, linguistic groups and religious groups. Their findings suggest that neither the ethnic, linguistic nor religious composition directly influences the respect for human rights in that country. This is a finding that is directly relevant to ongoing political debates in the United States and Europe. Anti-immigrant movements have sprung up in both of these regions, appealing to xenophobic sentiments, but making the more politically palatable argument that democratic governance is difficult, if not impossible, in ethnically and linguistically diverse states. The findings of this study show that such states are no more prone to the use of anti-democratic, repressive policies than other countries, once other important factors are controlled.

Whereas Lee et al. analyzed the impact of structural conditions on human rights violations, Sabine Carey concentrated on how different protest activities influence a government's decision to use repression against its own people. She distinguished between peaceful anti-government demonstrations, strikes, riots, guerrilla warfare and revolutions. The results suggest that governments group these five activities into two broad categories, namely into those that are non-violent and spontaneous and those activities that are violent and require a certain level of organization of the dissidents. The later category seems to trigger harsher and more violent responses from the state than the first one. The results support the theoretical framework put forward by Poe in Chapter 2, which suggested that governments use repression when they perceive themselves to be under threat. Protest activities that are violent and carried out by an organized group are particularly prone to triggering repression because governments are likely to perceive these as being more threatening than non-violent and spontaneous forms of dissent. This study is an initial effort to test the theoretical model presented in the Poe chapter, and the findings show that this model has promise and is worthy of future research.

The last two chapters by Pablo Policzer and Alette Smeulers take us in a completely new and different direction in our study of human rights violations by focusing on the organizations and the individuals that carry out these violations. By identifying characteristics of the perpetrators, their studies point towards signs that can be used by citizens, academics and human rights advocates as warning signals for potential human rights violations. Policzer characterized organizations according to the structures and procedures they put in place for the purpose of internal and external monitoring of human rights abuses. Smeulers focused on the individual, assuming that anyone can become a human rights abuser if s/he is subjected to certain kinds of training procedures. Whether or not the assumption that anyone could become a torturer is correct, adopting this supposition leads us to look inward, at ourselves and the practices within our own countries, searching for the seeds of human rights abuses within. Certainly this attitude would lead to more respect for, and a better protection of human dignity, if it were to be adopted by more people and their governments.

The Continuing Quest

The goals of this volume were to expand our understanding of why human rights abuses occur, to provide useful information for policy makers to end or at very least minimize human suffering and finally to contribute to an early warning system for human rights violations. As discussed above, most progress has been made towards the first goal. However, there are still many areas that need to be addressed in order to paint a more complete picture of why human rights are violated.

Firstly, one weakness in the literature to date is that it does not do justice to the richness of the human rights concept, as set forth in such human rights documents as the Universal Declaration of Human Rights. We agree with the arguments of Donnelly (2003) and Shue (1980) and others who argue that several classes of rights are normatively indivisible. However, most empirical, social scientific contributions to the human rights literature to this point have focused on the so-called 'right to personal integrity.' Meanwhile, other classes of rights have gone largely unexplored and unaddressed by human rights researchers. Clearly practical concerns dictate that it is oftentimes necessary to focus on one class of rights in a particular published work. It would be difficult to illuminate the empirical patterns underlying many different kinds of human rights, in a single scholarly book chapter or journal length article. That said, future work by human rights researchers should go further in examining the determinants of other classes of rights (as, for example, the chapters by Callaway and Harrelson-Stephens and by Milner et al. did in their investigations of subsistence rights, and the chapter by Abouharb and Cingranelli did in relation to workers' rights). In many instances they will find existing research has already addressed the issues of concern, albeit often without using the 'human rights terminology' (i.e., the large, existing literature on physical quality of life). Though it is not be possible to do justice to the entire concept of human rights in a single empirical piece, we can certainly work toward a body of human rights literature, which, as a whole, represents the concept more truthfully. The increasing number of scholars that are becoming interested in human rights can be a boon in this effort, allowing our developing scholarly subfield to diversify.

Secondly, systematic scholarly research needs to investigate a more diverse set of actors. Thus far the major focus has been on governments as the perpetrator of human rights abuses. But when we look at abuses of human rights around the world, we see that governments are only one actor among many that routinely abuse human rights. Future research needs to address how the behaviour of non-state actors, such as rebel organizations, terrorist groups and multinational corporations, abuse human dignity. Conversely, we should also investigate more carefully the effectiveness of various transnational and domestic actors in improving human rights conditions.

This is not to say that we should ignore the effects of nation-state governments on human rights. National governments will continue to be the greatest abusers of human rights. Though the human rights movement and globalization may each challenge some aspects of states' traditional role as the primary actor in world politics, nation-state governments are still the locus of great power and therefore arguably the greatest hope for improved human rights as well. The evaluation of government policies and their direct and indirect effects on human rights requires further attention from the research community. Along these lines, two elements that are likely to become increasingly important are the role of arms transfers and developed countries' policies concerning citizenship and asylum.

Human rights researchers also have work to do towards the second goal, conducting research that is more relevant to policy makers and other practitioners such as those who work with non-governmental and inter-governmental organizations. This goal overlaps so some extent with that of understanding, but all too often that overlap goes unrecognized in our discipline. We highlight our findings and the theoretical contributions of our studies, but fail to indicate how they speak to practitioners. We argue above that most of the contributions in this volume have some sort of practical application, or at very least, work in veins that could reasonably be expected to assist practitioners at some point in the future. In general, we believe, scholars should work on putting more emphasis on the relevance of their research even while emphasizing their contributions to theory. One means toward this end would be to give greater attention to the effects of variables that can be *manipulated* by practitioners, on human rights conditions. Some progress in this direction has been made in recent years, but clearly there is much work yet to be done.

We admit that not much progress was made in this volume directly toward the final goal we outlined for this research, the ability to give early warning to governments, IGOs, and NGOs who could use that information to lessen human suffering. None of the pieces in this volume addressed this question. That said, we are convinced that such efforts can be undertaken elsewhere. Several of the chapters of this book illustrated that reasonably well-specified models of various human rights phenomena have already been developed. A logical next step for the researchers who have built those models is to begin to use their models as vehicles to provide predictions, or at very least assessments of the risk of various human rights abuses, to practitioners who would want to use them. Obviously there are some obstacles that need to be overcome. One difficulty in applying these models, and those built elsewhere (e.g., Poe, Tate and Keith 1999) is that, as they stand, they cannot be applied directly to predict what will happen. Most of the models presented in the field thus far measure at least some of the independent variables, and the dependent variable at the same point in time. Of course, for a predictive vehicle to be of much real use to practitioners it must use *yesterday's* or *today's* data to forecast what is going to happen *tomorrow*, giving the decision maker some time to take remedial actions. Though this obstacle is a difficult one, we think it is one can be overcome with some effort and attention.

A Concluding Note

This volume brought together studies that applied the tools of social scientific inquiry to the quest for human dignity. Starting from the assumption that people matter and that they have human rights simply because of their being human, these studies set out to investigate how the protection of human rights has influenced policy decisions and what factors are likely to threaten the realization of such rights. Looking back now and evaluating its contents, it seems clear that much progress has been made, in a relatively short time, by those in the subfield that studies human rights issues. Yet there is a long path to travel before we reach the goal of using the knowledge we gain from our studies to provide significant useful information to the practitioners who are in a position to help. We will close simply by restating our hope for this volume, first stated in the introduction; that its publication will further increase the momentum of the scholarly movement that does systematic research on human rights, adding to our knowledge and, at the same time, stimulating future scholarly inquiry that will further human dignity.

Notes

1 See Chapter 11 of Donnelly's (2002) book *Universal Human Rights in Theory and Practice,* for a qualitative argument for this.

2 An exception is Walker and Poe (2002).

References

Donnelly, J. (2002), *Universal Human Rights in Theory and Practice,* 2nd edition, Ithaca, Cornell University Press.

Ellingsen, T. (2000), 'Colorful Community or Ethnic Witches' Brew? Multiethnicity and Domestic Conflict During and After the Cold War', *Journal of Conflict Resolution*, Vol. 44(2), pp. 228-49.

Most, B.A. and Starr, H. (1989), *Inquiry, Logic and International Politics*, Columbia, SC, University of South Carolina Press.

Poe, S.C, Tate, C.N. and Keith, L.C. (1999), 'Repression of the Human Right to Personal Integrity Revisited: A Global Crossnational Study Covering the Years 1976-1993', *International Studies Quarterly*, Vol. 43(2), pp. 291-315.

Sambanis, N. (2001), 'Do Ethnic and Nonethnic Civil Wars Have the Same Causes?' *Journal of Conflict Resolution*, Vol. 45(3), pp. 259-82.

Shue, H. (1980), *Basic Rights: Subsistence, Affluence, and U.S. Foreign Policy*, Princeton, NJ, Princeton University Press.

Walker, S. and Poe, S.C. (2002), 'Does Cultural Diversity Affect Countries' Respect for Human Rights?' *Human Rights Quarterly*, Vol. 24(1), pp. 237-63.

Index